796.156 SCH
Schleicher, Robert H.
Slot car racing

DATE DUE

AUG 0 9 2007

547
80663647

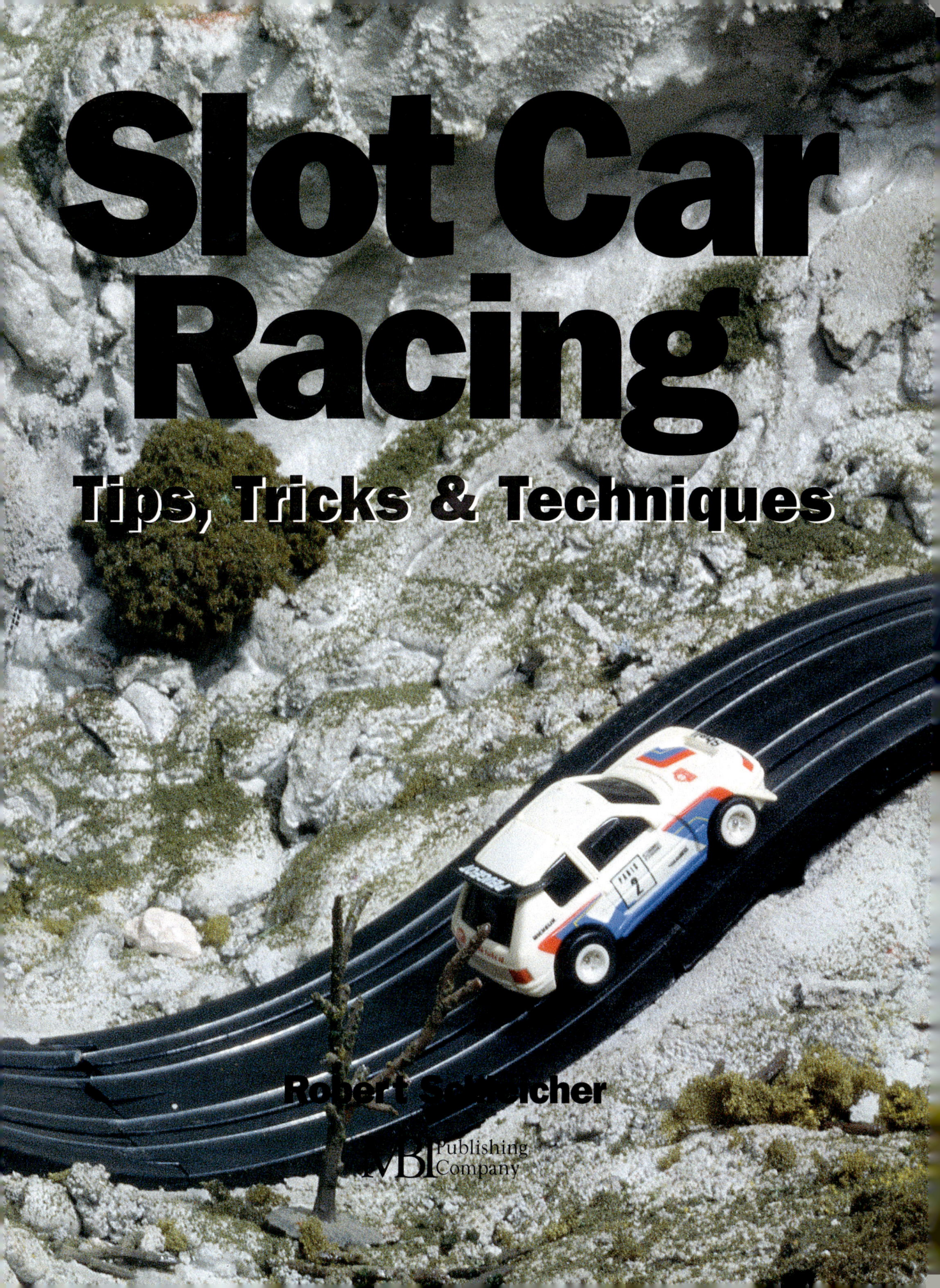

Slot Car Racing
Tips, Tricks & Techniques

Robert Schleicher

MBI Publishing Company

First published in 2005 by MBI, an imprint of MBI Publishing Company, Galtier Plaza, Suite 200, 380 Jackson Street, St. Paul, MN 55101-3885 USA

© Robert Schleicher, 2005

All rights reserved. With the exception of quoting brief passages for the purposes of review, no part of this publication may be reproduced without prior written permission from the Publisher.

The information in this book is true and complete to the best of our knowledge. All recommendations are made without any guarantee on the part of the author or Publisher, who also disclaim any liability incurred in connection with the use of this data or specific details.

This publication has been prepared solely by MBI Publishing Company and is not approved or licensed by any other entity. We recognize that some words, model names, and designations mentioned herein are the property of the trademark holder. We use them for identification purposes only. This is not an official publication.

MBI titles are also available at discounts in bulk quantity for industrial or sales-promotional use. For details write to Special Sales Manager at MBI Publishing Company & Distributors, Galtier Plaza, Suite 200, 380 Jackson Street, St. Paul, MN 55101-3885 USA.

Library of Congress Cataloging-in-Publication Data
Schleicher, Robert H.
   Slot car racing : tips, tricks, and track plans/ by Robert Schleicher.
      p. cm.
   ISBN 0-7603-2101-9 (alk. paper)
   1. Model car racing. 2. Slot cars. I. Title.

GV1570.S35 2005
796.15'6--dc22

On the frontispiece: You can stage a 24-hour Le Mans race with cars that have working lights like this SCX Le Mans Dome.

On the title page: The scenery on Slugger Canady's hillclimb layout is blown concrete.

On the back cover 1: Use a number five bit to drill two holes about 3/4 inch apart just ahead of the rear axle.
On the back cover 2: This is the qualifying grid of F1, CART, and IRL open-wheeled cars when the cars have magnets and all have silicone tires: Scalextric IRL Dallara-Chevrolet, NINCO F1 Stewart (scale-width), Scalextric F1 McLaren, NINCO F1 Arrows (wide), Scalextric F1 Williams, Carrera F1 Williams, NINCO CART Lola-Ford, SCX F1 McLaren (wide), Pro-Slot F1 Ferrari, and SCX F1 Arrows (scale-width).
On the back cover 3: Bob Dunkle's Scalextric raceway climbs about nine inches to a tight turn before heading back onto the flats. The trees are life-like model railroad accessories. The figures are porcelain and were found on eBay.

Editorial: Amy Glaser
Design: Brenda C. Canales

Printed in China

CONTENTS

Chapter 1	TODAY'S MODEL RACING CARS	.6
Chapter 2	WHAT'LL SHE DO? TRACK TESTS OF 39 CARS	.14
Chapter 3	REAL RACING ACTION	.28
Chapter 4	RACE CAR PREP AND PERFORMANCE	.48
Chapter 5	SIXTY CAR-BY-CAR COMPARISON SHOOT-OUTS	.74
Chapter 6	BUILD YOUR OWN RACE CAR	.88
Chapter 7	THE SNAP-TOGETHER HOME RACEWAY	.112
Chapter 8	RACETRACKS ON TABLETOPS	.130
Chapter 9	REAL RACETRACKS FOR YOUR HOME	.150
Chapter 10	SEDAN RACING: NASCAR, TRANS-AM, DTM, AND WRC	.184
Chapter 11	YOUR RACETRACKS	.190
Chapter 12	HO RACE CAR TRACK TESTS	.206
Chapter 13	HO TRACKS AND 11 TRACK PLANS	.214
	INDEX	.230

CHAPTER 1
TODAY'S MODEL RACING CARS

A 2001 Ferrari (a modified and repainted SCX Williams) and a Scalextric McLaren at Lowes on the Carrera version of Monaco.

Today's Model Racing Cars

Model car racing is now closer to real car racing than ever. The cars are almost indistinguishable from the real racing machines they replicate, but that's obvious. What's not so obvious is how well today's 1/32 scale racers perform.

First, you have a choice of speed, anything from true-scale miles-per-hour with infinitely controllable power slides, to the flat-out rail'n-it speeds that define the term "slot racing." There's no realism in rail'n it, but it is a thrill. At the realistic end of the speed spectrum, improved tires and the ability to run six cars in one lane make 1/32 scale model car racing virtually 1/1 racing.

Model Racing Cars

The list of available ready-to-race cars grows by about 100 (not counting different paint schemes) each year. The few that are not made can be assembled from cast-resin kits or you can buy a cast-resin, fiberglass, or clear plastic body and fit a suitable chassis to create your own.

Technology has reached tabletop racing in the form of digital cars and controllers that allow you to run up to six cars on a two-lane track. Controller-operated lane-changing tracks allow you to choose either the "fast" or "passing" lane at the flick of a button. No longer must you have a six-lane slot-car track to race six cars—two lanes are enough. The real racing element of having to wait for the best corner or straight to pass is now replicated on tabletop racing.

You can duplicate the real racetrack of your dreams in a space as small as 5x9 feet or have a full-house experience in as little as 8x16 feet. You can race at home against a lap timer or against a pace car like Scalextric Challenger, or race with a few friends or join (or create) a club.

You can stage a 24-hour Le Mans race with cars that have working lights like this SCX Le Mans Dome.

Bobby Isaac at the real Riverside Raceway in 1970.

It's a Game
Model car racing is, at heart, a game, as is Formula 1 racing with 1/1 scale cars or any other kind of racing. The cars are the playing pieces, the track the game board, and the race itself is the game. The rules can be as simple as racing against a clock to achieve the fastest laps in each lane or as complex as a race event with 20 drivers and cars that run qualifying heats, semi-main events, and main events as described in *Racing and Collecting Slot Cars* and *Slot Car Bible*.

Unlike most games, model car racing offers a near-infinite variety of contests to suit your personal whims and fantasies. Run a trading paint and a "no rules are good rules" NASCAR race for a few dozen laps or recreate the cars that ran at Le Mans in 1969 and rewrite history with you as one of the drivers. There are no limits.

Model Race Car Development
We have all learned a lot over the past 35 years, and that learning process is more focused with the cars that have been available, ready-to-race, over the past

Carrera's replica of Bobby Isaac's championship 1970 Dodge Charger Daytona is also available as a Pro-X Digital racer.

With the digital lane-changing systems shown in Chapter 3, you can race up to six cars at once.

five years or so. When *Racing and Collecting Slot Cars* was published in 2001, there was no American magazine devoted to racing 1/32 and HO cars at home. The first issue of *Model Car Racing* magazine appeared in December 2001, and it has continued to be published every other month.

Essentially, the magazine picks up where the two books leave off and it supplements the basic information in the books. The core of that new knowledge is in the pages of this book. We include plans for 12 replicas of real racetracks, another dozen smaller tracks for all the popular brands on these pages, and some examples of the exciting tracks that have been assembled across the land.

Cast-resin body kits, such as Modelmaker's 1964 289FIA Cobra, are easy to build and offer cars that you cannot obtain any other way.

Jason Boye created LeMonzaco, an HO track as realistic as the cars.

There are many new pit buildings, grandstands, control towers, and crowds of scale-model people available so you can make the track almost as realistic as the cars.

We have track tested both out-of-the-box and improved cars. The results of the track tests of 39 cars are in Chapter 2, and car-by-car shoot-outs of over 60 cars are in Chapter 5. There are ways of making nearly all the cars equal so you can win races with driving (and tuning) skill, rather than just a quick car.

Virtually all the material in this book was published in the January/February 2003 through November/December 2004 (Nos. 7 through 18)

Slot Classics cast-resin replica of the 1961 Ferrari 250GT SWB is a work of art, with etched-metal wire wheels and trim.

The prototypes for these two Scalextric Porsche 911GT-3R racers competed at Le Mans and the ALMS in 2003 and 2004.

issues of the magazine. The material in the first six issues still is available in special sets of limited-edition magazines that are sold as a package with a blue-and-white Scalextric Le Mans Cadillac for $85. About a dozen racetrack tests and a half-dozen racetrack plans (Riverside Raceway, Le Mans, Spa, Sebring, Brands Hatch, and Watkins Glen) are in those six issues but are not in this book. There's an index of the first six issues, as well as issues 7 through 18, on the *Model Car Racing* magazine website (www.modelcarracingmag.com). There is also an index of addresses for all the known manufacturers of model car parts and accessories and a list of dealers who carry these cars on the website.

Le Mans Miniatures produced a limited run of cast-resin kits and ready-to-race replicas of the 1967 Le Mans–winning Ford GT40 Mk IV.

This 1960s Indy classic is part of a series of handmade ready-to-race cars from D&G Osterero.

The limited production Slot Classics replica of the 1961 Le Mans Morgan Super Sport races a handmade Lotus 11, which is a clear plastic body on a modified Carrera chassis.

The Sheer Joy of It All

One of the joys of model car racing is that you can have a replica of just about any real racing car from almost any time period. You can even have the complete grid of cars from just about any race in history. The cars can be raced on a replica of any real racing track with the skill needed for power sliding, accelerating just this side of fishtailing, and picking the fastest lane around the track, even if it means taking the outside lane to pass—and you can have it all in your own home.

CHAPTER 2
WHAT'LL SHE DO?

A Monogram Daytona leads a Pink-Kar Ferrari GTO around a sweeping curve.

Track Tests of 39 Cars

If it's a race car, one of the first questions is, "What'll she do?" For model car racing, lap times are the measure of a car's performance compared to another.

I've had the chance to compare more than 100 1/32 scale model race cars by doing car-by-car comparisons or shoot-outs on a Sport Monaco track. Those comparisons are in Chapter 5. In addition, most of the cars are tested individually by Dan Wilson or Tom Dolan at the Model Car Racing Track Test Facility. The results of 39 tests are in this chapter. The tracks include two 35-foot-long 5x9-foot adaptations of the Indy Formula 1 track taken directly from *Racing and Collecting Slot Cars*. One track is assembled from Carrera sections, and the other is assembled from Scalextric Classic sections. We run about 50 laps on each track and record the fastest time in each lane.

We also have five skid pads, full circles of outer curves (we test on the inner lane of each) of Scalextric Sport, Scalextric Classic, Carrera, SCX, and NINCO track to test for ultimate cornering power on these brands. You can compare the skid pad numbers on Carrera and Scalextric Sport to the others to get a fair idea of how that car will corner on any brand. The surface of Artin's track is very similar to the Carrera track. That inner lane on the outer curve of each brand of sectional track represents a fair average of the corners on most home tracks. We use a Model Rectifier Tech III Power Command 30VA power pack for the skid pad test. We gradually increase the power until the car circles at the edge of traction, increase the power until the car spins out, and decrease it so the car circles just short of spinning out. The volt and amp readings from the gauges on the Power Command pack are recorded and interpolated into scale miles per hour.

For the two racetrack tests, we use a pure 12-volt DC power supply from Radio Shack. The power supply is more critical than you might think. You

continued on page 24

The Scalextric Lola-MG and Carrera Bentley with two magnets are two of the quickest cars currently available.

Pictured are the Carrera Formula 1 2003 Williams, Scalextric IRL Dallara, and NINCO 2002 CART Lola-Ford. The IRL and CART cars are considerably wider than the F1 cars.

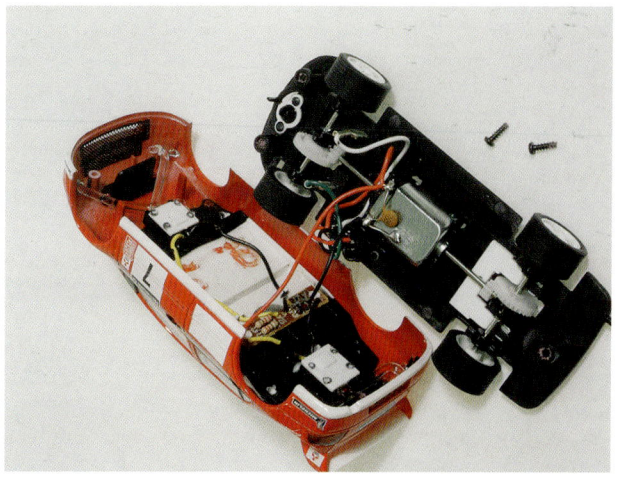

The Auto Art Subaru WRX has four-wheel drive.

Carrera 2003 Williams FW24 Formula 1 racer.

Ten of the many fifties-era sports/GT/Le Mans cars that are available (starting inside the front row): Top-Slot 1951 C-Type Jaguar, Petrolati Cad-Allard, MMK 1953 C-Type Jaguar, Carrera Mercedes 300SLR, Carrera 1954 Jaguar D-Type, Carrera 1951 Maserati A6GCS, NINCO 1949 XK120 Jaguar, Carrera Aston Martin DBR1, NINCO Ferrari Testa Rosa, NINCO Austin Healey 3000 Mk.III (back-dated to 1955 100S as shown in Chapter 4).

The Carrera Porsche 911 RSR is a reintroduction of a 1/29 scale 1970s-era model.

Ferrari 365 GTB/4 Daytona and an MMK Matra.

Left: The Fly version of the 1968 Ford GT40.

The MAXI-Models McLaren M6B is cast-resin and offered as a kit or ready-to-race.

The Fly 1998 Lola T98/10 dices with a Carrera Audi R8 at a recreation of the 1998 Le Mans race.

The Historic Racing Replicas McLaren M8D has a sidewinder motor and working steering.

Monogram's Greenwood Corvette and Fly's 1976 BMW 3.0 CSL.

A baver cast-resin Cheetah (number 36) uses the chassis from the MRRC 427 Cobra (number 10).

The NINCO BMW M3GTR has an anglewinder chassis to allow a sidewinder-style motor in a relatively narrow car.

The NINCO Subaru WRX rally car has four-wheel drive.

The NINCO Renault Clio has four-wheel drive with working suspension.

The NINCO 1977 Porsche 911 Turbo and Porsche 934 share a similar chassis, each with working front and rear suspension.

The coil-over suspension units on the NINCO Porsche 911 Turbo can be snapped off and replaced with softer or firmer units.

The Pro-Track Spyder inline chassis can be used to replace most ready-to-run chassis to provide quicker performance.

The NINCO 1998 Mercedes CLK has a quicker ProRace chassis.

The Scalextric Northstar Le Mans Cadillac (the 2001 Le Mans car and the *Model Car Racing* Limited Edition) can hold its own with added magnets.

The SCX Dome-Judd S101.

The motor and rear axle on the SCX Dome-Judd S101 are mounted in a separate pod that can be loosened to isolate vibrations for better cornering.

Slot.it Audi R8C Le Mans racer.

Slot.it 1983 Porsche 956.

will not achieve the same results with any of the power supplies furnished by the model car makers because some offer more power and others offer less, which is precisely why we settled on a generic power supply.

The Spec Sheet

The spec sheet is included with lithe track tests of model cars in *Model Car Racing* magazine articles so you can compare the model to its prototype. We list the dimensions of the real car first, followed by the 1/32 scale reductions of those dimensions and the dimensions of the model. You have a side-by-side comparison of the model's dimensions to an exact 1/32 scale version of the car. We weigh the front and rear of the car separately. We test the cars' magnetic down force on two special scales that are shown in *Slot Car Bible*.

MODEL CAR RACING TRACK TEST
RESULTS SUMMARY, ISSUE NO. 7 THROUGH 18

This is a summary of all the 39 track tests on 1/32 scale race cars we performed.

RACING

Car	Race Performance: Lap Time, 36-ft Scalextric Indy F1 Course	Scalextric Skid pad (32 1/4-in circle)	Cornering Speeds: Carrera Skid pad (35 1/4-in circle)	NINCO Skid pad (36 3/4-in circle)	Lap Time, 36-ft Carrera Indy F1 Course	Sport Skidpad (32 1/4-in circle)	SCX Skid pad (32 1/4-inch circle)
Maxi-Models McLaren M6B Performance:	4.7 sec.	4.34 sec.	10.13 fps	10.50 fps	9.55 fps	10.11 fps	9.65 fps
Scalextric Ford GT40 Performance:	4.30 sec.	4.28 sec.	9.05 fps	9.41 fps	7.51 fps	8.98 fps	9.49 fps
Slot.it Audi R8C Performance:	5.30 sec.	4.28 sec.	9.05 fps	9.41 fps	7.51 fps	8.98 fps	8.99 fps
NINCO BMW M3GTR Performance:	4.70 sec.	4.49 sec.	9.41 fps	10.12 fps	8.60 fps	9.37 fps	9.20 fps
NINCO Four-Wheel-Drive Subaru WRX Performance:	4.6 sec.	4.84 sec.	7.58 fps	8.62 fps	8.88 fps	9.08 fps	8.32 fps
Pro-Track Spyder Chassis Performance:	3.64 sec.	3.725 sec.	10.36 fps	11.59 fps	12.61 fps	10.48 fps	11.39 fps
Monogram Daytona Cobra Performance:	4.20 sec.	4.29 sec.	8.35 fps	8.51 fps	7.70 fps	8.85 fps	9.50 fps
Auto Art Four-Wheel-Drive Subaru WRX Performance:	4.10 sec.	5.10 sec.	9.55 fps	7.74 fps	7.38 fps	9.55 fps	.
Vanquish MG (1/29 scale) Lola T260 Can-Am Performance:	3.90 sec.	4.43 sec.	16.58 fps	10.05 fps	13.75 fps	16.99 fps	16.55 fps
Fly BMW M3GTR Performance:	3.95 sec.	4.25 sec.	9.98 fps	10.51 fps	7.69 fps	9.98 fps	8.50 fps
Carrera 427 'Vette (regeared 8/26) Performance:	4.30 sec.	4.0 sec.	9.34 fps	NA	9.52 fps	9.32 fps	8.70 fps
MRRC 427 Cobra Performance:	.29 sec.	4.35 sec.	9.28 fps	8.89 fps	9.02 fps	8.99 fps	9.20 fps
Scalextric Lola MG EX257 Performance:	3.75 sec.	3.90 sec.	11.88 fps	11.20 fps	10.35 fps	10.98 fps	11.00 fps
TSRF Super-Tuned Chassis (With NINCO F1 Le Mans Body) Performance:	4.10 sec.	3.95 sec.	10.15 fps	9.88 fps	11.03 fps	10.20 fps	10.36 fps
Spirit Lola B2K/10 Le Mans Performance:	4.22 sec.	5.76 sec.	"	8.93 fps	"	"	"
Artin Porsche GT-1/98 Performance:	5.867 sec.	5.731 sec.	6.29 fps	5.95 fps	6.01 fps	6.21 fps	7.38 fps
Scalextric IRL Dallara Performance:	3.54 sec.	3.67 sec.	11.94 fps	11.92 fps	10.73 fps	11.49 fps	11.62 fps
NINCO Renault Clio (With Suspension) Performance:	4.81 sec.	5.43 sec.	7.73 fps	8.69 fps	8.33 fps	8.32 fps	9.56 fps
Fly 1998 Lola T98/10 Performance:	3.05 sec.	3.57 sec.	12.52 fps	12.14 fps	10.82 fps	12.35 fps	12.98 fps
Scalextric 1972 L-88 Corvette Performance:	3.51 sec.	3.62 sec.	12.02 fps	12.41 fps	11.00 fps	10.94 fps	12.41 fps
Spirit 1971 Ferrari 512M Performance:	4.39 sec.	4.30 sec.	9.23 fps	9.32 fps	9.14 fps	8.78 fps	9.463 fps
NINCO 2002 Cart Lola-Ford Performance:	4.10 sec.	3.99 sec.	10.10 fps	9.50 fps	9.80 fps	9.43 fps	10.16 fps
SCX 2002 Dome-Judd S101 Performance:	3.86 sec.	3.94 sec.	10.94 fps	11.81 fps	9.83 fps	10.46 fps	10.60 fps
Slot.it 1983 Porsche 956 Performance:	4.24 sec.	4.10 sec.	10.65 fps	10.43 fps	9.90 fps	11.42 fps	10.72 fps
Fly 1969 Ford GT40 Performance:	4.05 sec.	4.35 sec.	10.53 fps	10.43 fps	9.66 fps	10.06 fps	10.44 fps
Monogram 1963 Corvette Grand Sport Performance:	3.91 sec.	4.21 sec.	10.80 fps	10.79 fps	9.90 fps	11.42 fps	10.72 fps
Fly 1972 Ferrari 365GTB/4 Daytona Performance:	4.62 sec.	4.50 sec.	9.14 fps	9.24 fps	8.68 fps	8.85 fps	9.00 fps
Carrera 2003 Williams FW24 Formula 1 Performance:	3.50 sec.	3.79 sec.	11.77 fps	12.05 fps	10.55 fps	11.46 fps	12.26 fps
Proteus Lamborghini Murcielago Performance:	3.61 sec.	4.07 sec.	10.49 fps	10.97 fps	9.79 fps	10.79 fps	10.61 fps
Vanquish MG (1/29 scale) 1972 Louts 72D Grand Prix Performance:	4.51 sec.	4.89 sec.	9.77 fps	9.16 fps	8.98 fps	9.75 fps	10.38 fps
Carrera (1/29 scale) 1974 Porsche 911 RSR Turbo Performance:	3.94 sec.	3.91 sec.	10.44 fps	10.37 fps	9.44 fps	8.67 fps	9.62 fps
Pink-Kar 1962 Ferrari GTO Performance:	4.24 sec.	4.98 sec.	9.24 fps	8.67 fps	8.908 fps	8.58 fps	9.67 fps
SCX 2003 Lola Ford-Cosworth Champ Car Performance:	3.48 sec.	3.82 sec.	12.28 fps	11.97 fps	9.56 fps	12.28 fps	9.84 fps
Scalextric Le Mans Cadillac Northstar (Modified—two round magnets) Performance:	3.71 sec.	3.64 sec.	10.73 fps	10.56 fps	10.35 fps	9.96 fps	10.20 fps
NINCO 1977 Porsche 911 Turbo Performance:	4.98 sec.	5.14 sec.	7.66 fps	7.40 fps	7.47 fps	8.22 fps	8.50 fps
Spirit 2000 Reynard 2KQ Performance:	3.39 sec.	3.51 sec.	13.02 fps	12.88 fps	11.78 fps	12.72 fps	13.07 fps
Historic Scale Racing Replicas M8D Performance:	4.82 sec.	4.61 sec.	8.40 fps	9.08 fps	9.12 fps	8.21 fps	8.51 fps
NINCO 1998 Mercedes CLK Pro Race Performance:	4.49 sec.	4.27 sec.	9.19 fps	9.27 fps	9.00 fps	9.12 fps	9.32 fps
Carrera 2001 Bentley Speed 8 LMP (two magnets) Performance:	3.80 sec.	3.81 sec.	12.01 fps	10.87 fps	10.60 fps	8.81 fps	13.24 fps

Key to Abbreviations: fps: feet per second sec: second

NOTES: * Car would not negotiate the NINCO skid pad, driving off at more than half-throttle.
** The sustained high speeds on the two tracks and on the Sport skid pad burned out the motor.

The motor and rear axle are mounted on a separate pod on the Slot.it Porsche 956 to isolate vibrations.

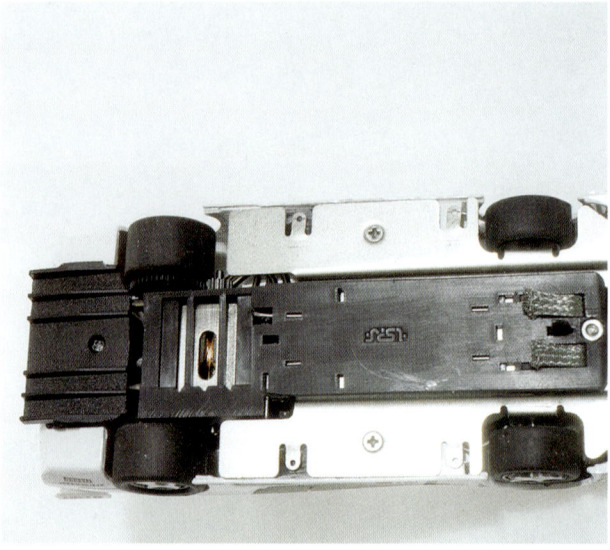

The TSRF Super-Tuned chassis is adapted to a Fly Saleen body.

The Spirit 1971 Ferrari 512M that is now in production has a quicker motor than the car we tested. The number 9 car is a Fly Lola T70.

Vanquish MG Lola T260 Can-Am models are a massive 1/29 scale.

The Vanquish MG Lotus 72 is also 1/29 scale.

The engine is fully detailed on the 1/29 scale Vanquish MG Lotus 72 Grand Prix car.

MODEL CAR RACING TRACK TEST RESULTS

(by brand and issue of *Model Car Racing* magazine with complete track test information)

- Artin Porsche GT-1/98, issue No. 11
- Auto Art 4-Wheel Drive Subaru WRX, issue No. 9
- Carrera 427 'Vette (regeared), issue No. 9
- Carrera 1970 Dodge Daytona Charger, issue No. 13
- Carrera Williams FW24, issue No. 15
- Carrera Porsche 911 RSR, issue No. 16
- Carrera (second-generation) 2002 Le Mans Bentley (with two magnets), issue No. 18
- Fly BMW M3GTR, issue No. 9
- Fly 1998 Lola T98/10, issue No. 12
- Fly 1968 Ford GT40, issue No. 14
- Fly 1972 Ferrari 365GTB /4 Daytona, issue No. 15
- Historic Racing Replicas McLaren M8D, issue No. 18
- MAXI-Models McLaren M6B, issue No. 7
- Monogram Daytona Cobra, issue No. 8
- Monogram 1963 Corvette Grand Sport, issue No. 14
- MRRC 427 Cobra, issue No. 10
- NINCO BMW M3GTR, issue No. 7
- NINCO 4-Wheel Drive Subaru WRX, issue No. 8
- NINCO Renault Clio (with suspension), issue No. 12
- NINCO 2002 CART Lola-Ford, issue No. 13
- NINCO 1977 Porsche 911 Turbo, issue No. 17
- NINCO 1998 Mercedes CLK ProRace, issue No. 18
- Pink-Kar Ferrari GTO, issue No. 16
- Pro-Track Spyder inline chassis, issue No. 8
- Proteus Lamborghini Murcielago, issue No. 15
- Scalextric Ford GT40, issue No. 7
- Scalextric Lola-MG EX257, issue No. 10
- Scalextric IRL Dallara, issue No. 12
- Scalextric 1972 L-88 Corvette, issue No. 13
- Scalextric Northstar Le Mans Cadillac with added magnets, issue No. 17
- SCX Dome-Judd S101, issue No. 13
- SCX 2003 CART Lola Ford-Cosworth, issue No. 17
- Slot-it Audi R8C, issue No. 7
- Slot-it 1983 Porsche 956, issue No. 14
- Spirit 1971 Ferrari 512M, issue No. 13
- Spirit 2000 Reynard 2KQ, issue No. 17
- TSRF Super-Tuned chassis (with NINCO McLaren body), issue No. 10
- Vanquish MG Lola T260 Can-Am, issue No. 9
- Vanquish MG Lotus 72 Grand Prix, issue No. 16

CHAPTER 3
REAL RACING ACTION

Four Grand National Plymouths and Dodges battle it out on a Carrera Pro-X track.

To me, racing defines fun. It's a belly-laugh-out-loud hoot to be driving at 101 percent of your capacity, with a friend doing exactly the same, and your two cars are moving so close that they seem to be linked with a half-inch-long bungee cord. It's almost as much fun to drive alone against the clock and discover you've just trimmed a full half-second off your best lap time. There are hundreds of other examples, including the special joy you feel when a car you have built or finely tuned is faster than its peers.

One Car at a Time

Nobody says you must race against another driver. For many model car racers, setting the fastest possible lap time is encouragement enough. The qualifying period for the races is one of the most exciting aspects of any race meet. Regardless of the brand of track, you can buy a plug-in electronic device that will count the number of laps and provide the time of the lap, usually down to 1/100 of a second. If you don't already have a lap counter/timer, buy one.

The lap-timing feature is perhaps the most useful because you use it to check the performance of the car. Just how much quicker is it if you move the traction magnet to the rear? Is it quicker with replacement silicone tires or just sanded-true stock tires?

The lap timer can help improve your driving techniques. With practice, you'll discover that there are certain sections of the track that you could take at a faster speed. It's only when you drive the quickest through every section of the track that you get the lowest lap times.

Scalextric Challenger, Never Race Alone Again

You have two choices of methods to race against yourself: Buy a Scalextric Sport Challenger and race against another car, or buy an accurate lap timer and

A photographer's darkroom timer, like this Cra Lab unit, can be used to turn the track on and off for timed races or heats. The laps are counted and the lap times are shown on the DS counter (right).

The Scalextric Challenger uses this Mercedes CLK DTM car. With a built-in computer, it will turn hands-off lap times that you'll be lucky to match.

The Carrera Pro-X chassis (bottom) is similar to the standard chassis, but the Pro-X has a printed circuit board, sensor, and longer guide shoe.

race against the clock. The Challenger replaces the Scalextric Pacer system.

The Challenger is designed to provide a second car that will race around the track as quickly as the best driver could race it by hand. Through the magic of computers and electronics, the Challenger learns the track and proceeds to crank off 50 flawless laps at the limits of tire adhesion. To get the most out of the Challenger, have lap counters on both its lane and yours. Sure, you can beat the Challenger for a lap, maybe even 10, but it takes real concentration to beat it for 50.

The Challenger is designed for Scalextric Sport or Classic track. If you use it on Carrera track, with the slightly smoother surface and less downforce, you may need to install silicone tires on the Challenger, and perhaps add additional magnets so the Challenger can come closer to the performance of standard racing cars on Carrera track.

Scalextric Sport World

Scalextric offers a PC interface program called Sport World. You can race at home, and you can compete

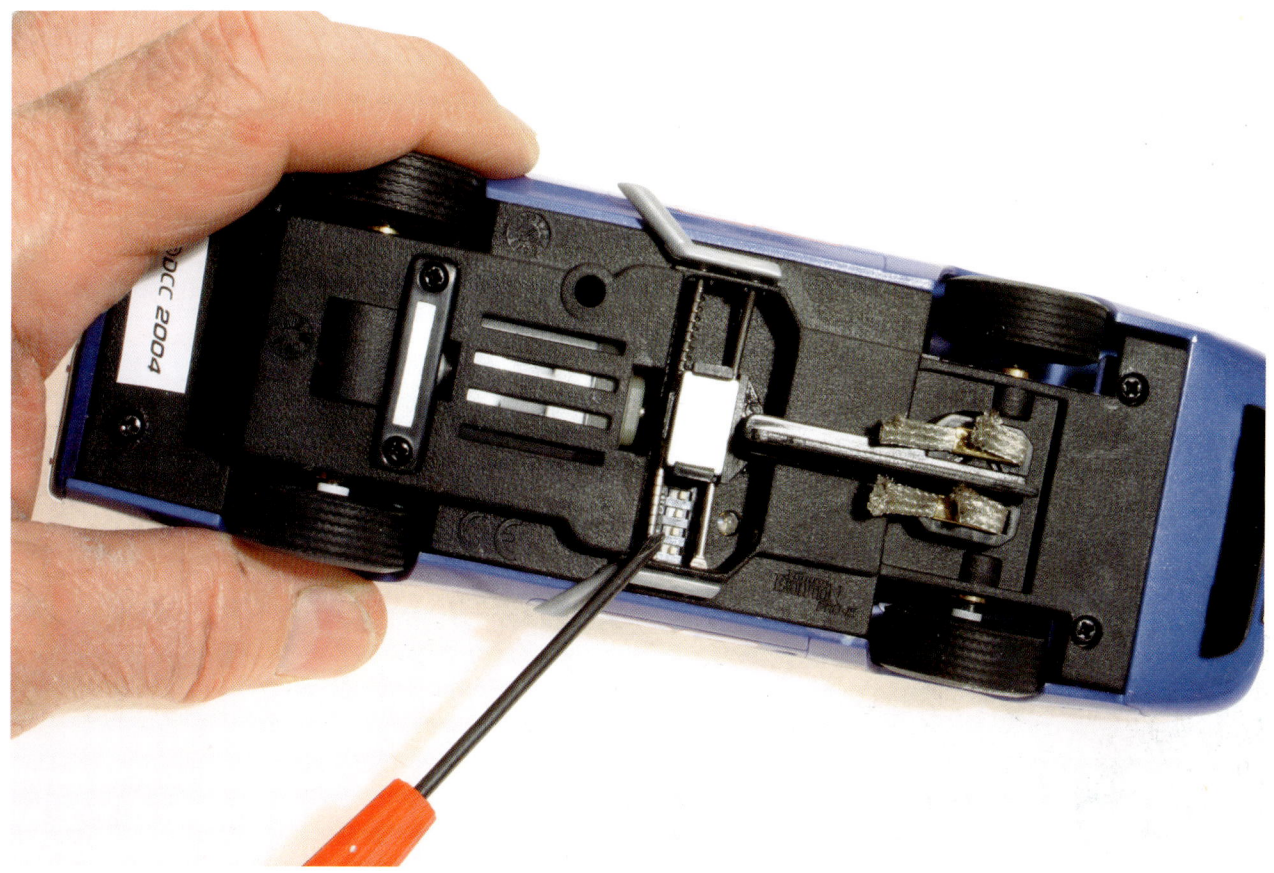

The four tiny slide switches on the dep switch on the bottom of the Carrera Pro-X cars are moved to set the cars either for Lanes 1, 2, 3, or 4; to program the car to be a pace car; or for pit lane sequences.

with other home racers worldwide on the Internet. The Sport World system includes a special connector track and PC software. The PC software provides real-time 3-D coverage of the racing on screen and a host of additional features to add realism to the racing. Software tools allow you to design and build circuits in 3-D, manage your car collection, and monitor and tune your cars performance. Online racing means you can race anyone anywhere in the world at anytime.

The immersive 3-D circuit design allows you to build a virtual eight-lane track. Circuits can be built from the full range of Sport and Classic track. The track can be lifted to form bridges and track twisted to close a circuit, just like in real life. You can also add buildings and accessories and sculpt the landscape.

The 3-D car catalog allows you to view a library of over 150 Scalextric cars, including more than 60 3-D models that allow you to view every detail of the latest cars. You can modify performance attributes of any car and take it for a virtual test drive to see the improvements before you apply them to your real 1/32 scale car.

The Sport World system allows you to load in data from previously saved races to view throttle versus speed graphs and compare them with your rivals or with your own best lap. Sport World hardware and software combine to keep track of exactly where each car is on the circuit so you can see the race from the trackside cameras or even ride on the bumper of the race leader. Pit boards constantly display race positions and the stats ticker keeps you updated on split times. Crashes, refueling, and tire changes are all covered in real time.

The Magic of Digital Racing

Now you can race 1/32 scale cars that perform more like the real cars than any tabletop racers in history. Scalextric, Carrera, and SCX have new cars and controllers that use digital technology to allow you

The tiny round bulb in the corner of the Carrera Pro-X lane-changing track is the sensor that receives the lane-change command from the car.

to drive the cars more like real racing machines than slot cars. The Scalextric Sport Digital, Carrera Pro-X, and SCX Digital systems are available now, and the NINCO system will be available in December 2005.

The new systems allow four to six cars to race at once in one lane, with each car under your complete control. There's no need for more than two lanes. With the digital systems, the better drivers will soon learn which is the fastest line around the track, and you will be the first of the losers if you can't figure out how to pass the leader. That's what happens on a real racetrack. It's a first for tabletop racing. Until now, tabletop racing was still slot racing with each car being able to zip along, more-or-less, without regard to any other car on the track. That's not the way it is on a real racetrack. These systems all have built-in car-identification systems for foolproof lap counting and timing.

How the Digital Systems Work

The new digital systems all feature a diagonal slot in a special track section to allow the cars to move from Lane 1 to Lane 2. There's a small metal flap that aligns either with the straight-ahead slot or crossover slot. A button on your controller opens that flap to the crossover when you want to change lanes. The Carrera Pro-X has a tiny button in the crossover that is activated by the car's guide shoe to return the flap to the straight route. The Scalextric Sport Digital flap has two solenoids, one to position the flap to straight and a second to move the flap back to the crossover position. The SCX digital system's lane-changing flap has a spring to return the flap to the straight position.

The Scalextric digital lane-changers are located on 90-degree standard (R2-size) curves. The Carrera Pro-X lane-changers are two special double-length pieces of straight. There are right- and left-hand versions, and with Scalextric Sport Digital, "in" and "out" sections. Many of the track plans in this book have Scalextric and Carrera lane-changers located at what I guess would be the best places to best simulate real racing action. So far SCX only offers standard (R2) curves and standard and half-length straights, so none of the plans in *Model Car Racing* can be used. SCX has promised a full line of curves

The Pro-X sensor provides the electrical signal to move the spring-loaded flap in the slot from straight to lane-change.

and shorter straights for future release, so you will then be able to use the Scalextric Sport plans for the SCX Digital track since both systems share the same geometry and nearly identical track section sizes of footprints.

All three digital systems (Carrera Pro-X, Scalextric Sport Digital, and SCX Digital) operate with a steady 12 to 18 volts of DC current through the rails. Both lanes are powered at all times. The commands to speed up, slow down, stop, or change lanes are carried through the pickup rails, and a decoder or chip inside the car implements those commands. This is the basic Digital Command Control system that has been proven in decades of use on model railroads. The difference between model racing cars and model railroads, however, is that the model railroad manufacturers have been foresighted enough to standardize a system, while the model race car manufacturers each have a system of their own. You cannot race one brand of car on any other manufacturer's track system.

It seems possible for a clever entrepreneur to develop a decoder module that would work with

A small wire-wound solenoid moves the Carrera Pro-X lane-changing flap from beneath the track. The coil spring pulls the flap back to the straight path as soon as the car's guide shoe leaves the flap.

I found that the basic Carrera Pro-X oval worked best with lane-changing tracks in the diagonal corners of the straights at the exits from the curves.

both Scalextric Sport Digital and with Carrera Pro-X, but so far that has not happened.

The Scalextric Sport Digital System offers a retro-fit chip to convert any brand of car to digital so that car can race on a Scalextric Sport Digital system, as well as on any conventional system. The car cannot, however, be raced on either a Carrera Pro-X or SCX Digital system.

None of the digital systems can be used with conventional cars. If you have an existing track, you must replace the connector track (where the controllers connect and power is supplied to the track) with the digital version. You must also replace the necessary track sections with lane-changing sections. Once converted, you cannot run any conventional cars—only digital cars. You can run Carrera or SCX conventional cars (or most other brands) that have been converted with the Scalextric Sport Digital retro-fit chip on Scalextric Sport Digital tracks. You cannot run anything but Carrera Pro-X cars on Carrera Pro-X track or SCX Digital cars on SCX Digital track.

The track plans in Chapters 8 and 9 often indicate two positions for the controller-connector track ("A" on the plans) so the drivers can be positioned at different areas of the track. If you are using digital systems, only one connector track can be used. If you try to use two, you will likely burn out some of the circuits in one or both of the connector tracks. SCX offers a cable to allow the second set of three controllers (SCX 2500 control unit) to be positioned a few feet away from the first three, but only one terminal track (where transformer is plugged in) can be used.

Lane-Changing vs. Conventional Racing

For the present moment, digital lane changing is a separate hobby. You can use the track sections from Carrera or Scalextric with their specific systems, but the track can include only the digital terminal or connector track—putting both conventional and digital terminal sections in the same track can destroy the digital system. The lane-changing tracks are, at present, only usable with digital cars. You cannot run older cars on the digital systems. Scalextric offers an $18 retro-fit chip (decoder) that will fit virtually any 1/32 scale car including conventional Carrera and SCX cars, as well as NINCO, Fly, Monogram, Auto Art, Slot.it, Spirit, MRRC, and

continued on page 37

This 45-foot, triangle-shaped track has room for four Carrera Pro-X lane-changers; two in the upper right, one in the far upper left (beyond the connector track), and one on the short straight in the upper center.

The Scalextric Sport Digital lane-changer tracks have two moving flaps that are visible as large metal triangles.

The Scalextric Sport Digital lane changers are located at the 90-degree standard curve with the sensor on a half-straight just before the curve.

The Scalextric Sport Digital connector Power Base track includes a seven-function lap counter and a timer.

most other brands. When installed, you can run the car on Scalextric Sport Digital, but not on Carrera Pro-X or SCX Digital. The Scalextric Sport Digital cars, whether out-of-the-box or converted older cars or other brands, will still run on conventional systems. The Carrera or SCX cars will not.

It is relatively simple to pull out the lane changers and a controller-connector track and replace them with conventional track and controller-connector tracks. I've changed over a 45-foot track in less than 30 minutes, including aligning borders and displaced scenery. The staff of *Model Car Racing* magazine is trying to work out some modifications that will allow you to leave the lane changers in place to run either all conventional or all lane-changer cars, but that is still in the future.

The Carrera Pro-X System

The Carrera Pro-X cars are essentially conventional Carrera cars with the addition of a decoder chip and a sensor to trigger the lane changer. Carrera has designed a rather complex guide shoe that moves the forward magnet from side to side and provides spring-loading to self-center the guide. The guide shoe is three times the length of a conventional Carrera guide to provide the length needed to trigger Carrera's lap-counting system.

When you press the lane-change button on the Carrera controller, a signal goes out from the car that is received by a tiny sensor at the corner of the lane-changing track. The metal flap that changes the lane from straight to crossover is triggered only by the signal from that car, and then only as the car is within a few inches of the lane changer. The system makes it possible for you to change lanes in front of your car without that car following you through the lane changer. The lane-changer flap reverts immediately to the straight position as soon as the car has passed. The lane-changing flap is operated by a small solenoid beneath the track with a coil return spring, much like similar systems for model railroad track switches. The Carrera lane-changing track has the

The SCX Digital track has a double-crossover lane-changer that can be used to move cars from either lane.

moving flap only at entry to the crossover. There is no flap at the exit. Carrera uses a long crossover that utilizes most of the length of two full straights. Their rationale is that cars can change lanes at higher speed than they could with a shorter lane changer.

All Carrera Pro-X digital cars have a built-in pace car option, as well as a pit stop function that can only be used if the optional track sections with a third slot for the pit lane is installed in the track. The Carrera cars are programmed to be Car 1, Car 2, Car 3, and Car 4 by moving the tiny buttons on a dep switch on the bottom of the car. That same switch is used to set the optional pace car mode into the "Fast" or "Slow" speeds to provide competition to match your driving skills. The pace car randomly selects lane changes to make it a more challenging competitor.

The Scalextric Sport Digital System

The Scalextric Sport Digital system operates very much like the Carrera Pro-X system. The primary difference is that the Scalextric system utilizes a 90 degree section of standard curved track ("R1") plus a half-straight. The half-straight includes a tiny sensor that the chip or decoder inside the car triggers. Scalextric Sport Digital controllers look like the standard Scalextric controllers, but they have a large button on the back to activate the lane-changer and a smaller black button that can be used to turn the brakes on or off. The guide shoe is similar to that in a conventional car. The sensor in each car triggers the lap counting and timing in the power base connector track.

The Scalextric Sport Digital system has a computer built into the power base controller-connector track. The Sport Digital system has seven

The guide shoe on the SCX Digital cars has a 1/4-inch-long tab that extends down into the slot 1/8 inch when the lane-change button on the controller is depressed.

A solenoid inside the car controls a lever that operates the actuating tab in the center of the guide shoe on the SCX Digital cars.

The tip of a toothpick demonstrates how the extended tab on the SCX Digital cars opens the flap in the track to allow the car to change lanes.

race modes that can be expanded with the Sport PC Interface system. Race information, including lap counting and timing, is displayed on each of the two rows of the LCD display.

The SCX Digital System

The electrical components that activate the lane-changing function in the SCX Digital system are in the cars, rather than the lane-changing tracks. The SCX Digital system does have a moving flap like the Carrera and Sport Digital systems, but the plastic flap is simply spring-loaded to the straight route. The guide shoe on the SCX Digital system cars opens the crossover-lane flap mechanically. The guide shoe on the SCX Digital cars has a 1/4-inch-wide center section, or plunger, that is extended about 1/8 inch below the bottom of the guide shoe to activate the lane change. On the lane-changing tracks, each lane changing flap has a 1/8-inch deeper slot to accommodate the deeper portion of the plunger in the car's guide shoe. The lower edge of the moving flap that changes the lane is reachable only by that extended guide shoe plunger. It's a very clever system that means only your car is going to open that flap and it will spring shut until the next car with an extended length guide shoe plunger opens the flap. The guide shoe's extended depth plunger is actuated by a lever and a small solenoid inside the car.

The track supplied with SCX Digital system is all new. It is dark gray instead of black, and has a new snap-in connection system for the track sections, borders, and retaining walls or guard rails. The track is only about 1/8 inch wider than conventional SCX track, but it is not interchangeable. There is a third electrical strip in the SCX Digital track that runs below the bottom of the slot with a third set of copper connectors at each track joint. The third power strip (SCX calls it a power line) is used to carry current to the lap counter/timer and other accessories. The SCX Digital cars receive their power

continued on page 44

The basic SCX Digital set includes three cars and four lane-changers that can be expended to race up to six cars with the addition of three more SCX Digital cars, three 20060 controllers, a 20070 electronic transformer, a 25000 control unit, a 25010 lap-counter expansion module, and a 20090 connecting cable.

With 8 SCX Digital lane-changers, there are 16 opportunities to pass on this 6x15-foot track.

The basic Scalextric Sport Digital set includes an elevated overpass for a figure-8-shaped track that, if used, can bend the track pins. It's best to arrange the track in a flat oval like this.

from the pickup rails like all the other model racing car systems. The SCX Digital cars have a special guide shoe that, in addition to the extending center plunger, has metal faces on each side. Those metal faces are used to contact brass tabs near the moving flaps on the lane-changer tracks to provide stall-free electrical power through the lane-changer track. The brass tabs are spring-loaded below the track to maintain electrical contact with the guide shoe. Carrera and Scalextric use long metal flaps to provide stall-free operation through the lane-changing track.

The SCX Digital system includes a separate lap counter, which is sold with most sets. The SCX Digital lap counter displays the total number of laps, the positions of each car in the race, and lap times. The SCX cars are programmed by placing them on the connector track and depressing the

Top Right and Above: The Scalextric Sport Digital system's sensors (located inside the cars) trigger the lane-changer and the digital decoder chip to allow six cars to operate at once.

controller brake button to match the car. SCX Digital will have a variety of programs and track sections for pit stops and rally competition in the future.

Tips for More Multi-Car Racing Fun

Install the lane-changers at the beginning of any long straights. On a simple oval, put the lane-changers diagonally apart in the two opposite corners of the track at the exits of the curves.

The terminal or controller-connector tracks on SCX, Scalextric, and Carrera are directional so the cars will only run in the direction indicated by the marks on the track surface of the starting grid of each brand.

The lane-changing tracks for Carrera and Scalextric are also directional. If you want to run cars in the opposite direction, you must rotate the lane changers 180 degrees.

To prevent loss of electrical power on the track, I strongly recommend that you install Scalextric Sport C8248 track power booster cables or Carrera 20584 additional supply cables to connect every 15 feet of track.

When a car deslots, you no longer have to worry about putting it in the correct slot. Just slap it back onto the track and align the guide with either slot on either lane.

I do not claim to be the most coordinated person on the planet, but I cannot effectively make

The receiver to signal the Scalextric Sport Digital system to change lanes is located in a circular cutout in the slot on the sensor track section.

my thumb operate independently from my index finger. I found it far easier to change lanes by holding the controller (regardless of whether it was Carrera, SCX, or Scalextric) in both hands, operating the speed trigger with one hand and hitting the lane-changer button with other.

The "Ten-Count" Penalty

The experience of hundreds of hours of real car racing helped us develop a simple rule to prevent lane-changing from becoming a destruction derby. If your car causes an accident by either ramming the rear of another car or sideswiping a car, your car is removed from the track for 10 seconds. That one rule virtually eliminates the demolition derby that experienced model car racers were oh-so-sure would doom lane changing. In over 100 races, there were only four penalties.

Digital Lane-Changing Systems, Pros & Cons:

I can, as with different brands of track (see *Slot Car Bible*), make a very good case for any one of the brands of digital racing. Conversely, each brand has its own Achilles' heel. Here are some pros and cons.

Scalextric Sport Digital

Pros: The system uses standard Scalextric Sport track, which means that with Sport track adaptors, you can also use it with Scalextric Classic or standard SCX. Or, you can use NINCO adaptors to connect Sport to NINCO track. Only the new digital terminal track with new controllers and the lane-changing track sections need to be added to any existing or proposed race track. Having the lane changers on a curve makes it easier to fit them into a smaller track. Up to six cars can be raced at once, and an additional power base plugs into the controller-connector track to provide the power needed for three more cars. So far, Scalextric is the only system to offer retrofit kits that should work on a Carrera, Fly, NINCO, or most other car brands as they do on a Scalextric car. There's also the option of running six cars at a time.

Cons: The lane-changers are 90 degree standard-size (R2) curves and need a half-straight before the turn, so you may need to modify the track plan to get that two-piece set of track in place. Also, there are "in and out" sections so you will not be able to change lanes if you want to race in the opposite direction on the track. Cars are around $59.95 each.

Carrera Pro-X

Pros: The system uses standard Carrera track except for the terminal track and the lane-changing track sections. The lane-changers on a straight allow the cars to pass at relatively high speeds. Likely the least expensive system, the cars should be about $5 more than conventional Carrera cars. Any Carrera Pro-X car can be converted into a pace car so you can race against yourself by setting the miniature dep switch on the bottom of the car as shown in the instructions.

Cons: It can be difficult on a small track to find the space for the two straight lane-changers. Only four cars can be run at a time. No additional power is available, and a slight power surge can be felt when four cars are racing. The Pro-X cars do not have brakes. There is no retrofit available, which means you may not be able to run any other brand on the Carrera Pro-X track unless you swap chassis. So far, Carrera only offers three F1 cars and the Dodge and Plymouth 1970-era NASCAR cars, but most new Carrera cars will be available as Pro-X racers. There are no retrofit kits for Carrera or any other brand.

SCX Digital

Pros: The lane-changer is short, includes right, left, in, and out turns so you can fit it into just about any track plan and have the option of changing directions. The lane-changers are relatively inexpensive so you can install more of them to provide more places to pass with less forethought about where to pass. The new digital track is more realistic than standard SCX track. You can race up to six cars at once, and additional power supplies plug into the connector track.

Cons: The SCX track is not interchangeable with conventional SCX track. There are no retrofit kits so you cannot run conventional SCX or any other brand or cars. At the moment, only standard straight and standard curve track sections are available, but more are promised. The cars are a bit more costly because more of the electronic gear is in the car. There is limited choice of cars. The larger number of lane-changing possibilities does not accurately imitate real racing. It's a bit too easy to pass.

The lane-changer flap on the Scalextric Sport Digital system is actuated by pair of solenoids that push the flap to either straight or crossover position.

NINCO Digital

NINCO's system will allow you to use conventional NINCO track for all except the lane-changers and terminal tracks. NINCO will also offer retrofit decoders or chips so you can convert a NINCO and most other brands to run on the NINCO track. NINCO promises to address the pros and cons of the other brands, but it is too early to tell if you can run a NINCO digital car on the Carrera or Scalextric Sport Digital track.

CHAPTER 4
RACE CAR PREP AND PERFORMANCE

Fly's BMW 3.0CSL races with a Monogram Greenwood Corvette, perhaps at Daytona in 1976.

No model racing car runs its best right out of the box. Most will run around the track, but none are race-ready. Every experienced model car racer goes through a mental check list of things to do to be sure each new race car is truly ready to race. Blueprinting is what most of the real car racers call the process of bringing the car up to the near-perfect performance within any racing rules.

The car will become quicker if you drive it long enough to work in the bearing surfaces and gear mesh. If you really want to assess how performance-improvements work, I strongly suggest you invest in a lap counter/timer so you can time how fast the car is going before and after you make each change.

Perfect Preparation

There are dozens of things you can do to improve the performance of any model racing car. Most of them are in this chapter. There are two approaches to getting more speed from a model car: I call the first approach "pick of the litter," and the second, "perfect preparation." The pick-of-the-litter approach is the one I personally use as often as possible. You simply try all the cars you have and race the best one. I adjust the braid and usually replace the tires with silicones and sand the rear tires, but that's about all I do to tune the majority of my cars. There are many racers who go through the entire tuning and setup procedure, right down to new axles, wheels, gears, and tires, with every car.

More Motor

Today, changing motors or gears is hardly ever necessary. About 90 percent of the cars have the same motor, and SCX and NINCO (two of the motors that look different) are built to match the performance of the others. There are differences among stock motors from the same production batch that can be as high as 10 percent. The best of the stock motors is better than the worst of the higher-revving motors.

Chassis Perfection

First, inspect the edges of the tires where they are closest to the body. In my experience, at least one tire will rub the body on at least half of the Fly cars, but the problem can occur on any brand. In some rare cases, the rear tires may rub on some chassis part on the inside. Use a hobby knife to shave away slivers of plastic at the point where the tire is rubbing.

Next, place the car on a perfectly flat piece of Carrera or Artin hard plastic track or a block of wood with a slot cut in the wood to accept the guide. Be sure all four tires touch. Gently lift each front wheel and tire to see if there is any upward movement. If there is no upward movement, you might want to correct that (this is described later).

When you are satisfied that the tires are true, apply a drop of cyanoacrylate cement (ACC or Super Glue) to each of the rear axle bearing mounts and to the front and rear motor mounts. Wipe off any

continued on page 53

Rest the car on a perfectly flat piece of track to be sure all four tires touch the track surface.

Wet the inside of the tire and wheel rim with saliva to lubricate the tire so it will snap into place.

If you are perfectly satisfied with your choice of tires, they can be glued to the rims with Walthers Goo, Pliobond, or Elmer's Probond.

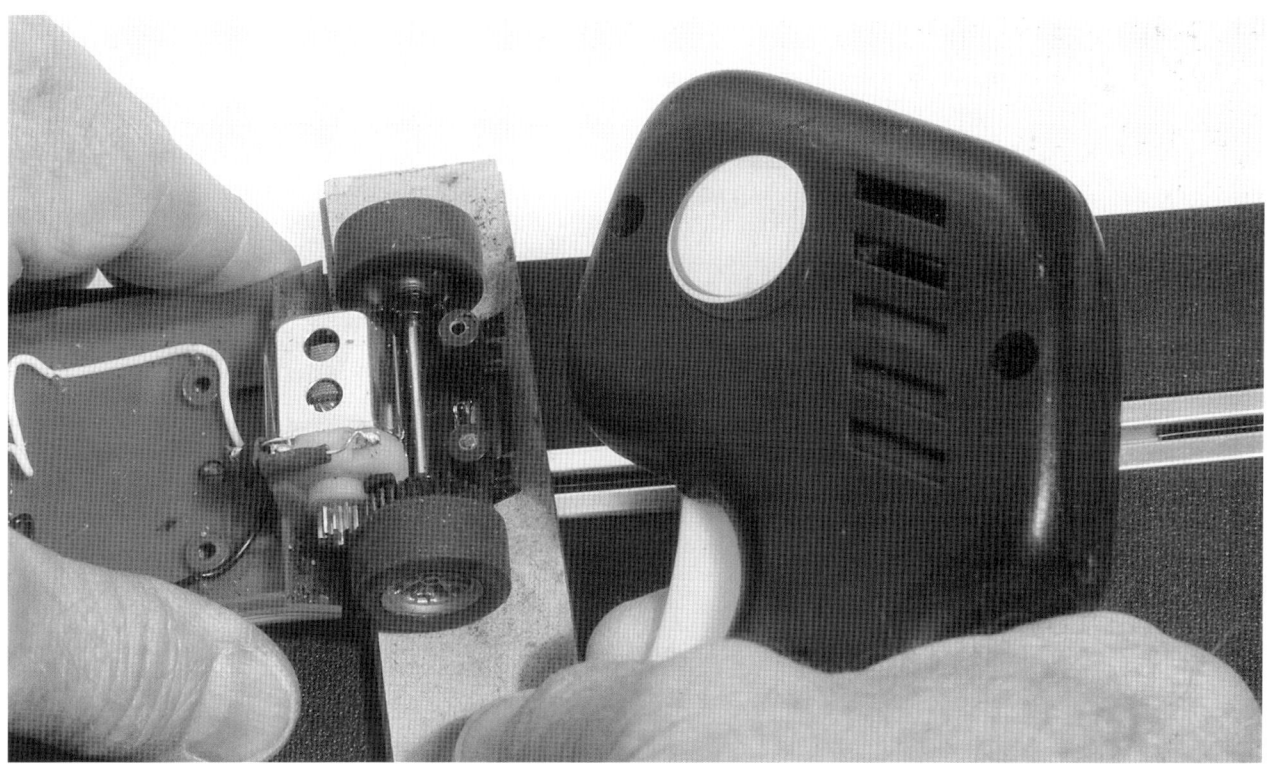
Set the throttle on full speed and gently lower the car onto a block of fine-grit sandpaper so that the spinning tires barely touch.

Pry out the coil spring that serves to self-center the pickup shoe on the Scalextric cars and discard the spring.

On Scalextric cars, insert the braid and pull the long and short ends down so you can trim the short end.

There's only a subtle difference in the shape and angle of the braid, but it's enough to ensure no-stall performance and full-power pickup.

If the wheels will not twist off by hand, remove the tires and grip the wheels as gently as you can and use a slight twisting motion.

excess glue with a tissue, spray the areas with kicker to set the cement, and wipe off any excess fluid.

Wheels and Tires

The most important speed secret for any model race car is round tires. It may sound obvious, but there is at least some wobble in every car I have seen, and some are considerably worse than others.

First, spin each tire and wheel by hand and push and wiggle the tire firmly all around its circumference to be sure it is seated properly. Even if the tires are round, the sanding will roughen up the tread surface to provide better traction. Artist supply stores sell small wood sticks with fine-grit sandpaper that are great for sanding rear tires.

Wrap a rubber band around the throttle trigger to keep it on full speed. Hold the rear of the car in one hand while you hold the sandpaper with your other hand. Gently lower the car with its spinning rear wheels onto the surface of the sandpaper. The object here is to just touch the tires so the high spots touch the sandpaper first and are sanded away. Slowly lower the car onto the sandpaper, placing a bit more pressure on one tire and then on the next. Finally, apply equal pressure to both wheels to be sure the tires are flat across their widths.

You can actually hear an out-of-round tire because it produces a vibrating noise that a round tire does not. If the vibrating noise does not go away after about 30 seconds of light sanding, the wheel or tire is probably too far out of round to correct. A really out-of-round tire is usually caused by a crooked wheel or a wheel that has a lump of plastic on the rim that should be sanded smooth. You can remove the tire and use the throttle to slowly spin the rear wheels to see if the wheel is out of round. Sometimes you can bend the wheel back into true-running with firm finger pressure.

Silicone Rubber Tires

Years of experience racing 1/32 scale cars has proven beyond doubt that most cars will be quicker if you use something other than stock tires. Look at the lap times in the shoot-outs in Chapter 5 for the cars without magnets and you'll see that the stock tires seldom work well unless there's a strong magnet to

continued on page 58

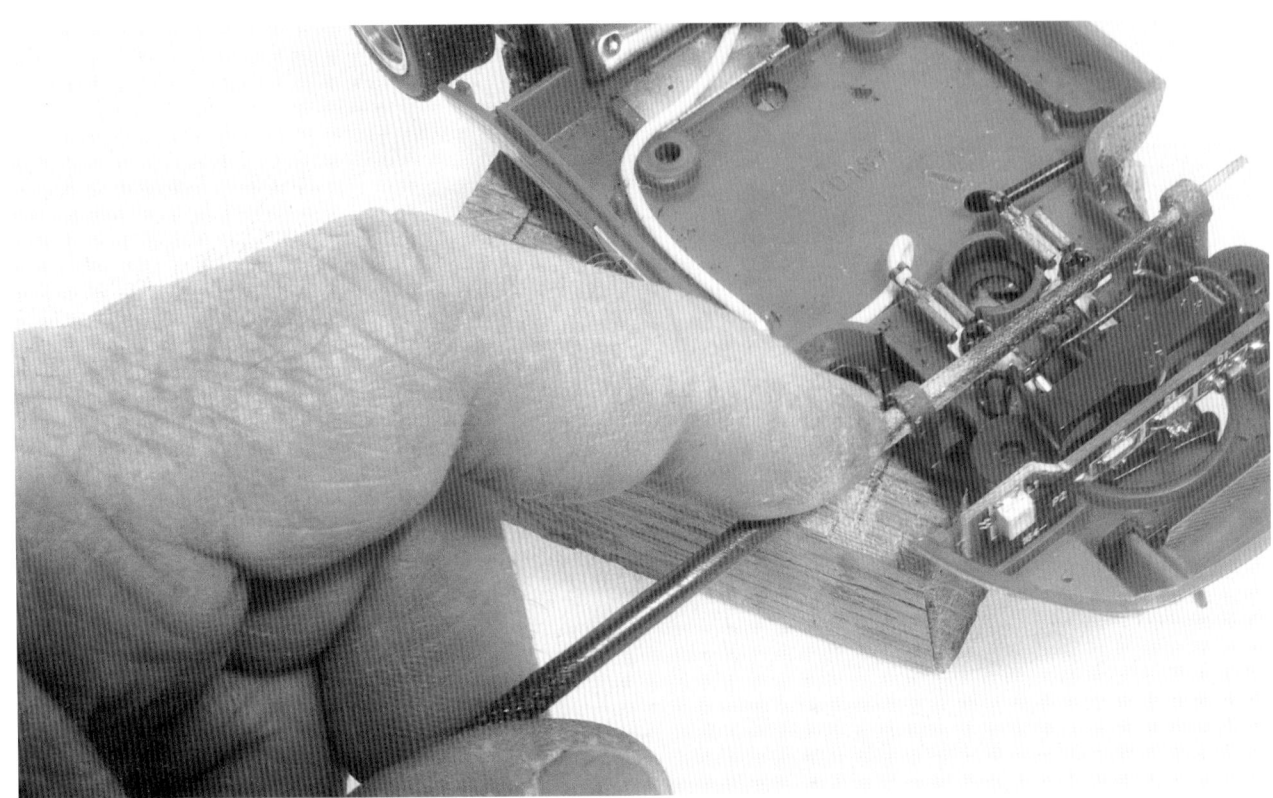

Use a jeweler's file to remove about 1/64 inch of plastic from the bottom of each front axle hole.

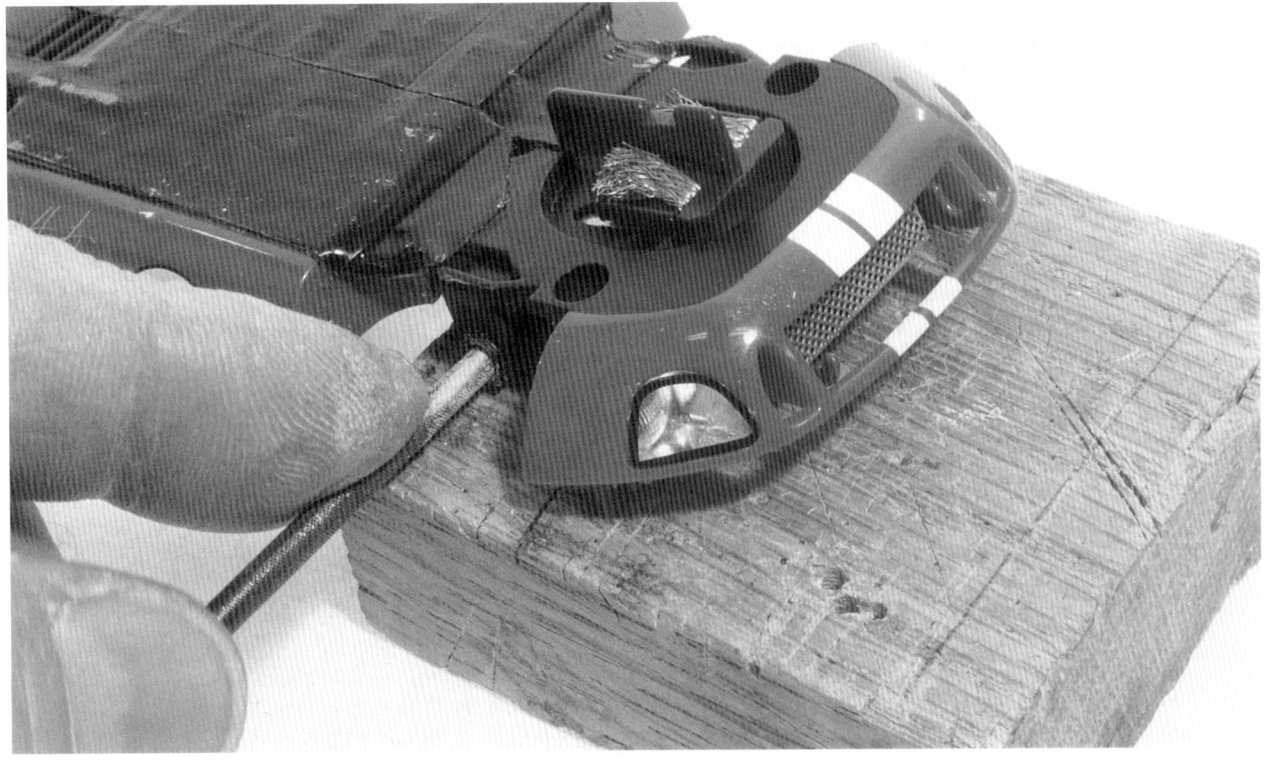

Turn the car over and file off about 1/64 inch of plastic from the bottom of the axle hole.

When you are finished filing the axle, it should be free to move up and down a total of about 1/32 to 1/16 inch.

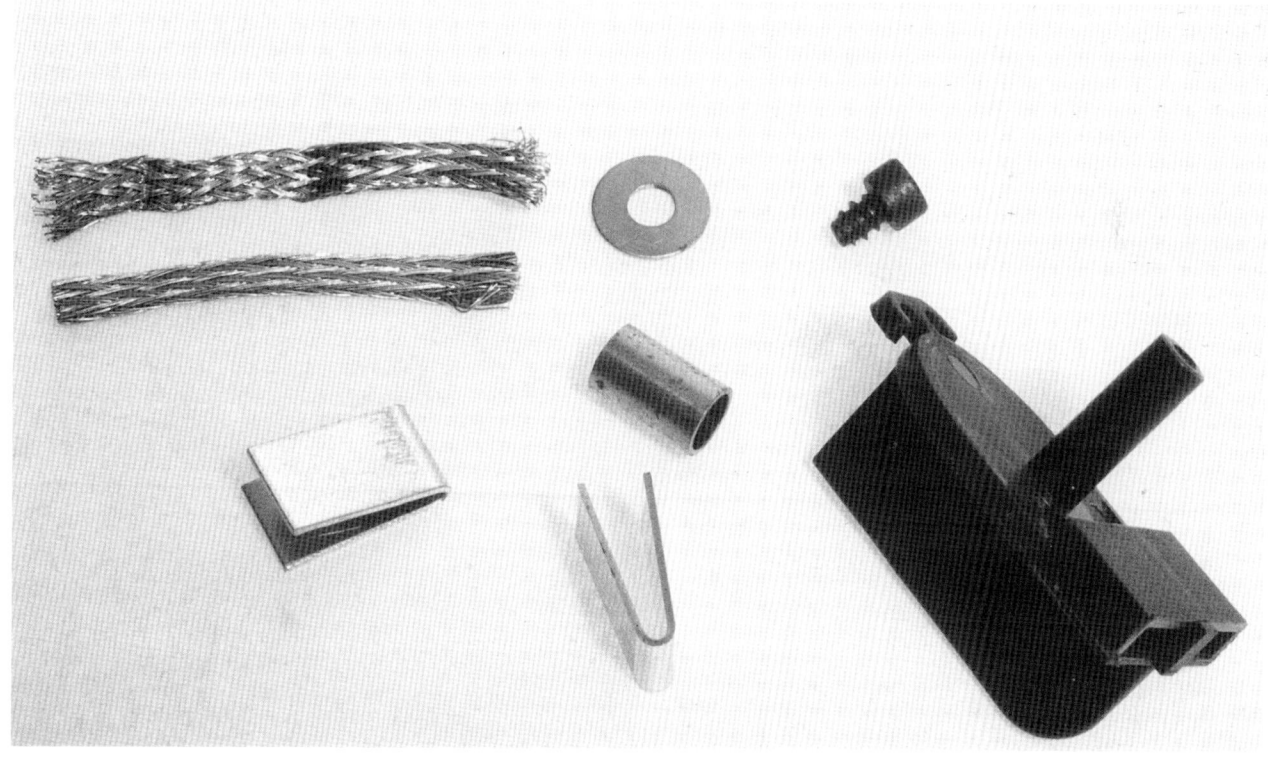

The Electric Dream's number TSP-1 Carrera Pickup conversion kit with Super Slot brass clips.

Press the brass tube completely into the Carrera pickup pivot hole with needlenose pliers.

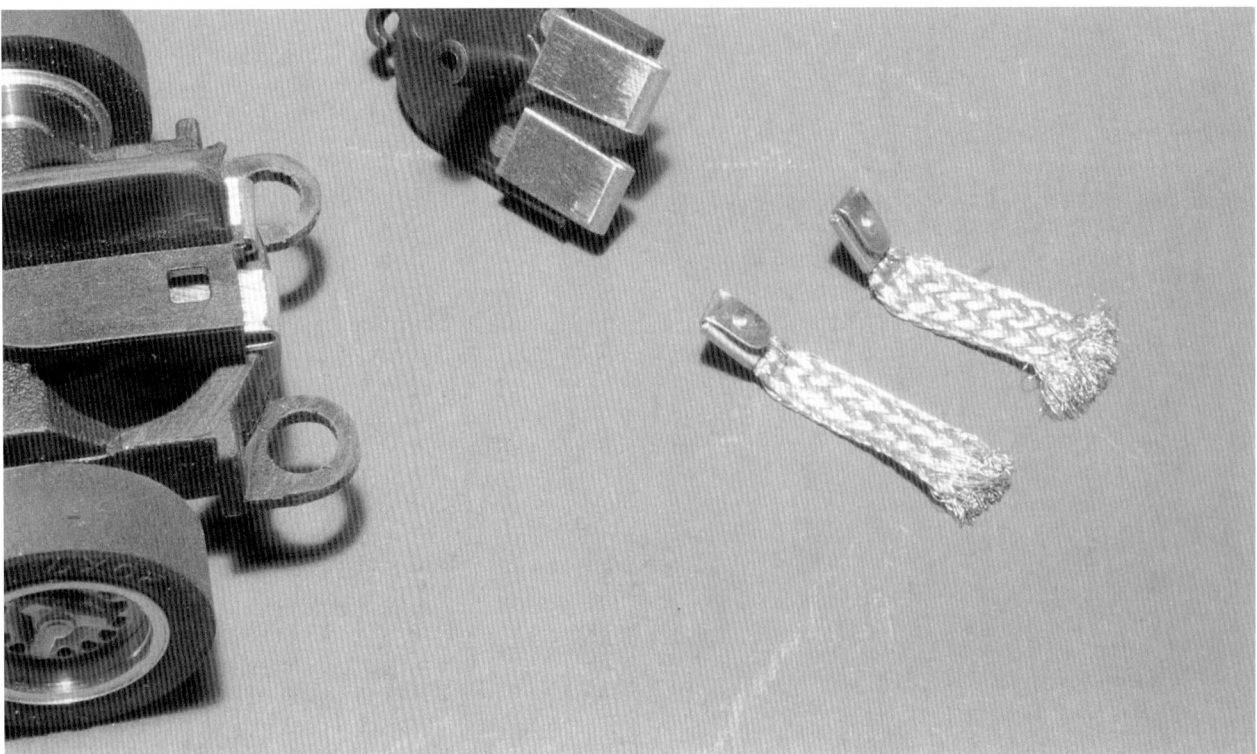
For a quick-change braid, insert the brass clips as shown.

Solder the motor-led wires to the top of each of the brass clips.

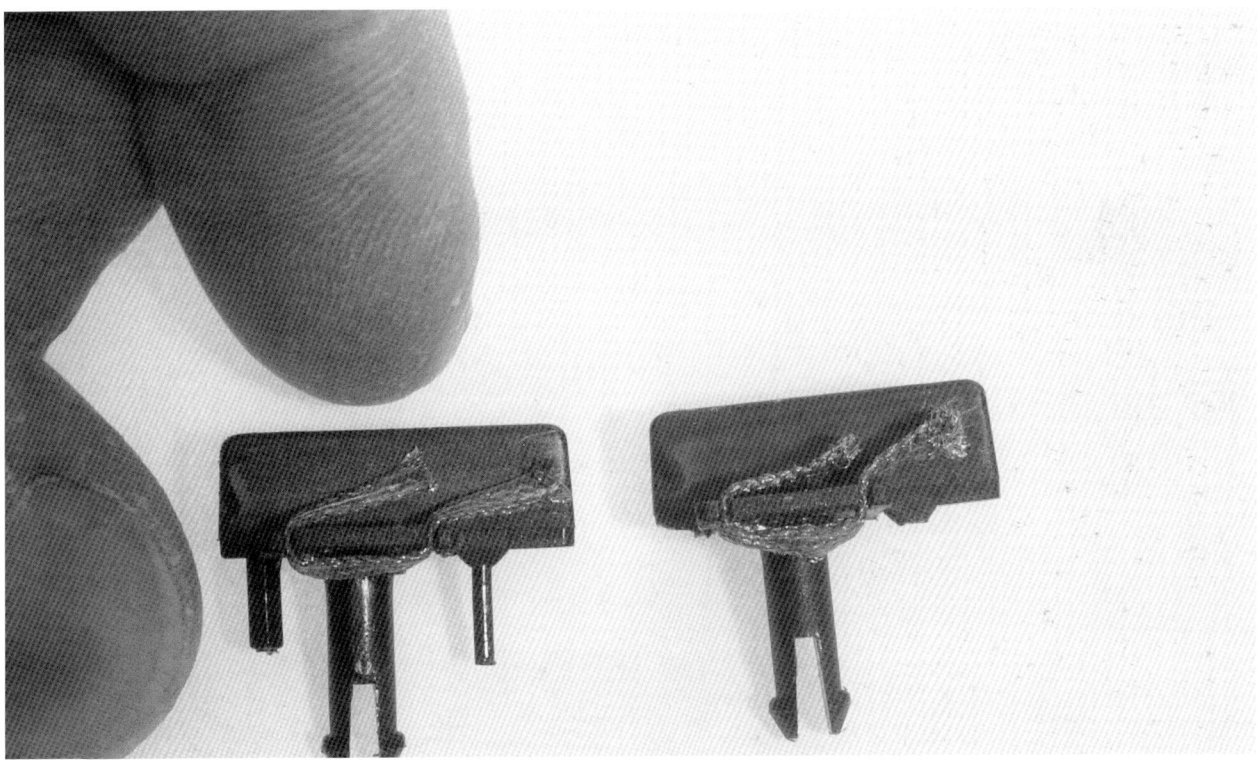
The new SCX pickup is on the left. The SCX pickup on the right has a broken stop pin and steering-actuating pin. Usually just the stop pin breaks.

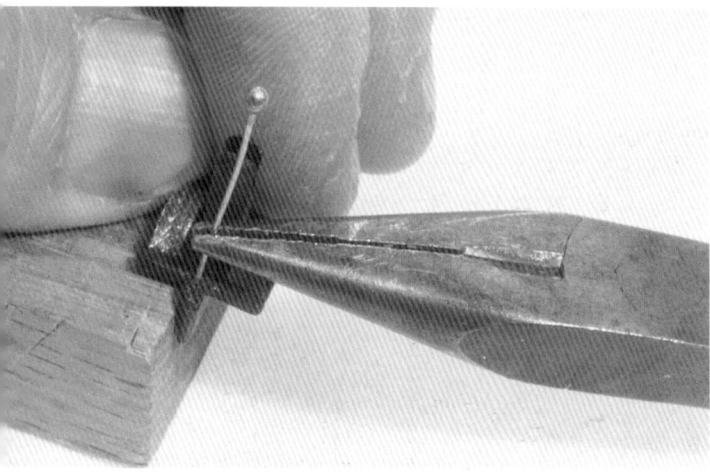

Use a straight pin, held by a pair of needle-nose pliers, to make a 1/64-inch-deep dimple in the center of the SCX pickup at the precise locations of the two broken pins.

keep them from hopping and sliding. The aftermarket tires are both more round and offer better traction, which shows up big time in reduced lap times. At the moment, the most commonly available aftermarket tires are silicone rubber replacements. Puma Paws and Indy Grips are the most common brands in the United States, but there are others.

Generally speaking, softer rear tires (such as NINCO, Slot.it, P-B-Ls Hot Shoes, Ortmann, and Buffalo Hobby's Super Tires) will work as well as and sometimes even better than silicones, but be prepared to lose some of the advantages of softer tires if you run against cars that are fitted with silicone tires. In the interests of equal racing, I recommend that you pick one brand for each race to minimize the variables. That's what I did for the shoot-out tests.

Three-Point Suspension

There are dozens of theories about why one model car corners better than another. One suggests that the car is primarily a three-point device, with the rear tires and the pickup being the critical points of contact. The front tires are there to serve much like training wheels on a bicycle. Some cars are designed so that the weight of the car rests on the pickup, with the front wheels and tires touching the track, but carrying only their own weight. In a corner, the front wheels do not touch until the car starts to lean at the extreme edge of traction. Another theory is that the slightly loose or rattling body also takes a set as the body leans to the limit of its very slight movement.

To set up a car with three-point contact, you may need to enlarge the holes for the front axle. Remove the front axle (which usually requires the removal of one of the front wheels). Use a round jeweler's file to enlarge the front axle holes about 1/64 inch on the top and on the bottom. Do not remove any material from the sides of the holes. You want to allow the axle to move a total of about 1/32 inch. The axle can actually move up until the top of the tire hits the inside of the fender, but there is seldom that much plastic on the axle bearings. When you're finished, there should be at least 1/32 inch of plastic left at the top of the bearing so the axle cannot break through the bearing.

Use a number 60 drill bit in a pin vise to drill a hole about 3/32 inch deep—just deep enough so you can see the edges at the base of the SCX pickup blade. The 0-80 screw will cut its own thread in the soft plastic.

Cut off the head of the new screw in the SCX pickup with needle-nose pliers.

Use sprue cutters to trim about 1/32 inch from any posts or ridges that prevent a loose body from rattling on the chassis.

Better Pickup Action

The pickup or guide shoe used in Scalextric cars is also used by some of the other makers, including MRRC, Pro-Track, and MAXI-Models. Scalextric uses a rubbing contact on the tops of the pickup brushes so there are no wires to flex and break. The rubbing contact is part of the chassis, however, and is not available from other makers, although SCX and Auto Art have similar no-wire contact systems. Some model car racers prefer to bypass the Scalextric (or SCX or Auto Art) metal wipers and connect wires directly to the pickup, just like the "old days." It can be difficult to measure the effect of bypassing the Scalextric contact system in actual racing, but it can prevent an occasional lack of power if the contacts are not touching.

To "hard wire" the braid, I recommend soldering the wires to the top of the braid. If the braid wears out, soften the solder and resolder it to the new braid. MRRC, Pro-Track, and MAXI-Models all supply hard-wired Scalextric pickups and use a small brass ferrule to connect the wires without solder. There is a problem with solder in that it can provide a weak link where the solder ends on the pickup wire. The wire will flex only at that spot and can break quicker than if the wire is attached with the ferrules. If you elect not to solder the wires directly to the braid, the ferrules are available from Pro-Track.

To use a no-solder technique with these brass ferrules, strip about 1/4 inch of insulation from the wires and install the ferrule. Bend the individual strands back over the ferrule and spread them apart so they fill about 180 degrees of the round ferrule's edges. Use small-tipped needle-nose pliers to start each ferrule into the round hole at the top of the pickup in front of the braid.

Gently squeeze the edge of the ferrule to push it into the hole. Honestly, I am only able to perform this operation successfully about half of the time. I often bend the ferrule beyond repair or enlarge the hole so the ferrule does not fit tightly. I solder the wires on and try to remember to renew the wires every 30 hours or so by unsoldering them, cutting-off the end

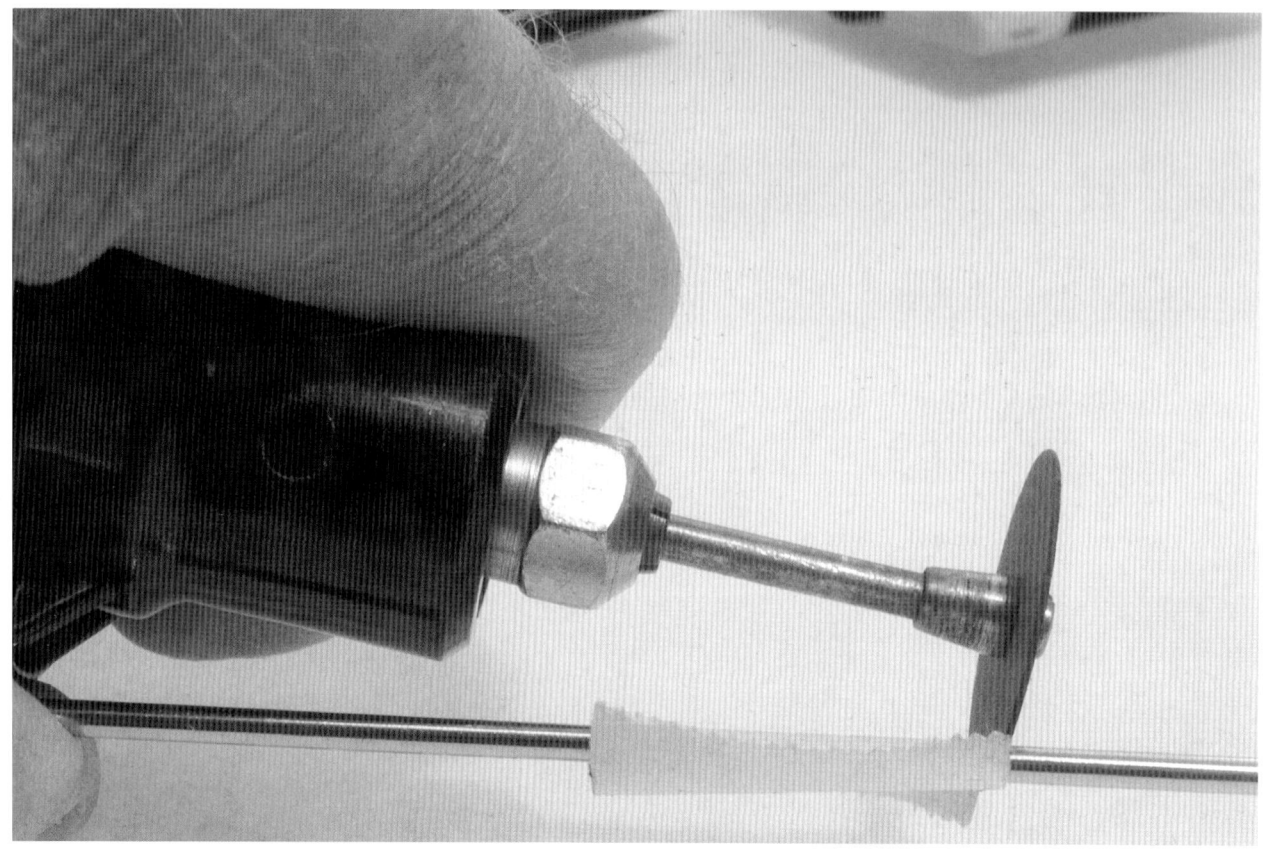

Use a cut-off disc in a Dremel motor tool to cut the replacement axle to fit the model. Always wear eye protection when working with motor tools.

1/16 inch beyond the point where the older one stopped, stripping another 1/4 inch of insulation, and resoldering the wires.

Chris Walker and many others who have experienced racing 1/24 scale cars on commercial raceways have developed a system of braid installation that works quite well. You will need to purchase a complete new pickup shoe from Electric Dreams and brass clips from Slot Sports. You can use any type of pickup braid.

The Carrera cars have pickup or guide blades that are so loose they practically rattle in the chassis. They are loose enough to be forced at something less than a 90-degree angle with the slot, which means they can slide up and out of the slot too easily. You can shim the hole in the Carrera chassis with a short piece of brass tubing from the TSP-1 pickup conversion kit from Electric Dreams. The kit includes a new pickup complete with braid. The kit also includes a piece of brass tubing that will jam in the Carrera pickup pivot. The clever brass spring clips are available from Slot Sports (www.slick7.com). The new installation forces the pickup to remain vertical in the slot to allow quicker cornering speeds.

You can convert the Electric Dreams pickup with a quick-change braid by inserting the Slot Sports brass clips without the braid. Solder the pickup wires to the brass clips. It's best to do the soldering with the clips out of the pickup so you don't melt the pickup. With soldered-on wires and braid with metal clips (Carrera offers it), you can change the braid by pulling the braid out the end of the pickup. You usually don't have to remove the body or pickup.

The pickup or guide shoes on the SCX Formula 1 and CART cars guide the car and actuate the working steering. The pins that stop the guide from pivoting are easily broken, which allows the guide to swivel so far it gets hooked on the copper contacts and will not center at all. Replacement guides are available from SCX, or the broken guides can be repaired by replacing the top and steering pins with 0-80 steel screws. Your hobby dealer can

The Slot.it, BWA, Pro-Track, and MRRC replacement aluminum wheels are attached to the axles with Allen socket screws in the wheels.

order Woodland Scenics number 808 or Walthers number 1016 brass 0-80x1/2-inch screws or Kadee number 1649 stainless steel 0-80x1/2-inch screws, which I like the best. You will also need number 53 and 60 drill bits and a pin vise to hold the drills and tap.

Bodywork Basics

You can sometimes smooth out the performance of a car by leaving the body slightly loose. Simply turn back all the mounting screws a few turns each until you can feel that the body can barely rattle. You may need to file all around the edges of the body to remove the snap-in fit on most chassis. There are posts or stops inside some cars that also must be trimmed back with sprue cutters or a hobby knife to allow the body to rattle about 1/64 inch or less on the chassis.

Removing Rear Axle Slop

If the rear axle moves more than the thickness of a piece of paper, the shifting can cause the car to hop and deslot. You can remove the side-to-side slop with clip-on washers. You should be able to feel, but not actually see, the side-to-side movement or slop at the rear axle. If you can see the movement, the car will often corner unpredictably with noticeably slower lap times. The side-to-side movement on this out-of-the-box Scalextric car is typical of most model racing cars. There is so much slop that you can actually see the axle shining between the gear and the chassis. Look carefully to see if the axle should be moved slightly to the right or left to align each tire the same distance from the edges of the body. Plastic polymer axle spacers are sold by Slot Sports. The number SS0-13 package contains about a dozen spacers. Use sprue cutters or an X-Acto knife to cut through one side of each spacer. Use tweezers to spread the spacer sideways so it will slip over the axle. Install the spacers between the bearing and the gear and between the gear and the bearing, or on the opposite side between the gear and the wheel. I guessed that one washer was enough and tried it. There was still side-to-side slop so I snapped

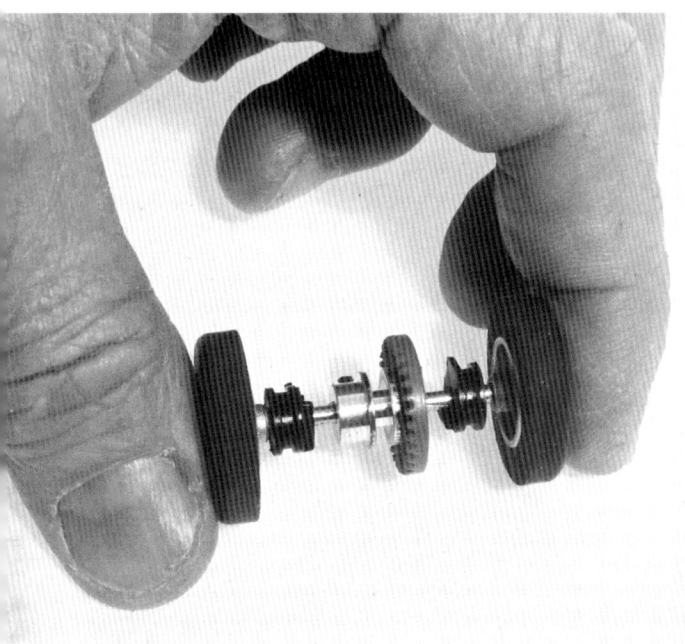

The stock crown gear on this Carrera D-Type Jaguar has been replaced with a Slot.it crown gear.

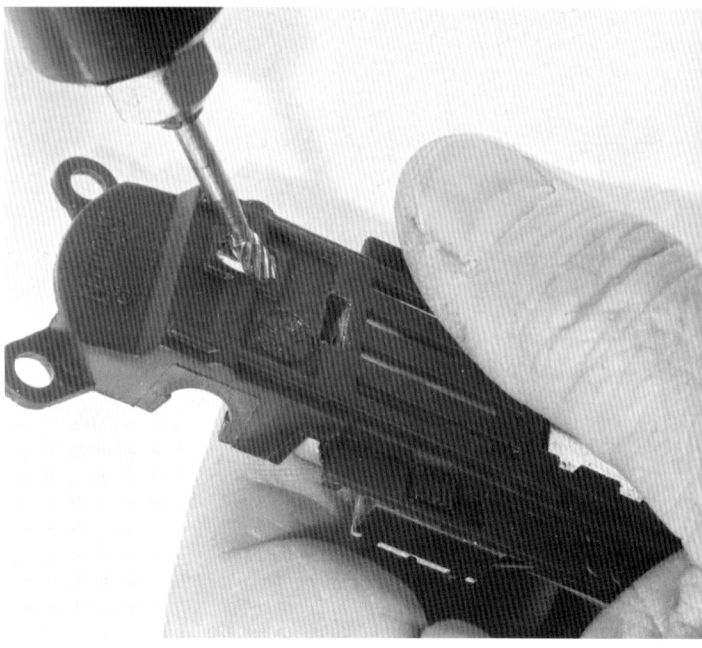

The Slot.it gears are sometimes larger than the stock gear, and the chassis must be cut away with a milling bit in a Dremel motor tool to provide clearance for the gear.

the axle out and installed a second washer. Two were just right so I snapped the axle back in place. You can see the shiny black washers next to the gear.

New Gears for More Speed?

The terms *gear-swapping*, *gearing-up*, or *gearing-down* are common jargon in a race car garage. Real racing cars have gearboxes and rear axle gear sets that are changed to match each track, and often they match the changing weather and traction conditions between the practice and the race. You can change the gears in any model car.

Generally speaking, most 1/32 scale cars are geared relatively high. On a 1/32 scale model racing car, the high-revving motor must be geared down to produce the most usable power at the rear tires. Most 1/32 scale model cars have a crown gear or spur gear on the rear axle that has about three times the number of teeth of the pinion gear on the motor. The gear ratios approach 3:1, which means that the motor revolves three times for each revolution of the rear axle. It's a nice compromise ratio for home tracks because it never allows the motor to reach full power for long enough to overheat the motor.

If you are trying to run a 1/32 scale car on one of the commercial raceways with a 30-foot straight, a 3.0:1 ratio is too low and something like 2.75:1 or even 2.5:1 might produce faster lap times, and because the motor won't be running at peak revs for as long, it will have a longer motor life.

For most home racers, however, the 3:1 ratio is an excellent compromise. The early Carrera 1/32 scale cars with a single magnet in front of the motor have relatively high 2.6:1 gear ratio, with a 10-tooth pinion gear on the motor driving a 26-tooth crown gear on the axle.

The gears in the Carrera cars have a smaller gear pitch (more teeth per inch) than most, so you must replace both the pinion and the crown gear. You can buy replacement Carrera motors and rear axles for most of the older cars and swap motors.

The simplest way to try new gear ratios is to use a new 26-tooth Slot.it crown gear to replace the stock Carrera 26-tooth crown gear and try an 8-tooth pinion gear (for an 8/26 or 3.25 ratio) and a 9-tooth pinion (for a 9/26 or 2.89 ratio) without modifying the car in any way except for installing the crown gear.

The SCX cars have 9 teeth on the pinion gear and 27 teeth on the crown gear for a 3:1 ratio. I wanted to try a lower ratio for some of the shorter and tighter tracks. It would be possible to replace the SCX pinion gear with a Slot.it SIPI08 8-tooth pinion

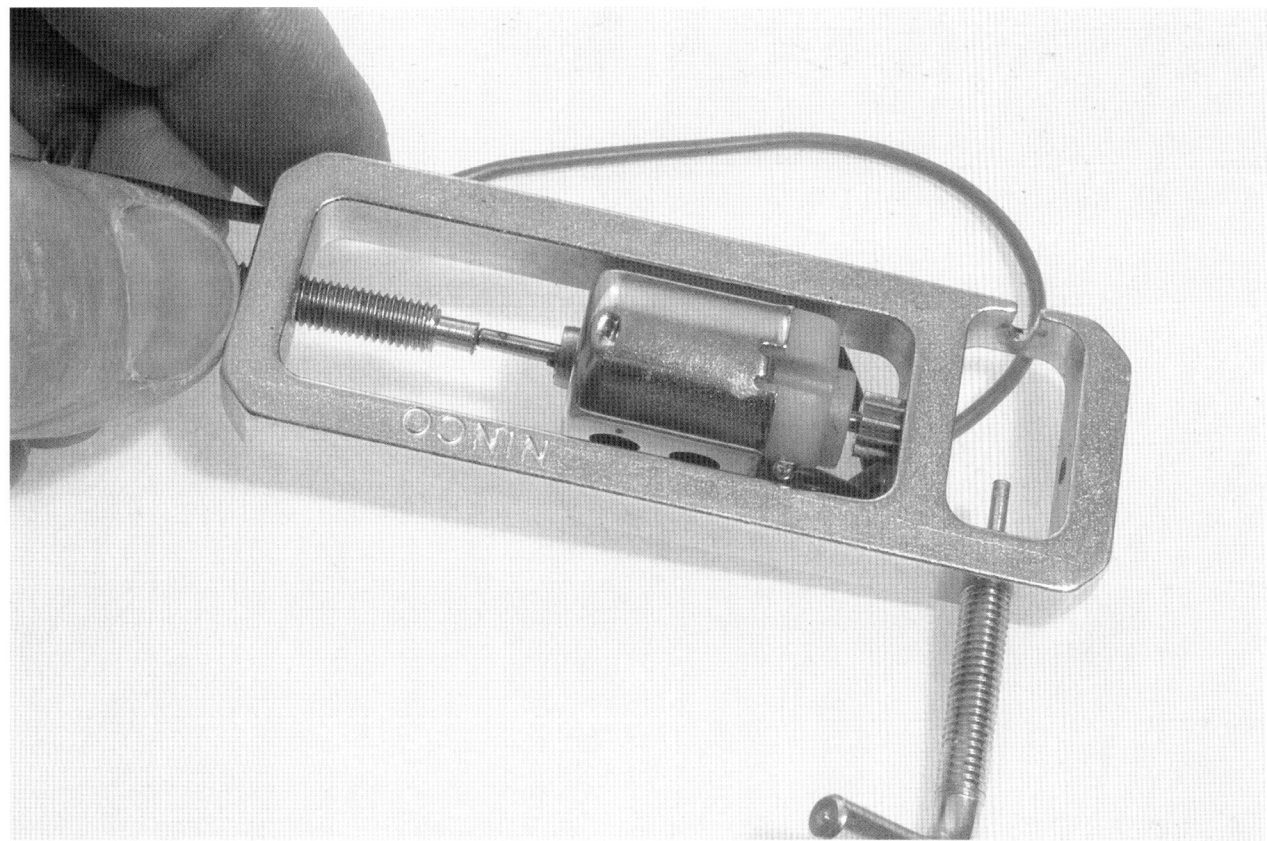

Use a NINCO number 70201 gear puller to remove the pinion gear.

gear, but the mesh between the SCX gear and the Slot.it gear is not precise and you'll have some gear noise unless you also replace the crown gear with a Slot.it part.

I wanted the smoother mesh of the Slot.it crown gear, so I replaced the SCX crown gear with a Slot.it SIGI06 26-tooth crown gear. I chose the one-tooth smaller gear so it would clear the gear cavity on the SCX chassis, and the single tooth difference has no noticeable effect on the performance.

On the Carrera cars, the larger crown gear rubs the chassis and the upper plate on the Carrera chassis, so the upper plate must be cut open into a U-shaped axle retaining piece with barely enough room to hold one of the attaching screws. A notch must also be cut into the bottom of the frame. By using the 30-tooth gear, I had three more choices of gear ratios by simply changing the pinion gear: 8/30 or 3.75:1, 9/30 or 3.33:1, and 10/30 or 3.00:1.

It is not easy to change the crown gear because it takes some real effort to remove the pressed-on wheels and to get them back on reasonably straight. You can buy replacement set-screw aluminum wheels from Slot.it, BWA, or Pro-Track. BWA even offers an entire range of wheel inserts so you can match the appearance of virtually any real race car wheel. To remove the pinion gear, use a NINCO number 70201 gear puller to pull off the 9-tooth SCX brass pinion gear from the motor and to press on the new Slot.it 8-tooth gear.

Slot.it makes special pinion gears to mesh with their crown gears and a different set of pinion gears to mesh with their spur gears for sidewinder motors. These are the gears I used for these inline chassis cars: SIGI06 26-tooth crown gear, SIGI04 30-tooth crown gear, SIPI08 8-tooth pinion gear, SIPI09 9-tooth pinion gear, SIPI10 10-tooth pinion gear.

I determined that the 8/30 combination was too low, even for our 5x9-foot test track. If you are running on a really tight course with a lot of inner-radius curves, you may find the 8/30 combination best. I was extremely pleased with the performance of the Carrera cars with the 9/30 gearing. The performance numbers are listed in Chapter 2.

BWA offers three wheel widths and a choice of over 15 cast-resin inserts to duplicate American Mags Halibrand six-spoke modern mags, and a dozen others.

Slot.it (lower right and bottom left) supplies inserts with most of their wheels with the set screw in the tire-mounting area. The Pro-Track wheels (left, center) have deep recesses and the extended set screw hub is at the rear of the wheel. The BWA wheels (top) have the set screw in the tire-mounting area.

To remove the magnet from Monogram cars, simply pry in one of the front or rear tabs and snap out the bracket and magnet.

Use scissors to cut two 2 1/4-inch (57.3 mm) strips of golf club lead weight, weighing about 1/4 ounce.

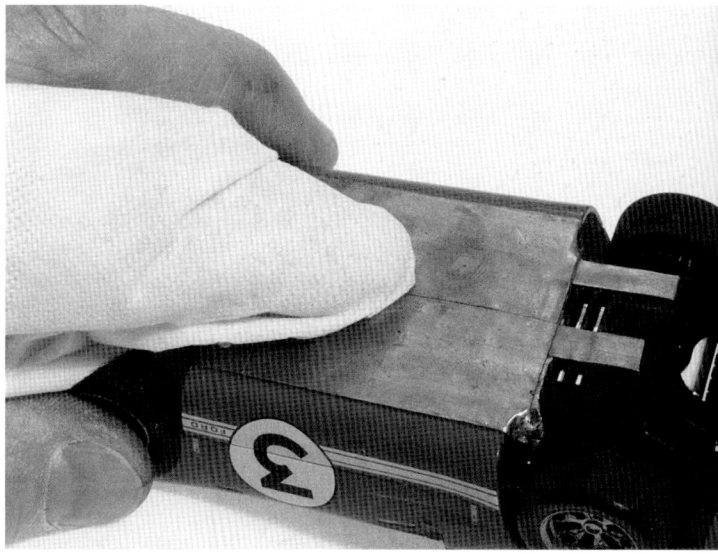

Wrap a piece of cloth around your finger and press any wrinkles out on a smooth block of wood before you remove the self-adhesive plastic backing.

Better Wheels

Nearly all the plastic wheels on every brand of model racing car are crooked. Some are much worse than others. Crooked wheels promote wheel hop, which in turn means lower cornering speeds. The smoother the car, the quicker it will power through corners, with or without magnets. You can improve the performance of nearly any car by installing new aluminum wheels, especially on the rear.

The ends of the axles are knurled to better grip the wheels on most model cars. The teeth on the knurls must be filed down to allow an aluminum wheel to fit on the axle. Be very careful so you remove only the raised knurls without actually biting into axle to create a flat spot that can force the wheel to run crooked.

You may want to replace the axle. It is possible to pull the gear from the stock axle with a NINCO number 80201 Gear Puller, but the knurls will tear up the inside of the gear and it may not fit tightly on the new axle. Slot.it offers new crown gears (for inline motors) and spur gears for sidewinder motors like the GT40.

If you replace the axle, try to buy bearings from the same source for a better fit. Slot.it, NINCO, and some other aftermarket firms offer replacement bearings to fit most model cars. The axle diameter of Scalextric, Slot.it, and Pro-Track drill rod at 2.3 mm is 0.090 inch. Drill rod at 3/32 inch is 0.092 inch, MRRC at 2.9 mm is 0.116 inch, and EJ's at 3.1 mm is 0.125 inch.

The 3/32-inch drill rod is the straightest, but it's a few thousands of an inch too large for BWA or Slot.it wheels. The K & S 3/32-inch (which measures 0.091 inch) stainless-steel drill rod (number 7133) is the best fit, but like all wire, it is slightly crooked. Cut three or four axles and roll each across a flat tabletop to select the straightest one of the batch.

Replacement aluminum wheels are available in a large range of sizes. You can find a width and diameter to match just about any model. Tires are another matter. The replacement wheels will not necessarily fit the stock tires, which means they will not fit the replacement aftermarket tires either, so you may need to do some experimenting. Measure the wheel width and diameter on the stock car and hope that the inner rib on the replacement tire matches. You can, however, order Puma Paws or Indy Grips silicones for most wheels.

You can find wheels at Pro-Track Corp. (417 Oak Place # 2, Port Orange, FL 32127; protrack@bellsouth.net; http://www.slotcar.org/protrack) in several sizes. There is a 12.7x8.5 mm (0.502x0.338 inch) or 12.7x5.7 mm (0.502x0.225 inch).

These wheels have a 0.136 in. (3.4 mm) wide boss on the back to accommodate the set screw. The

design allows a very deep wheel, which is perhaps the most realistic available, but they can be a difficult fit on narrower cars. These are the wheels used with the Le Mans Miniatures cut-down-wheel inserts on the Ford Mk IV in Chapter 6. Pro-Track offers a medium-density rubber tire, and Indy Grips has silicones for both widths. You must, however, glue the tires to the rims because there is no rib or flange. You'll have to cut down plastic wheels for inserts, which can be found at BWA Wheels (http://trak.to/bwaslotcars/; bwapenrose@hotmail.com).

BWA positions the set screw inside the wheel to make them as narrow as stock plastic wheels. Three widths are offered to fit either Slot.it soft rubber tires or Puma Paws or Indy Grips silicone tires. The narrow BWA wheel will fit most NINCO Classic tires and Scalextric Ford GT40 tires. The wider wheels may fit some of the wider stock tires if you want to use them for front wheels. The sizes available are 13.9x7.5 mm (0.547x0.296 inch), 13.9x9.6 mm (0.547x0.378 inch), and 13.9x11.7 mm (0.547x0.460 inch).

The magnets on SCX cars and on the rear of newer Carrera cars can be removed by loosening the two mounting screws.

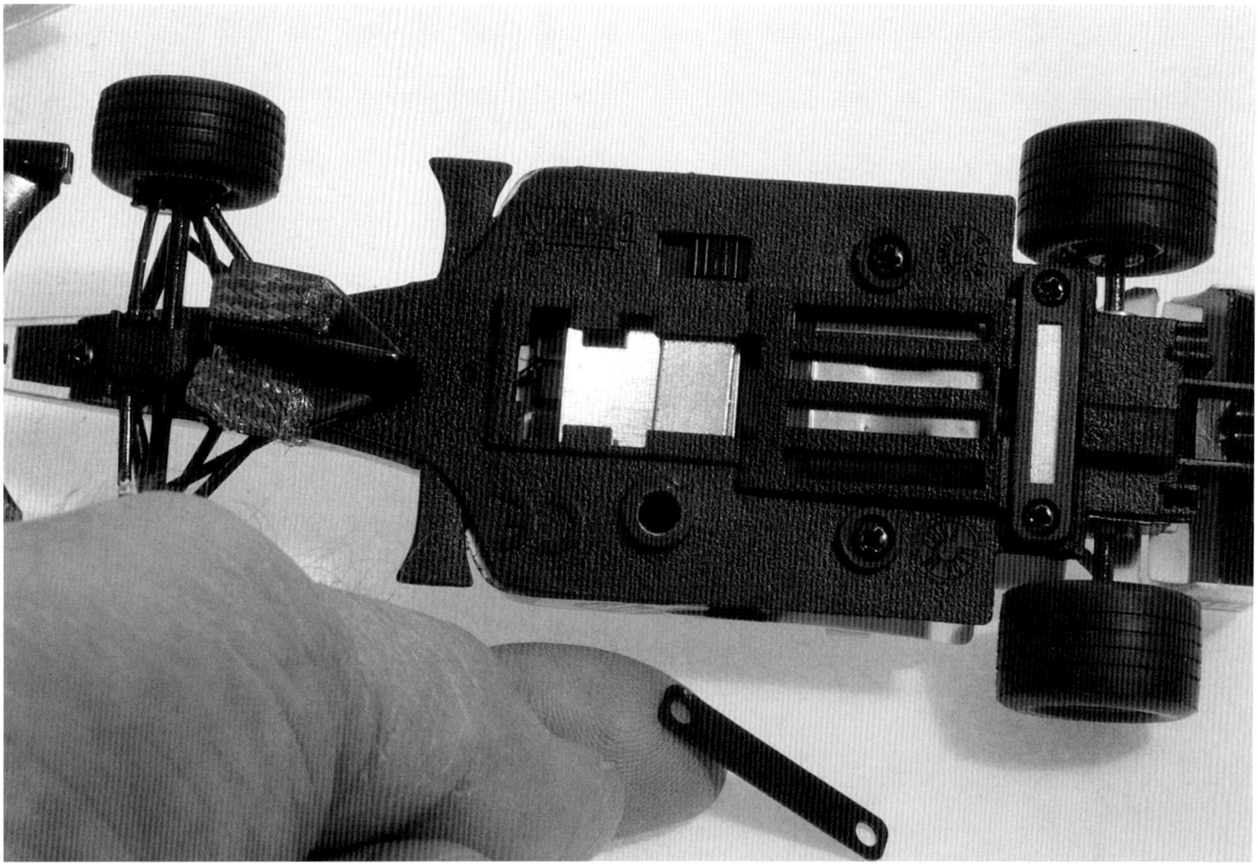

The new Carrera cars have an extra plastic shim that can be inserted between the rear magnet and chassis to lower the magnet for more downforce.

Locate the hole for each new magnet by drilling a pilot hole first with a 1/16-inch drill bit in a pin vise, and then enlarge the hole to lower the magnet on NINCO cars with a number 5 drill bit.

Slot.it (http://www.slot.it/) offers 1/32 scale motors, magnets, gears, wheels (see Scalextric USA for the nearest dealer). This Spanish firm makes a full line of wheels with matching soft rubber tires. Puma Paws and Indy Grips offer silicone tires for most Slot.it wheels. The set screw is positioned inside the wheel to make them as narrow as stock plastic wheels. The sizes available are 13.2x8.1 mm (5.522x0.322 inch) and 14.8x9.8 mm (5.84x0.386 inch). The Starter Kit number 04 has large hubs (wheels), and Starter Kit number 02 has small hubs (wheels) and 36-tooth spur gear with bearings and axle.

MRRC International Hobbies Ltd. (P.O. Box 790, St. Heiler, JE4 0SW, Jersey, Great Britain; see Scalextric USA and REH for locations) makes superb wheels and axles and soft tires. The odd axle size, however, makes them most suitable for scratch-built chassis. The wheels are similar to the Monogram wheels of the 1970s, but with set screw mounting. The set screw is inside the wheel so they are narrow enough to replace plastic wheels. MRRC also offers gears and bearings to fit their axles.

EJ's Hobbies (7017 Cascade Road SE, Grand Rapids, MI 49546-7304; http://ejshobbies.com) offers aluminum wheels similar to Revell's front and rear wheels from the 1970s with 5-40 threads to fit EJ's own 1/8-inch axles. EJ's also offers gears and bearings. The odd size makes them more suitable for scratch-built chassis than for converting plastic wheels on plastic chassis.

Finding Traction With Weight

If you are running a car with traction magnets, there's seldom any gain by adding weight. If, however, you do opt to remove the magnet, about 1/4 ounce of lead on the bottom of the car between the front and rear wheels will help keep the pickup braid compressed and provide more traction. The lead will also lower the car's center of gravity. Real

Place a piece of 0.060x0.125-inch plastic between the track and magnet to be sure the magnet rests 0.060 inch above the track. Secure the magnet with a 1/16-inch bead of metal-filled epoxy.

The lowered NINCO magnet is clearly visible beneath the CART (shown) or F1 chassis.

Formula 1 cars use exotic metals to provide a similar center of gravity reduction. If you add more than 1/2 ounce, the car will be slower—usually 1/4 ounce is enough. Shops and sporting-goods stores that carry golf supplies can supply self-adhesive lead about 0.006 in. (2 mm) thick and 0.78 in. (19.8 mm) wide. The lead is used to weigh golf clubs on a trial-and-error basis until the best weight is found. There are examples of cars with stick-on lead in Chapter 5.

The Laws of Magnetic Downforce

Magnetic downforce on a model racing car is produced in two ways: by the strength of the magnet and by how close the magnet is to the steel rails. The steel used in the rails affects the downforce as well. The alloy that Carrera uses has less iron than the steel used in other brands. This makes the magnetic downforce less on a Carrera track, but it's the same for all the cars, so their performance relative to one another will be similar.

The magnet should not be placed so low that it touches the track or else it can short-circuit the track and burn out the power pack. I don't recommend that you place a magnet any closer than 0.020 inches from the track. Use 0.020x0.125-inch Evergreen Scale Models or Plastruct strip styrene as a feeler gauge to determine the ground clearance.

I would suggest you also buy a steel scale ruler from a hobby shop that carries model railroad products. So far, I have not seen any 1/32 scale rulers, but the HO scale model railroad rulers are usually 0.020 inch thick, and the ruler's magnetic properties can be helpful in positioning the magnets.

Matching Magnets

Magnets can be used to provide truly realistic performance to match the incredible detail of the models. The real 1960s-era cars were noticeably slower than the cars of the early 1970s, when motor racing reached a peak, and the speeds dropped to match the tighter rules, only to climb again in the mid-1980s and 1990s.

From a model car racer's point of view, however, it is reasonable to stipulate that cars from 1971 to the present should be quicker than earlier cars. It would also be wise to stipulate that GT-class cars, like the various Porsche 911s, Ferrari GTBs, BMW 3.0CSLs, and similar cars, should be slower than the less-restricted prototype cars, although taller and heavier bodies will slow the coupes as long as the magnetic downforce is minimal. With strong magnets, it doesn't matter much if the car is a low-slung coupe or a NASCAR or DTM sedan. The simplest way to do that is to stipulate that the pre-1971 cars should race with no magnets and that later cars should race with a limited amount of magnets to keep things as simple as possible and still provide an opportunity for any car to win.

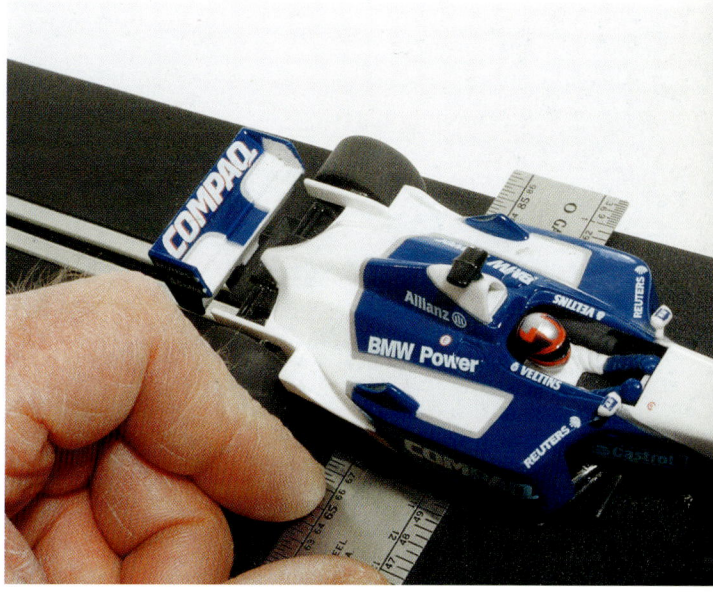

Use a number 5 bit to drill two holes about 3/4 inch apart just ahead of the rear axle.

Place a 0.020-inch-thick steel ruler between the track and the tape so the steel attracts the magnets but provides a 0.020-inch ground clearance.

It is difficult to dictate equality with rules alone. It can also be difficult with 1/32 scale model racing cars. Downforce magnets can significantly alter the performance of a 1/32 scale car so that two brands of cars with nearly identical motors, gears, and tires can provide models with vastly differing performance, based primarily on how strong the magnet is and where it is positioned in each of the cars. Even among the same brands, a different magnet can make an incredible difference in performance. Out of the box, the Scalextric MG Lola is much faster than the Scalextric Cadillac on most home tracks, and the major reason is magnets.

One Simple Solution for More Downforce

I wanted to find a relatively mild magnet to provide realistic downforce without turning the cars into projectiles. Some model car racers are every bit as competitive as those who race full-size cars, so I wanted a magnet that could be placed anywhere (behind the axle, on the pickup shoe, on top of the driver's head) to make it so simple that it would be impossible to cheat. The only limitation was a need for 0.020 inch or greater ground clearance. Some clubs skirt around the problem by specifying specific brands of cars, but that can lead to one-make, one-model racing.

I opted for Radio Shack 64-1895 1/8-inch Rare Earth magnets because they are easy to find and install. To make the installation easier, however, buy a number 8 drill bit (0.199 inch) or a 7/32-inch (0.2187-inch) drill bit so the magnet will be tight fit. A 1/8-inch drill is just a bit too large, but it will do if you cannot locate the number 8 drill bit.

Drill a pair of holes in front of the rear axle about 5/8 inch apart, center to center. Run a 1/32-inch bead of metal-filled epoxy around the hole. Press each magnet into a small square of masking tape, and then insert the magnets into the epoxy-lined holes. Place a steel ruler over the tape to grip the magnets. Place the car on the track on top of the steel ruler with the pickup in the slot and all four wheels resting on the track. Pull the steel ruler down, if necessary, to get the ruler squeezed between the tape on the magnets and the rails of the track. That will provide the necessary 0.020 inch of clearance. When the epoxy cures overnight, remove the ruler and tape, and double-check to be sure you really have 0.020 inch or more of ground clearance by sliding that piece of 0.020-inch plastic between the magnets and the rails on the track.

The magnets will work on any model racing car. I applied them to a few of the open-wheeled F1/IRL/CART cars in the shoot-out in Chapter 5. The techniques are the same for any sports or GT car.

The Radio Shack magnets will press into the number 5-size holes, but they need to be fixed in place with metal-filled epoxy.

Use metal-filled epoxy to attach a piece of 0.020x0.125-inch styrene between the Scalextric IRL car's magnet and the chassis to raise the magnet.

Carrera F1 Cars

Carrera has a revised chassis in the 2003 F1 Williams and the F1 Sauber, which has a second bar magnet similar to the one beneath SCX cars. The new Carrera cars also have lower gearing. These cars will run with the Scalextric F1 cars and all the other cars in the 11-car F1/IRL/CART shoot-out right out of the box if you insert the black plastic spacer that's in the box to lower the magnet to within 0.020 inch of the track.

You can update the earlier Carrera cars with a pair of Radio Shack magnets. The car is quick, but the higher gearing makes it a bit different to drive than the other 10 cars. It's actually just a bit quicker than the newer Carrera F1 Williams.

Pro-Slot F1 Cars

We used the techniques described above to install two of the Radio Shack 1/8-inch magnets in the Pro-Slot Ferrari. The additional magnets did their job, and the Pro-Slot motor has the power to pull them.

NINCO F1 and CART Cars

Do not try to lower the NINCO magnets to within 0.020 inch of the track like other brands. We tried placing the magnet at 0.040 inch above the track and got a whopping 70 grams (6 ounces) of downforce on a Scalextric Classic track and 55 grams (2 ounces) of downforce on a Carrera track. It was way too much force for the NINCO motor to overcome, and the lap times actually increased to 6.61 seconds. The NINCO motor, like the SCX motor, is not strong enough in the F1 or CART cars to pull a much stronger magnet. By lowering the magnet too far, you increase its effective strength enough to overcome the motor's power. On the NINCO cars, the magnet can only be lowered to about 0.070 inch above the track. That's enough to make the NINCO cars competitive with all the other F1 cars. To lower the magnet, simply push the magnet-mounting hole on through the chassis with a 21/64-inch drill (0.3281 inch) bit or use a 5/16-inch bit and whittle the hole a bit larger. Buy a piece of 0.040x0.125-inch Evergreen styrene strip and use it on top of the 0.020-inch-thick steel scale ruler to install the magnets in the NINCO cars. Run the 1/32-inch bead of metal-filled epoxy around the hole, press the magnet into a piece of tape, and then press the magnet into the hole and cover it with a steel ruler. Place the car on the track with a piece of 0.040x0.125-inch styrene strip between the ruler and the track to provide a minimum 0.060-inch clearance.

Scalextric F1 Cars

Just for fun, we tried installing a pair of the Radio Shack magnets in a Scalextric F1 car, using the same techniques described for the older Carrera and

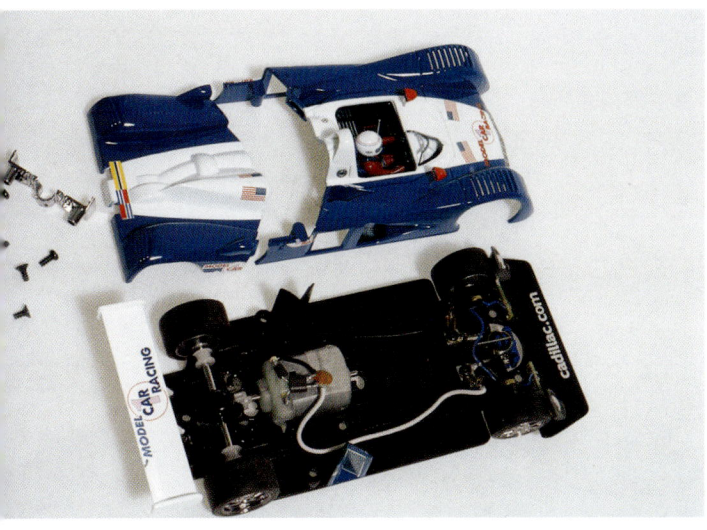

Remove the Phillips-head screws that secure the Scalextric Le Mans Cadillac Northstar LMP body.

Use a pin vise to drill a 1/16-inch pilot hole in the two rear corners of the chassis. Then turn the chassis over and use a number 5 drill bit to enlarge the 1/16-inch pilot holes.

Pro-Slot cars. The downforce nearly doubled and the lap times dropped from 5.59 seconds to 4.96 seconds. That's close enough to the out-of-the-box Scalextric IRL car times. If you want to increase the speed of the Scalextric F1 cars, rather than decrease the speed of the IRL car, you can add a pair of magnets, but you will be left searching for a way to bring the NINCO or Carrera or Pro-Slot cars up to that pace without swapping motors. The purpose of this exercise is to get as many of the open-wheeled cars to potentially the same speed to avoid one-brand, one-car races.

Scalextric IRL Cars

The Scalextric IRL cars are a bit lower than the Scalextric F1 Williams, McLaren, or Toyota (and presumably the Renault) cars. The lower car brings the magnet closer to the track, which in turn provides more downforce that provides more tire grip and results in quicker lap times. The out-of-the-box Scalextric IRL cars will turn 4.72-second laps on the Sport Monaco track. It's easy enough to decrease the downforce, just raise the magnet. Pry the magnet out of the car. Cut a piece of 0.020x0.125-inch styrene the length of the magnet. Apply some metal-filled epoxy to the bottom of the styrene strip and place it where the magnet had fit. Spread some more metal-filled epoxy on top of the styrene strip and push the magnet into the epoxy. Press the magnet firmly into the chassis by squeezing it tightly with needle-nose pliers.

When the epoxy cures overnight, the magnet will be about 0.020 inch farther from the rails. The raised magnet allowed the Scalextric IRL car to turn a 5.39-second lap so it was competitive with the other 10 cars in this shoot-out. Actually, we might have gone just a bit too far. I suggest you try a piece of 0.015x0.125-inch styrene shim in place of the 0.020x0.125-inch shim (to lower the magnet 0.005 inch compared to our test car) and you can probably reduce the IRL car's lap time to the 5.20-second range.

SCX F1 Cars

All the SCX F1 cars, including the Arrows, Minardi, Williams, McLaren, and Jaguar, have nearly identical gearing, motors, and magnet positions. You can lower the SCX magnets by loosening the two screws that retain the magnet box. Turn the screws out an equal amount until a piece of 0.020-inch styrene will slide between the track and the bottom of the magnet. Unfortunately, it's not quite that simple because the SCX motor, like the NINCO motor, does not have enough power to pull that much downforce. In this case, we opted to swap motors and fit the SCX Turbo Pro motor, which can be ordered by any SCX dealer.

More Magnetic Downforce for Scalextric Cars

The model car manufacturers are producing faster cars. The Scalextric Lola-MG, SCX Dome-Judd

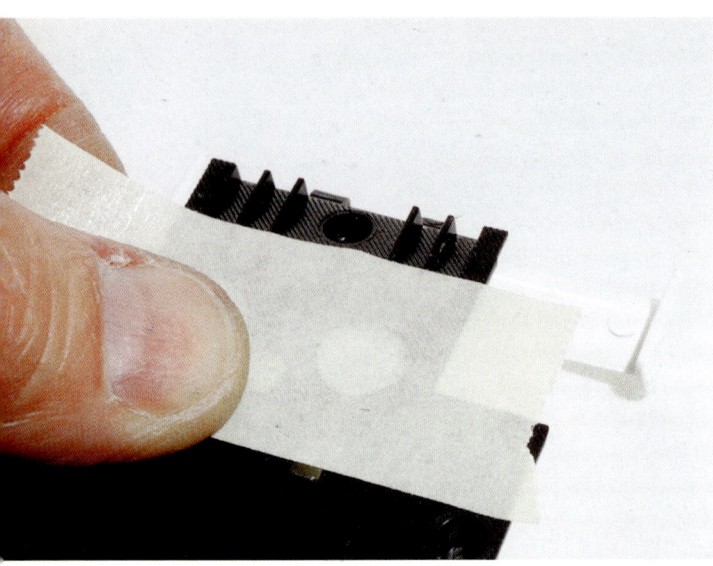

Press a piece of masking tape over the bottom of the car to cover the holes.

S101, Fly Lola B98-10, NINCO Honda NSX, Spirit Reynard B2KQ, and the Carrera Le Mans Bentley (with second bar magnet) are the current quickest racing cars. It's a whole new generation of performance that makes everything else obsolete.

To create this new generation, more magnetic downforce was added by lowering the magnet closer to the track or using a more powerful magnet, although in Carrera's case, a second magnet was added. There are those who feel that these cars are too quick and that they fly around the track at speeds several times faster than their real-world equivalents. The simple solution to that is to pull the magnets on all the cars (including the Scalextric Le Mans Cadillac Northstar LMP car) that are represented by the models in the Sport/GT/Le Mans shoot-out in Chapter 5. An alternative solution is to standardize on a weaker magnet like the Radio Shack 64-1895 1/8-inch Rare Earth to provide a more realistic amount of downforce on every car in this class.

It is possible to increase the magnetic downforce on some of the older cars to match the newer racers. The Scalextric Le Mans Cadillac Northstar LMP, Porsche GT3, and Caterham 7 have the small circular magnet mounted just ahead of the rear axle. Later Scalextric cars, such as the Lola-MG, the sidewinder NASCAR cars, and the Le Mans Lister, have a single bar magnet and are quicker. You can easily modify the Scalextric Cadillac to match the performance of the fastest Scalextric, SCX, Fly, Carrera, and NINCO cars by drilling two holes and adding a pair of magnets. You can see the effect of the extra magnet in the results of the modern-era Sports/GT/Le Mans shoot-out in Chapter 5.

The Scalextric Le Mans Cadillac Northstar LMP is also available as a collector car in American racing colors of white and blue as part of a package that includes the first six issues of *Model Car Racing* magazine, each with "Scalextric Limited Edition" logos. At the moment, that's the only source of the Le Mans Cadillac.

Scalextric offers a number W8449 replacement pack of five different magnets for $9.95 that includes one each of the thin and thick bar and round magnets. You'll need just one pack because you can use the existing thin round magnet from the Cadillac. To match the performance of the Scalextric Lola-MG, you'll need a pair of the thin round magnets. You could use two of the thick magnets, but that's too much downforce, and you would then need to increase the downforce of all the other cars to match. We tried both the thick and the thin magnets, and two thick magnets were too much. The car would not move around the track unless we increased the power to 23 volts. We do know folks race cars with this much downforce, but it is not something I recommend. The two thin magnets bring the performance of the Scalextric Le Mans Cadillac Northstar LMP car up to the level of the fastest cars you can buy. From there on, it will be up to you to tune the car and drive it fast enough to win races.

To install the magnets, remove the Phillips-head screws that retain the body. The chassis is the same on all four versions of the Scalextric Le Mans Cadillac Northstar LMP cars. The Scalextric Porsche GT3 and Caterham 7 also have the single round magnet so you can increase their magnetic downforce by using these same techniques. Use a pin vise to drill a 1/16-inch pilot hole in the two rear corners of the chassis where the cross rib and the lengthwise ribs join. The photos of the finished chassis show you where the holes should be located. Turn the chassis over and use a number 5 drill bit to enlarge the 1/16-inch pilot holes. You only want to drill into those lengthwise and cross ribs about 1/8 inch to help retain the strength of the chassis. Use a number 11 blade in an X-Acto

When you remove the masking tape, the two magnets should be perfectly flush with the bottom of the chassis.

knife to shave away any burrs from the edges of the two holes. The third hole is where the stock magnet is located. The stock magnet is raised above the track by the thickness of the plastic chassis. The two magnets we are installing will be flush with the bottom of the chassis to provide more than twice the magnetic downforce. The spread of the magnetic downforce will also make the car much easier to drive at the limit of tire adhesion. Press a piece of masking tape over the bottom of the car to cover the holes. Use a toothpick to apply a thick bead of metal-filled or J-B Weld epoxy around the edges of each magnet and press the magnets into the holes so the masking tape grips them. Rest the chassis on a steel ruler or iron scrap so the magnet will hold the chassis to the iron. Push the tops of each magnet down firmly into the tape with tip of a screwdriver, and push the chassis down as well. You want the magnets to be perfectly flush with the bottom of the chassis when the epoxy cures. Apply some additional beads of epoxy around the chassis ribs to compensate for the strength you removed by drilling the two holes. Let the epoxy cure overnight and remove the masking tape. The two magnets should be perfectly flush with the bottom of the chassis. The masking tape leaves the surface slightly rippled, similar to the surface of the stock chassis. Reassemble the car and you're ready to go racing.

You could carve a rectangular cavity to fit the Scalextric bar magnet in the same position as it is in the Lola-MG. It is much easier to drill the two holes. It is also possible to put a thicker, round magnet in the stock location and/or drill through that hole to lower the magnet. The two thin round magnets work best because the downforce is spread so the car can slide a bit to give you some warning of impending crashes. More important, the performance of the Scalextric Le Mans Cadillac Northstar LMP with two thin round magnets is a close match for the other cars that compete in the same class in the real world.

CHAPTER 5
SIXTY CAR-BY-CAR COMPARISON SHOOT-OUTS

The 1960s-Era Sporst/GT/Le Mans cars. With the magnets removed and silicone tires snapped on, there's less than a half-second difference in lap times from the fastest to the slowest. This is the order they finished: NINCO Austin Healey Mk III, NINCO 427 Cobra, Fly Ford GT40, Slot Classics Morgan, MRRC Porsche 904, Carrera 427 Corvette, Reprotec 427 Cobra, Carrera Mustang GT350, MRRC Ferrari 275P, Scalextric Ford GT40, Monogram Daytona Cobra, MRRC 427 Cobra, Monogram Corvette Grand Sport, and Scalextric Lotus 7 (Caterham).

Unpredictability is what makes racing yell-out-loud exciting. The surprise element is the root thrill of real racing action, which is what makes NASCAR and IRL and motorcycle road racing so exciting. Any one of a dozen drivers can win. Ditto for the automobile or engine brands. Conversely, predictability is what makes Formula 1 and Le Mans so difficult to get all fired up about. There's no surprise.

With 1/32 scale racing cars, there is almost always one particular brand and body style in each real race car class that outruns everything else. For example, if you are racing 1965–1995 Sports/GT/Le Mans cars, Fly's Porsche 908 or Lola T70 is going to be the car that wins most often. What happens next is that everyone wants to have a crack at winning so you see nothing but Fly 908s. If you race current Formula 1 cars, you'll soon discover that on most home tracks, the Scalextric Renault and Williams are quicker than any other model. Some club members simply repaint their Renault Williams in Ferrari red or Renault blue and yellow to add some variety.

If you want to run more than one-car racing classes, you have two choices. With magnet cars, sort through them and find which ones are competitive in each class. You can also remove the magnets to provide more equal racing.

Car-by-Car, Class-by-Class Shoot-Outs

We divided the model racing cars you can buy into five categories: 1960s-Era Sports/GT/Le Mans, 1950s-Era Sports/GT/Le Mans, 1970s-Era Sports/GT/Le Mans, Modern-Era Sports/GT/Le Mans, and Open-Wheel F1/IRL/CART.

Each category includes examples of every available brand of model car and any major variations in chassis design. For example, cars in the "Sports" classes include chassis with inline front motor, inline rear motor, and sidewinder rear motor. If any one manufacturer makes two or more of these types of chassis, I included them. If the manufacturer offered both coupes and roadsters, I tried to include examples of both because the coupes can sometimes be a bit slower. I tried to include examples of just about everything so

After running the first weighted tests, we determined that the front-motored 1960-era cars might perform better with less weight on the front. We repositioned the weight on front-motored cars to just the rear. MRRC supplies a screw-on steel plate that was used to add weight to the MRRC Porsche 904.

With magnets removed, this is how the 14 1970s-Era Sports/GT/Le Mans cars finished: Carrera Porsche 911RSR (1/29), Fly Lola T70 Mk III, NINCO Porsche 911 Turbo, Fly Porsche 917/10 Can-Am, Fly Porsche 908/3, Monogram Greenwood Corvette, Scalextric L-88 Corvette, Fly Porsche 917, Fly Ferrari 512S, GB Track Porsche 917PA, Fly Ferrari 365 GTB/4, Fly BMW 3.0 CSL, MMK Matra M670 (Fly 908), and Spirit Ferrari 512M.

Track Testing on the Sport Monaco Track

All the cars in this chapter were track tested on the Scalextric Sport Monaco track (plans in Chapter 9). All the track tests in Chapter 2 were conducted on the standard Scalextric Classic and Carrera 5x9-foot tracks (plans are in *Slot Car Bible*) and on circular skid pads assembled from Scalextric Sport, Scalextric Classic, Carrera, SCX, and NINCO track. For these shoot-outs, I wanted to try all the cars on the larger Sport Monaco track under racing conditions, as well as running against the times posted by the DS lap timer.

Each car was disassembled, the tires trued, and the bearings and other working parts were checked for alignment. I did not make any of the modifications except for running the cars around the truck for about five minutes, sanding the stock and replacement silicone tires, and adding about 1/4 ounce of lead sheet to each car for the later tests. Essentially, the cars were tested right out of the box.

1960s-Era Sports/GT/Le Mans Shoot-Out

If you are interested in racing cars from the 1960s, you probably care how the cars look. The point of racing a historic machine is to recreate both the appearance of that individual car and the cars it competed with in its era. These 1960s-era cars are considerably slower than the cars of today and would look pretty absurd flying around Le Mans at the same pace as a 2004 Audi R8R (such as SCX's model). However, with magnets most of these 1960s-era cars can match or exceed the performance of the Audi. In the words of a current television commercial, "That's just not natural!"

It makes more sense, and it certainly looks more real, to replicate the limits of tire adhesion and horsepower that were current in the 1960s. The good news is that you can come very close to matching the performance of the real racing cars of this era and include the advantages of having all the cars more or less equal.

If you can match all the 1960s cars' performance, the driver, not the car, can claim the right to the win. By removing the magnets, removing the stock tires and replacing them with silicone tires, and adding some peel-and-stick lead weight, all of the cars can turn qualifying lap times within 0.49 second (that's about 5 percent) of one another.

On the relatively smooth Scalextric Classic track, the NINCO Cobra benefited the most from silicone tires. The MRRC Ferrari has some very hard and slip-

you could win with the car you chose or with any body style on that type of chassis from that model maker. There are 60 cars in these shoot-outs, which is enough to give you an example of the chassis that are fitted beneath about 90 percent of the 1/32 scale model racing cars that are currently available.

There are sub-classes within these classes, but we were able to tune these cars so that any one of them could win races, especially without magnets. On the actual tracks, nearly every one of them has won races.

1960s-ERA PUMA PAWS AND INDY GRIPS SILICONE TIRES

Model Car	Puma Paws Tire No.	Indy Grips Tire No.
Carrera 427 Corvette Stingray	01006	7005
Carrera Mustang GT350	01006	7005
Fly Ford GT40	04005	3007
Monogram Corvette Grand Sport	04005	1304
Monogram Daytona Cobra	05002	1303
MRRC 427 Cobra	06002	5001
MRRC Ferrari 275P	06001	5003
MRRC Porsche 904	06003	NA
NINCO Austin Healey Mk III	00701	2002
NINCO 427 Cobra	07004	2002
Pink-Kar Ferrari GTO	08001	2002
Reprotec 427 Cobra	11001	NA
Scalextric Ford GT40	13005	1010
Scalextric Lotus 7 (Caterham)	13009	1006

pery tires so silicones helped it as well. The ribs and out-of-true tires on the Pink-Kar Ferrari GTO were equally worthless compared to the silicones. The newer Carrera Corvette with the second bar magnet in the rear would probably have been as quick as the Monogram Corvette. Conversely, the MRRC Porsche 904 was much quicker with the stock tires.

Even with silicone tires, there is about a 3-second difference per lap between the fastest and the slowest cars. In other words, the Monogram Grand Sport would lap the MRRC or Reprotec Cobras about every third lap. The newer Carrera and Monogram cars are in a class by themselves for the simple reason that they have more magnetic downforce than the other cars of this era. If you want to race 1960s-era cars with magnets, you're going to have to accept the fact that only 2 of the 15 could break 5 seconds, 4 of the 15 could break 6 seconds, 4 more were in the low to mid-6-second range, and 4 more were slower than the rest. You could divide the races into those four different sub-classes. Actually, you could go a step further and actually add magnets to the slower cars to bring them up to the speeds of the faster cars, but we'll discuss that later in the chapter.

For the next series of tests, we put the stock tires back on each of the cars. We also removed the magnets from each car. We then ran them all to achieve the best qualifying lap time for each car. With the exception of the MRRC Porsche 904, the stock tires don't work well without a magnet to force them onto the track. The Reprotec, MRRC Ferrari 275P, and Pink-Kar tires were especially slippery. Removing the magnets is not enough to make model car racing fun because most of these tires are designed to work with the extra weight or load of the magnetic downforce.

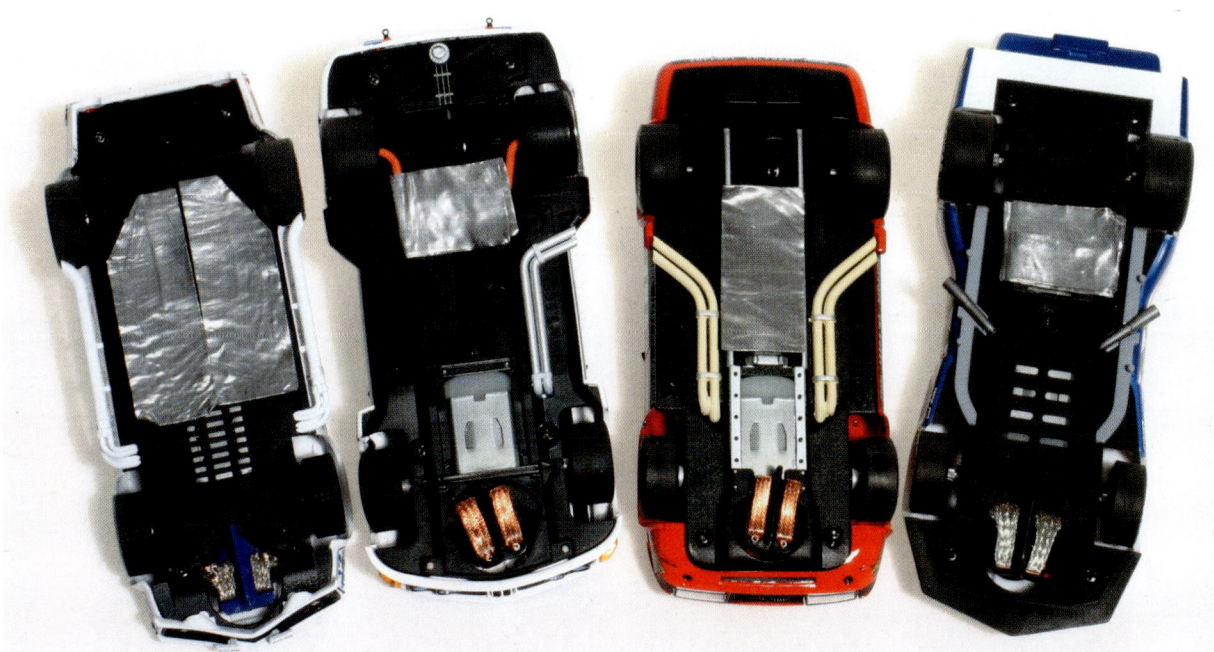

The thin golf club–weight self-stick lead was applied to the rear of the four front-motored 1990-era cars: the Scalextric L-88 Corvette, Fly BMW 3.0 CSL, Fly Ferrari 365 GTB/4, and Monogram Greenwood Corvette.

1960S-ERA SPORT/GT/LE MANS SHOOT-OUT

Model/Real Car	W/ Magnets		No Magnets	
	Tires: Stock	Silicones	Tires: Stock	Silicones
Carrera 427 Corvette Stingray*	6.78	6.35	8.82	8.08
Carrera D-Type Jaguar	5.42	4.70	8.72	7.88
Carrera Mustang GT350*	7.59	6.96	9.78	8.10
Fly Ford GT40	6.66	5.80	8.98	7.96
Monogram Corvette Grand Sport**	5.78	4.97	8.91	8.29
Monogram Daytona Cobra**	5.88	5.73	9.11	8.24
MRRC 427 Cobra**	7.43	7.65	9.03	8.76
MRRC Ferrari 275P	8.68	5.59	21.75	8.07
MRRC Porsche 904**	5.79	7.92	9.14	7.91
NINCO 427 Cobra	7.28	6.61	8.75	7.77
NINCO Austin Healey Mk III	6.82	6.52	8.71	7.92
Pink-Kar Ferrari GTO	8.07	6.96	9.37	8.06
Reprotec 427 Cobra	8.36	7.77	8.62	8.03
Scalextric Ford GT40	5.80	5.52	9.16	8.16
Scalextric Lotus 7 (Caterham)	6.41	6.07	9.07	8.20
Slot Classics Morgan**	NA	NA	8.65	7.99

NOTES:
*The new Carrera cars with a second magnet are much faster than the older cars. The newer car, however, is much slower without any magnets (it turned an 8.19-second qualifying time) than the older car without magnets, which turned the 7.92-second qualifying time. The Carrera Mustang GT350 was one of the older Carrera models with a single magnet. The later cars with the second rear magnet should be just a bit slower than the Carrera 427 Corvette Stingray because the Mustang is a bit more top heavy.

**The MRRC Porsche 904 was quicker on the stock tires than on silicones. So far, MRRC has only shipped the 904 kits to Europe, but they were supposed to be in the United States in fall 2004. The same chassis will be offered beneath an ex-Monogram King Cobra and a Ferrari 250 GTO LM. The MRRC 427 Cobra and Ferrari 275P are available to dealers from REH Distributors.

***Cars with the magnet in front of the motor were slowest, but often improved (relative to other cars) with magnets removed.

****The Slot Classics Morgan (with a NINCO motor, gears, wheels, and tires) was included as an example of how the slightly greater weight of a cast-resin body can affect performance. The Le Mans Miniatures Ford GT Mk IV (see issue No. 11) has Scalextric Ford GT40 motor, gears, wheels and tires; and the Bauer Cheetah (see issue No. 10) has an MRRC 427 Cobra chassis; and the MAXI-Models McLaren (see issue No. 12) and the Modelmaker's 289FIA Cobra (see issue No. 14) have MRRC 427 Cobra chassis. The Carrera GT350 can be modified with the Slot Car World kit to recreate the racing version, the GT350R as shown in the No. 6 issue (Monogram was expected to have a replica of the GT350R in early 2005). The Top-Slot Lightweight E-Type Jaguar uses an MRRC Ferrari chassis so its times are just slightly slower than the MRRC 275P Ferrari. Similarly, the Top-Slot cast-resin Shelby Daytona Cobra (a replica of a different car than Monogram's model) uses the MRRC Cobra chassis, so its lap times should be similar to the MRRC 427 Cobra. You can usually expect these resin cars to be comparably slower than the sources of their chassis that have lighter weight injection-molded plastic bodies.

We ran a fourth series of tests with silicone tires on all the cars and no magnets. The performance of some of the cars can be improved even more by adding a bit of weight to help the pickup brushes work properly and provide just a bit more load on the tires. First, we added a single layer of golf club lead between the rear of the pickup and the front of the rear axle. That only added about 1/4 ounce (7 grams) to the weight of the car, but all the cars except the MRRC Porsche 904 ran better. The spread in lap times was reduced to just 0.84 seconds between the fastest and the slowest, and we can get it even closer.

Balancing With Weight

The weight distribution of the cars with front motors left the rear tires with proportionally less load than the cars with mid-motors, so we removed the weight we had installed from the front half of the Scalextric Lotus 7, MRRC 427 Cobra, Monogram Daytona Cobra, and the Monogram Grand Sport and installed it in three or four layers in front of the rear axles. It seems that about 40 percent of the weight needs to be on the pickup. With less weight, the rear of the car tends to swing too easily and too wide (call it "oversteer" to compare it to real car's handling).

You'll need two postage scales to check the weight of the front, rear, and entire car. You may need to adjust the scales until either scales read the same total weight. I added about 10 grams of the self-adhesive golf club–weight lead over the rear axles of each of these cars. It worked well on the MRRC 427 Cobra and lowered its lap time from 8.62 seconds with 7 grams all across the bottom to just 8.22 seconds. Conversely, we were able to cure the Morgan's tendency to hang the tail out by adding about 2 grams near the front.

Every one of these cars has a near-equal possibility of winning a race. Some will respond to tuning better than others. The cars with front motors are particularly difficult to drive because they are twitchy compared to the cars with rear motors. A skilled and practiced driver can win with any of these. An MRRC 427 Cobra, with just a bit of weight and silicone tires, won the local club's championship against examples of virtually every other car in this shoot-out.

Without magnets, the cars look and feel like the power-sliding or four-wheel-drifting cars of the 1950s and 1960s. You drive through every foot of every corner, varying the throttle just enough to keep the car

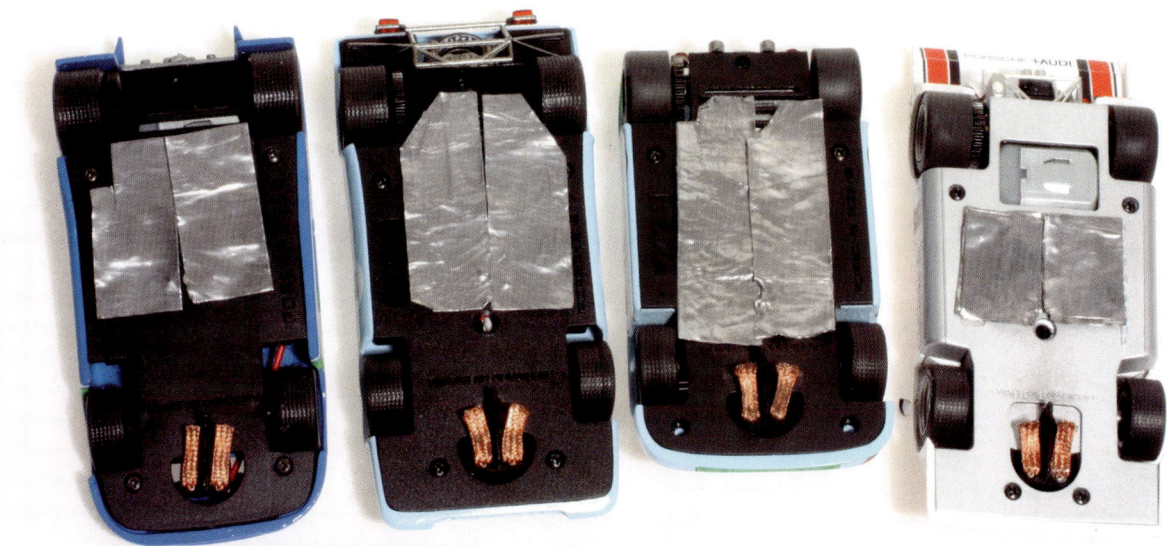

The sheet lead was applied to the center of the rear-motored sidewinder 1970-era cars: the MMK Matra (with Fly Porsche 908 chassis), Fly 917, Fly 908/3, and Fly 917/10.

Weight Distribution: Total/Front/Rear (in grams)

Model Car	Weights (in grams): overall/front/rear		
	Stock	Weighted	Balanced
Carrera 427 Corvette Stingray	83/45/38	88/48/40	90/40/50
Carrera Mustang GT350	85/46/39	90/45/45	90/42/48
Fly Ford GT40	70/31/39	75/32/43	75/32/43
MRRC 427 Cobra	65/28/37	70/31/39	70/30/40
MRRC Ferrari 275P	52/22/30	57/25/32	57/24/32
MRRC Porsche 904**	78/32/46	95/40/55	95/40/55
Monogram Corvette Grand Sport*	74/39/35	80/32/48	82/42/50
Monogram Daytona Cobra*	74/37/37	80/40/40	90/40/50
NINCO Austin Healey Mk III*	70/29/41	76/33/43	76/33/43
NINCO 427 Cobra	76/34/42	82/37/45	82/37/45
Pink-Kar Ferrari GTO	63/22/41	68/24/34	68/24/34
Scalextric Ford GT40	70/31/39	75/32/43	75/32/43
Reprotec 427 Cobra	72/30/42	77/33/44	77/33/44
Scalextric Lotus 7 (Caterham)*	55/26/29	60/28/32	66/30/36
Slot Classics Morgan	85/35/40	85/35/40	87/43/54

NOTES:
*The extra weight was too much for the Scalextric Lotus 7 and the Monogram Daytona and Grand Sport, and increased their lap times by about 5 percent. It would seem that the optimum weight for a car without magnets, but with silicone tires, is about 2 1/2 to 3 ounces (70 to 85 grams). If you increase the weight more than that, the cars are marginally slower when accelerating and are slower to brake, which is just enough to increase the lap times. There is, however, no hard and fast rule to this. The Austin Healey was one of the lightest cars and the Porsche 904 was the heaviest, but both turned lap times well below eight seconds. We needed a lap timer to discern this because the extra weight certainly made these three easier to drive.
**The MRRC Porsche 904 includes a steel plate with two small steel strips that can add about 3/4 ounce (10 grams). We tried it, but it increased the car's lap time from 7.92 to 8.06 seconds.
With the final bit of weight added, the spread in lap times between the fastest and slowest tumbled to less than a half-second (0.49 second) per qualifying lap.

sliding just enough to gain maximum traction, but not so much as to scrub-off speed, which is precisely what the drivers of the real cars did.

Road Racing in the 1950s-Era Sports/GT/Le Mans

There is a resurgence in interest in the sports and GT cars that really jump-started road racing after World War II. There are enough models available to allow you to establish an excellent representation of a typical 1950s-era sports car race. Most of these have been mass-produced over the past few years and should be available, although you may have to search a number of dealers for some of them. The cast-resin and clear bodies are available now. We have not done a 1950s-era shoot-out, but a number of the cars use chassis that are in previous shoot-outs (specifically, the Scalextric Caterham 7, NINCO Austin Healey, and

16-CAR 1060s-ERA SPORTS/GT/LE MANS SHOOT-OUT

Model/Real Car	With Magnets		No Magnets		With Weight
	Tires: Stock	Silicones	Tires: Stock	Silicones	Silicones
Carrera 427 Corvette Stingray*	6.78	6.35	8.82	8.08	7.92
Carrera D-Type Jaguar	5.42	4.70	8.72	7.88	7.97
Carrera Mustang GT350*	7.59	6.96	9.78	8.10	8.01
Fly Ford GT40	6.66	5.80	8.98	7.96	7.87
Monogram Corvette Grand Sp.	5.78	4.97	8.91	8.29	8.23
Monogram Daytona Cobra	5.88	5.73	9.11	8.24	8.10
MRRC 427 Cobra	7.43	7.65	9.03	8.76	8.62
MRRC Ferrari 275P	8.68	5.59	21.75	8.07	8.03
MRRC Porsche 904	5.79	7.92	9.14	8.42	7.91
NINCO 427 Cobra	7.28	6.61	8.75	7.77	7.85
NINCO Austin Healey Mk III	6.82	6.52	8.71	7.92	7.78
Pink-Kar Ferrari GTO	8.07	6.96	9.37	8.06	7.95
Reprotec 427 Cobra	8.36	7.77	8.62	8.03	7.97
Scalextric Ford GT40	5.80	5.52	9.16	8.16	8.10
Scalextric Lotus 7 (Caterham)	6.41	6.07	9.07	8.20	8.29
Slot Classics Morgan	NA	NA	8.65	7.99	7.88

NOTE:
The standard tires for the Carrera 427 Corvette Stingray and Mustang GT350 are 1/4 inch wide, as are the Puma Paws and Indy Grips replacement silicone tires. The best lap time was 8.08 seconds. I wanted to see how much a Corvette or Mustang would improve if the street wheels and tires were replaced with racing wheels and tires, so I replaced the stock wheels with MRRC wheels (as described in the November/December 2003 No. 6 issue) and matching 3/8-inch-wide Puma Paws tires. The Corvette's lap time was reduced to 7.92 seconds. I did not try the wider tires on the Mustang, but I would guess that it would turn about a 7.94-second qualifying lap with wider tires.

Carrera 427 Corvette), so you can get a rough idea of how these cars perform. Without magnets, but with silicone tires, the 1950s-era cars should run about the same as the 1960s-era cars.

There is also a selection of models to recreate Grand Prix racing in the 1950s: Scalextric has released a pair of Grand Prix cars, a 1957 Maserati and Vanwall, and Cartrix has a 1955 Mercedes W196. Pre-Add has a series of 1950s-era GP bodies that includes the Lancia-Ferrari D50, Ferrari 625 and Squalo, Mercedes W196, and 1956 Maserati 250F.

1970s-Era Sports/GT/Le Mans Shoot-Out

The same tests that were conducted with 1960s-era cars were conducted with a 15-car group of 1970s-era cars. Again, I tried to include examples of all the different chassis so you could have a choice of any car that brand offers. I included four different Fly (and GB Track) sidewinder chassis because all four are slightly different. I also included the Fly Ferrari 365 GTB/4 and BMW 3.0CSL, even though both are front-motored, because the BMW might be slightly more top-heavy and corner somewhat slower. The Spirit Ferrari 512M had the slightly slower motor. Newer Spirit 512Ms should be just as quick as the Fly sidewinders. The first series of tests on the Sport Monaco track were the out-of-the-box cars with stock tires, and then I retested them with Puma Paws silicone tires.

The silicone tires changed the order of the differences in lap times. Out-of-the-box, there were 1.51

1/32 SCALE 1950S-ERA SPORTS/GT/LE MANS CARS

Allard J2X (Petrolati body, see issue No. 18), Aston Martin DBR1 (Carrera), Aston Martin DB4GT (Carrera DB5), Austin Healey 100S (modified NINCO 3000 Mk III, see Chapter 4), Ferrari 166 roadster (NINCO), Ferrari Testa Rosa (NINCO), Ford Thunderbird (Carrera), Lotus 7/Caterham (Scalextric), Jaguar D-Type short nose (Carrera), Jaguar D-Type long nose (Auto Art), Lotus 11 (Carrera chassis, Pattos body; see issues 4 and 5), Maserati A6GCS (Carrera), Mercedes 300SLR roadster (Carrera), Porsche 60K10 (Lovespeed body), Porsche 356 (NINCO), Porsche 550 Spyder (Revell/Monogram).

There are also a number of limited-production cars and bodies that have been available recently. These may be a bit more difficult to find, but most are worth searching for.
MMK: Aston Martin DBR1, Ferrari 500 and 740 Monza, 1953 Jaguar C-Type, Lister Jaguar (Costin).
Slot Classics: Alfa Romeo Guiletta Spyder, Morgan Super Sports, and Mercedes 300SL Spyder and coupe.
Top Slot: Austin Healey 100, Ferrari 166 coupe, and 1953 Ferrari 340MM.

seconds difference in the lap times from the fastest to the slowest. With new silicone tires, 1.61 seconds separated the slowest and fastest cars. In all the tests, that's a pretty equal field. The other shoot-outs have produced similar ranges: the 14-car modern-era Sports/GT/Le Mans shoot-out were separated by 1.52 seconds a lap, even with silicone tires. About half of these 1970s-era cars were competitive with the modern-era cars, but the four quickest modern-era racers ran away from the quickest of these earlier-era racers.

In theory, the Fly Porsche 908/3, Lola T70 Mk III, Porsche 917/10 Can-Am, GB Track Porsche 917PA, Porsche 917, Ferrari 512S and 512M, and the MMK Matra MS670 (Fly 908) should all have nearly identical performance because they all have nearly identical chassis, sidewinder motor locations, motors, gearing, tires, and weight. In this shoot-out, and in real-world racing, that's not necessarily true. The MMK Matra will be difficult to bring up to match the others because its cast-resin body is heavier. It is, however, possible to make any of these Fly cars a match for one another if all the cars are tuned to perfection to eliminate out-of-round wheels, wobbly wheels, excessive side play in the rear axle, and all the other things that blueprint a model racing car.

Similarly, the Monogram Greenwood Corvette, Scalextric L-88 Corvette, Fly BMW 3.5 CSL, and Fly Ferrari 365 GTB/4 should all have similar performance because they share very similar inline front-mounted motors, gear ratios, and weight. The relative positions of these cars in this shoot-out, particularly after all have the same spec tires, is about what we see in actual model car races.

The NINCO Porsche 911 Turbo or 934 is slower because it has less downforce than the other cars. You can fix that by removing the magnet, drilling through the mounting hole, and gluing the magnet about 0.060 inch above the rails (any lower and the motor won't pull the downforce). The original Spirit Ferraris were fitted with relatively slow motors. The newer cars have a much faster motor like that in the Spirit Reynard. The heavier Ferrari won't be as quick as the Reynard, but it should be as quick as the Fly sidewinders.

For the next series of tests, I removed the magnets and put the stock tires back on the cars and ran a series of qualifying laps. Next, I replaced the stock tires with the same Puma Paws silicones that were used for

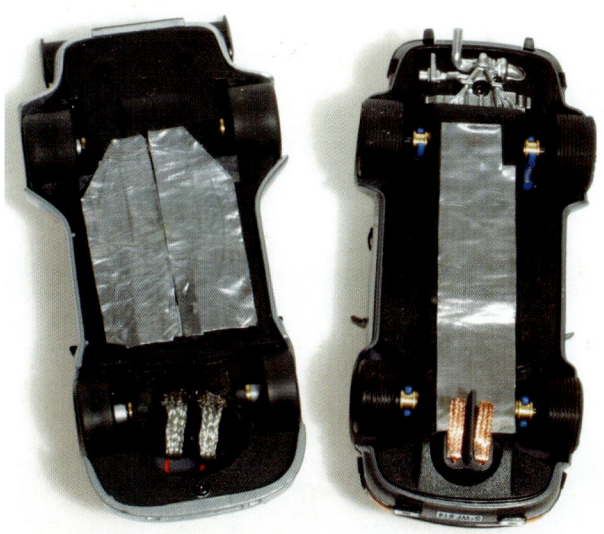

The Carrera Porsche 911 Turbo RSR and NINCO Porsche 911 Turbo both have inline front motors.

the previous tests. Finally, I added about 1/2 ounce of weight to better balance the cars and positioned the weight a bit more toward the front of the sidewinder-style chassis and a bit more toward the rear for the inline-style chassis.

There are some anomalies here, just as there are with the 1960s-era cars. The Porsche 917 and 908/3 were some of the fastest cars ever produced, quick enough to complete with current Le Mans cars.

1970S-ERA PUMA PAWS AND INDY GRIPS SILICONE TIRES

	Puma Paws Tire No.	Indy Grips Tire No.
Carrera Porsche 911RSR	01007	NA
Fly BMW 3.5CSL 1976	04008	3008
Fly Ferrari 512S	04001	3003
Fly Ferrari Daytona 365 GTB/4	04005	NA
Fly Lola T70 MKIII	04001	3003
Fly Porsche 917	04001	3003
Fly Porsche 908/3	04001	3003
Fly Porsche 917/10	04001	3003
GB Track Porsche 910PA	04001	3003
Historic Scale Racing Replicas	27001	NA
MMK Matra MS670 (Fly 908)	04001	3003
Monogram Greenwood	05004	1305
NINCO Porsche 911 Turbo (934)	07006	1305
Scalextric L-88 Vette	13014	1009
Spirit Ferrari 512M	04001	3003

16-CAR 1970s-ERA SPORTS/GT/LE MANS SHOOT-OUT

Model Car	With Magnets		No Magnets		Weight
	TIRES: Stock	Silicones	TIRES: Stock	Silicones	+5 grams
Carrera Porsche 911RSR (1/29)*	7.15	5.91	7.98	7.08	6.98
Fly Lola T70 Mk III	6.58	5.39	9.25	7.42	7.40
NINCO Porsche 911 Turbo****	7.86	6.93	8.35	7.44	7.42
Fly Porsche 917/10 Can-Am	7.30	5.68	9.17	7.95	7.63
Fly Porsche 908/3	7.38	5.36	9.25	8.29	7.66
Historic Scale Racing Replicas M8D	6.94	6.92	7.72	7.68	7.68
Monogram Greenwood Corvette	6.23	5.71	9.10	7.97	7.90
Scalextric L-88 Corvette	6.68	5.79	9.34	8.14	7.98
Fly Porsche 917	7.48	6.68	9.35	8.30	7.99
Fly Ferrari 512S	7.19	6.74	9.43	8.36	8.05
GB Track Porsche 917PA	7.40	6.26	9.57	8.40	8.08
Fly Ferrari 365 GTB/4	7.17	6.18	9.61	8.48	8.23
Fly BMW 3.0 CSL	6.55	5.80	9.44	8.27	8.24
MMK Matra M670 (Fly 908)**	7.74	6.49	9.58	8.41	8.39
Spirit Ferrari 512M***	7.27	7.01	9.70	8.52	8.45

NOTES:
The Historic Scale Racing Replicas McLaren M8D was tested after the shoot-out with other 1970s-era cars, but its performance numbers are included here.
*The Carrera Porsche 911RSR (and the similar Porsche 935) are much larger than any of these cars and are closer to 1/29 scale. The extra width and length produces predictably quicker lap times.
**The MMK Matra has a cast-resin body that weighs about 1/2 ounce more than the typical injection-molded plastic body. The model has a Fly 908 chassis.
***Spirit now supplies a much faster motor in its cars, so newer editions of the Ferrari 512M should be quicker than the car we tested.
****We tested the NINCO Porsche Turbo with the stock blue spring, but with spring units removed from the front axle.

Conversely, the L-88, Greenwood, Ferrari Daytona, and BMW 3.5CSL were quick, but were far outclassed by the sports-racing cars. Those differences between the real cars are not reflected in the qualifying lap times between the real cars from this test. There is a rather random arrangement of performance based not on how well the real car performed, but how well the model performs. Removing the magnets is a major help to bring the performance of all these cars close enough to make a race of it. The prototype cars, such as the 917 and 512M, should be relatively quicker than they are. One way to make them quicker would be to allow the models of the truly fast real cars to run magnets (or more magnets) than the replicas of production-based cars. In effect, the GT cars would run in a separate class, just as they do in real life. It would be your choice whether to run them in the same race with the replicas of prototype cars as they do at Le Mans.

Modern-Era Sports/GT/Le Mans Shoot-out

The modern-era sports and GT cars, most of which competed at Le Mans, are the most popular choices among the various model car firms. Every 1/32 scale model race car manufacturer offers at least a few Le Mans replicas.

I selected the cars that were the most competitive from each maker. The Fly Saleen, for example, is large and heavy and is really not as fast as the Fly Corvette, so I picked the Corvette. The Corvette is large and heavy compared with the Fly Panoz Esperante, so I included it and the smaller Fly Viper for comparison to the Corvette. I wanted to see if there was a noticeable difference between Fly front-motored coupes (the 'Vette and Esperante), so we included the Fly Panoz Roadster S. Similarly, I wanted to compare a Fly sidewinder to these inline and front-motored pair, so I opted for the Fly Joest. Fly produces rear-motored inline cars, so I added the Fly Lola B98-10. The Scalextric Lola MG is one of the fastest cars on home tracks and we wanted to compare it, especially without magnets, to the very similar Scalextric Cadillac since both are inline cars. I also wanted to compare a Scalextric sidewinder to the rest of the cars, so I included the Porsche GT3R. The Carrera Bentley is their only GT coupe, so we compared it to their 1999 Le Mans–winning replica of the BMW because the BMW is a bit quicker than the Carrera Panoz. Similarly, I compared the NINCO version of the Le Mans–winning BMW to the NINCO replica of the McLaren F1 GT car. SCX currently offers the Le Mans–winning Audi, a Ferrari 333SP, and a Dome, but all four should run about the same, so I opted for the Audi R8 from SCX. The Slot.it Porsche 956C is from the 1980s, but most racers will run it with these more modern cars.

MODERN-ERA PUMA PAWS AND INDY GRIPS SILICONE TIRES

Model/Real Car	Class	Weight: ounces (grams)	Puma Paws Tire No.	Indy Grips Tire No.
Carrera Bentley EXP	GT	3 1/4 (92)	7003	N/A
Carrera Bentley EXP	GT (2 mags)	3 3/8 (97)	7003	N/A
Carrera BMW V12LM	SP	3 (85)	7003	N/A
Fly Corvette C5R	GT	3 (85)	3002	04005
Fly Lola B98-10	SP	2 3/8 (65)	3003	04002
Fly Panoz Esperante	GT	2 7/8 (80)	3001	04002
Fly Panoz Roadster S	SP	2 7/8 (80)	3001	04002
Fly Porsche 1997 Joest	SP	2 7/8 (80)	3002	04002
Fly Viper	GT	2 1/2 (70)	3001	04002
NINCO BMW V12LM	SP	3 1/2 (100)	2004	07002
NINCO McLaren F1	GT	3 1/2 (100)	2001	07002
Scalextric Cadillac	SP	2 3/4 (78)	1007	13008
Scalextric Lola MG	SP	2 1/2 (70)	1007	13008
Scalextric Porsche GT3R	GT	3 (85)	1010	13007
SCX Audi R8	SP	3 (82)	4005	14002
Slot.it Porsche 956C	GT	2 1/2 (70)	N/A	15003
Spirit Reynard 2KQ	SP	2 3/4 (80)	N/A	16001

Easy To Drive

These tests do not reveal the easy-to-drive factor that can make the difference between winning and finishing third or fourth. When the cars were fitted with magnets, the really quick ones only required your attention at two or three points on the track where you would let off on the throttle to about half and then get back on as quickly as you could move the trigger. The Fly Lola B98-10, Scalextric Lola MG, Slot.it Porsche 956C, SCX Audi R8, Spirit Reynard, Carrera Bentley (with two magnets), and Fly Viper were in a class by themselves. The Audi was the easiest to drive, and racing over 25 laps, it would be more likely to win than the more nimble Fly Lola.

The cars without magnets were all very close. Top lap times over two-minute heat races were turned by the Fly Viper, Scalextric Porsche, Scalextric Lola MG, Spirit Reynard 2KQ, Slot.it Porsche 956C, SCX Audi R8, and Fly Lola. Examples from the quickest to the slowest of individual lap times reflect the easy-to-drive factor. I found I turned the most consistent lap times with the SCX Audi and NINCO McLaren. The Carrera Bentley was smooth, but had a disconcerting rumble and banged the Sport guard rails far too often. The Fly Lola and Spirit Reynard were easily the most nimble of all the cars—both felt like they weighed half as much as any of the other cars as you drove it—but they were easy to deslot. Oddly, the Scalextric Cadillac was easier to drive and quicker than the Lola MG.

The quickest cars with magnets are still about one second per lap faster than the cars without magnets. The difference in lap times among different brands—and even cars from the same brand—is so great that you end up having races that are populated only with Slot.it Porsches or Fly Lolas. Only four other cars (Spirit Reynard 2KQ, SCX Audi R8, Fly Viper, and Scalextric Lola MG) could compete with the Slot.it Porsche and Fly Lola with out-of-the-box magnets and were about a second per lap quicker than the others. By dumping the magnets, fitting silicone tires, and adding golf club lead weights, 10 of these 14 cars can win, and the four "slower" cars are close enough that proper tuning and a better motor would bring them up to the standards of the other 10.

Open-Wheel F1/CART/IRL Car Shoot-out

When the cars run with magnets, the race for out-of-the box cars is most likely going to be won by the Scalextric IRL car, primarily because it has the strongest magnetic downforce of the bunch. Really, out-of-the-box has come to mean that the car with the strongest magnet wins. Carrera's newer F1 cars with the second magnet are quicker than the other F1 cars and almost as quick as the Scalextric IRL car.

MODERN-ERA SPORTS/GT/LE MANS SHOOT-OUT

Model/Real Car	Class	With Magnets Tires: Stock	Silicones	No Magnets Tires: Stock	Silicones
Slot.it Porsche 956C	GT	5.63	5.80	7.02	7.06
Carrera Bentley EXP	GT (2 mags)	5.38	5.22	10.10	7.11
Carrera Bentley EXP	GT	7.90	7.65	10.10	7.11
Carrera BMW V12LM	SP	6.95	5.99	8.82	7.13
Fly Porsche 1997 Joest	SP	7.10	6.27	8.88	7.29
Fly Corvette C5R	GT	7.05	6.17	9.45	7.32
Fly Lola B98-10	SP	5.40	5.28	8.20	7.33
Scalextric Cadillac	SP	6.98	6.06	8.09	7.36
Scalextric Cadillac	SP (2 mags)	6.05	5.19	8.09	7.36
NINCO McLaren F1	GT	7.89	6.64	8.97	7.37
SCX Audi R8	SP	5.45	5.23	8.03	7.38
Spirit Reynard 2KQ	SP	5.48	5.32	8.30	7.43
Scalextric Porsche GT3R	GT	6.49	6.28	7.79	7.46
NINCO BMW V12LM	SP	7.43	6.44	8.39	7.51
Fly Panoz Roadster S	SP	7.35	6.18	8.18	7.70
Fly Panoz Esperante	GT	6.94	5.94	7.90	7.73
Scalextric Lola MG	SP	5.44	5.28	8.71	8.11
Fly Viper	GT	5.33	5.12	8.22	8.12

(From fastest to slowest, without magnets, with silicone tires)
Lap Times (on Sport Monaco track, in seconds)

The sheet lead was also applied down the center of the 1970s era GB Track Porsche, Fly Ferrari 512S, Fly Lola T70, and the Spirit Ferrari 512M.

There are two solutions to this problem: Add more magnets so whatever car you are racing against the Scalextric IRL Dallara (or the two-magnet Carrera) is as quick, or remove the magnets from all the cars.

Out-of-the-Box, With Silicone Tires

In some cases, the stock tires are so bad that even the strong magnets cannot overcome their slipperiness. Remember, we are testing on a Sport Monaco track and the stock tires will work much better on the rougher surface of the SCX track, the older Scalextric Classic track, or the rough surface of NINCO track. The rougher the track, the less advantage silicone tires are likely to have. What owners of NINCO tracks tell us, however, is that the silicones allow quicker lap times, even on NINCO track. With silicone tires, the Scalextric IRL Dallara-Chevrolet flies. On the tight Sport Monaco track, the car was so stuck-down it was only necessary to let up on the throttle once a lap. You could, quite literally, drive with your eyes closed. The Scalextric F1 and NINCO F1 cars were nearly as quick and it was only necessary to let up twice on each lap. The newer Carrera F1 cars were even quicker. The addition of a second magnet by the Carrera factory is a mass-production example

The Historic Scale Racing Replicas McLaren M8D was not included in the original 1970s-era shoot-out, but its performance numbers indicate it would be competitive with most of the cars when all run without magnets.

The modern-era Sports/GT/Le Mans car shoot-out results, from fastest to slowest, without magnets, and with silicone tires: Carrera Bentley EXP, Carrera BMW V12LM, Fly Porsche 1997 Joest, Fly Corvette C5R, Fly Lola B98-10, Scalextric Cadillac, NINCO McLaren F1, SCX Audi R8, Scalextric Porsche GT3R, NINCO BMW V12LM, Fly Panoz Roadster S, Fly Panoz Esperante, Scalextric Lola MG, and Fly Viper.

Shown here are 14 cars, each with identical tires and weight, and no magnets. The sheet lead weights have been left unpainted to make them visible. I suggest you paint them flat black so they don't look so crude.

of what you can do at home with just a smear of epoxy and a spare Scalextric bar magnet. Just slap the second magnet on the bottom of the car, and you can also drive with your eyes closed. I hope you detect a prejudice here. A strong magnet might have a place on a track with nothing but broad curves and 20-foot straights, but on most home tracks, the majority of the cars already have such strong magnets that you can drive with your eyes closed. That's great for beginners because they won't lose patience chasing after desloted cars, but it produces performance where the cars are a blur, much like the neo-magnet HO cars. It is racing, but it's not what I would call model car racing—projectile racing, perhaps.

No Magnets, Stock Tires

When you pull the magnets, the slippery tires show up in a hurry. Very few model racing cars have tires that are sticky enough to keep the car from sliding. The spread in lap times with stock tires is 1.66 seconds, but the numbers alone don't convey the whole story. The Carrera, SCX, and Pro-Slot cars are really no fun to drive without magnets when the cars have stock tires. Conversely, the NINCO tires and the treaded tires on the Scalextric Williams work almost as well as the silicones. In fact, the lap times on the NINCO CART Lola-Ford were nearly identical with the stock or silicone tires. The silicone tires work magic for most of the cars. The lap times of all the cars are reduced, and of much more significance, the spread from fastest to slowest is just 0.38 seconds a lap. For most drivers, any

INDY GRIPS AND PUMA PAWS TIRE NUMBERS

Model/Real Car	Indy Grips Silicone Tire No.	Puma Paws Silicone Tire No.
Carrera F1 Williams	7004	01001
NINCO CART Lola-Ford	2003	07005
NINCO F1 Stewart (scale)	2003	07005
NINCO F1 Arrows (wide)	2003	07005
Pro-Slot F1 Ferrari	1601	10001
SCX F1 Arrows (scale)	4006	14001
SCX F1 McLaren (wide)	4006	14001
SCX CART Lola-Ford	4006	14001
Scalextric F1 McLaren	1008	13010
Scalextric F1 Williams	1008	13010
Scalextric IRL Dallara-Chevrolet	1008	13010

TEN-CAR GRAND PRIX F1/CART/IRL SHOOT-OUT

Model/Real Car	With Magnets		No Magnets	
	Tires: Stock	Silicones	Tires: Stock	Silicones
Carrera F1 Williams	8.08	6.01	8.24	7.46
Carrera F1 Williams (2 mags)	7.28	5.01	8.24	7.46
NINCO F1 Stewart (scale)	6.38	5.52	7.69	7.58
Scalextric F1 McLaren	6.42	5.59	7.89	7.59
Pro-Slot F1 Ferrari	7.81	7.35	7.87	7.62
NINCO F1 Arrows (wide)	6.46	5.61	7.73	7.63
Scalextric F1 Williams	6.36	5.62	7.85	7.67
SCX F1 Arrows (scale)	NA	NA	7.81	7.69
Scalextric IRL Dallara-Chevrolet	5.69	4.72	8.10	7.74
NINCO CART Lola-Ford	6.24	6.12	7.76	7.78
SCX CART Lola-Ford	7.62	6.26	8.05	7.64
SCX F1 McLaren (wide)	7.03	6.46	9.35	7.84

(From fastest to slowest, with magnets removed, with silicone tires)
Lap Times (on Sport Monaco track, in seconds)

one of these 10 could win a race. The cars are even more fun to drive because you really do have to pay attention to every corner—forget closing your eyes; you cannot even blink. The lap times are only about a second a lap slower than the out-of-the box cars, so you are not giving up much performance.

Accurate Scale F1 Cars

The NINCO and SCX F1 cars have front and rear track widths that are about a foot wider than those of the real cars the models recreate. There's no reason I can see for this difference, and it makes the F1 cars look like CART and IRL cars. Ironically, NINCO has a CART car and its track isn't any wider than NINCO's F1 cars. It's not terribly difficult to reduce the front and rear track widths on either NINCO or SCX, but you do lose the steering, which does absolutely nothing to help the cars' handling, but it probably doesn't hurt much either. There's information on how to narrow the track on NINCO and SCX F1 cars in Chapter 4. For whatever reason, the narrower versions of the NINCO and SCX cars handle better than the wide versions. It could be because the steering hinders lap times. It's nice to know you can have a realistic car that handles well.

The Strata of Speed

In the real world, the open-wheeled cars are designed to be the fastest cars around any given track. An F1 car is supposed to be faster than a Le Mans car, and a CART or IRL car is supposed to be faster than a NASCAR car. Modern cars are also supposed to be faster than cars from the 1970s, which are supposed to be faster than cars from the 1950s. With model cars, magnets can be used to provide real racing performance that matches the real cars, regardless of the era. To make the F1, CART, and IRL cars quicker than the other cars, the simple solution is to pull the magnets from the other cars and fit "spec" (in this case, silicone) tires.

We selected the Scalextric F1 Williams as the benchmark for open-wheel car performance. The Scalextric IRL cars are faster, but in the real world, that's not true, so there was some logic to the choice. The real reason was that it will require some major modifications to make the other open-wheel cars as quick as those IRL cars, and why should they be? It's relatively simple to reduce the speed of the IRL car, and it's an example of how you can reduce the speed of any car.

The shoot-out produced another wild card in that the SCX F1 cars have a simple magnet adjustment that allows you to lower the magnet by loosening two screws. The SCX magnet is so strong that the motor won't pull it, so we were forced to swap motors in the SCX car, and fitting the SCX replacement Turbo-Pro motor. So, we have 12 cars that include the full range of magnet modifications from strictly stock (Scalextric Williams and McLaren) to reducing the magnetic grip (Scalextric IRL car).

Carrera has introduced a new F1 chassis for the 2003 Williams, McLaren, and Sauber. Carrera also makes a 2002 Ferrari F1 car that also has the two-magnet

GRAND PRIX F1/CART/IRL SHOOT-OUT, ADDED MAGNETS

Model/Real Car	with Stock Magnets		with Added Magnets
	Tires: Stock	Silicones	Silicones
SCX F1 Arrows (scale)	6.83	NA	5.20
Carrera F1 Williams 2003 (stock)	NA	NA	5.21
SCX F1 McLaren (wide)*	7.03	6.46	5.22
Carrera F1 Williams 2002*	8.08	6.01	5.26
SCX CART Lola-Ford	7.62	6.26	5.28
Scalextric IRL Dallara-Chevy**	5.69	4.72	5.39
NINCO CART Lola-Ford*	6.24	6.12	5.51
NINCO F1 Stewart (scale)*	6.38	5.52	5.52
Scalextric F1 McLaren (stock)	6.42	5.59	5.56
NINCO F1 Arrows (wide)*	6.46	5.61	5.60
Scalextric F1 Williams (stock)	6.36	5.62	5.61
Pro-Slot F1 Ferrari*	7.81	7.35	5.76

(From fastest to slowest, *with added magnets, ** with raised magnet)
Lap Times (on Sport Monaco track, in seconds)

The qualifying grid of F1, CART, and IRL open-wheeled cars when the cars have magnets and all have silicone tires: Scalextric IRL Dallara-Chevrolet, NINCO F1 Stewart (scale-width), Scalextric F1 McLaren, NINCO F1 Arrows (wide), Scalextric F1 Williams, Carrera F1 Williams, NINCO CART Lola-Ford, SCX F1 McLaren (wide), Pro-Slot F1 Ferrari, and SCX F1 Arrows (scale-width).

DOWNFORCE: GRAND PRIX F1/CART/IRL SHOOT-OUT, STOCK MAGNETS

Model/Real Car	Clearance: Scalextrix	Carrera	Downforce: Scalextrix	Carrera
Carrera F1 Williams 2002	0.040	0.035	38 gm (1 oz)	42 gm (1 oz)
Carrera F1 Williams 2003	0.020	0.025	110 gm (3.8 oz)	58 gm (2.0 oz)
NINCO CART Lola-Ford	0.070	0.075	45 gm (2 oz)	45 gm (1.5 oz)
NINCO F1 Stewart (scale)	0.070	0.075	78 gm (2.8 oz)	45 gm (1.5 oz)
NINCO F1 Arrows (wide)	0.070	0.075	78 gm (2.8 oz)	45 gm (1.5 oz)
Pro-Slot F1 Ferrari	0.035	0.040	15 gm (0.5 oz)	0 gm (0 oz)
Scalextric IRL Dallara-Chevy	0.010	0.015	100 gm (3.5 oz)	72 gm (2.5 oz)
Scalextric F1 Williams	0.020	0.025	127.6 gm (4.5 oz)	90.1 gm (3.2 oz)
Scalextric F1 McLaren	0.020	0.025	113.4 gm (4.0 oz)	85.1 gm (3.0 oz.)
SCX F1 Arrows (scale)	0.060	0.065	98 gm (3.5 oz)	70 gm (2.3 oz)
SCX F1 McLaren (wide)	0.060	0.065	98 gm (3.5 oz)	70 gm (2.3 oz)
SCX CART Lola-Ford	0.045	0.040	155 gm (4.75 oz)	70gm (2.5 oz)

DOWNFORCE: TWELVE-CAR GRAND PRIX F1/CART/IRL SHOOT-OUT, ADDED MAGNETS

Model/Real Car	Clearance: Scalextrix	Carrera	Downforce: Scalextrix	Carrera
Carrera F1 Williams 2002*	0.040	0.035	98 gm (3.5 oz)	42 gm (1.5 oz)
Carrera F1 Williams 2003	0.020	0.025	110 gm (3.8 oz)	58 gm (2.0 oz)
NINCO CART Lola-Ford*	0.070	0.075	170 gm (6 oz)	55 gm (2.0 oz)
NINCO F1 Stewart (scale*)	0.070	0.075	170 gm (6 oz)	55 gm (2.0 oz)
NINCO F1 Arrows (wide)*	0.070	0.075	170 gm (6 oz)	55 gm (2.0 oz)
Pro-Slot F1 Ferrari*	0.015	0.020	120 gm (4.2 oz)	80 gm (2.8 oz)
Scalextric IRL Dallara-Chevy**	0.025	0.030	83 gm (2.8 oz)	70 gm (2.3 oz)
Scalextric F1 Williams (stock)	0.020	0.025	127.6 gm (4.5 oz)	90.1 gm (3.2 oz)
Scalextric F1 McLaren (stock)	0.020	0.025	113.4 gm (4.0 oz)	85.1 gm (3.0 oz)
SCX F1 Arrows (scale)*	0.060	0.065	127 gm (4.5 oz)	70 gm (2.5 oz)
SCX F1 McLaren (wide*)	0.060	0.065	127 gm (4.5 oz)	70 gm (2.5 oz)
SCX CART Lola-Ford	0.045	0.040	155 gm (4.75 oz)	70gm (2.5 oz.)

NOTES: *with added magnets, ** with raised magnet

chassis. The Carrera F1 cars should perform the same as the 2003 Carrera Williams. The new cars do not make the older single-magnet Carrera F1 cars obsolete; however, if you are willing to modify the older cars, you can drop in a pair of magnets, as shown in Chapter 4.

CHAPTER 6
BUILD YOUR OWN RACE CAR

The MAXI-Models M6A McLeagle is a complete cast-resin kit.

Rent-a-racers are great fun. What's even more delightful is to own your own car. Perhaps the best of all is to race your own hand-built machine. Dan Gurney and Jack Brabham did in 1/1 scale Grand Prix racing, and you can do it with your own 1/32 scale machine.

The ready-to-race models are near perfect, so there's little point in trying to duplicate something you can buy ready-to-run. However, there are several hundred race cars that you can have only if you are willing to build, or at least repaint, to get the specific replica of real racing cars you crave.

Sometimes, a simple repaint can get you what you want. There are very few Ferrari F1 ready-to-race model cars with cigarette or alcohol sponsors. At present, there are few available. If you want a current-era F1 Ferrari as an alternative to the Carrera F1 Ferrari, you can repaint another F1 car and apply Ferrari decals.

Virtually any real race car you might want is available as a clear plastic, fiberglass or cast-resin body. The cast-resin bodies usually have the best shapes and details. There are about 50 race cars I want but cannot get as ready-to-run cars. My list included the 1988 Le Mans–winning XJR9 Jaguar that was in *Slot Car Bible* and the Austin Healey 100S, M6A McLeagle, 289FIA Cobra, and Cadillac-Allard that are in this chapter. The XJR was a clear plastic Pattos body on Fly Porsche chassis, and the other cars are cast-resin bodies on a variety of ready-to-run chassis.

Body Damage

Even the best drivers of real racing cars crash occasionally. When parts break off on your slot cars, you can glue them back on. There are several choices of glues, and each works best for some specific component. I prefer metal-filled epoxy for really strong joints or tiny parts, such as mirrors. Shoe Goo or clear silicone is good to hold motors in place. The cyanoacrylate cements such as Super Glue have relatively limited use because they rely on a perfect fit. Super Glue is fine for reattaching things such as broken-off spoilers on Scalextric GT40s. Weldbond is a flexible form of white glue that works well for

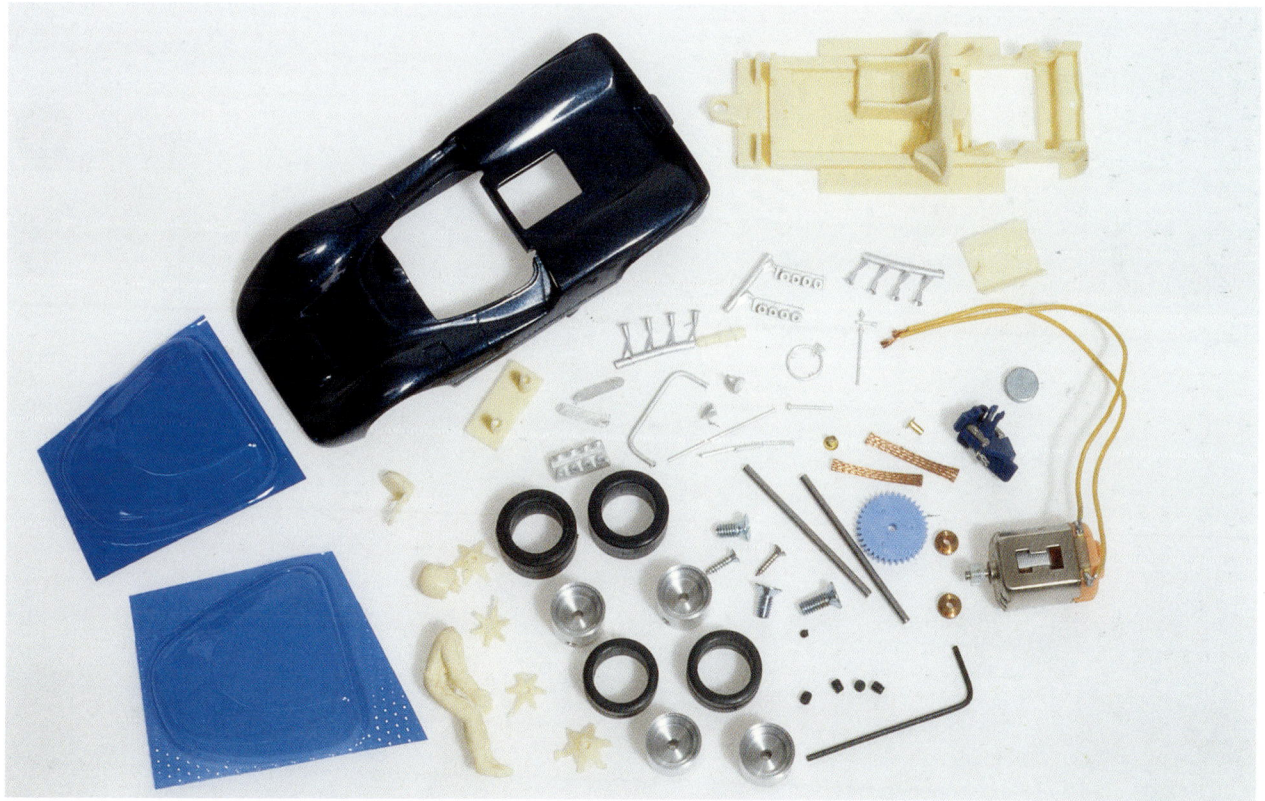

The MAXI-Models kits include the cast-resin body with etched and cast-metal parts, decals, gears, chassis, motor, pickup, axles, wheels, and tires.

This is the out-of-the-box Scalextric 2003 Renault F1 without cigarette-sponsor markings.

The Pattos decals fill-in the areas where "Mild Seven" appeared on the full-size 2003 Renault F1 at most of that season's races.

The 2001 Ferrari (a rebuilt and repainted SCX Williams) is lower and slimmer than the Scalextric McLaren.

retaining clear parts because unlike Super Glue, silicone, and some other cements, it will not etch or craze the clear plastic.

Custom-Decal Markings

You can create a model racing car that is truly unique by applying additional or new markings. Since many model cars are sold to youngsters, few are available with the cigarette or alcohol product sponsors that made the cars famous. The decals are usually available. Sometimes you will need to completely repaint the car, but it's not always that difficult. I wanted to race a 2003 Renault F1 with cigarette sponsor Mild Seven markings so I applied Pattos Mild Seven decals to Scalextric 2003 F1 Renault. You will need photographs of the real car to determine exactly where to place the decals.

To apply decals, clean the model with detergent, and then dry it completely. Cut the decals from the sheet and dip one at a time in warm water for a few seconds. Set the decal on a piece of facial tissue for a few minutes until the water soaks through the paper backing. Place the decal and paper backing on the model and hold the decal itself with a small paintbrush while you pull the backing from beneath it with tweezers. Position the decal perfectly, then cover it with a coat of Microscale's Microsol to soften the decal so it will adhere like paint. Let the decal dry overnight and gently clean the surface of the model with warm water on a cotton swab. Dry the model. Spray on one or two very light coats of Testors GlossCote and let it dry. Protect the model with a brush-on coat of Future-brand vinyl floor covering. Let that dry overnight and you are ready to go racing.

Correct Colors

An accurate replica of a real racing car includes an accurate rendering of the colors of the real car. The body shape may be correct, but the car won't look quite like the real one if the color is not close to the color of the original.

For one example, the Shelby American Cobras appeared in two shades of metallic blue. The cars that were raced in early 1964 were painted Guardsman Blue, a standard Ford production car color, and the late 1964 cars and 1965 cars were painted in Ford's standard (but darker) Viking Blue.

MCW Automotive Finishes repackages original automotive lacquer paint in aerosol cans or 3-ounce bottles, especially for modelers. They offer both Guardsman and

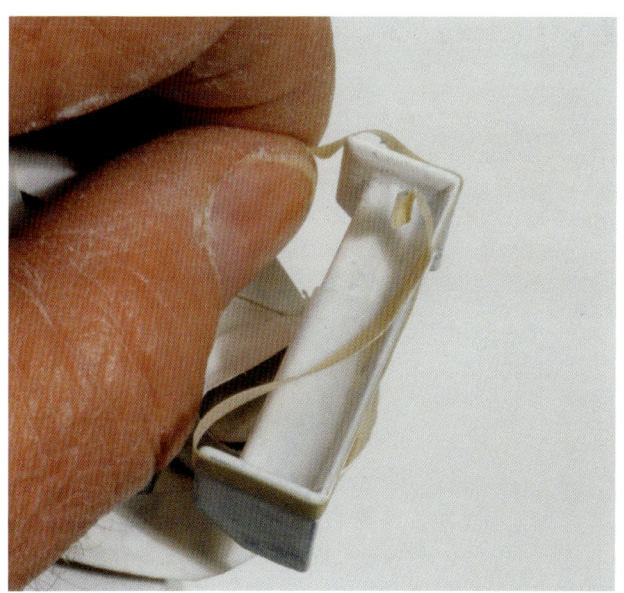

Mask off the areas that are to remain white with 1/8-inch 3M automotive masking tape.

Make loops of masking tape with the sticky side out and press them onto a scrap of wood, then press the body parts onto the tape so you can hold the stick while you spray the parts.

Viking Blue, as well as just about every other racing color, including the Mecom Blue used on the Grand Sports and the metallic blue used on Scarabs.

You may be able to find automotive paint suppliers by looking in the Yellow Pages. The larger automobile paint supply stores have Ford's Viking Blue to the original formula, but you will have to buy a quart can. Most shops will allow you to specify the size of the metallic particles so you can pick "fine" and have a near-scale shine. Most shops can pour that quart into a special aerosol can for about $16. The less-expensive route is to try to find a pre-packaged aerosol can such as Dupli-Color or Plasti-Kote. The Plasti-Kote FM8089 Ford Blue was a bit too silver to match the Viking Blue, and the Dupli-Color T338 Light Blue was a bit too blue. The Dupli-Color Ford Medium Blue was quite close, however, to the Guardsman Blue. Fred Martin used Dupli-Color Ford Medium Blue to match the darker Guardsman Blue on the larger Cobras.

I sprayed samples of DuPont Viking Blue, Plasti-Kote FM8089 Ford Blue, and Dupli-Color T338 Light Blue. The Plasti-Kote shade was very close to what Monogram selected for its first Daytona Cobra coupe. I opted for the DuPont paint for the 289FIA Cobra's colors at the Targa Florio.

Painting Your Race Car

It might seem odd to paint an already painted body, but sometimes that is the only solution when you

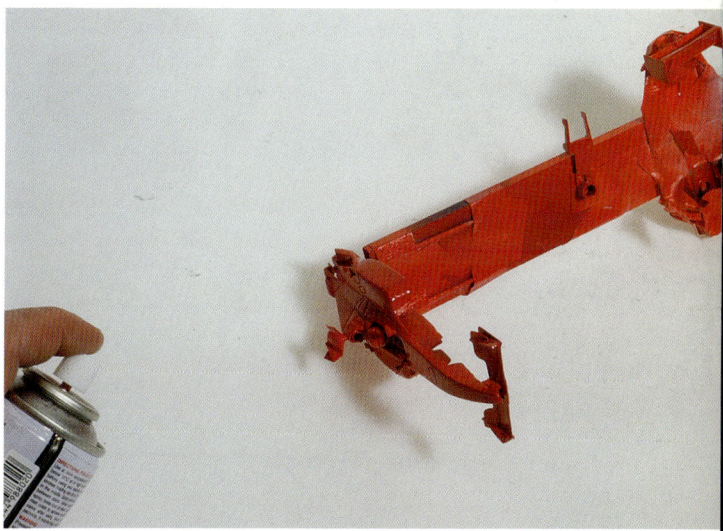

After masking off the white, spray the second color (red).

want a car you cannot buy. I wanted a 2001 Formula 1 Ferrari so I repainted an SCX Williams after extensively reworking the body. A quicker solution would be to repaint and decal a Scalextric 2003 Renault F1. The finished model is a close replica of 2002 Ferrari F1 racer.

Ferrari F2001 F1

I opted to recreate the 2001 Ferrari because I liked the earlier graphics and the anteater nose. I modified

Most of the white on my model needed to be retouched to obtain a sharp, cleaner color line.

The completed 2001 Ferrari captures the slim and lean appearance of the real race car.

an SCX Williams by trimming the nose, changing the barge boards, replacing the wheels and tires, and narrowing the overall width. Decals for both cars are available from Pattos. Tamiya's Red is very close to the color photos of the real cars, so that was the color I selected.

Dan Gurney's 1970 AAR Trans-Am 'Cuda

The Carrera Hemi 'Cuda is very close to the AAR 'Cudas that Dan Gurney and Swede Savage raced in the 1970 Trans-Am. The model, like the real car, looks a lot meaner if you lower it about 1/8 inch. Use the milling bit in a Dremel motor tool to remove 1/8 inch from both rear mounting posts. The Carrera reversing switch interferes with the interior on the lowered car, so I removed the switch. First, unsolder the wires from the motor brushes and the reversing switch. Resolder the black wire to the right motor brush, and the red to the left, but check the car on the track to see that it

Make the chin spoiler for the Trans-Am 'Cuda from 0.020-inch-thick Evergreen styrene plastic sheet and attach it with metal-filled epoxy. After the epoxy cures, use a 1/8-inch drill bit to locate the holes for the front body-mounting screws.

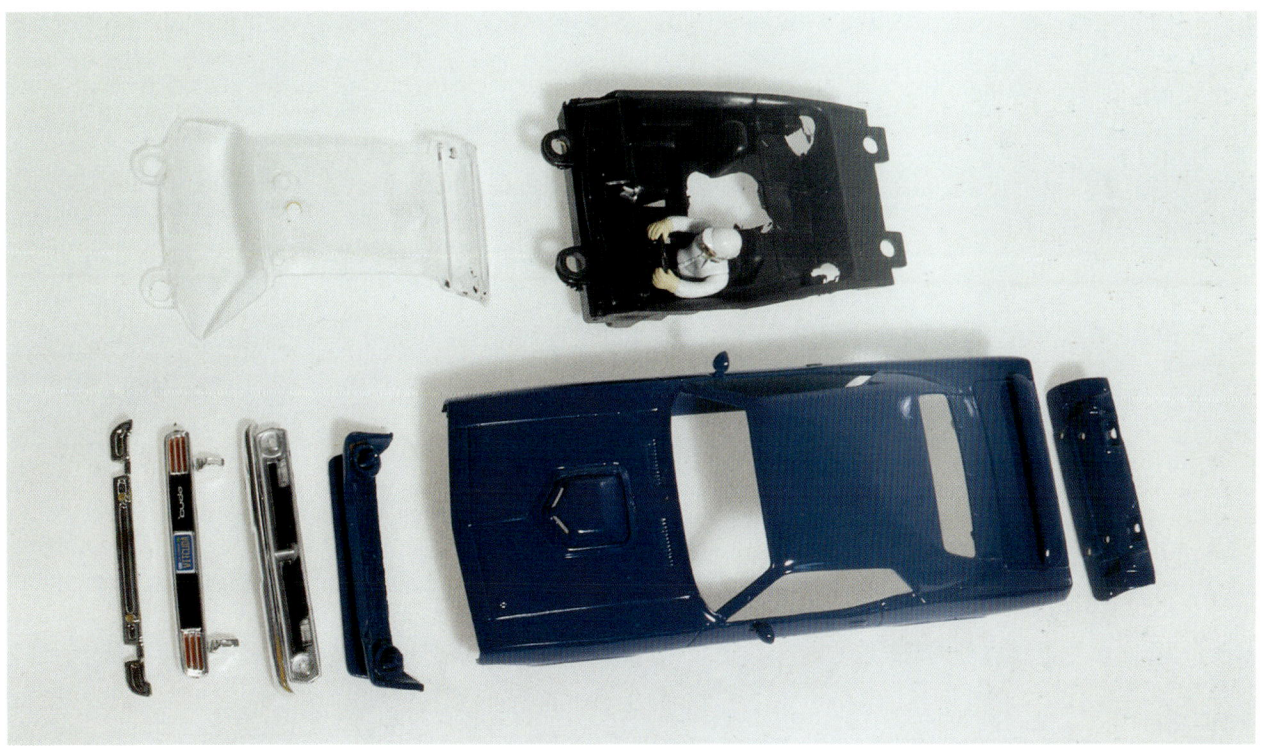

Paint the parts for the Trans-Am 'Cuda as individual pieces before you assemble the car.

Here is Dan Gurney piloting his own AAR Trans-Am 'Cuda at the 1970 Laguna Seca race.

runs in the right direction. You can skip the body-lowering process and just go with the painted car and new tires. I also added the front air dam or chin spoiler and replaced the wheels with MRRC American mag-style.

The first AAR Trans-Am 'Cuda was raced with huge square numbers (usually 48 for Gurney and 42 for Savage). The paint is available from MCW as 2084 Gurney Trans-Am Dark Blue Metallic. I decided that Testors Model Master "Blue Angel Blue" was close, but it is not metallic. Swede's car usually had the orange and yellow splash on the hood, but the team used whichever car was available during the season—the numbers peeled off. I used the Pattos Plymouth decals with the "Dan Gurney" decal from the Fred Cady 1/24 scale sheet.

Two-Color Painting, The Marlboro-Sponsored Racers

The bright orange and white Marlboro vee has become the trademark of some of the most successful race teams and cars in the history of open-wheeled racing. Roger Penske has been using it recently on his successful Indy 500–winning IRL cars, but its history goes back to the 1980s. The McLaren F1 cars used it from 1981

Dan Gurney tries hard at the 1970 Trans-Am on a 1/32 scale recreation of the Laguna Seca race.

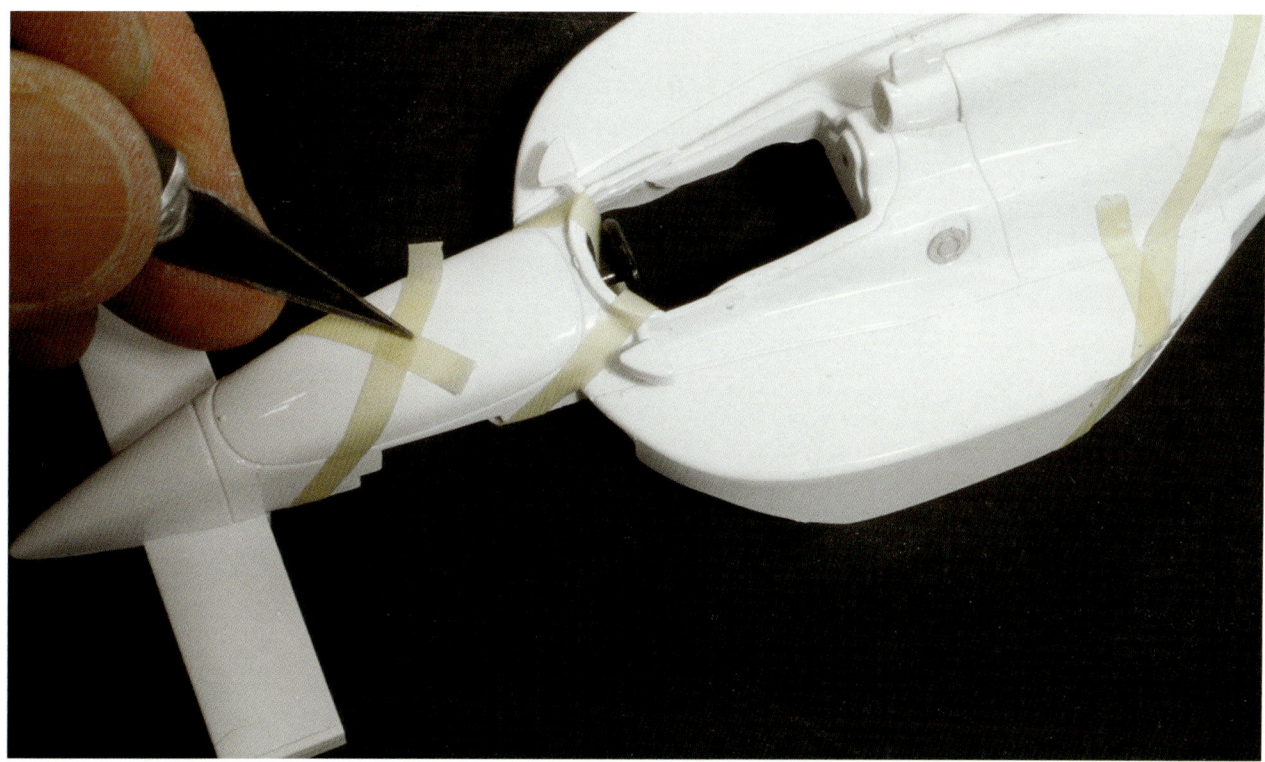
Cross the 1/8-inch automotive masking tape, then use a hobby knife to slice the edges of the vees.

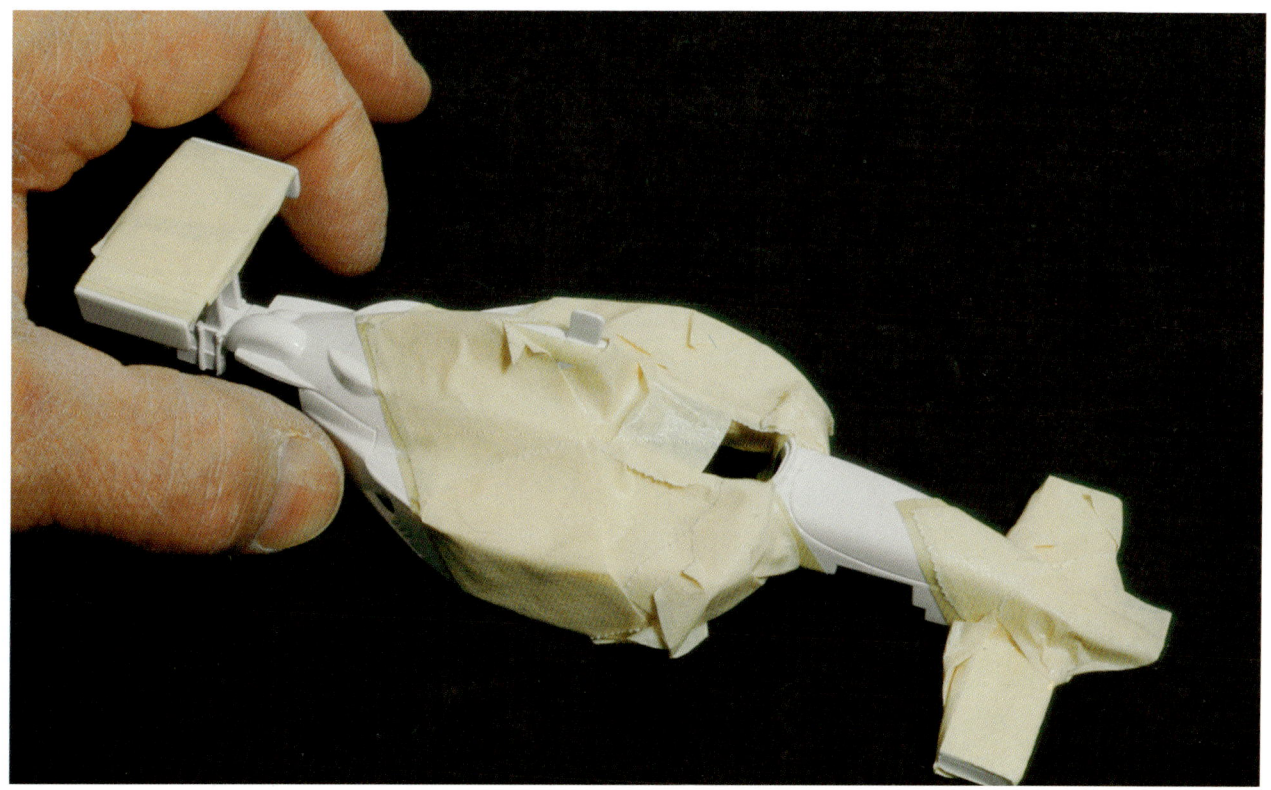
Cover the remaining areas that will be left white with Scotch Magic tape or masking tape.

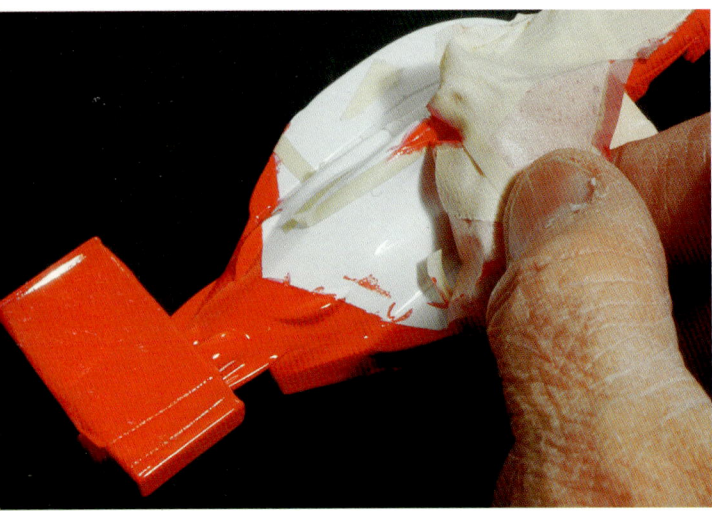

Most of the white on my model needed to be retouched to obtain a sharp, cleaner color.

Scalextric offers the IRL Dallara unpainted as car number C2548. It is the same car as the Pennzoil- and Conseco-sponsored cars. Marlboro decals are available from Indycals for this 2002 Indianapolis 500-winning 1/32 scale car. Each set costs $9, but there are enough to do both the number 2 and number 3 cars.

The Scalextric IRL cars have smaller-than-scale end plates on the ends of the wings, presumably to limit damage. I found some black Champ model railroad decals for the Colorado & Southern (number HON-5) and cut the number 3 from the ampersand (&), but Woodland Scenics MG746 dry transfer numbers could also be used. Pattos has decals for the earlier Marlboro-sponsored cars with the standard logo and Honda power.

To paint the model, remove the screws that retain the body and chassis. Use fine-grit sandpaper to roughen the areas of the body that will be painted red. Use 1/8-inch-wide automotive masking tape to cover the white, exposing only the areas to be painted red. Cross the tape and use a hobby knife to slice the edges of the vees. The photographs will provide a guide to the placement of the edges of the red/white color separation. Cover the remaining areas that will be left white with Scotch Magic tape

through 1996 when Marlboro switched to Ferrari. The red-and-white Marlboro scheme also appeared on the Dallara in 1972, as well as on the Alfa Romero and BRM Formula 1 cars. Marlboro's sponsorship of Ferrari goes back to the 1980s, but Ferrari never allowed more than the relatively small Marlboro logos on the sides of the cars and the small white patches.

With new decals and touch-up paint, the Scalextric IRL Dallara can be an excellent replica of the Marlboro Team Penske car that Helio Castroneves drove to win the 2002 Indianapolis 500.

Compare the grilles on the Austin Healey 100S (left) and the stock NINCO 3000 Mk.III.

or common masking tape. Tape the body and rear wing to a scrap of wood and spray it with three light coats of Tamiya Fluorescent Red. Let the paint dry for about an hour and slice along the edges of the 1/8-inch tape to cut the paint clear from the tape. Gently remove the tape by pulling the tape back over itself. The red will likely bleed beneath the masking in a few areas, but you can use a pipe cleaner dipped in lacquer thinner to remove the minor overspray patches. Use a sharp hobby knife to scrape any rough edges to provide a clean color separation line between the red and white. The supports for the rear wing can be touched up with flat black paint. The exposed upper surfaces and trim tabs on the chassis are also painted Fluorescent Red. Mask the areas that are to remain unpainted. Spray some of the Tamiya Fluorescent Red in the can lid and paint the gearbox with a brush to represent the cover on the real car.

Real Chrome

Bare-Metal is an ultrathin aluminum foil with a very light adhesive backing. The material is thin enough

Use Post-It notes to align the louvers, and position the edge of the Post-It note precisely where you want the edge of the louvers.

Here are the louvers on the hood of the Austin Healey 100S. The hood strap is a piece of beige paper with Bare-Metal chrome buckles.

For small raised details such as gas filler caps, door handles, and the parking lights on this Morgan, cut a 1/4-inch-square of Bare-Metal, pull off the backing, and press the metal only onto the very top of the light with your fingertip. Then tuck in the foil with a toothpick.

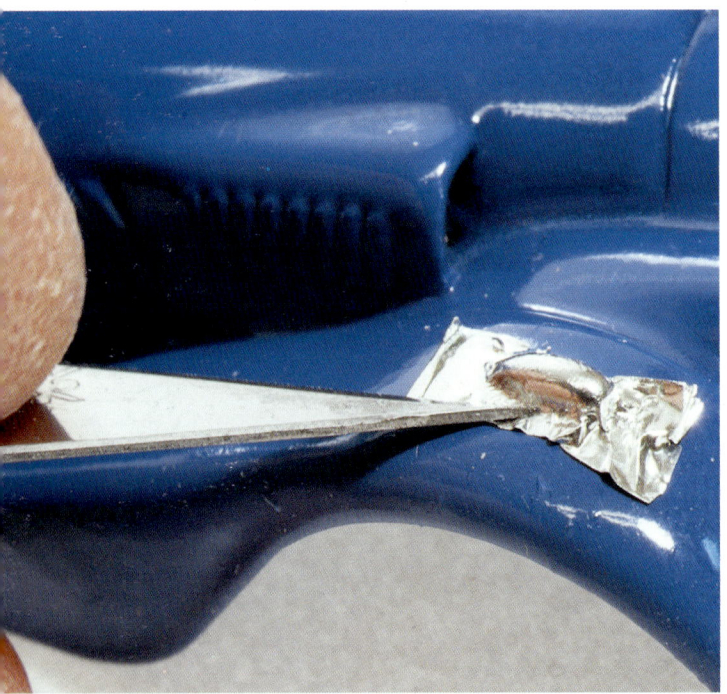

Use a brand-new number 11 X-Acto blade to carefully slice along the vertical edges of the parking light so you will leave the chrome on the vertical sides, and none on the flat portions of the body.

to literally stretch around something as small as a 1/32 scale parking light or driving light without tearing. The polished aluminum that Bare-Metal calls "chrome" is bright enough to look more like real chrome than painted parts. In truth, the plated parts are really far too shiny for 1/32 scale. The shine of the Bare-Metal is far more realistic.

To apply the foil, cut a piece near the size of what you want to chrome. Press the foil in place, slice around the edges, and peel off the excess. If you cut a bit too much, you can easily trim off the excess. Using Bare-Metal is considerably easier and vastly more realistic than trying to paint on chrome details. I still use a dot of silver paint to simulate a small knob or snap, but everything else is Bare-Metal.

Use scissors to cut a piece of Bare-Metal about twice as wide as and a bit longer than the part you want to cover. Pick at the edge of the foil to free one corner from the paper backing, then pull the rest of the foil away with tweezers. Apply the Bare-Metal sticky side down and gently press the Bare-Metal onto *only* the uppermost side of the part to be "plated." The idea is to get the Bare-Metal stuck to the sides of the part, not to the surrounding areas of the body. Next, use a toothpick to gently press the Bare-Metal into the horizontal edges of the part. Draw the toothpick slowly and gently down the sides of the part. Buy a new number 11 X-Acto blade (then never use it for anything else) and hold the blade in your fingers so you can control it perfectly. Carefully slice along the vertical edges of the part you are plating so you will leave only chrome on the vertical sides with none on the flat portions of the body.

The Austin-Healey 100S Le Mans Racer

The NINCO model is a 1/32 scale replica of the 1963–1968 Austin-Healey 3000 Mk. III. The 1953–1956 production Austin-Healey 100 (the early cars had a simple "100" model designation) had a shield-shaped grille. The Austin-Healey 100S was the competition version of the earlier street 100. The prototype for the 100S finished third at Sebring in 1954, hence the "S" designation. The 100S had a grille with a shape very similar to the later 3000 Mk III. There were some minor differences in the shapes of the front fenders of the 1953–1956 cars compared to the later models. The doors and body (and the wheelbase) on the 3000-series cars were 2 inches longer. The primary visible difference between the

100S and the later 3000 models was a hood scoop that appeared on all the cars from 1956 onward.

The NINCO Austin-Healey 3000 Mk III is a 2+2-seater, while the 100S was strictly a two-seater. The rear deck on the 100S extended forward to about the rear of the seats. It is possible to use a NINCO tonneau cover reshaped to curve upward rather than being flat, but it was more work than I wanted to do. I also did not change the driver's position from right hand to left hand. The seat is there and a paper tonneau could cover the entire opening if you want to do the conversion.

To match the 100S, I filed off part of the scoop, including both the ribs along the sides of the hood bulge, but left a bit of the front of the scoop so I did not file through the plastic. I filled in the small remaining dent at the front of the original scoop with automobile body spot putty. I wanted a crash-proof Brooklands windscreen, so I sliced into the body with a razor saw and inserted a piece of the flexible clear plastic used to hold photos in billfolds. I used metal-filled epoxy to fill in the saw cut and retain the Brooklands screen. I masked the screen while the body was being painted. I used the automobile body spot putty to fill in the holes from the bumpers, windscreen, window wipers, and the front edges of the hood opening. The hood on the 100

Use tweezers to gently pull the excess Bare-Metal from the body.

was about 9 inches shorter at the front than the hood on the 3000. When the car was complete and painted, I simply sliced in a new hood line, along with the other door, trunk, and hood lines, and filled in the hairline with black India ink.

I used a razor saw to cut the 3000 Mk III grille in half, and then cut off the four center bars to reduce the width of the grille from 1.07 inches to 0.95 inch.

All the chrome trim on the Morgan Super Sports (see Chapter 1) is Bare-Metal chrome foil.

MRRC's (number 00) 427 Cobra and Modelmaker's (number 98) 289FIA Cobra.

I filled in the joints with a dab of metal-filled epoxy after using the epoxy to install the grille. It is just wide enough so the recesses on each side for the stock grille look like shadows. You could fill in the recesses on either side of the grille. The grille is still too wide to match the 100S, but it matches the too-wide proportions of the NINCO model. Two rows of louvers were stamped into the hood on the real 100S and on the modified production 100M.

I tried to duplicate Lance Macklin's 1955 Le Mans 100S as closely as possible, right down to the NOJ 393 number plate, which I made using Champ model railroad decal alphabet set L-42 applied to a scrap black decal. The letters and black decal were sealed with Testors GlossCote before soaking the black decal to apply it the model. I used Detail Associates 1711 Clear Headlight lenses for the driving lights. I painted the chrome NINCO wheels with Eastwood's (www.eastwoodcompany.com) number 12852 Detail Silver for full-size car wheels. It is very close to the gray-tinted silver that Dunlop used on these wheels in the 1950s.

Race Car Louvers

In the 1950s and 1960s, the real racing cars had louvers stamped into their hoods. There was a practical use for them because most of the sports cars that were raced in the 1950s and 1960s were either Italian or British, and had engines that overheated easily. The louvers helped release some of the under-hood heat.

The louvers on the hood of the modified NINCO Austin-Healey 100S were cut from Cary Locomotive Works LV-424 embossed aluminum louvers. Your hobby dealer can order them from the Cary Locomotive Works, a division of Bowser Manufacturing Co. The louvers are intended for HO scale diesels, but are almost the perfect scale for 1/32 scale model cars.

To install the louvers, cut an entire row of four sets of louvers at once. This is a critical step because your scissors must be right at the edge of the rounded tips of the louvers and the cut must be perfectly straight. You may want to substitute a steel ruler and an X-Acto knife to make a more precise cut. Each louver set was curved slightly to help them conform to the curve of the hood. Use Post-It notes to align the louvers. Position the edge of the Post-It note precisely where you want the edge of the louvers. Align the sets of louvers by butting each set against the edge of the Post-It note. You may need to trim the edges of some of the sets to get perfect alignment. Use a second Post-It note to pick up the aligned set of louvers without disturbing its alignment. Apply a bead of cyanoacrylate cement (Super Glue) to the area where the louvers will be fitted, then gently lower the Post-It note with the louvers onto the glue. You may need to use a toothpick to apply a bit more glue along the edges of the louvers. Let the glue cure for a few hours. You can sand the edges of the rows with a piece of 600-grit sandpaper wrapped around a round toothpick to soften the edges. The model can be painted with a coat of primer so you can sand off any scratches or glue with 600 wet-or-dry sandpaper dipped in water.

Custom-Built Models

The easiest way to start building your own model is to buy a kit that is intended to fit an existing chassis. Modelmaker's 289FIA Cobra is a good place to start. Petrolati, Noisy Muse, Top-Slot, Bauer, Proto Slot-Kit, Resilient Resins, Pre-Add, A2M, and MMK also make cast-resin bodies designed for specific chassis. The instructions supplied vary from excellent with diagrams (Top-Slot and Petrolati) to typed words. MAXI-Models, Le Mans Miniatures, Slot Classics, Proto Slot-Kit, and Top-Slot make complete kits that include the chassis.

Dan Gurney fights a car with a broken spring at a 1/32 scale recreation of the 1964 Targa Florio.

The Modelmaker 289 FIA body kit includes crispy-molded clear and colored parts, but with lots of flash.

To remove the flash, slice along the edges of the parts with a sharp hobby knife, then break off the excess flash.

The Modelmaker 1/32-scale 289FIA Cobra

One of the anomalies of racing in the 1960s is that the Cobra that spearheaded the Cobra-Ferrari wars has been largely ignored by real racing fans. The car most envision when you say "Cobra" is the later 427, but the 427 was a street machine. Sure it won some SCCA races, but the 289FIA Cobras were the real international race winners.

The Modelmaker 289FIA Cobra body kit includes a separate chin scoop that was fitted just below the D-shaped grille on many of the 289FIA cars, including the Targa Florio machines. There were some 289FIA cars that had less bulbous rear fenders with more pronounced lips, and some rear fenders extended out more in front of the tires near the body sills. The Modelmaker body will do just fine for any of them because it has the characteristic bulbous rear matched to the slimmer front fender flares with the all-important D-shaped front grille opening—all the significant changes that characterize the 289FIA cars compared to the 427s.

The Modelmaker body is a finely detailed cast-resin body material that is quite flexible and feels very much like styrene. You just can't glue it with anything but epoxy or Super Glue. The body kit includes a one-piece body that literally snaps onto the MRRC 427 Cobra interior/body mount so you are replacing the MRRC 427 Cobra body with Modelmaker's 289 FIA Cobra body. You can certainly adapt the body to other chassis like NINCO's, but you'll have to devise your own body

Test fit the body on the MRRC 427 Cobra chassis.

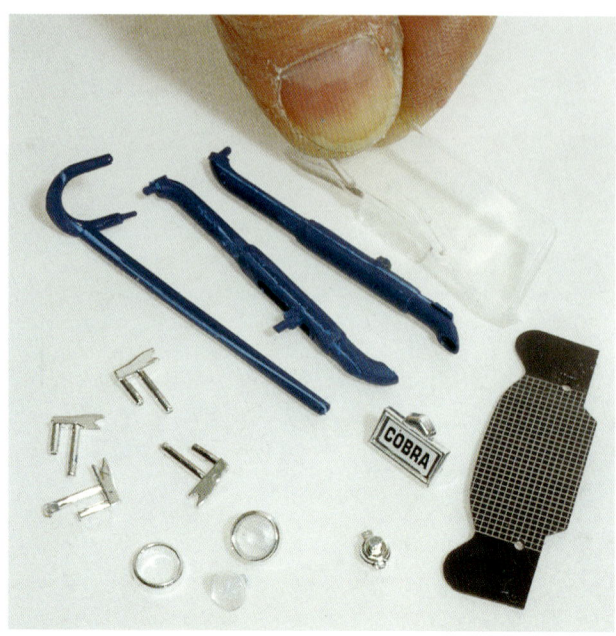

I used the windshield, exhausts, and most of the chrome parts left over from the MRRC 427 Cobra to detail the Modelmaker 289FIA Cobra.

The Noisy Muse Javelin is shown here in a recreation of the Trans-Am series, circa 1968, on John MacKenzie's Seattle Hill Raceway (see Chapter 11).

The Noisy Muse 1968 Trans-Am Javelin is a cast-resin body to fit a modified Scalextric Camaro chassis.

mounts. The kit also includes a clear full-width windshield, a small clear one-person windshield, headlight lenses, taillight lenses, parking lights lenses, exhaust pipes, license plate holder, rear view mirror, gas cap, front and rear jacking pads, and a rollbar. I took the headlights, jacking pads, gas cap, mirror, rear license plate light, and the full interior from the MRRC model. I also use NINCO Halibrand-style wheels front and rear with NINCO front tires and Indy Grips rear tires.

The body is simple to assemble; just shave away any casting flash. The smaller parts can be snapped off their molding sheet and the seams can be cleaned up with a file and sandpaper. The only tricky component is the clear windshield, which must be filed away at a smaller radius for about 1/16 inch at the center to fit the contour of the cowl. Use a half-round machinist's file to reshape the bottom edge of the windshield. There's no method of attaching the full windshield, so I scratched through the paint and used metal-filled

The chassis for the Cad-Allard is a lengthened Scalextric Caterham 7 with NINCO wire wheels and tires.

The Caterham 7 chassis must fit inside the Petrolati Cad-Allard cast-resin body so the lower edges of the two are flush with one another.

Bill Pollack's Cad-Allard as it was raced in 1953, recreated in 1/32 scale.

epoxy. It snapped off when I spread the body to insert the interior, but tore off some paint. I reattached it with more metal-filled epoxy, and this time it bonded directly to the bare body and has lasted. The half-round, single-person screen on the number 98 model is a better solution and the Modelmaker body has holes to accept the part—it was used in America when the cars were contesting modified or USRRC events. The European cars all had full windshields.

The MRRC driver sits about a scale 6 inches too tall in the cockpit. I removed about 1/8 inch from the bottom of the seat so it could rest on the floor of the interior. I also removed the two seat-attaching ribs from the floor. I bent the driver's arms inward so he could still grip the steering wheel in his lowered position. Fred Martin removed about 1/8 inch from the bottom of the driver in his Guardsman Blue number 98 car and filed and fitted both arms to create a more realistic racing posture.

Trans-Am Javelin

Noisy Muse produces a cast-resin body kit to mount on the Scalextric Camaro chassis. The kit includes decals to recreate the Trans-Am Javelins that were raced in 1968 when Jim Jeffords, of Purple People Eater fame, and Ronnie Kaplan ran the AMC factory road racing effort out of Kaplan Engineering. The Noisy Muse kit includes the cast-resin body with vacuum-formed clear plastic windows and decals. You will need to epoxy some body mounts and adapt the Scalextric chassis and interior to fit.

The Cadillac-Allard in 1/32 Scale

Greg Petrolati produced a cast-resin replica of the Cadillac-Allard. The kit includes the body, steering wheel, front fenders, two choices of hood bulges with decals for Fred Wicker's number 8 car, an Allard decal for the nose, and an Allard decal for the driver's uniform. You will also need a Scalextric Caterham 7 or Lotus 7 with cycle fenders and a NINCO 70133 driver, 80706 wire wheels, and 80503 tires.

The body is very clean with minimal flash on the lower edges. The front axle is cut out and the inner rear fenders are deliberately left blank so you can fit the body to the chassis of your choice. The instruction sheet is very complete and has full-size templates. The recommended chassis is the

The chassis for the Cad-Allard is a lengthened Scalextric Caterham 7 with NINCO wire wheels and tires.

The Caterham 7 chassis must fit inside the Petrolati Cad-Allard cast-resin body so the lower edges of the two are flush with one another.

Rocky Russo's 1/32-scale EJ's Indy Roadster.

Scalextric Caterham or Lotus 7 with cycle-style fenders. The Allard's fenders can be cemented right on top of the Caterham's fenders, and the edges can be ground to conceal the overly thick fender. The Caterham chassis must be cut to insert two pieces of 0.040-inch-square Evergreen styrene strip across the width and up the sides to extend the chassis length by 0.080 inch. It takes a bit of fitting to get the chassis to fit the body, but take your time and remove no more than 1/32 inch of material at a time before test-fitting to be sure you're close.

It took me longer to get a halfway decent set of white sidewall tires than it took to assemble the entire model. I applied white fingernail polish to the tire. It needs to be applied with the tire on the wheel, but any excess polish that reaches the rim can be scraped off with the tip of a toothpick and red paint applied to touch up the wheel. The outer edges of the whitewall can be sliced to size by spinning the tire in the chassis while holding an X-Acto blade against the edge of the tire. This is dangerous, so wear eye protection, Kevlar gloves and sleeves, and a Lexan face mask. Be sure the tip of the blade faces away from the tire's direction of travel so the tip cannot dig into the tire. An easier solution is to use the white sidewall tires from Carrera's 1957 Thunderbird and slice off a bit of the width from the back of each tire with a razor saw.

Bill Pollack's black car with the white sidewalls and five red wire wheels has been one of my top 50 favorite cars of all time. If you prefer red, you can recreate Wacker's red 8 Ball, or recreate Sydney Allard's green car, or Roy Richter's number 1 silver car. The Allard was paneled in aluminum and at least one vintage racer is polished aluminum. This is relatively easy enough to do with Bare-Metal over the entire body. I used Bare-Metal chrome for the porthole trims, hinges, grille, fuel filler, license light, fender lights, and taillights.

Steve Bunkey used an EJ's reproduction brass chassis with an Arii Porsche 911 body for this model.

Steve Bunkey's Porsche 911 races against a Scalextric Lotus7.

Building Your Personal Chassis

Back in the 1960s and 1970s, there were very few slot cars available ready-to-run, but there were lots of 1/32-scale kits, most with brass chassis. You can still buy reproductions of the Monogram and Strombecker brass chassis from EJ's. There are a number of other chassis available from EJ's, Slot Classics, Pendle, MRRC, Pro-Track, Pattos, TSRF, and others. You can also buy bearings, axles, wheels, and other components and solder your own chassis together. You can use a ready-painted body from a current ready-to-run car or buy a clear plastic, fiberglass, or cast-resin body to complete your personal racing machine.

EJ's Classic Indy Roadster Kit

This Indy roadster is assembled from a one-piece brass chassis and a clear plastic body. The decals are replicas of those supplied with Strombecker's 1970s-era Indy Roadster kit. The kit includes high-quality aluminum wheels, bronze bearings, and an NOS Cox crown gear. The tires are well detailed and the kit includes chrome inserts for the wheels; a chrome exhaust, gas cap, and roll bar; and decals with three-view drawings to show where the decals are to be placed for each of the five optional paint schemes.

Rocky Russo opted to drop in a NINCO NC-2 motor in place of the faster Fox motor supplied with kit. He also added about a half-ounce of lead automotive wheel weights between the pickup and the motor. The body is clear plastic. Trim the body from the base with cuticle scissors. Use a hole punch to open the holes for the front and rear axles, and use an awl or ice pick to open four holes (they are marked on the body) for the two wire clips that retain the body to the sides of the chassis. The 0.030-inch thick clear Lexan plastic body is designed to be painted on the outside using the special paint designed for R/C race cars. A separate clear plastic windshield is supplied with a driver's head and torso that can be painted before cementing them to the top of the body.

Converting Display Models to Racers with EJ's Chassis

Steve Burkey's model is a replica of the Porsche 911 that Jerry Titus drove to the 1966 SCCA D Production Championship, and was assembled from an Arii static model and an EJ's chassis. The 911 was first offered as a 1/32 scale static model by LS, later by Entex, and then Arii. The chassis is an EJ's copy of the original Monogram frame with EJ's 1/8-inch threaded axles. He used vintage Atlas wheels and tires and a Dynamic guide and Wilson's gears, but EJ's has similar items.

The body was assembled and then modified with a Dremel tool and milling wheel to clear the chassis. The chassis is mounted with 4-40 threaded brass inserts from EJ's and 4-40 flat pan head screws now available from EJ's. The 4-40 brass inserts are pushed into a slightly bored-out Plastruct 1/8-inch

Chuck Lawrence's fiberglass 1954 Ferrari 375 and a 1957 Maserati 450S are mounted on modified NINCO chassis.

Chuck Lawrence's Maserati 450S, Ferrari 375, and Elva Mk VII.

There are many body manufacturers and any of their bodies can be adapted to modified ready-to-run chassis. Some clubs specify a chassis, such as NINCO's Classic (like that used under their 427 Cobra, XK120 Jaguar, and 356 Porsche), and the members can use either the bodies that come on the chassis or remove the body and replace it with another not available from NINCO.

Chuck Lawrence races with the PSSRA club in Washington. The club members are allowed to cut the chassis or lengthen it to match the new body. Pieces of 0.060-inch-thick sheet styrene are used to provide fill-in pieces and the cut parts are held together with JB Weld's metal-filled epoxy. Chuck's cars include a 1954 Ferrari 375 and a 1957 Maserati 450S, both made from fiberglass bodies hand-carved by Chuck and produced by Classic. The chassis under the Maserati 450S and the Ferrari 375 are modified NINCO chassis. The chassis beneath the Elva Mk VII is a Monogram front with an MRRC rear chassis and an older open-frame Clubman motor.

Super-Tuned Chassis: Pro-Track

The Pro-Track Spyder chassis is designed so it can be used to power a hand-made car with a clear plastic or cast-resin body or the chassis can be used to repower a ready-to-run model like the Fly Joest Porsche. The chassis runs much quicker than any conventional ready-to-run model and falls into what we are calling the Super-Tuned class. These cars are really too fast for most home tracks. They are more at home on a commercial-size raceway with a 20-foot or longer straight. For those looking for the ultimate in performance, the Super-Tuned cars provide a ridiculously high level of speed and handling that is closer to the mad hummingbird look of HO cars than most 1/32 scale cars. The Pro-Track chassis is an excellent machine that finds favor even with those who prefer to race with no magnets.

The Pro-Track chassis is cut from a lightweight fiberglass-reinforced material with threaded posts to clamp the sideplates together. There's a clever magnet adjustment feature to allow the magnet to be raised or lowered. The wheels are turned aluminum with set screws, the rear bearings are sintered bronze, and the floater-style front axle rides in notches in the frame. The chassis is adjustable down to 75 mm (2.95 inches; 94.4 inches in 1/1 scale) for the wheelbase, and a 56.9 mm (2.25 inches, or 72 inches in 1/32 scale) overall width. The backs

plastic tube. The tubes were cut over-length and mounted to the chassis, then shortened to lower the body to the correct height inside the body. The driver is an old Monogram with a braced roll bar from 1/16-inch Plastruct rod. The wheel inserts are vintage Strombecker items, but the kit's wheels could be modified. You could also settle for EJ's American mag five-spoke inserts. The body was painted with Tamiya paints, and the sponsor lettering was applied with dry transfers. The numbers and logos are from Steve's scrap box.

Custom-Cut Plastic Chassis

The chassis from one ready-to-race model car can sometimes be used with a new and different body.

The Pro-Track chassis with the side-mount body posts are installed to snap into Pro-Track's body-mounting tabs inside the Fly Le Mans Joest body.

The TSRF chassis is available as a kit, assembled, or assembled with a painted and ready-to-run body.

of the wheel bosses could be filed to reduce the width, and the chassis can be cut or filed for shorter wheelbases. Pro-Track also provides a very clever set of four mounting pads that can be cemented inside the sides of the body for a snap-on installation. I used the Pro-Track posts to mount the Fly Joest Porsche body. I cut the Fly rear wing from the Fly chassis and attached it to the Fly body with metal-filled epoxy.

Super-Tuned Chassis: TSRF

Philippe de Lespinay is one of the pioneers of the Super-Tuned cars, which he usually calls Euro-Racers. Philippe is a model car racing engineer and he designed the later plastic chassis for Cox slot cars in the 1970s. The TSRF chassis is his baby. TSRF has ready-to-run chassis in both 1/32 scale (shown) and 1/24 scale. The chassis is designed to compete with the Fly Racer, Slot.it Porsche 956, NINCO ProRacer, and the Pro-Track Spyder. The TSRF chassis has a stamped-steel pan for a low center of gravity. The pickup guide shoe is a solid-mount (no pivot) 1/4-inch-long pin with the braid mounted to the chassis on either side of the pin. The front wheels are mounted to the steel pan, which is also the body mount. The steel pan is free to rattle a few thousands of an inch on the plastic portion of the chassis to isolate motor and rear tire vibrations from the body. The chassis includes a body-mount system for injection-molded plastic or pin-mounted clear plastic bodies. The components are all high quality with 64-pitch gears and ground axles. The wheels are true-running plastic, but metal wheels are available at an extra cost.

The TSRF chassis has adjustable wheelbase, and to some extent, adjustable pickup guide length. The motor, rear axle, and pickup pin are mounted in the injection-molded plastic chassis. The pickup pin is the most unique feature of this car because it does not pivot. It's a fixed pin that is 0.812 inches (4.5 mm) long and about 0.056 inches (1.4 mm) wide. The pickup pin location is fixed at 3.65 inches (92.7 mm) from the rear axle. There are three positions available to mount the plastic chassis to the metal chassis. There are also three positions to mount the front axle.

The TSRF chassis fits more modern sports and GT cars, but the sidewinder motor can interfere with the rear body sections on some open-cockpit cars such as the SCX Audi R8, Carrera BMW V12LMR, and the Scalextric Cadillac Northstar LMP or Lola/MG. The GT cars usually have enough clearance above the TSRF motor, so the chassis will fit the Fly Porsche GT-1/98, Fly Saleen S7R, NINCO McLaren F1, NINCO Panoz Esperante GT, and NINCO Porsche Evo or Callaway C12-R, but there's not enough room beneath the Carrera Bentley Speed 8 LMP or Slot.it Audi R8R coupes to clear the TSRF sidewinder motor. The TSRF chassis is large enough to fit under NASCAR sedans and most Touring car racers. The chassis is too wide for the 1970s sports and GT cars such as Fly's Lola T-70, Porsche 917, Ferrari 512, and GB Track's Porsche 910

Attach the two TSRF plastic body-mounting angles to the sides of the chassis and test fit the body.

Stick on two strips of self-adhesive foam poster stickers to attach the TSRF plastic angles to the inside sills of the NINCO McLaren F1 body.

unless you fit narrower wheels and tires and remove the edges of the steel pan.

The TSRF chassis kit includes two alternate body mounting systems: a pair of pin tubes for mounting clear or injection-molded plastic bodies with straight pins. A pair of plastic angles with screws and nuts are also included if you want to remove the body. It is possible to grind away parts of the donor body's interior, or you can use a piece of flat black card with a driver torso from NINCO. I've managed to fit the TSRF chassis beneath the Fly Saleen S7R and retain all the visible interior and engine detail.

The TSRF body-mounts will also accommodate clear plastic bodies from firms such as Betta, Booth, EJ's, MacLeod Western, Pattos, Pro-Track, and True Scale. TSRF is also produces some clear plastic bodies.

Solder-Together Brass Chassis

For some model car racers, constructing the car from the tires up is as much a pleasure as finishing the body or racing the car. There is a special thrill when a car you've designed and soldered together is quicker than the expensive factory jobs. Dan Wilson is a master at soldering chassis together from bits of brass. He's won races and *concours d'elegance* at MESAC (see Chapter 11) back in the 1960s and he thinks he is still competitive.

Dan's techniques for laying out the chassis, cutting holes, bending, and soldering the brass chassis appeared in the first six issues of *Model Car Racing* magazine. You can buy brackets similar to those he creates from brass bars from EJ's and Pattos, but you'll need to learn to solder.

Here are three of Dan's favorite 1/32 scale chassis. All the cars are fitted with Revell-style wheels from EJ's with either EJ's wheel inserts or old Revell or Monogram inserts that Dan has copied in RTV molds to create resin replicas. The front tires are EJ's, and the rear are Indy Grips silicones. The gears are usually NOS Tradeship or Cox from EJ's or NINCO, and all three cars have Plafit Rabbit Mabuchi motors.

Iso-Pivot Chassis

Dan's Ferrari 750 Monza is a clear plastic body from Pattos. The chassis is a 0.032-inch-thick brass sheet. The chassis pivots from just below the rear axle. The chassis is basically two pieces: (1) the motor/rear axle/pickup guide and (2) the body-mounting pan and front axle carrier. It's a design that has become known as an iso-pivot, and the Cox fantasy slot cars of the 1970s had a similar chassis. The front axle is mounted in the center so it is free to pivot upward on either side.

Fate Pivoting Front Axles

Dan Wilson subscribes to the theory that the weight of the car should be carried on the two rear tires and the pickup, with front tires just along for the ride. Rocky Russo developed a leading-link-style front

With some careful grinding with a Dremel motor tool, the interiors of many models, such as this Fly Saleen S7R, can be modified to clear the TSRF motor and chassis.

Dan Wilson's Ferrari 750 Monza features a modified iso-pivot pan and a low-pivot front axle.

The Ferrari 750 Monza body is clear plastic (available from Pattos) that is painted on the inside.

The Fate front axle is free to pivot upward to place all the front weight on the pickup shoe.

axle that is referred to as the Fate (after an old comedy race movie, *Professor Fate*) axle because the front axle is free to move upward and to pivot down to about 1/16 inch below the track (when the car is off the track). Dan's Ferrari 750 Monza and DKW sedan (another Pattos body) have this leading-link front axle.

First, assemble the front axle with a piece of brass tubing running from the back of one wheel (or wheel lock nut) to the other. Cut a piece of K&S 1/16-inch pin tube the same width as the chassis. Slip the piece of 1/16-inch pin tube over a piece of 0.020-inch steel piano wire. Bend the piano wire into a rectangular shape the width of the chassis (usually about a 1/2 inch) and about 1/2 to 3/4 inch long. Solder the one 1/2-inch end of piano wire to the brass tube that serves as the front axle bearing. Solder the 1/16-inch piece of tube (with the piano wire rectangle and front axle now attached) to the chassis at the correct position to obtain the desired wheelbase. Dan uses Harris Sta-brite low-temp silver solder for all his joints and makes sure that both surfaces to be soldered are polished-clean.

Pin-Guide Chassis

Dan's 250F Maserati Grand Prix chassis reverts to the solid pin guide, rather than a pivoting guide shoe. This was a design that dates back to the dawn of

The Fate front axle is essentially a leading-link system that places most of the car's weight on the pickup shoe.

Dan Wilson's 1954 Maserati 250F is a clear plastic body from Pattos with a brass chassis and pin guide.

model car racing, but it is still viable. In fact, a modified version is standard on the TSRF chassis, shown earlier in this chapter. The pin is 0.047-inch steel piano wire mounted in a solid 3/8-inch block of clear Plexiglas. The Plexiglas is mounted to the 0.060-inch thick brass chassis with 2-56 screws. The pin itself is covered with a piece of plastic tube from a WD-40 spray can. The pickup braids are positioned so the trailing edges are directly across the track from the pin to minimize the chances of the brushes missing the pickup strips on the track if the car gets too sideways in a corner. The wheels, tires, gears, and axles are from NINCO, and the clear plastic body is from Pattos.

Mounting Injection-Molded Plastic Bodies

Injection-molded plastic bodies can be mounted with threaded 4-40 screws using the same system Revell, Monogram, and Cox had in the 1970s. EJ's sells the brass inserts and 4-40 screws. Smaller 2-56 and even smaller 00-80 inserts and matching flathead screws are available from the PEM Pemserts website (http://www.pennfast.com/reps_and_distributors/na distributebystate.html)

The mounts for the injection-molded plastic body are three-point for stability and strength. Dan used the same style post system that was common with the slot car kits of the 1960s. For this model Dan used 0-80 thread-size Pem inserts.

This Pink-Kar Ferrari GTO body is mounted on a handmade 0.060-inch-thick brass strip chassis similar to the Iso-Pivot under Dan Wilson's Ferrari 750 Monza. The front body mounts are attached to these chassis pans. A number 1-size washer is soldered to a piece of 1/16-inch brass rod, which is soldered to the rear of the chassis to provide the mounting for the rear of the body. Dan used three 0-80 flat-head screws with countersunk holes so the screw heads are flush with the bottom of the chassis. Two 1/4-inch-square blocks of Evergreen styrene are cemented to the inside edges of the body to provide the side mounting posts, and the built-in Pink-Kar rear post provide the rear body mount. The chassis is positioned inside the body to determine the height of these pads. The holes drilled in the chassis are marked on the pads so the pads can be drilled to match the chassis. The threaded EJ's or Pemserts inserts are pushed into the holes with pressure from a soldering iron to slightly soften the plastic. The rear body mounting post is molded into the Pink-Kar body. Pemserts for 0-80 inserts are inserted into holes in the plastic body mounts to provide the threads for the three body-mounting screws. The flathead screws and matching countersunk holes allow the side pans to be as low as possible with no chance of the screw heads rubbing the track. The countersunk holes also allow the screws to be left about a half-turn loose so the body can rattle (for smoother running, to isolate vibrations) and still be centered on its mounting screws.

Mounting Clear Plastic Bodies

The time-proven method of mounting clear plastic bodies on a brass chassis is to use four straight pins

A simple acrylic block supports the guide pin and the front axle, and it also provides an insulated mounting platform for the pickup brushes.

The brass plates on the sides of this DKW model provide places for corner marshals to grip and provide interior buffer beams to protect the body from hard crashes. Four straight pins are used to retain the body.

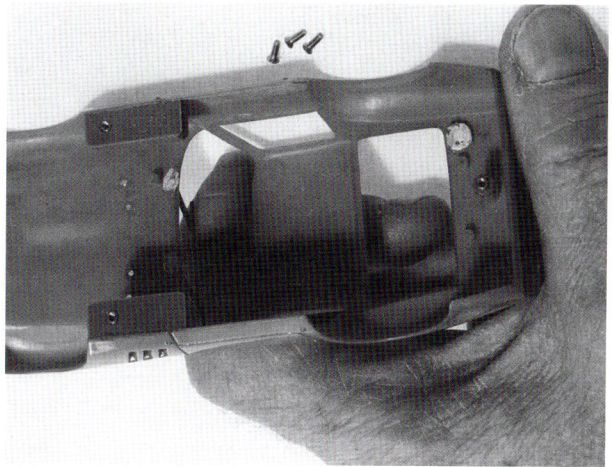

Two 1/4-inch-square blocks of Evergreen styrene are cemented to the inside edges of the body to provide mounting pads. The rear body mounting post is molded into the Pink-Kar Ferrari GTO body.

pushed into the ends of K&S 1/16-inch brass tubes. Temporarily prop the body over the chassis to determine where the 1/16-inch brass tubes, often called pin tubes, should be placed. Also determine the length of the tubes. Try to locate the ends of the tubes so they are at least 1/4-inch above the lower edges of the body so you do not tear the clear plastic body. It may be necessary to bend the pin tubes upward slightly into a gullwing shape if the chassis is too low. When you are satisfied, solder the tubes to the chassis. You can protect the body from the relatively sharp ends of the pin tubes by soldering small washers to the ends of each tube. Protect the inside of the body with a strip of filament tape. The pins themselves can be bent slightly to provide a tight fit. Finally, the heads of the pins can be painted to match the body.

CHAPTER 7
THE SNAP-TOGETHER HOME RACEWAY

The Sport Monaco track rises to a 9-inch elevation at Mirabeau with flats for the major structures.

Your home racetrack exists for two reasons: to provide a place to race and to provide a realistic setting for the cars. First, the track needs to provide reliable and constant electrical flow. Once the track is operating to perfection, you can add a host of details to make the track more realistic.

The race cars are always going to be more realistic than the tracks we build for the simple reason that there's never enough space for a realistic track. Jason Boye and Brad Bowman have created some of the most realistic tracks with LeMonzaco and the Katz-Pa-Ring in Chapter 13, but they are built in relatively vast spaces. However, you can create a high degree of realism, even on a Ping-Pong-table-sized track.

Assembling Scalextric Sport Track

The rounded end tabs on Scalextric Sport track are slightly longer than the two center tabs so you can assemble the track by holding a piece in each hand and aligning the two joining surfaces. It's much easier to place both pieces flat on the tabletop and slide them together. You'll hear a click when the locking tabs are fully engaged.

I also suggest that you buy the Sport C8241 Power and Control Multi-Lane track for two reasons. First, it includes track wiring and controllers with built-in brakes. Second, the track connects to any half-length of full-length straight with two push-on clips. You can then position the plug-in box a few inches from the edge of the track so sliding cars won't bump into it.

Sport also offers an 8215 lap counter/timer or you can opt for the 8147 Sport RMS PC Interactive Multi-Lane computer-controlled lap counting, timing, and race programming.

Trouble-Shooting Sport Track

The locking tabs are not as strong on the Sport track as they were on Classic track, which is one of the reasons why Sport track is quicker and easier to assemble. If you try to assemble a track that does not fit properly, the joint can come apart and damage the locking tabs. You can often restore a damaged tab by bending the smallest locking portion of the tab downward to give it more "spring."

Assemble Sport track by laying both pieces on the table and slide the two pieces together until the tabs click shut.

Pinch the clamping tab tightly around the joining pin on Sport track with needle-nose pliers.

You'll know you've got it right when the Sport pin feels tight, but you haven't squeezed so hard that the metal has ripped into the plastic.

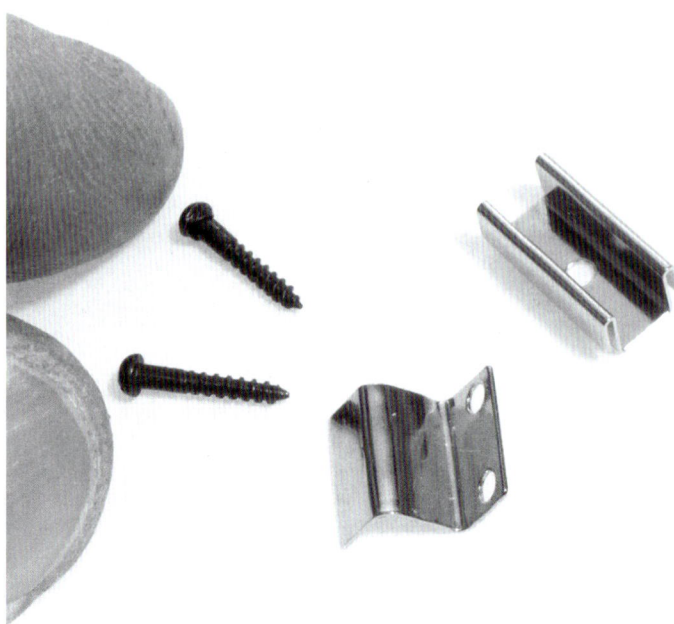

The Scalextric C8232 Side Track Clips are Z-shaped (bottom), and the C8255 Middle Track Clips are U-shaped (top).

Secure Scalextric Sport track to a tabletop with C8232 side track clips.

The Scalextric Sport track-joining system is designed to be strong enough to hold the track sections on a tabletop or floor, but it is nowhere near strong enough to hold the track while you move it. If you try to pick up a long section of assembled track, the track is going to sag. When the track sags, there is a definite chance you will loosen the square metal track joining pins, which can result in no electrical connection at all or a track connection that works some of the time.

With Sport track, you need a pair of small needle-nose pliers to reach inside each metal joint to crimp the joint tighter around the pin. You may also need to squeeze the female end inward slightly.

The loose-joint problem also exists with Scalextric Classic and SCX track. You can fix loose metal track connections on Scalextric Classic and SCX track by gently prying the rails apart with a screwdriver.

Secure-Mounting for Scalextric Sport Track

If you are going to elevate part of a Scalextric Sport, Scalextric Classic, or SCX track, I strongly recommend that you mount the part of the track that will be elevated on a piece of 1/8-inch plywood so the plywood can be elevated. The plywood will support the track and borders, and will save a lot of frustration. If you want to attempt to bank any turn, you will have to attach the track to a piece of 1/8-inch plywood and bend the plywood and track into the bank.

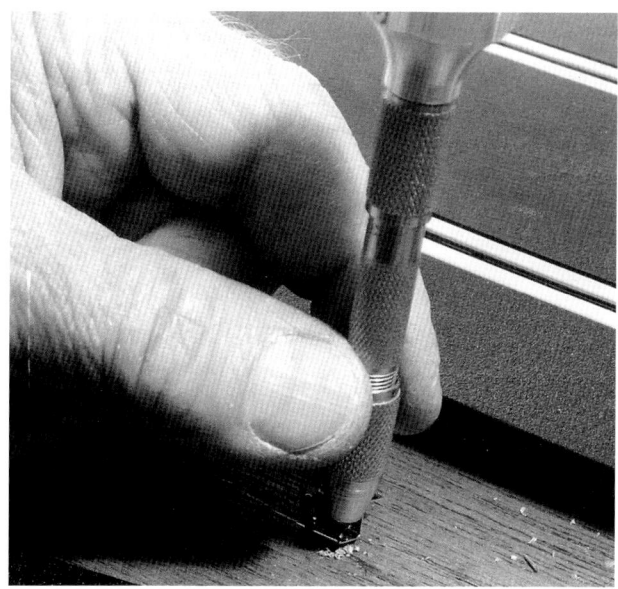

Use an awl or a pin vise with a 1/32-inch drill bit to make a 1/8-inch deep starter hole for the wood screw.

To install the border, lift the edge of track in the midsection, insert the edge of the border, then slide the border toward the clip.

Use a felt-tipped pen to mark the edges of the track, including the borders on the 1/8-inch plywood. Use a saber saw to remove the excess plywood. You can attach the track to the plywood with Scalextric (or SCX or NINCO) track clips or cement the track to the plywood with silicone caulking cement or Shoe Goo. The plywood can then be elevated with either blocks of wood or with the Woodland Scenics system. Do not elevate the track without supporting it because you will ruin every track joint, perhaps permanently.

Make Room for Power Slides

If you are going to run cars without magnets for traction, the cars are going to slide more in the corners than they do with magnets. I strongly recommend borders or extensions or skid aprons for the outside of every corner on every brand of track for at least 2 feet on either end of any straight.

The outside of the curves on Scalextric Sport, Scalextric Classic, or SCX track is too narrow, even with borders installed, for the larger cars like NASCAR sedans and modern Le Mans cars with long wheelbases and longer tails. If you are running the larger cars on SCX track, consider using Scalextric Sport Borders because they are about 1/4 inch wider than the SCX borders.

You can extend the width of the Scalextric Classic and Sport borders by another half-inch with the

Mount the C8255 middle track clips to the tabletop with number 0x1/4-inch round head wood screws.

Scalextric number C8212 Barriers pack that includes five full-straight-length guard rails and 15 clips to attach them to the edges of the track. Frankly, Scalextric designed these to clip onto the edge of the track in place of borders, but the clips work just as well clipped to the outside edge of any border as shown in the photos. You can also mix and match the straight barriers in the pack with the

Push the border down the track and over the clip.

You can also use duct tape to attach the borders on a temporary track.

The borders on any piece of Scalextric Classic or Sport or SCX track can be effectively widened about 1/2-inch by using the Scalextric C8212 barriers and clipping the supports to the bottom of the guard rails and to the outside edges of the barriers.

leftover barriers from the curves to provide a continuous barrier (guard rail) around every corner.

Homemade Borders and Skid Aprons

All the current manufacturers of 1/32 scale track make borders (some call them extensions or skid aprons) for the outside of the curves. Skid aprons are no longer available for Revell, Monogram, Strombecker, or Riggen track, and even when these tracks were new, the skid aprons were relatively scarce so they are even harder to find today. Aurora once made a few for their HO track curves, but they have been out of production for a long time.

HO racers have known for years that you can fabricate skid aprons from model railroad cork roadbed. That's fine as long as you are willing to cement the track and the cork roadbed to the tabletop, but it defeats the purpose of having sectional track. If you cement the track sections to a piece of plastic, cement the cork roadbed to the plastic and you have the best of both worlds: skid aprons and a portable track. Buy a 15x19-inch plastic "For Sale" sign for curves or straights you want to extend.

For HO tracks, a single strip of HO scale model railroad cork roadbed will be enough for 180 degrees of a 15-inch radius curve. You will also need a package of Evergreen Scale Models 0.060x0.125-inch strip styrene to shim the cork up to the thickness of the HO track.

If you wish to make skid aprons for 1/32 scale track, buy the O scale cork roadbed. Depending on the brand, you may need to buy Evergreen styrene strips to shim the cork to match the thickness of the track. You will only be able to get about one skid apron on each "For Sale" sign. If you have trouble locating O scale

The extended guardrails provide just enough room so the longer cars don't ricochet off of them.

cork roadbed, you can use two layers of HO scale roadbed, but do not split it along the diagonal seam. Use it full width for 1/32 scale.

Perfect Power

There is nothing more frustrating than to find dead or slow spots due to a loose track connection, so the track joints are the first place to start to eliminate a low power section of track. The quickest way to check the track is to disconnect the section where you know you have power. Disconnecting that one section forces the power to flow from just one direction into that suspect loose track. Then hold the throttle down with a rubber band while you slide a car around the track. If there is a loose joint anywhere, it will show up in the sound of the car.

If your track length is longer than 20 feet, you will find there is a loss of power the farther you get from the terminal track. The best solution is to install jumper cables from the terminal track to carry direct power to the distant portions of the

Carrera's 20578 (size 4) curve is nearly 7 feet in diameter and is a delight to drive.

The SCX 88420 safety protectors are simulated tire barriers made of foam to minimize damage to cars, especially at the end of a straight.

track. A jumper cable should be installed about every 15 to 20 feet of track. Jumper cables are available from all the major track suppliers to plug into their specific brands.

Be absolutely certain you are connecting the rails correctly or else you will create a short circuit that can damage the power pack. It is possible to make the connections with the track in place, but it is far safer to turn the track sections over, as shown, so you know you have made the proper rail-to-rail connections. Be sure that you are connecting the rails from Lane 1 to the rails in Lane 2.

Hillclimbs for Home Tracks

There are really two ways to make uphills and downhills for model race car tracks. The most obvious is to support the track on 1/8-inch plywood, cut to match the contour of the track. Elevate the plywood,

continued on page 121

The finished track section allows the T-Jet cars to slide around the corner like real racing cars.

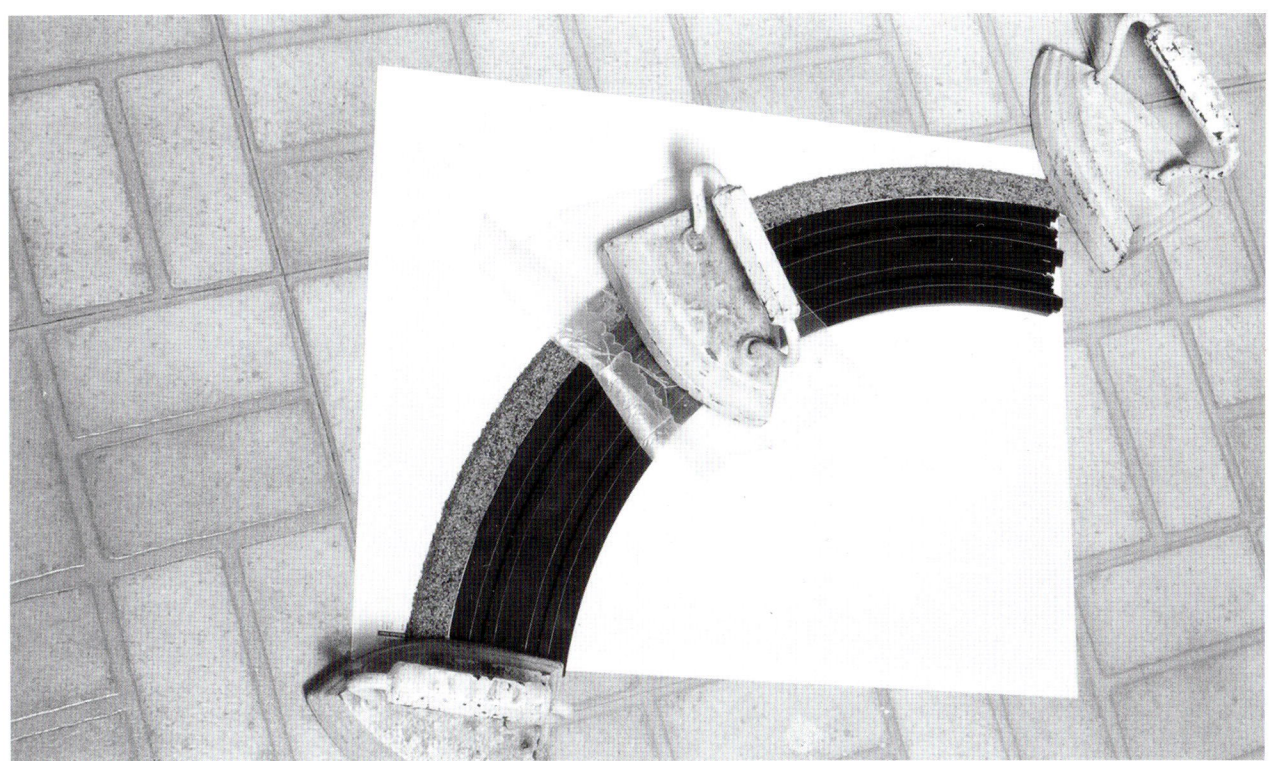

Use Weldbond or silicone cement to attach the track to the sign, and then cover the track and cork with waxed paper and weigh it down while the glue dries.

Slice off the excess sign and paint the inside edge of the white sign flat black.

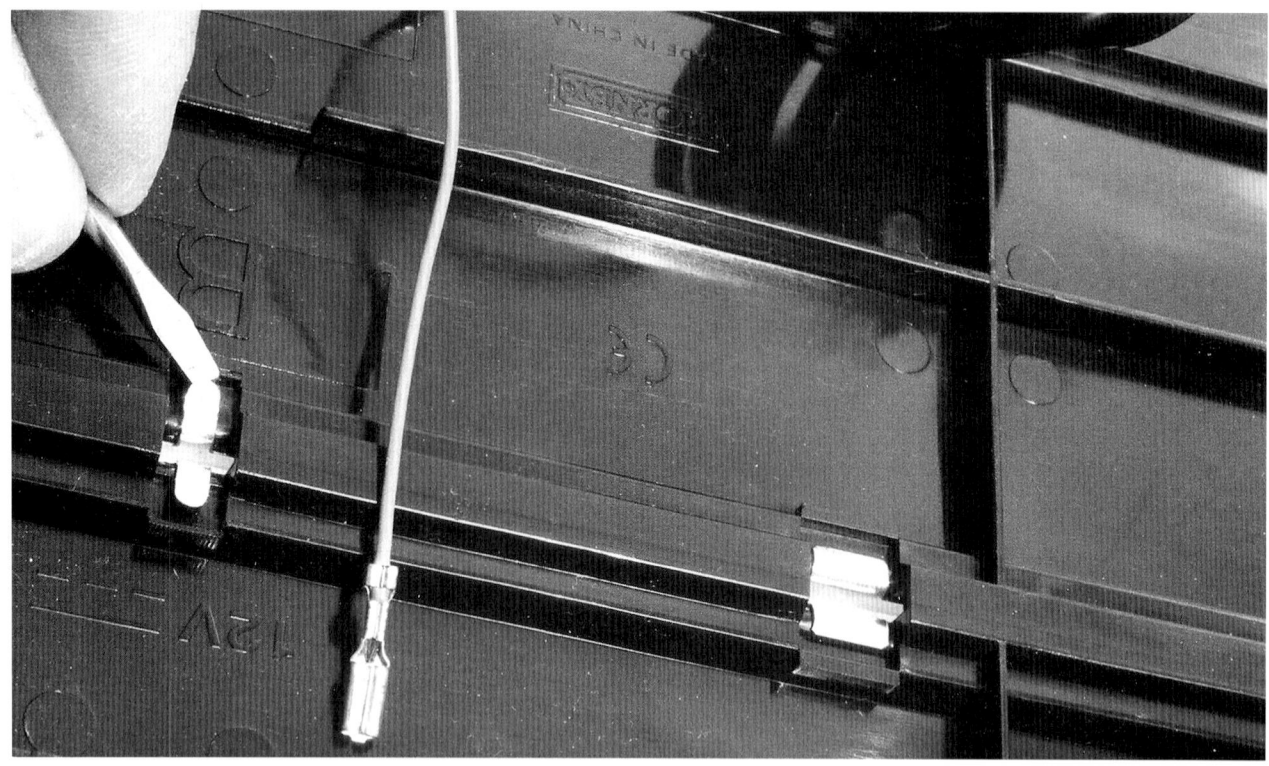

The Scalextric Sport track straight sections have small gravestone-shaped tabs that can be gently pried up to accept the terminals on the ends of the C8248 Scalextric Sport Track Power Booster Cables.

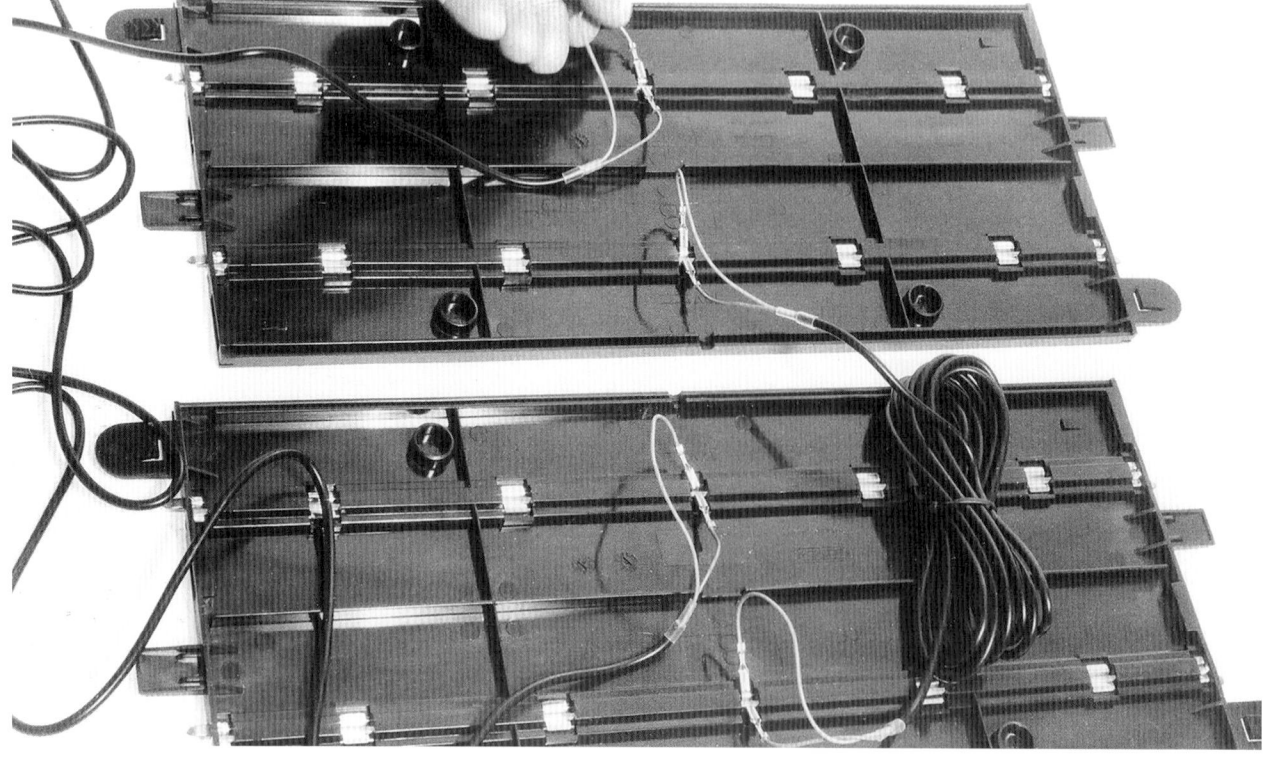

The Booster Cables are designed to connect the terminal track to another straight track section.

along with the track, with vertical 1x4-foot risers like a model railroad right of way. That's the kind of system that Bob Dunkle used for the uphill section of his 5x12-foot Scalextric Sport raceway in Chapter 11. It works great, but it compromises the portability of the track.

I adapted the Woodland Scenics' model railroad right of way support system to model car racing tracks as described in *Slot Car Bible*. Woodland Scenics offers a series of very lightweight expanded-polystyrene risers shaped like crinkly noodles for flexibility in right or left directions. The system uses Woodland Scenics ST1409 4-inch risers for the vertical support and their 1/2-inch thick ST1423 12x24-inch plain foam sheets.

All of this is illustrated in *Slot Car Bible*, as installed on a Carrera Monaco track. That track uses the Carrera number 20545 crossing with one half turned 180 degrees to produce a vertical ess curve to bring the track down from 9 inches to zero in less than 3 feet. It's a bit like a roller coaster, but it is great fun to race on. It's a simple way to gain or lose elevation with Carrera track.

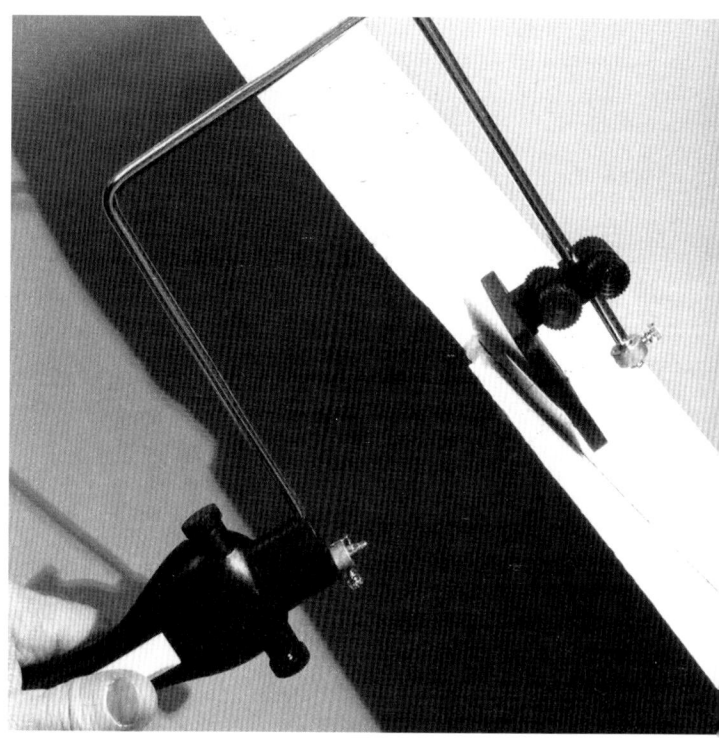

Use the Woodland Scenics ST1435 hot wire foam cutter with the ST1437 foam cutter bow and guide to cut along the marked lines.

Cover the downhill portion of the track with as many overlapping 12x48-inch foam boards as necessary to reach across the outside borders of track.

On this version of Monaco, the track in the upper left will be supported by two sets of standard curves to elevate it to 9 inches so the first downhill jog is from 9 to 4 1/2 inches at the R1 curve in the left foreground.

Cut four pieces of the 4-inch riser diagonally from one corner to the 2 inches in from the opposite end as shown.

I wanted to recreate a similar Monaco plan for Scalextric's Sport track, but with a downhill to match the relatively gentle uphill and to better simulate the real downhill through the turns at Monaco from Mirabeau to Lowes to the waterfront. This meant custom-cutting the supports so a few of these supports will be reused.

I did make another standard support, this one for the Scalextric Sport Classic R1 curve to elevate it 4 1/4 inches. I simply traced the half-round pair of curved outer aprons and cut a 180-degree support from 1/2-inch foam. I then hot-glued the 4-inch-high Woodland Scenics risers around the curve and across the straight end to make a D-shaped box. This is the Standard Inner Curve Support.

The remainder of the downhill section of the Sport Monaco track in the photos is made from custom-fitted versions of the above standard supports. I'd strongly suggest you assemble all the standard supports you need and work them into the track to see how they fit before you begin custom cutting. The Standard supports fit easily, but the custom ones will require trial-and-error and a bit of trimming and adding to get a perfectly smooth downhill flow through the curves.

Carrera and Artin track does not seem to need to be secured to the tabletop or portable foam supports. If, however, you want to build uphill grades for Sport, Classic, SCX, or NINCO track, the track must be mounted on 1/8-inch plywood, but the plywood can be supported by this system using Woodland Scenics risers and inclines.

Rally and Off-Road on "Real" Dirt

Several of the World Rally Cup (WRC) events, as well as the Baja 1000 and the Paris-Dakar races, are held on dirt roads. If you try to use real dirt, you will discover that the dirt will be converted to grinding paste, especially if attracted by oil or grease, to wear out your car's bearings. Metallic particles in the dirt can short out the motor, but you can make fake dirt from cornbread flour.

To make the corn flour brown, toast it in an oven. Line a flat baking pan with foil and spread about 1/4 cup of corn flour over the pan. It takes about three hours at 300 degrees Fahrenheit to get the corn flour to brown completely.

The "dirt" works the best on the rougher surface tracks such as NINCO, SCX, or Scalextric Classic (in descending order of roughness). You can apply it to Scalextric Sport, Carrera, or Artin, but the cars' tires will quickly wipe it from the smooth surfaces.

You can use just enough to color the track surface and provide the look of dirt, or you can apply a good 1/16 inch and let the cars dig their way through. The most realistic effect comes from spreading about 1/64 inch over the track, then running a car to provide a racing line through the dirt. Brush any excess dirt from the slot.

You can use a vacuum cleaner with a flexible hose to remove any excess dirt. Tape a nylon sock over the flexible extension hose to catch the dirt and tap the trapped dirt onto a piece of foil to be reused.

The corn flour dust is extremely fine and pervasive. I suggest you use it outdoors because it gets on everything. Also, buy enough track sections to make a dedicated dirt track instead of trying to apply it, clean it, and reapply it to an existing track. Also, with enough running, the dust can reach inside the motor to insulate the commutator from the motor brushes. If that happens, squirt a small amount of WD-40 into the motor while you turn the motor using the rear wheels to solve the problem. Also remember that corn flour is food and will attract mice, ants, and other pests, so you'll need a pest-free place to store the track.

Realistic Pit and Paddock Scenes

Scalextric, SCX, and Carrera each offer a range of realistic pit garages, grandstands, and control or press towers. Bauer offers some die-cut card replicas of pits and towers based on structures at the Nurburgring track.

SCX also has 1/32 scale tents they call rally boxes. They are designed to replicate the portable repair facilities set up for the World Rally Cup (WRC) events around the world. Similar tents are used at races just about everywhere outside Formula 1 or NASCAR, so the rally box has a greater use for adding realism to any home raceway than to serve as a base for rally teams. I felt that the SCX rally boxes were unrealistically tall, so I removed about 1 1/2 inches from each support leg before assembling them. I also painted over the rally car brands on the edges of the tents.

Technically, the pit is where the cars stop for fuel or driver changes. The places where the cars are repaired are usually called paddocks. Today, the driver's pit signals and the laptop computers are sited on what are called pit walls, like the pit lanes produced by GB Track (a division of Fly). A series of three Fly (GB Track) pit walls are just across the pit lane track from the SCX paddock tents—an odd combination of modern pit walls and archaic paddock tents, but something you could see at Monaco or tracks like Laguna Seca.

The GB Track 79708 pit wall provides a site for two cars with a railing, simulated electrical connection box, and covered drain/cable access hatch. The model has notches for possible future lighting or other electronics. You can join as many of the pit walls as you wish. There would be 10 of them for a current Formula 1 race, but for a model racetrack, two is probably enough to control four cars. The right and left ends of the pit wall need to be finished with the GB Track 79716 pit wall set. You'll only

Do not allow Sport track to sag because it will loosen the track joining pins. Use 5-foot-long pieces of 1/4x2-inch lathe to provide temporary support for the track so it cannot sag. Fill this area with the diagonally cut risers.

The descent from 9 inches to 4 1/2 inches is complete and installed. Note that there are areas near the tabletop with 2- to 4-inch gaps, but the track itself is supported by the foam board.

need one set of the number 79716, regardless of how many 79708 pit walls you use. The 79708 team control paddock is the bench and sunshade where two team members sit with laptop computers to control and monitor the cars.

Cardboard Structures

The Nurburgring had its own massive scoring tower, a tall Shell-sponsored tower, and a Continental

Spread about 1/32 inch of the corn flour with a wide paint brush, then dust the excess from the pickup rails and slot.

The deep "dirt" is a natural environment for the NINCO Pajero Paris-Dakar racing SUVs.

tire-sponsored press tower at the end of the pits. Bauer has recreated the three towers and the pit buildings in two cardboard kits. Cardboard seems an odd choice, but it is a very popular modeling medium in Europe. For a model car raceway, it's just fine because it offers easy assembly and pre-colored and -lettered surfaces.

These Bauer structures were available in HO scale in the early 1970s as plastic kits from Faller, but they have been long out of production. If you want them bad enough for HO tracks, you could make color photocopies of the Bauer 1/32 scale kits and reduce them to 1/64 scale.

Scalextric has three Sport building kits: the C8152 grandstand, a C8150 pit garage, and C8151 control tower. The kits are full-color, die-cut from thick cardboard. The "spectators" in the grandstand are actually photographs of a crowd at a real race and are worth examining closely for some truly realistic faces. It's about the easiest and quickest way possible to cram nearly 300 scale-model people into a grandstand.

The Scalextric Sport grandstands, like any other model grandstand, look a bit odd standing alone. Three or four of them look far more realistic. The scalloped roof on the Sport grandstand looks quite similar to the roof on the Sepang, Malaysia, F1 track.

You can assemble any of the Sport or Bauer structures with rubber cement, white glue, or any of the thin cyanoacrylate adhesives such as Super Glue (also referred to as ACC). ACC is the quickest, but you need to be careful to avoid assembling your fingertips to the building. Use some scraps of waxed paper to press down on the seams and to back up the walls while you assemble the components. ACC gives more fumes when you work with cardstock or paper, so work outdoors or in a well-ventilated area and wear a respirator.

Carrera Modern-Era Buildings

Carrera has a range of modern-era grandstands and pit buildings that can be used to provide a realistic setting for current Formula 1 or Le Mans cars. The Carrera 21101 grandstand is an example of a modern curved grandstand with no roof. The 21100 has a curved roof and optional supports so it can be placed above the 21101 grandstand to create a two-story grandstand. Carrera also offers three sets of figures to populate the grandstands: 21106 set of figures small, 21107 set of figures big, and 21108 set of figures grandstand. The grandstands in the photos are occupied with two of all three sets.

Carerra also has a series of pit buildings that can be stacked to create an infinite variety of pit scenes. The 21104 is the basic two-door pit garage unit with a 21105 two-bay window VIP floor that can be stacked above the garage. The 21102 press tower has three stories of D-shaped glass walled viewing rooms that stack on a two-window version of the pit lane. There is also a

The modified SCX Rally boxes are similar to the awnings found at nearly every real car race. SCX sells separate sets of Rally car mechanics that are shown in the photos, or you can use mechanics from Scalextric or Monogram.

21103 press tower extension that has a D-shaped viewing room with an outside balcony. The set of pit lane structures in the photo was assembled from two 21104 pit lanes, three 21105 VIP floors, one 21102 press tower, and one 21103 press tower extension. The two open pit garages are populated with a set of 21110 and 21111 mechanic figures. The three pairs of red-, black-, and white-roofed pit walls are Fly/GB Track kits described earlier in this chapter.

Populating the Pits

Most of the people you would want to "populate" a 1/32 scale racetrack are the ones who would be closest to the track. There are a number of sources of spectator figures, including Scalextric, Carrera, SCX, Preiser, and MRRC. SCX, Scalextric, and Carrera also have modern-era spectators and a set of modern

The SCX Rally boxes are easy enough to assemble. The vertical posts simply plug into the plastic floor and the cloth tent.

Use sprue cutters to shorten each of the four vertical posts to 3 1/4 inches.

pit crew figures with safety helmets. Some of the most charismatic figures have not been available. The GB Track division of Fly now has four sets of modern-era figures to bring life to your track.

You will want to have at least one engineer sitting on the pit lane's stool. GB Track offers a series of unpainted cast-metal figures, including 79714, which includes an engineer with a laptop and a manager with an etched-brass signal board. The figures are shown in these photos. An alternative is to use one of the unpainted sitting figures from the MRRC 5092 spectator set or the sitting figure from the MRRC 5091 track officials figures. If you would rather not paint the figures, use the two seated men from the Preiser 63054 seated-people set of three figures.

The MRRC 5090 drivers and pit crew figures has one figure holding a pitboard that would fit nicely on the GB Track 79708 pit wall. If you prefer painted figures, you could use the standing man (with his red vest repainted in a suitable team color) from the Preiser 63071 set of four

A GB Track 79709 team control paddock with 79716 pit wall pieces to finish off the ends. The two figures are from the GB Track 79714 pit wall engineers set of unpainted metal figures.

These are Bauer's models of the Nurburgring control tower and Shell tower.

Use a long ruler to help guide the fold lines on the tower so the edges are perfectly straight.

I used thin cyanoacrylate cement (Super Glue) to assemble the grandstands in less than an hour. Squeeze the glue-soaked seams together with a scrap of waxed paper so you don't cement your fingertips to the model.

The Shell tower, Continental scoring towers, and pits are long-out-of-production HO Faller plastic kits on Gary Merrifield's track (see Chapter 13). Today you can buy color cardboard versions of all three from Bauer.

truckers. The corner worker and one of the two seated men from the pre-painted SCX 88320 set could also be used.

There is, however, no source of modern-era corner workers—those orange-coated folks who wave the flags and push and pull the cars off the verges of the track. Preiser makes a variety of 1/32 scale figures. Many of these figures are perfect for use as spectators on a model race car track. The Preiser 63051 men in hard hats and 63052 men in

127

Three or more of the card Sport C8152 grandstands can be placed side-by-side for a far more realistic scene than a single grandstand.

The LaRascasse restaurant at Monaco was copied from a book and glued to 1/8-inch Foamcore with 3M Spray-Ment to create one of the dozens of flats on the Sport Monaco track.

Six Preiser construction workers were transformed into six modern-era racetrack corner workers with some paint.

hard hats waving arms can be easily converted to exact 1/32 scale modern-era corner workers by snapping off the side and back edges of their hard hats with sprue cutters or an X-Acto knife to change the hard hats into caps. Your dealer can order them from Walthers.

The Preiser worker figures are in random colors. Paint their coats and pants orange with any brand of model railroad Reefer Orange (I used Floquil). I used Testors 1123 green enamel for the caps. Since you do not have to worry about the fine details like faces, hair, hands, or shoes, the painting is quick and easy. I did six of them in less than an hour.

The two of the Carrera modern-era grandstands are filled with Carrera figures.

This pit complex is assembled from an assortment of Carrera kits with a GB-Track "pit wall" in the foreground.

CHAPTER 8
RACETRACKS ON TABLETOPS

A Scalextric Renault, with Mild Seven decals from Pattos, is chased by a Carrera Williams around a bend on a tabletop track.

You can assemble a challenging track for 1/32 scale cars in a space as small as 4x8 feet. Frankly, a 5x9-foot Ping-Pong table offers far more possibilities, or you can place a pair of portable conference tables side by side for a 5x10-foot area. There's room for tables that small in just about any spare room, even if they are placed temporarily over a bed. You only need to be able to walk around two long sides and one short end; the other short end can butt against the wall.

How Much Space?

A 4x8-foot piece of plywood is a convenient size that's easy enough to handle. You can support it on a pair of sawhorses. Buy the sawhorse brackets and you can install your own wood to elevate the track to 36 inches for less strain on the back muscles. There are several plans in this chapter for a pair of 4x8-foot boards, placed end-to-end or placed offset, side-by-side.

The plans are marked with two "L" letters that indicate the track joints where you can insert a pair of straight track pieces (one on each side of the track) to expand the track. The letters "W" indicate where you can insert additional pairs of straight track pieces to expand the width of the plan. If, for example, you like one of the 5x9-foot plans, but you have two 2 1/2x10-foot conference tables, you can add a pair of straights to expand the plan from 5x9 feet to 5x10 feet.

Portable or Permanent?

All these tracks are designed to be portable. You can set them up on a Ping-Pong table and cover the table with green felt to simulate grass. The scenery can be Life-Like's rugged number 1871 giant oak trees, plus your choice of pit buildings, grandstands, control towers, and spectator vehicles. There are lots of ideas in Chapter 7, and all are portable. If you buy one of the fold-up Ping-Pong tables on its own casters, you can store the track and scenery inside the folded-up table.

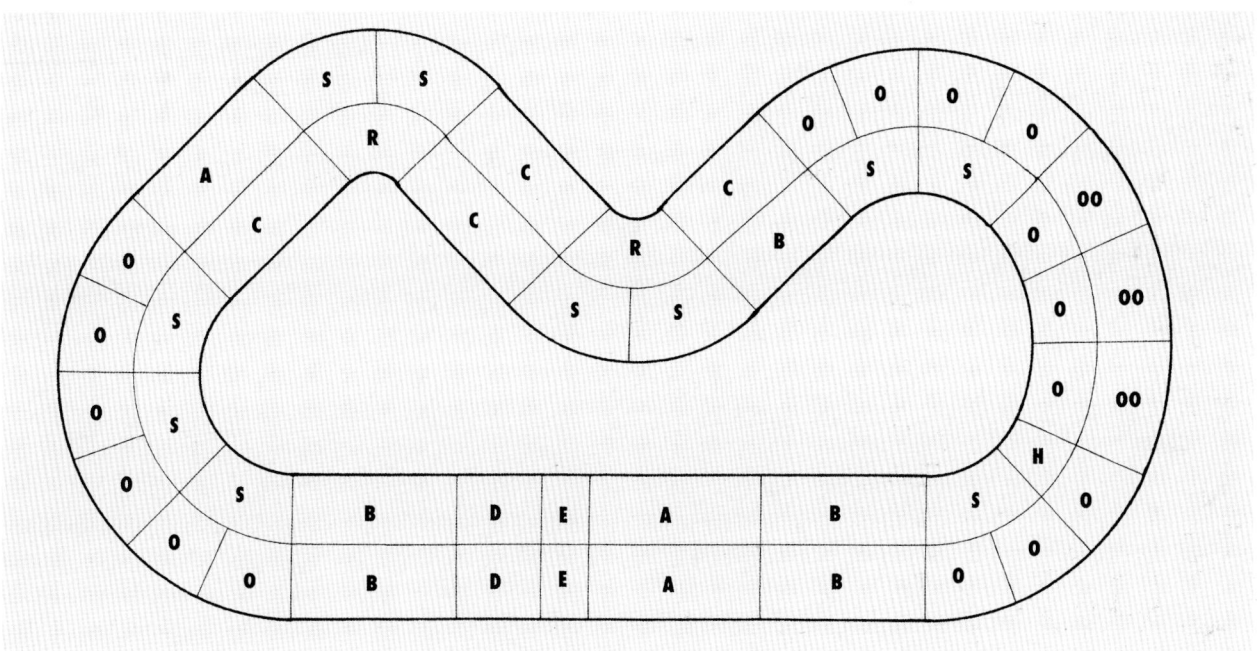

Scalextric Sport, Classic, or SCX track required for a 4x8-foot compact raceway.

Key	Quantity	Description
R	2	Sport-brand C8201 Hairpin Curve
H	1	1/2 Standard Curve
S	10	Standard Curve
O	16	Outer Curve
OO	3	Outer-Outer Curve
E	2	1/4-Straight
D	2	1/2-Straight
B	5	Full-Straight
C	4	Sport-brand C8246 -Side Swipe Straights
A	2	Connector Track

This is racing action in 4x8 feet. The cars seem to tuck in behind each other when they negotiate the crossover and squeeze track (chicane) sections on a raceway assembled with Scalextric Sport track sections.

Most of these plans are for just two lanes. You can squeeze a four-lane track onto a tabletop, but there are not many variations possible. With two lanes, however, you also have the option of using the digital lane-changing systems described in Chapter 3 to race four or six cars on a two-lane track.

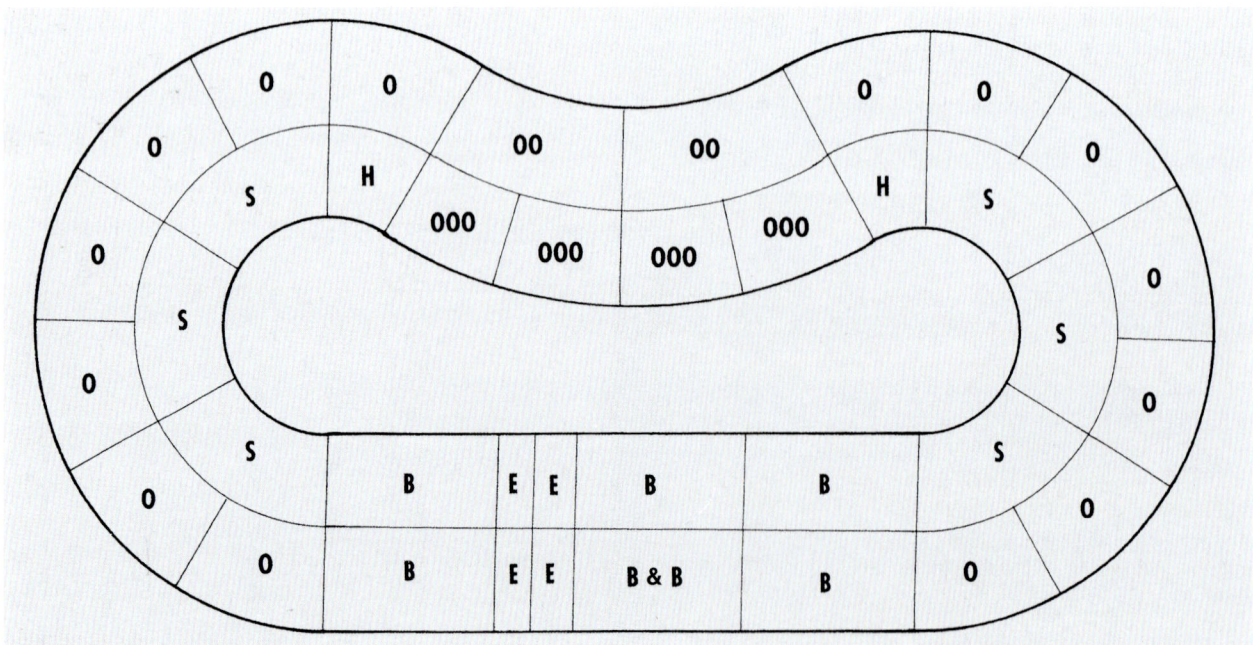

Carrera track required for a 4x8-foot compact raceway.

Key	Quantity	Description
H	2	1/2 Inner Curve
S	6	Inner Curve
O	14	Middle Curve
OO	2	Outer Curve
OOO	2 pair (4)	Outer-Outer Curve
N	0	Banked Outer Curve
E	4	1/4-Straight
D	0	1/3-Straight
B	4	Full-Straight
A	2	Connector Track

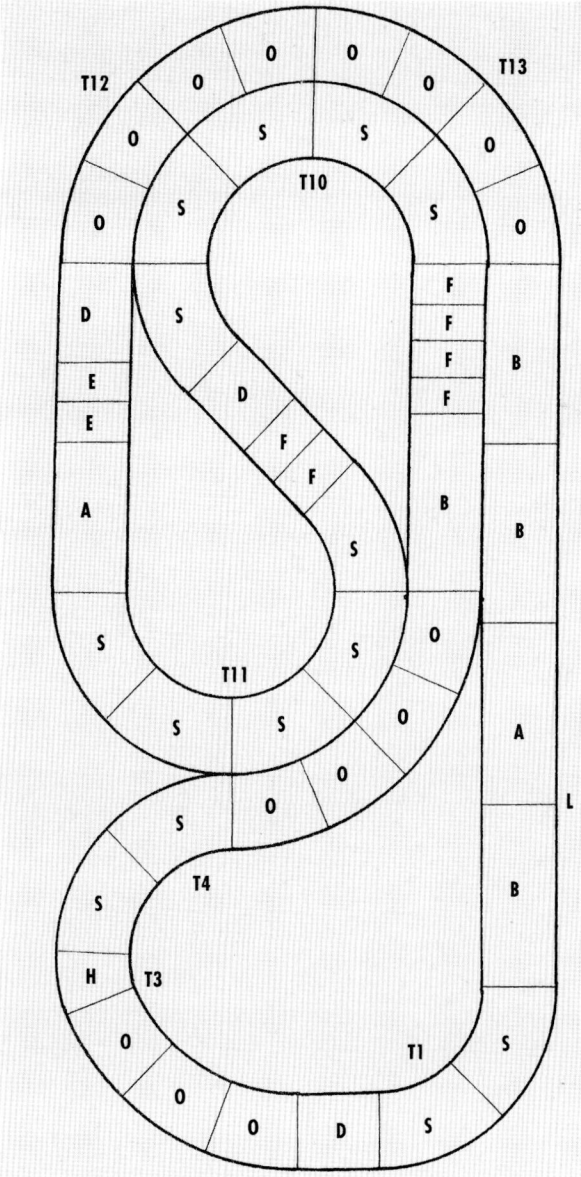

Scalextric Sport, Classic, or SCX track required for a 4x8-foot Indy F1 circuit.

Key	Quantity	Description
H	1	1/2 Standard Curve
S	14	Standard Curve
O	15	Outer Curve
OO	0	Outer-Outer Curve
D	3	1/2-Straight
E	2	1/4-Straight
F	6	"Short" Straight
B	4	Full-Straight
A	2	Connector Track

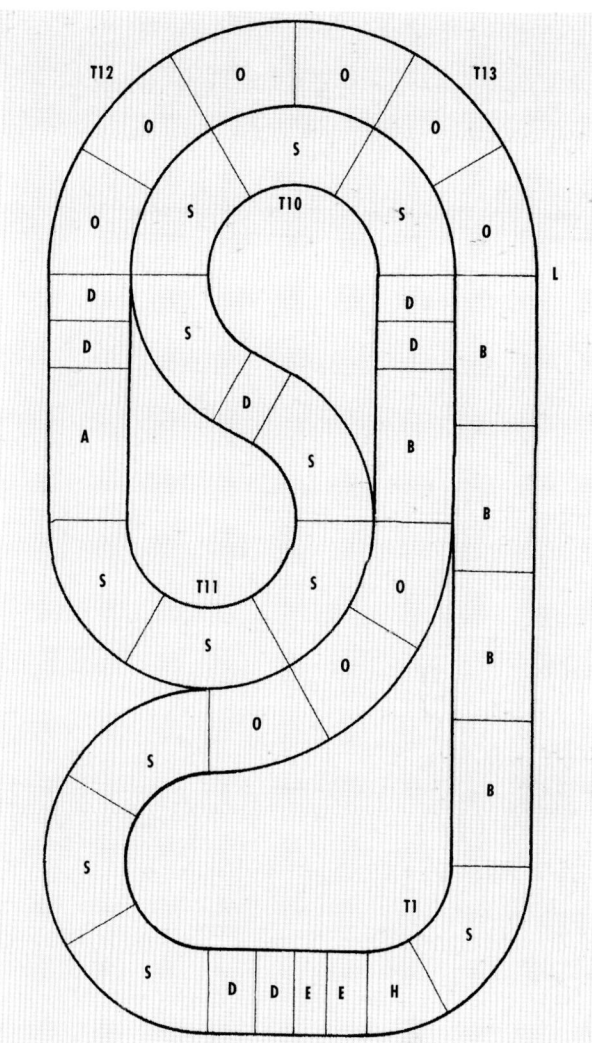

Carrera track required for a 4x8-foot Indy F1 circuit.

Key	Quantity	Description
H	1	1/2 Inner Curve
S	12	Inner Curve
O	9	Middle Curve
OO	0	Outer Curve
OOO	0	Outer-Outer Curve
E	3	1/4-Straight
D	6	1/3-Straight
B	4	Full-Straight
A	2	Connector Track

Picking the Best Brand of Track

I cannot pick one brand as the "best." Each brand has a particular advantage that is not shared by the others, and each has a fault unique to its own brand. There's a comparison chart in *Slot Car Bible* that provides my personal pros and cons.

NINCO track has the same geometry as Scalextric and SCX, so you can use the Scalextric plans as a

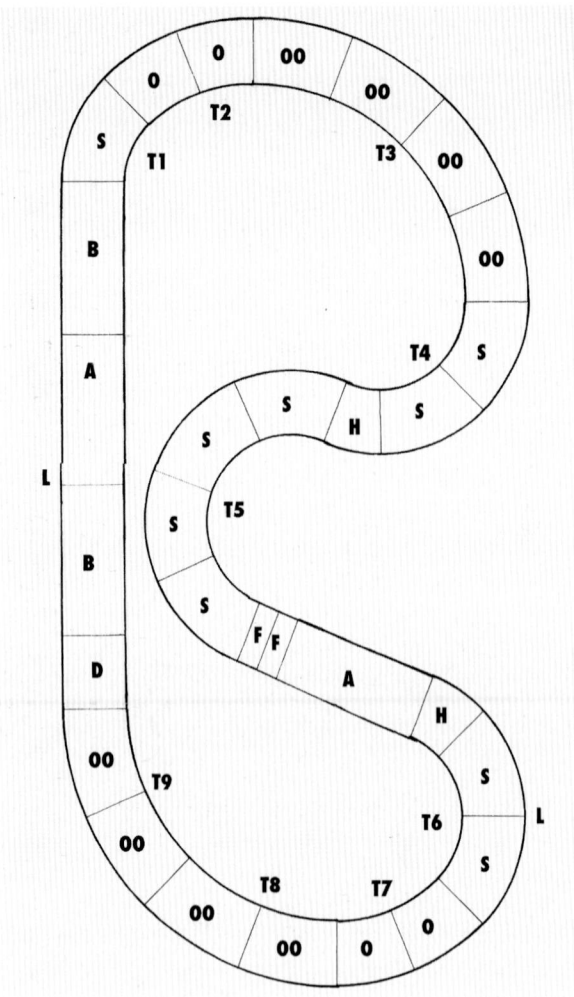

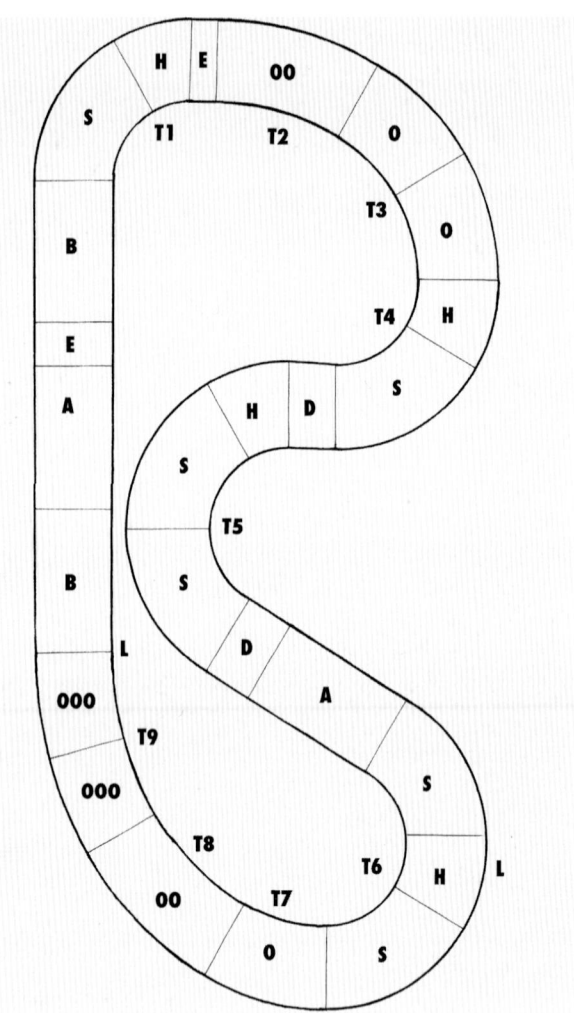

Scalextric Sport, Classic, SCX, or NINCO track required for a 4x8-foot parabola duo.

Key	Quantity	Description
H	2	1/2 Standard Curve
S	9	Standard Curve
O	4	Outer Curve
OO	8	Outer-Outer Curve
F	2	"Short" Straight
E	0	1/4-Straight
D	1	1/2-Straight
B	2	Full-Straight
A	2	Connector Track

Carrera track required for a 4x8-foot parabola duo.

Key	Quantity	Description
H	4	1/2 Inner Curve
S	6	Inner Curve
O	3	Middle Curve
OO	2	Outer Curve
OOO	1 pr. (2)	Outer-Outer Curve
E	1	1/4-Straight
D	2	1/3-Straight
B	2	Full-Straight
A	2	Connector Track

guide for assembling a NINCO track. The NINCO track is somewhat wider, so the track may require more space. You may also need to insert some short filler pieces of straight track to get the final joints to align perfectly. Some of the plans require a half-length curve "H," which NINCO does not offer. You will need to cut one half-length standard curve (at "H"), as shown in *Slot Car Bible*, to use NINCO track for these plans.

Artin track has the same geometry as Carrera, so you can use the Carrera plans as a rough guide to assembling an Artin track. The Artin track sections are smaller than Carrera's, so you will need more straight track sections, and the finished track should require less space. You will likely need to use some sort of straight track sections or even custom-cut a straight track section (as shown in *Slot Car*

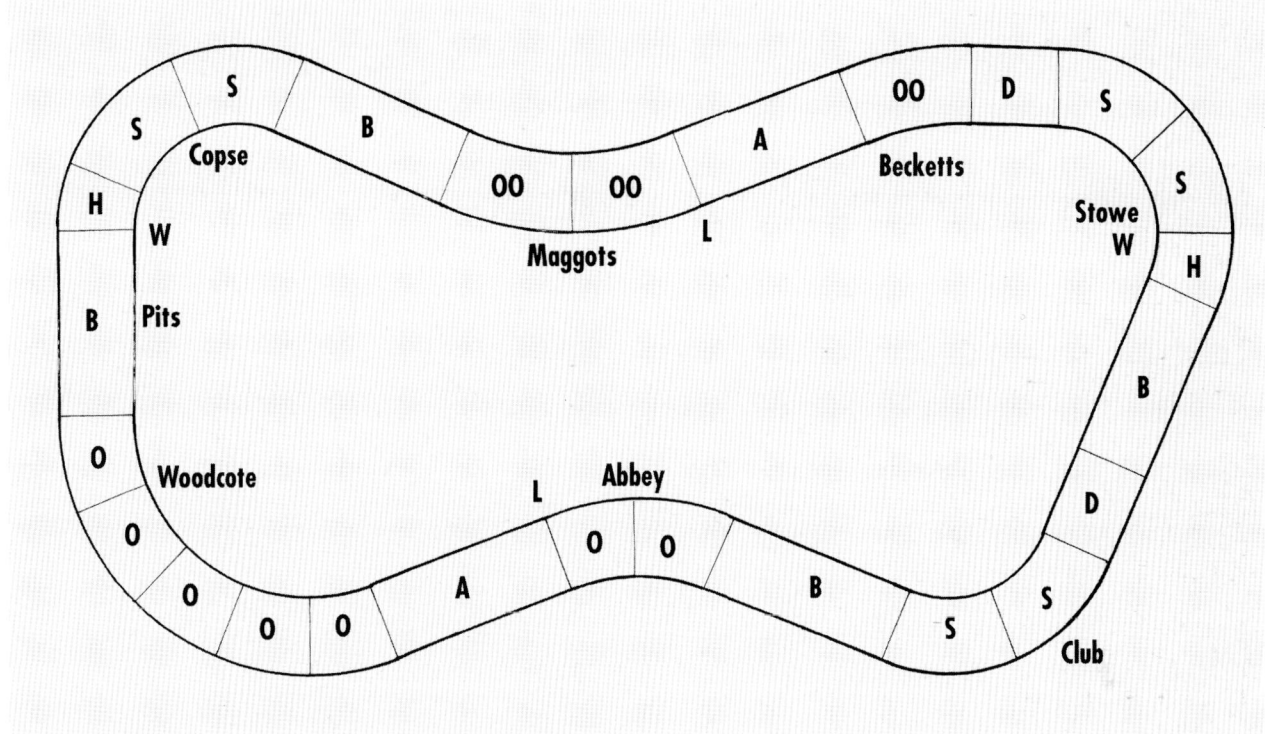

Scalextric Sport, Classic, or SCX track required for a 4x8-foot Silverstone circuit.

Key	Quantity	Description
H	2	1/2 Standard Curve
S	6	Standard Curve
O	7	Outer Curve
OO	3	Outer-Outer Curve
D	2	1/2-Straight
E	0	1/4-Straight
F	0	"Short" Straight
B	4	Full-Straight
A	2	Connector Track

Bible) to get the track to match these plans and still align properly at every joint.

Borders, Skid Aprons, and Extensions

The track plans in *Slot Car Bible, Racing and Collecting Slot Cars,* this book, and *Model Car Racing* magazine identify the track sections with letters, not part numbers. We also use a single plan to apply to Scalextric Sport, Scalextric Classic, SCX, and NINCO. On that plan we listed four different part numbers for each track section. If you are building one of these larger tracks, the charts in the *Slot Car Bible* provide the part numbers for all the brands that correspond to the letters on the plans.

I strongly suggest you buy a catalog for the brand you are using. You can also log onto the company's website so you can familiarize yourself with part numbers of both the track and the borders. Your dealer may also have a catalog, but you have to create your own shopping list.

The 4x8-Foot Four-Lane Track

This four-lane track for 4x8 feet has the same left-right series of ess bends that were part of the Watkins Glen track in the November/December 2002, number 6 issue of *Model Car Racing*. The combination allows a racing line through the corners.

The 4x8-foot Four-Lane for Scalextric Sport, Classic, SCX, or NINCO

These track sections are designed to fit as much racing as possible into the smallest possible space. This particular plan uses the tight R1 curves, so I don't recommend that you assemble it with Scalextric Classic at the places marked "R." You can combine Classic and Sport, using the smoother Sport C8201 hairpin curves at those two locations.

I have included one of the Scalextric Sport number C8201 hairpin (chicaned) curves at "R" in the ess bends on each lane, with straight chicane track sections C8246 side swipe straights at "C." If

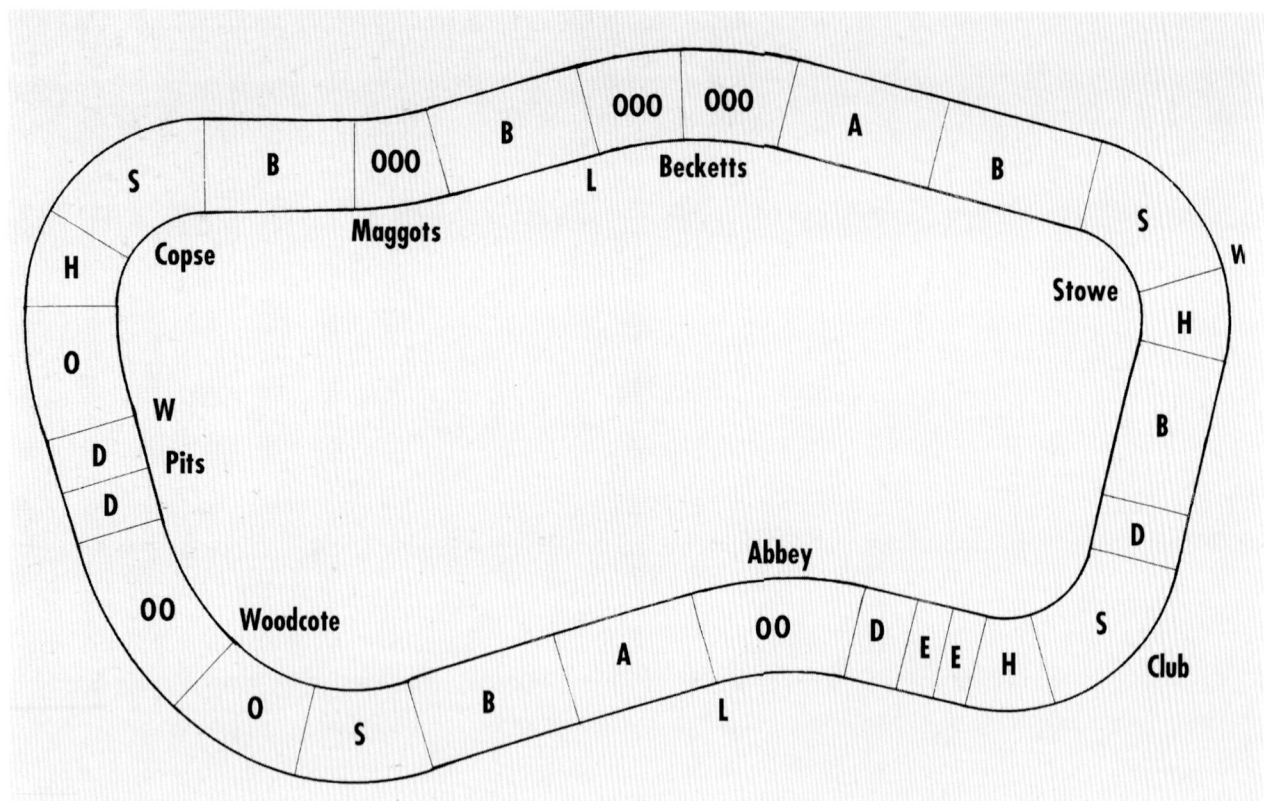

Carrera track required for a 4x8-foot Silverstone circuit

Key	Quantity	Description
H	3	1/2 Standard Curve
S	4	Standard Curve
O	2	Outer Curve
OO	2	Outer-Outer Curve
OOO	3	Outer-Outer-Outer Curve
D	3	1/3-Straight
E	2	1/4-Straight
B	5	Full-Straight
A	2	Connector Track

you assemble the track with SCX or NINCO sections, you will need to use standard and outer curves in this area and replace the straights with half-length straights. You can also use the Scalextric Sport C8201 racing curve crossovers at "V" to provide a racing line through that section of the course.

The 4x8-foot Raceway for Carrera

Carrera provides really broad curves, and this plan is designed to take advantage of the smooth racing flow as much as possible. The two end curves are as tight as they can be for a four-lane Carrera track, but the bend in the center of the track is assembled from the giant Carrera number 4-size curves (on the outside lane). The track should provide exciting racing, and the lap times for each lane will be closer than you might imagine because it's a long way around the outside.

Indy F1 Circuit in 4x8 feet

The turns are all numbered to correspond to somewhat similar turns on the real Indy F1 track. There was just enough room to include a decreasing-radius turn (T3 and T4). There are two terminal tracks so drivers can be positioned on opposite sides of the track so each can serve as a corner marshal. If you have the space, consider assembling the track on two 4x8-foot boards placed end-to-end to produce a 4x16-foot track. The longer straights will provide the speeds of a much larger track in a relatively compact space.

Indy F1 Circuit in 4x8 feet for Scalextric Sport, Classic, or SCX

There's enough room on a 4x8-foot piece of plywood for a great Scalextric Sport, Scalextric Classic, SCX, or Carrera track. I strongly suggest

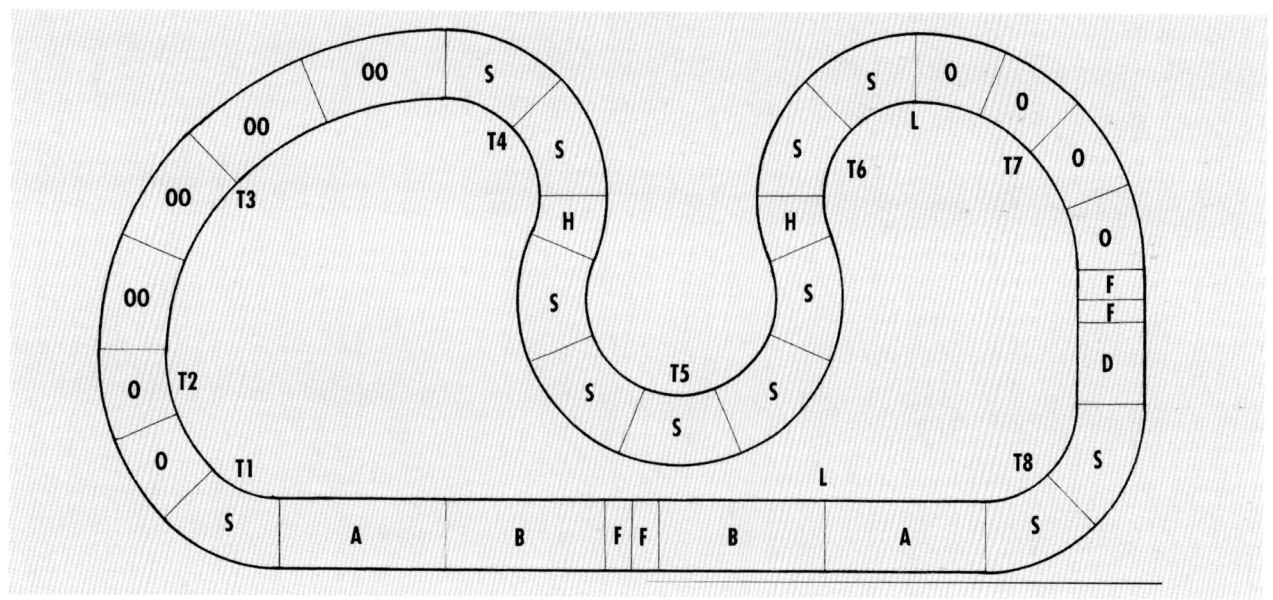

Scalextric Sport, Classic, SCX, or NINCO track required for a 4x8-foot parabola uno.

Key	Quantity	Description
H	2	1/2 Standard Curve
S	12	Standard Curve
O	6	Outer Curve
OO	4	Outer-Outer Curve
F	4	"Short" Straight
E	0	1/4-Straight
D	0	1/2-Straight
B	2	Full-Straight
A	2	Connector Track

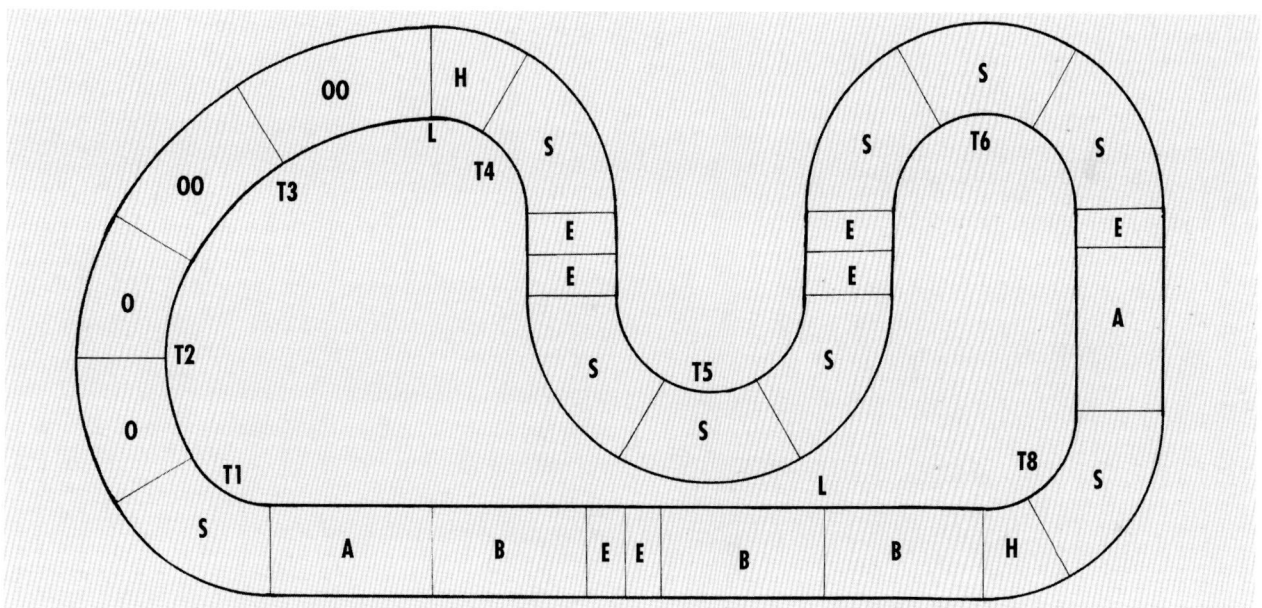

Carrera track required for a 4x8-foot parabola uno.

Key	Quantity	Description
H	2	1/2 Inner Curve
S	9	Inner Curve
O	2	Middle Curve
OO	2	Outer Curve
OOO	0	Outer-Outer Curve
E	7	1/4-Straight
D	0	1/3-Straight
B	3	Full-Straight
A	2	Connector Track

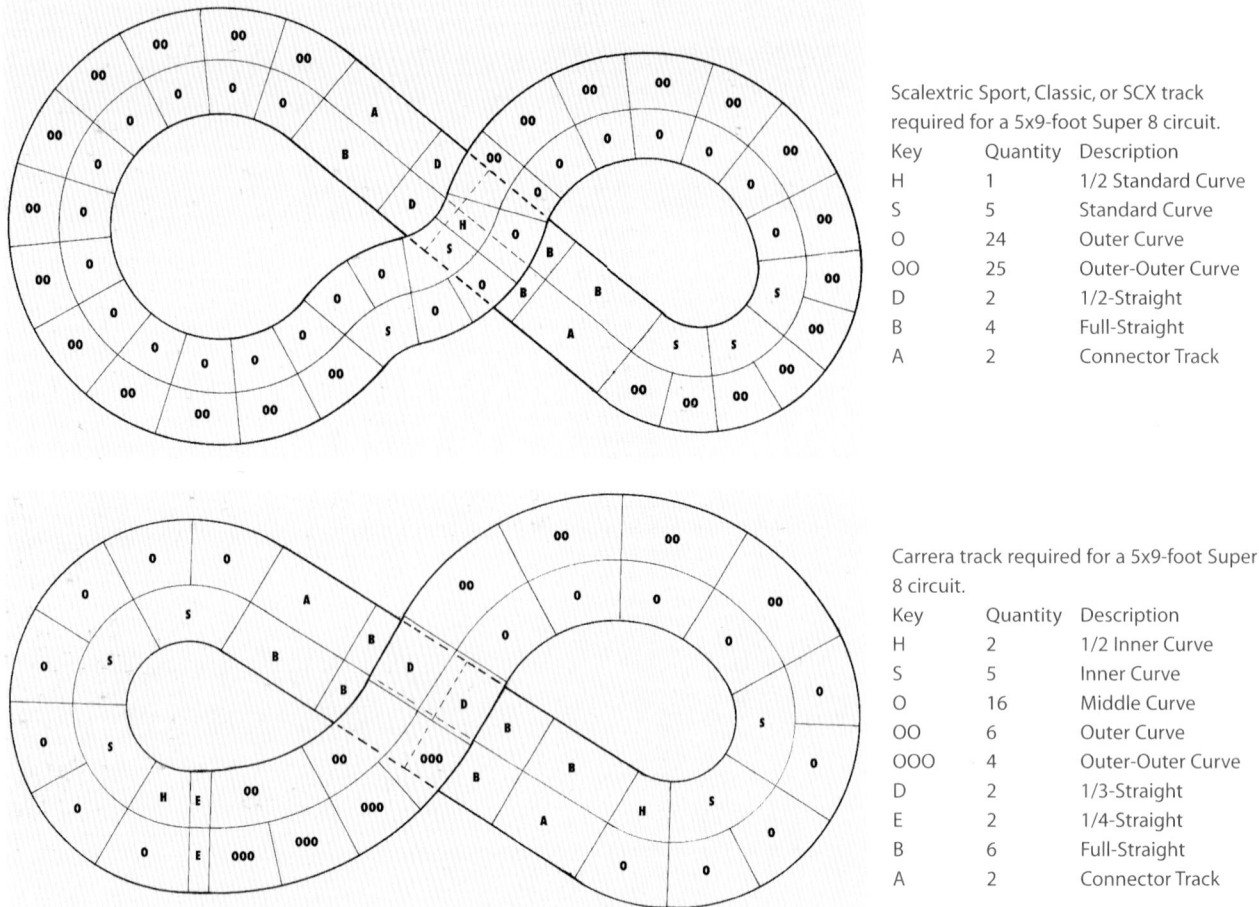

Scalextric Sport, Classic, or SCX track required for a 5x9-foot Super 8 circuit.

Key	Quantity	Description
H	1	1/2 Standard Curve
S	5	Standard Curve
O	24	Outer Curve
OO	25	Outer-Outer Curve
D	2	1/2-Straight
B	4	Full-Straight
A	2	Connector Track

Carrera track required for a 5x9-foot Super 8 circuit.

Key	Quantity	Description
H	2	1/2 Inner Curve
S	5	Inner Curve
O	16	Middle Curve
OO	6	Outer Curve
OOO	4	Outer-Outer Curve
D	2	1/3-Straight
E	2	1/4-Straight
B	6	Full-Straight
A	2	Connector Track

that you attach the track to the tabletop with Scalextric (or SCX or NINCO) clips and/or Shoe Goo or silicone caulking once the track is perfectly aligned. The adjacent tracks serve as skid aprons (borders) for each other so you will want perfect alignment of the side-by-side areas. You will also need to cut the borders to fit in the wedge-shaped areas at the ends of the adjacent turns.

Indy F1 Circuit in 4x8 feet for Carrera

With Carrera track, the borders will actually hang off the edges a bit, but it will fit on that 4x8-foot piece of plywood. The basic configuration is the same as the 5x9-foot Indy F1 track we use for track tests, and the plan is shown in *Slot Car Bible*. There's room for a banked Turn 12 (T12 on the plan) on the 5x9-foot version, but the turn should be flat on this 4x8-foot track. There's also room for a corkscrew through turns T3 and T4 on the 5x9-foot version that will not fit on the 4x8-foot plan.

The turns are numbered to roughly correspond to similar turns on the real Indy Formula 1 track. You will need to cut the outer edges of the borders around T4, the right end of T10, and both ends of T11 into wedge shapes to fit the track. You may also need to substitute some "E" 1/4-straights for "D" 1/3 straights (and vice versa) to get the track to fit together firmly. With Carrera, you can use the four-lane locking pins to pull everything together. I have included two terminal tracks so drivers can be positioned on opposite sides of the track so each can serve as a corner marshal.

Parabola Duo in 4x8 feet

The simple spiral is called a parabola in geometry. For real car racing fans, the word sounds very much like the Parabolica curve at Italy's Monza racetrack, and for good reason. That curve is one of the fastest on the Formula 1 circuit because it is a large curve and it gets larger as the car progresses

The original Indy F1 circuit overhangs the edges of the Ping-Pong table. Use the plan in this chapter to reduce the overhang.

through it. It is a parabola, or in racer terms, an increasing radius curve.

The 4x8-foot plans include a pair of parabolic curves. I have labeled the individual segments of the curves with "T" and numbers. Turns T1, T2, and T3 are increasing radius turns, but the curve through T3 and T4 is a decreasing radius. On a real racetrack, this 270-degree series of curves (T1 through T4) would probably have two apexes for most drivers; one near T2 and the other near T4 on the plan. The curve through T6, T7, T8, and T9 is another increasing radius curve. For sheer fun, there is also a tight, ess curve through T4 and T5.

Parabola Duo in 4x8 feet for Scalextric Sport, Classic, SCX, or NINCO

The track in this plan is far more difficult to drive than it might appear. The combinations of curves are tricky because most cannot be negotiated with a steady throttle setting. The transition from right to left through turns T4 and T5 is more abrupt on this version of the track.

Parabola Duo in 4x8 feet for Carrera

The increasing radius curve through turns T6, T7, T8, and T9 is more pronounced on the Carrera version because Carrera offers an outer/outer/outer broad-radius curve (000 on the plans) to provide four stages of increasing radius through this turn.

Silverstone in 4x8 feet

There's a larger version of Silverstone, with some more information on the real track, in Chapter 9. Because the earlier version of the real track is so simple, it can be reduced to just 4x8 feet and still recreate the correct look and feel. The plan can be expanded infinitely at "L" and "W" if you have a longer and/or wider space.

Silverstone in 4x8 feet for Scalextric Sport, Classic, SCX, or NINCO

To keep the track on a compact 4x8-foot layout, there is no Chapel curve and Becketts is a mere jog in the straight, but this allows the straight to be taken flat-out with most cars all the way from Copse

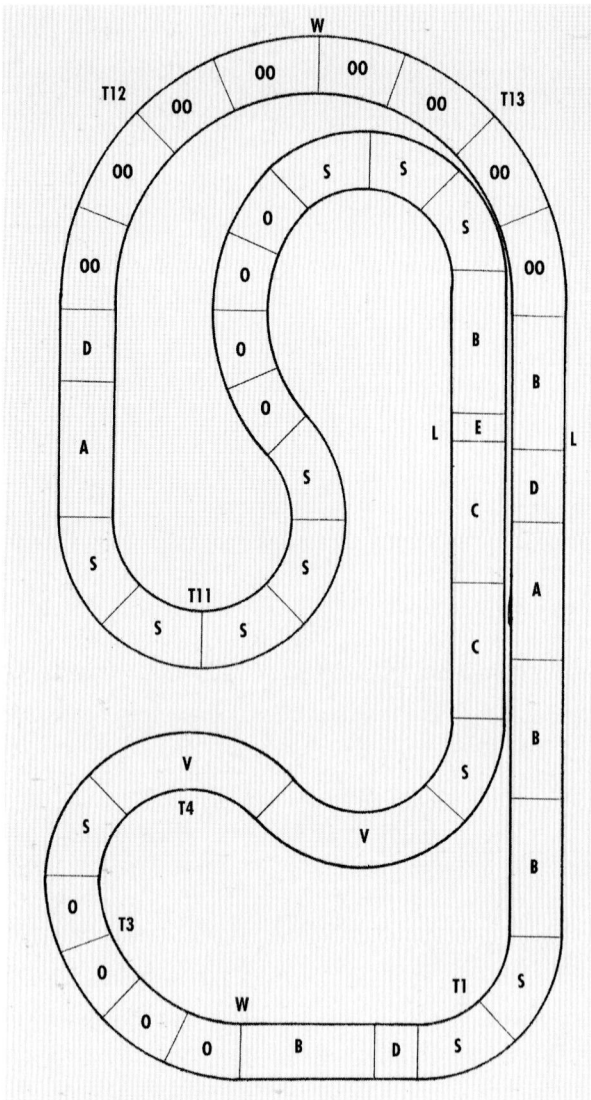

Scalextric Sport, Classic, or SCX track required for a 5x9-foot Indy F1 circuit.

Key	Quantity	Description
H	0	1/2 Standard Curve
S	12	Standard Curve
V	2	Optional Crossover curves (replaces four pieces of "S")
O	8	Outer Curve
OO	8	Outer-Outer Curve
D	3	1/2-Straight
E	1	1/4-Straight
B	4	Full-Straight
C	2	Chicane (Sport C8246 side swipe straights)
A	2	Connector Track

to Stowe. The 4x8-foot plans can be lengthened to 20 feet or more by inserting pairs of straight track sections at the points marked "L," and it can be expanded to 12 feet or more in height by adding pairs of straight track sections at the points marked "W" on the plan.

The plan is designed so most cars can make it through Maggots and Becketts without the need to pull back on the throttle. The cars should also make it through Abbey at near full-throttle, although Abbey is a bit tighter than Maggots or Becketts. The curves are a constant radius on all the corners on the Scalextric/Classic/SCX/NINCO version.

Silverstone in 4x8 feet for Carrera

The Silverstone circa-1950s track for Carrera in 4x8 feet is also designed so most cars can negotiate the gentle curves at Maggots and Becketts at full throttle and convert it into a table-length straight. Most cars will be able to negotiate Abbey curve with just a slight let-off on the throttle. The plan utilizes all four sizes of Carrera curve track sections to produce an increasing radius curve at Woodcote and a decreasing radius curve at Copse.

Parabola Uno in 4x8 feet

This version provides a longer main straight with tighter series of ess curves for a different driving challenge in a minimum space. There is just a single parabola on each of these 4x8-foot tracks, hence the Parabola Uno title. On both versions, the turn at T1 is a standard-size curve, followed by a medium-size curve at T2, and a broad-radius curve at T3. However, at the exit from T3, there is a much tighter standard radius curve at T4. In effect, the path through turns T1, T2, T3, and T4 is from an increasing radius turn to a decreasing radius turn.

Parabola Uno in 4x8 feet for Scalextric Sport, Classic, SCX, or NINCO

There was enough space on the Scalextric Classic, Sport, SCX, and NINCO version to include a second increasing radius turn through T6 and T7.

Parabola Uno in 4x8-feet for Carrera

The broader curves that Carrera offers provide a somewhat smoother path around a track that is particularly noticeable on this plan. Still, there should be no part of the circuit that a car can take flat-out except for the entrance to a straight.

Super 8 Raceway on a Ping-Pong Tabletop

It would seem that 5x9 feet isn't much space, but it's

enough for a four-lane figure 8 using any of the popular brands of 1/32 scale track. That's the size of a common Ping-Pong table, but you can also assemble a 5x10-foot version from two 2 1/2x10-foot portable conference tables placed side-by-side.

Super 8 Raceway for Scalextric Sport, Classic, SCX, or NINCO

I have tried to include as many broad radius curves as possible to make this compact track a fast one. One lane has a full 270-degree of broad radius and the other end has a decreasing radius from outer/outer (R4) to outer (R3) radius curves (or an increasing radius if you are racing the opposite direction). There's also an interesting ess bend in the middle that may be negotiated with a quick blip of the throttle. The upper level track must be supported on 1/8-inch plywood.

Super 8 Raceway for Carrera

The Carrera plan utilizes all four of Carrera's curves. There is a short four-section set of the massive sweeper number 4-size curves that leads to a 210-degree curve at one end, and an increasing radius curve at the opposite end. If you are racing in the other direction, it is a decreasing radius curve. The track will be quite different to drive in each direction, thanks to the two increasing and/or decreasing radius curves.

Indy F1 Circuit on a Ping-Pong Tabletop

A version of this plan appeared in *Racing and Collecting Slot Cars*, and it is the track we use to test every 1/32 scale race car, but it doesn't have banked turns on the broad end.

Indy F1 Circuit on a Ping-Pong Tabletop for Scalextric Sport, Classic, SCX, or NINCO

The plan is a distorted recreation of the Indy F1 course with the turns from the real track marked as "T" on the plan. On the original plan, there is a straight track section in the middle of the broad-radius, 180-degree turn made from eight "O" outer curves and are replaced with "OO" outer-outer curves (Sport R4, part number C8235; SCX number 84030). On this modified plan, the straight is eliminated to make for a smoother powerslide through that curve. The track utilizes all but the innermost sizes of curves that are available from Scalextric

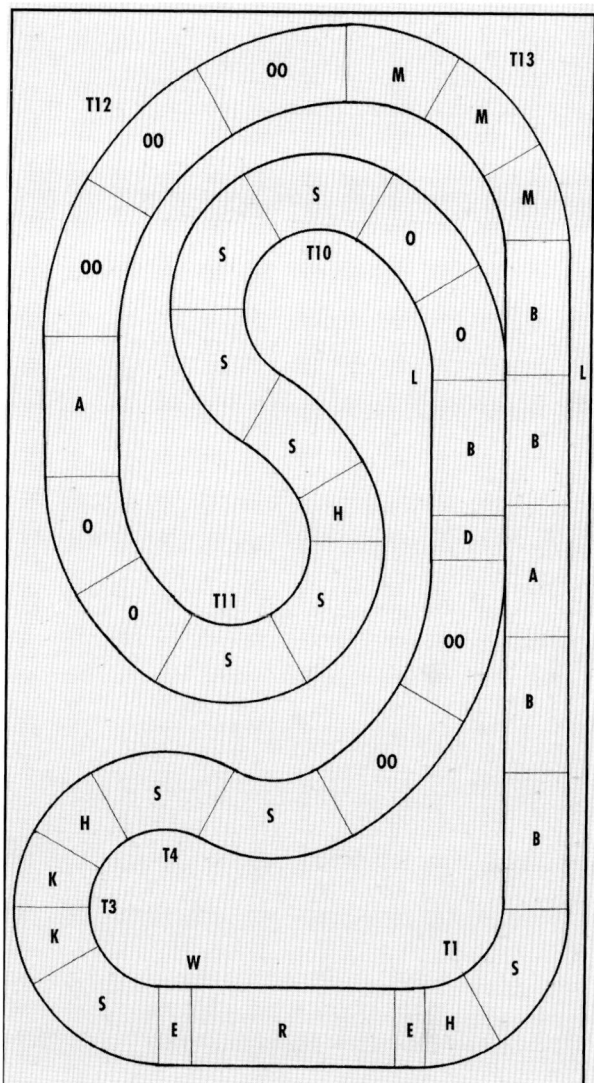

Carrera track required for a 5x9-foot Indy F1 circuit

Key	Quantity	Description
H	3	1/2 Inner Curve
S	10	Inner Curve
K	2	Banked Inner Curves
O	4	Middle Curve
M	3	Banked Middle Curves
OO	5	Outer Curve
OOO	0	Outer-Outer Curve
E	2	1/4-Straight
D	1	1/3-Straight
B	5	Full-Straight
A	2	Connector Track
R	1	Half of Overpass Bridge set

Sport, Scalextric Classic, SCX, or NINCO for a variety of different corners. If you race clockwise around this circuit, turns T3 and T4 are decreasing radius, and turn T10 is an increasing radius. This

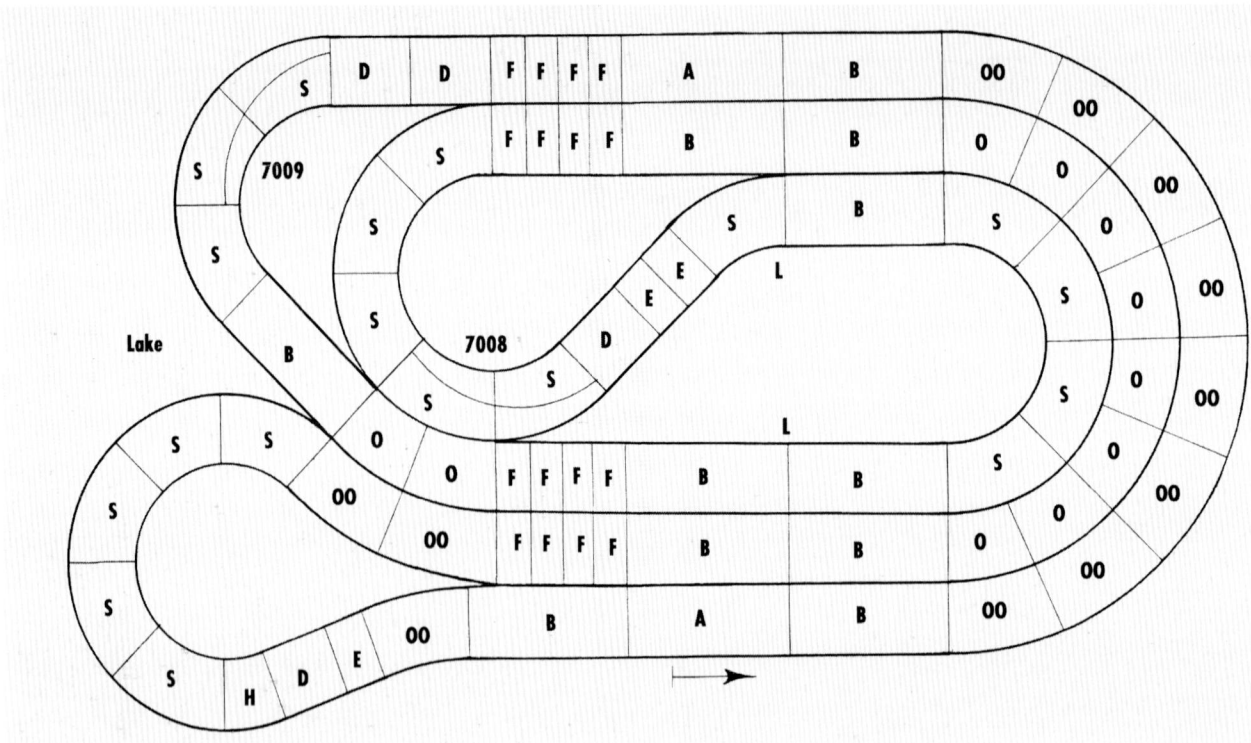

Scalextric Sport, Classic, or SCX track required for a 5x9-foot Interlagos circuit.

Key	Quantity	Description
H	1	1/2 Standard Curve
S*	18	Standard Curve
O	10	Outer Curve
OO	11	Outer-Outer Curve
D*	3	1/2-Straight
E	3	1/4-Straight
F	16	"Short" Straight
B	12	Full-Straight
A	2	Connector Track

*NOTE: If you are using the Scalextric Sport Digital lane-changing system, some of these "S" standard curves may be replaced by lane-changing tracks, along with the adjacent half-straight "D" as a sensor track.

track is one of the most challenging and fun-to-drive tracks possible in this small of an area.

Indy F1 Circuit on a Ping-Pong Tabletop for Carrera

You can reduce the amount of overhang with this slightly modified plan. Because of the wide skid aprons, the track overhangs the 5-foot sides of the table about 4 inches. It features a broad 180-degree turn that, on this plan, has three number 3-size flat curves leading immediately into three Carrera banked number 2-size curves to complete the bend. The curve is a decreasing radius, but because of the bank, cars may be able to negotiate the 180-degrees at more or less the same throttle setting. The track also has the corkscrew at the bottom through the turns marked T3 and T4 that was featured in *Racing and Collecting Slot Cars*. A Carrera overpass bridge track section ("R" on the plan) leads the cars uphill so they can descend through the corkscrew.

Interlagos, Brazil, in 5x9 feet

The Interlagos track near Sao Paulo, Brazil, was one of the most convoluted real racetracks on the planet. There's more information on the real track in Chapter 9. The design can be compressed to squeeze onto a 5x9-foot Ping-Pong tabletop. If you want to put it on two 2 1/2x10-foot (or two 3x10-foot) conference tables, you can add six pieces of straight track to the list of track required.

The curve at the right end looks like six lanes, but it is just three pairs of adjacent lanes. The adjacent tracks serve as skid aprons (borders) for each other, so you will want perfect alignment of the side-by-side

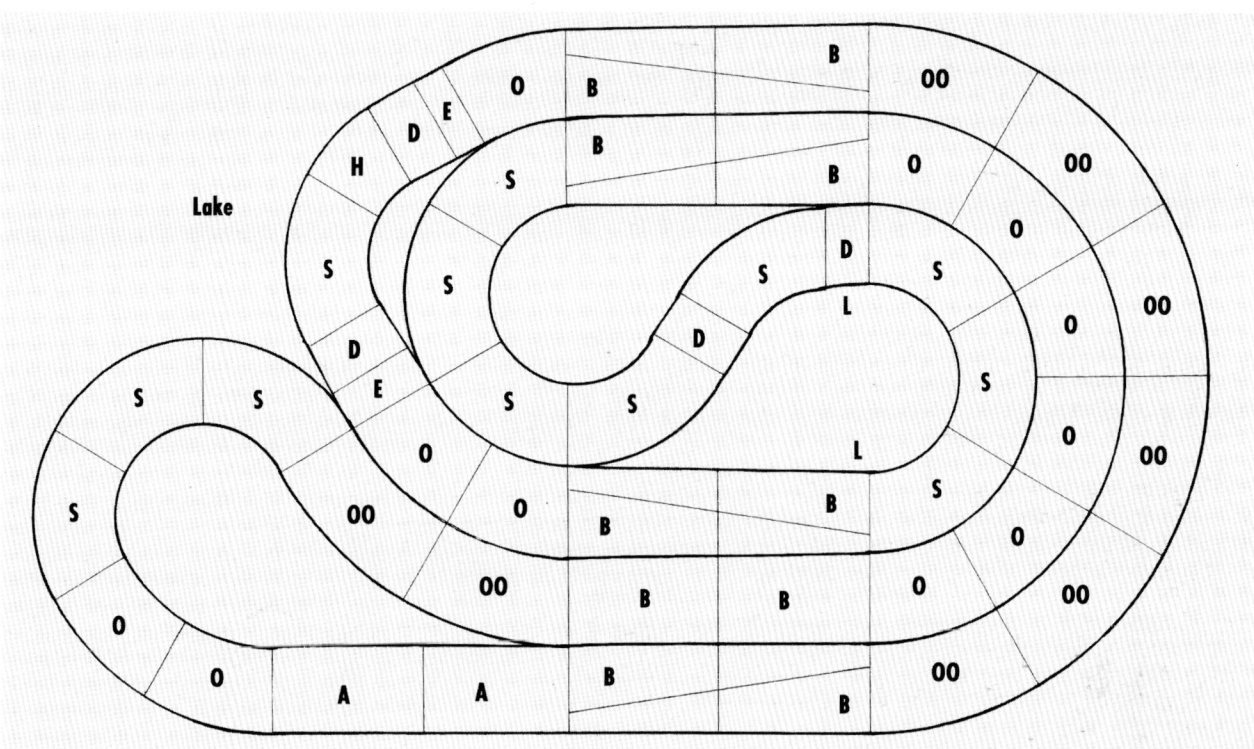

Carrera track required for a 5x9-foot Interlagos circuit.

Key	Quantity	Description
H	1	1/2 Standard Curve
S	18	Standard Curve
O	10	Outer Curve
OO	11	Outer-Outer Curve
D*	3	1/2-Straight
E	3	1/4-Straight
F	16	Short Straight
B*	12	Full-Straight
A	2	Connector Track

*NOTE: If you are using the Carrera Pro-X lane changing system, some pairs of standard-length straights ("B") may be placed with Carrera Pro-X lane-changing tracks.

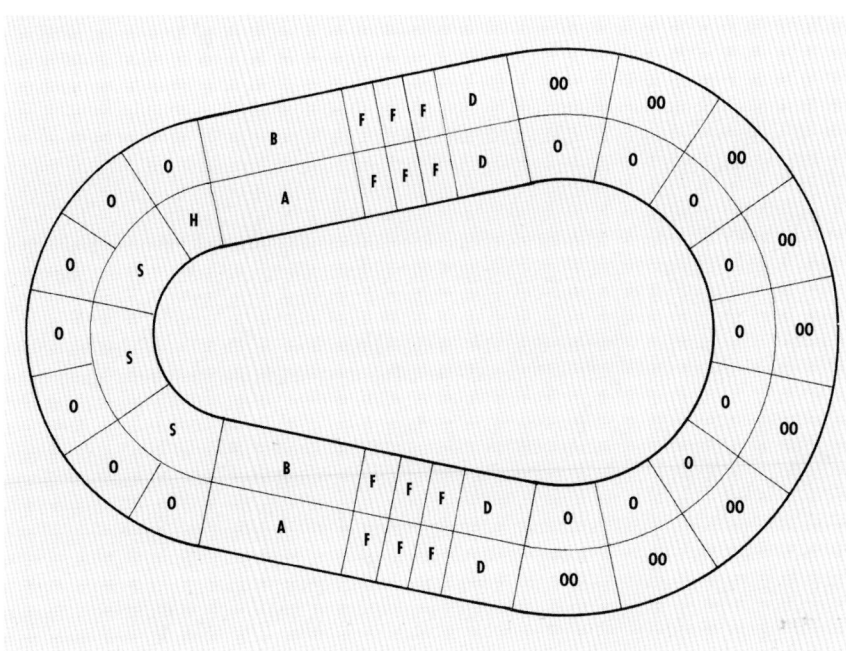

Scalextric Sport, Classic, or SCX track required for a 5x9-foot four-lane Darlington Raceway.

Key	Quantity	Description
H	1	1/2 Standard Curve
S	3	Standard Curve
O	16	Outer Curve
OO	9	Outer-Outer Curve
E	0	1/4-Straight
F	12	"Short" Straight
D	4	1/2-Straight
B	2	Full-Straight
A	2	Connector Track

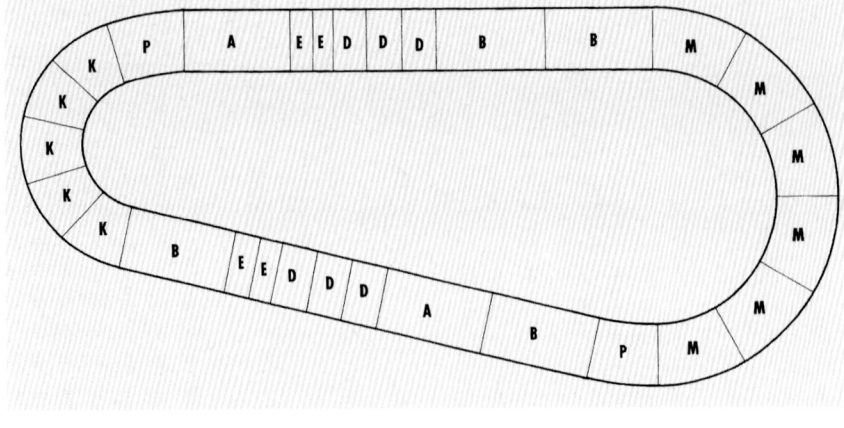

Carrera track required for a 5x9-foot, two-lane Darlington Raceway.

Key	Quantity	Description
K	5	Banked Inner Curve
M	5	Banked Outer Curve
P	1 pair (2)	Banked Outer-Outer Curve
E	4	1/4-Straight
D	6	1/3-Straight
B	4	Full-Straight
A	2	Connector Track

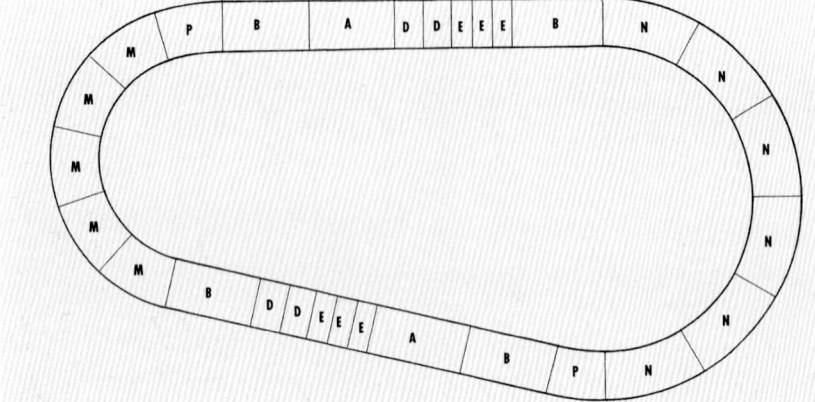

Carrera track required for a 6x11-foot, two-lane Darlington Raceway.

Key	Quantity	Description
M	5	Banked Standard Curve
N	5	Banked Outer Curve
P	1 pair (2)	Banked Outer-Outer Curve
E	6	1/4-Straight
D	4	1/3-Straight
B	4	Full-Straight
A	2	Connector Track

areas. You will also need to cut the borders to fit in those wedge-shaped areas at the ends of the adjacent turns. Both versions have a broad-radius curve at the left. On the Carrera version, there's an increasing radius on the lower left. All other curves on both versions of Interlagos have a constant radius.

Interlagos, Brazil, in 5x9 feet for Scalextric Sport, Classic, SCX, or NINCO

If you decide to assemble the track from Scalextric Classic, Scalextric Sport, or SCX track, I strongly suggest that you attach the track to the tabletop with Scalextric, SCX, or NINCO clips and/or Shoe Goo or silicone caulking once the track is perfectly aligned.

Interlagos, Brazil, in 5x9 feet for Carrera

The Carrera version is a tight squeeze on a 5x9-foot Ping-Pong table. The borders will hang over the edges on three of the four sides of the table. If you assemble the track on a pair of 3x10-foot folding conference tables, there will be plenty of room for the borders to fit within the confines of the table edges.

Darlington Raceway on a Ping-Pong Tabletop

Darlington Raceway is a popular track for NASCAR fans because it's egg-shaped and a break from the traditional ovals. There are plans for simple four-lane ovals for Scalextric Classic and Sport, SCX, and NINCO in *Slot Car Bible*. You can prop up the ends of these brands of track to simulate banking on one end with the other end flat to somewhat create Darlington. With the Carrera version of Darlington in the *Slot Car Bible*, I suggest banking one end with Carrera's banked curve sections and assembling the opposite end flat to simulate the effect of two different size turns.

Darlington Raceway on a Ping-Pong Tabletop for Scalextric Sport, Classic, or SCX

The four-lane plan for Darlington can be assembled from Scalextric Classic and Sport and SCX track except for the two groups of six short straights "F" on the plan. Only Scalextric Classic (part number C8039) and Sport (part number C8236) offer these very short sections. Sport makes a half-straight adapter track, which could be used to mate the track

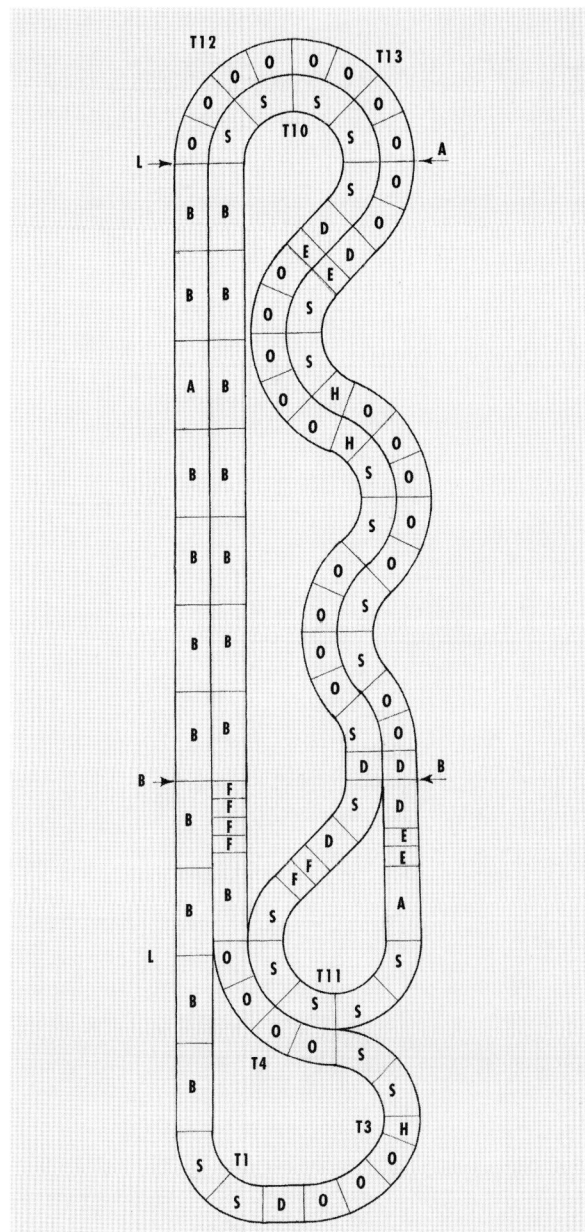
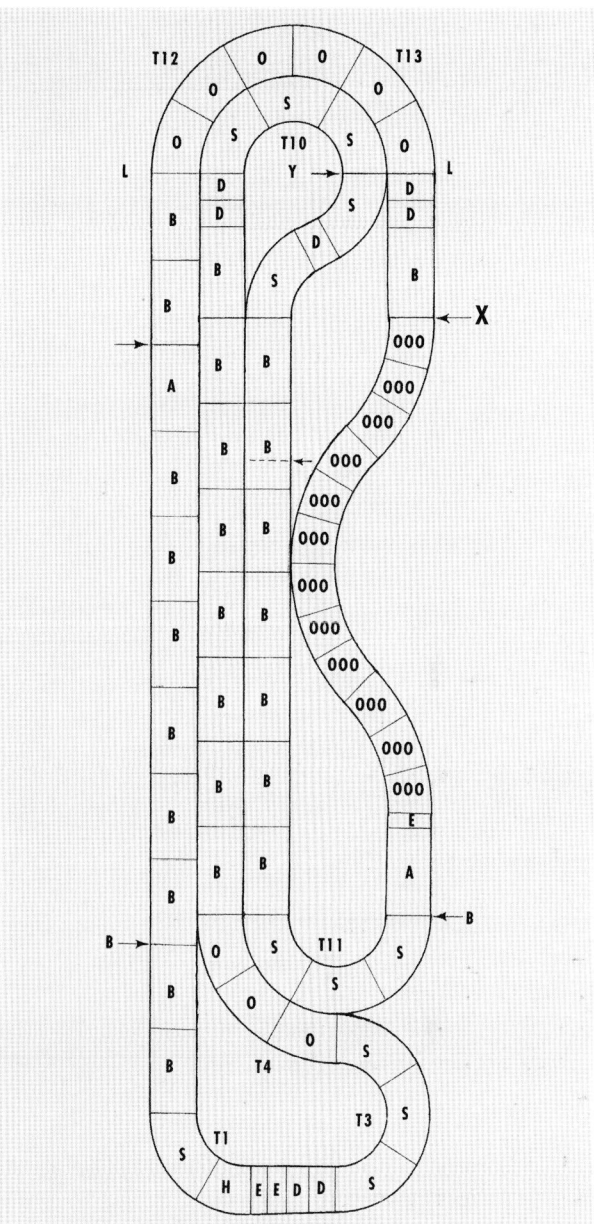

Scalextric Sport, Classic, SCX, or NINCO track required for a 4x16-foot King Snake circuit.

Key	Quantity	Description
H	3	1/2 Standard Curve
S	22	Standard Curve
O	33	Outer Curve
OO	0	Outer-Outer Curve
D	5	1/2-Straight
E	4	1/4-Straight
F	6	Short Straight
B	18	Full-Straight
A	2	Connector Track

Carrera track required for a 4x16-foot King Snake raceway.

Key	Quantity	Description
H	1	1/2 Inner Curve
S	12	Inner Curve
K	0	Banked Inner Curves
O	9	Middle Curve
M	0	Banked Middle Curves
OO	0	Outer Curve
OOO	6 pair (12)	Outer-Outer Curve
E	3	1/4-Straight
D	7	1/3-Straight
B	26	Full-Straight
A	2	Connector Track
R	0	Half of Overpass Bridge set

to SCX. I do not recommend this plan for NINCO because you would have to cut special curves and straights, so it would be far easier and probably just as much fun to drive by making a simple four-lane oval and propping up one end to simulate a banking.

Darlington Raceway on a Ping-Pong Tabletop for Carrera

The Carrera 20579 banked curve ("P" on the plans) with border 20580 is the only curve in the Carrera system that is a half-length curve. The short length makes the near-perfect replicas of Darlington possible. Since the new curve is banked, it can be used with any of Carrera's other banked turns. By using Carrera's number 1-size banked turn (which I feel is too sharp for a banked turn) on one end and their number 2-size banked curve on the other end, you can fit Darlington on a Ping-Pong table. You can try it, but I'd opt for the bank one end/flat the other from *Slot Car Bible* because it would be more fun to drive, at least on the outer three lanes.

Darlington Raceway in 6x11 feet for Carrera

The Carrera banked turns are enjoyable to drive in the 3-size and 4-size (and the outer lane of the number 2-size is fine; the inner is still too sharp for banked turn, in my opinion). You can use the 2- and 3-sized Carrera banked turns to make Darlington, but it will require 6x11 feet, which is an awkward size unless you cut up three sheets of plywood to make a 6x12-foot surface, which could be supported by a Ping-Pong table. It looks like you could drop the 5x9-foot Carrera plan inside the 6x11-foot version. You could do this, but there would be no possible way to make the inner and outer tracks fit snugly. The problem is that Carrera only makes one number 4-size half turn, and you'd need a number 3-size. You could cut your own 3-size half-curve, as shown in *Slot Car Bible*, but the banks put a lot of stress on the track, so this is not recommended. You have two other choices: Use all flat curves with the two plans in this issue, or settle for two lanes or assemble the four-lane Darlington from *Slot Car Bible*.

King Snake Raceway in 4x16-feet

There's enough room on a pair of 4x8-foot pieces of plywood for a pretty fantastic raceway. There are two parallel straights, each almost 13-feet long. The ess bends might seem a bit boring to look at, but the car in the outer lane is constantly moving from a broad radius right turn to a sharp radius left and back to a broad radius right as it negotiates the esses. If you are racing in a clockwise direction around the outer loop, there's only one decreasing-radius turn, and all the other turns have a constant radius. It's the combinations of left-right-left turns that make this track an interesting raceway. Like any other track, it becomes a completely different animal when you race in the opposite direction.

King Snake Raceway in 4x16 feet for Scalextric Sport, Classic, SCX, or NINCO

This track is designed to take advantage of the relatively compact "footprint" of Scalextric Sport, Scalextric Classic, SCX, and NINCO track. At a glance, it's more like a parking lot autocross for two cars, rather than a meander through the woods, but this is about as much racetrack length as you could possibly squeeze into just 4x16 feet.

King Snake Raceway in 4x16 feet for Carrera

The borders will actually hang off the edges a bit if you use Carrera track, but it will fit on that 4-foot-wide table. The turns are numbered to roughly correspond to similar turns on the real Indy Formula 1 track with the addition of the giant ess bend. You will need to custom-cut borders in the areas where the track begins to run parallel to an adjacent track. Cut the outer edges of the borders around T4, the right end of T10, and both ends of T11 into wedge shapes to fit the track. You may

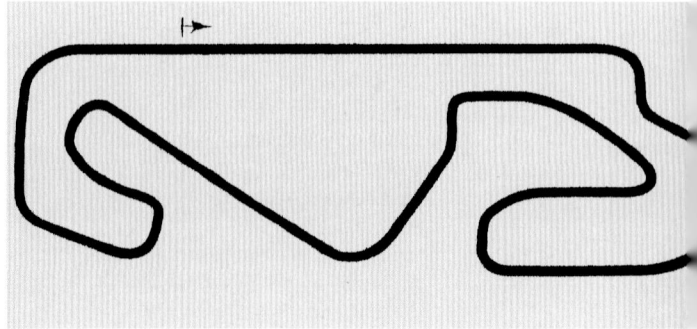

The Catalunya (Barcelona), Spain, F1 Track

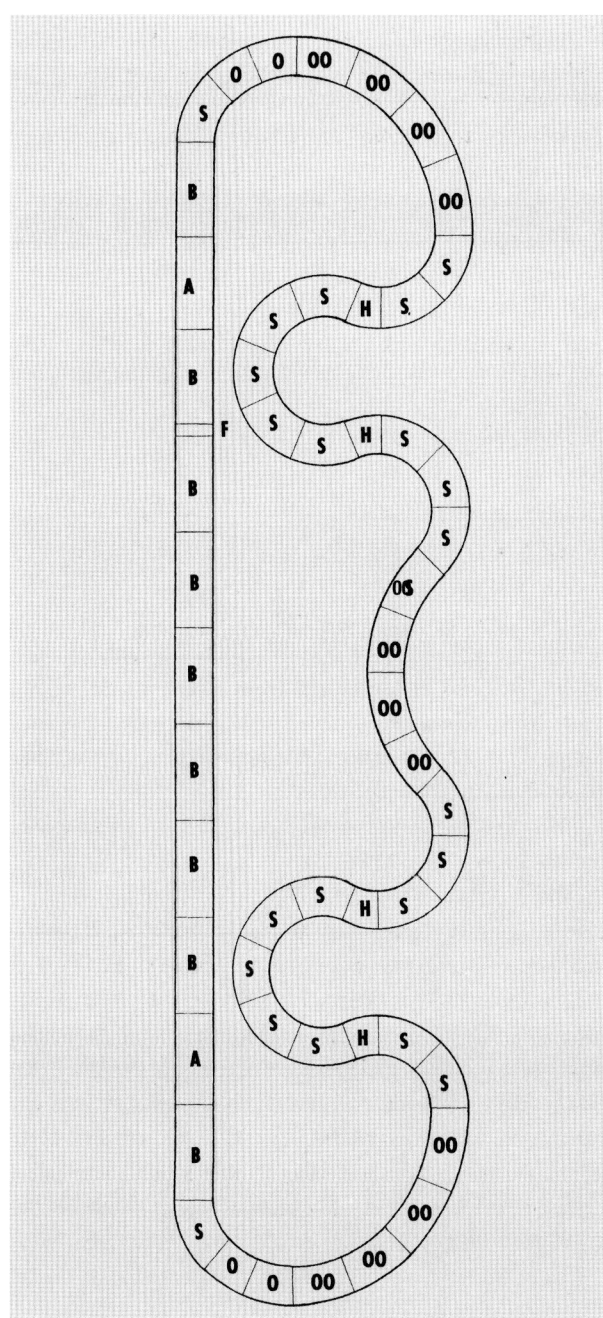

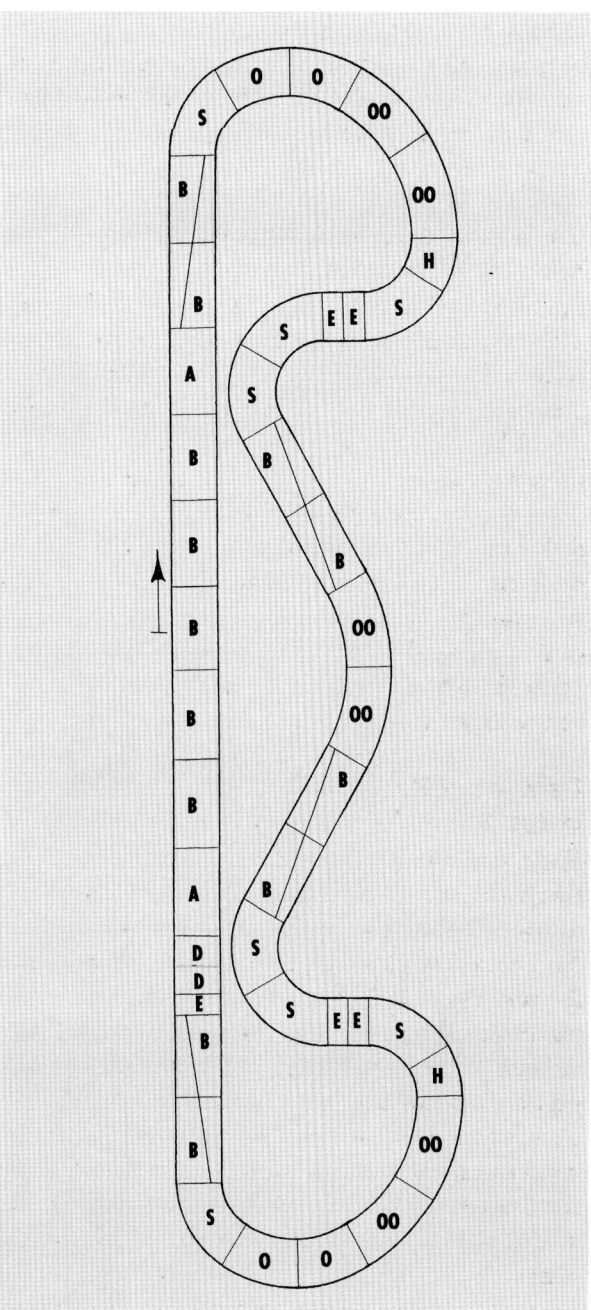

Scalextric Sport, Classic, SCX, or NINCO track required for a 4x16-foot Catalunya (Barcelona) F1 track.

Key	Quantity	Description
H	4	1/2 Inner Curve
S	22	Standard Curve
O	4	Outer Curve
OO	12	Outer-Outer Curve
F	1	"Short" Straight
E	0	1/4-Straight
D	0	1/2-Straight
B	9	Full-Straight
A	2	Connector Track

Carrera track required for a 4x16-foot Catalunya (Barcelona) F1 track.

Key	Quantity	Description
H	2	1/2 Inner Curve
S	8	Inner Curve
O	4	Middle Curve
OO	6	Outer Curve
OOO	0	Outer-Outer Curve
E	5	1/4-Straight
D	2	1/3-Straight
B*	13	Full-Straight*
A	2	Connector Track

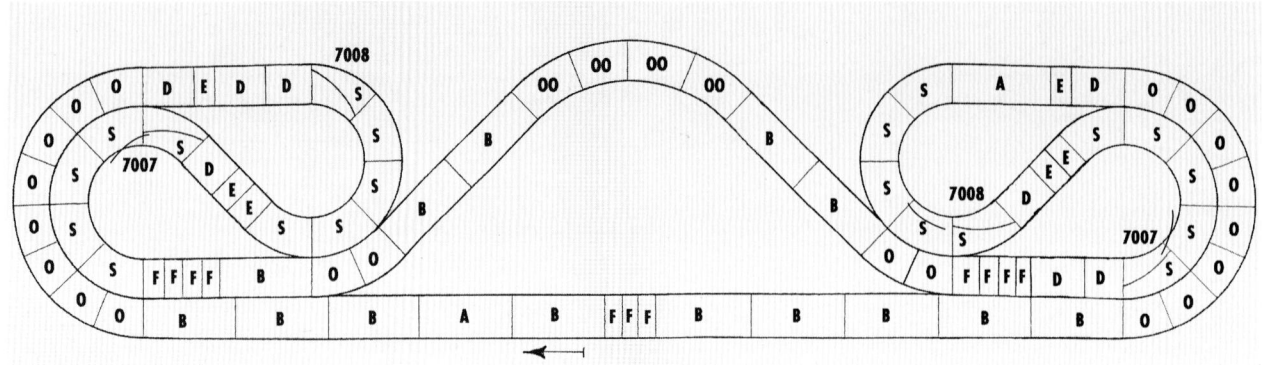

Scalextric Sport, Classic, or SCX track required for a 4x16-foot Double Indy F1 circuit.

Key	Quantity	Description
H	0	1/2 Standard Curve
S*	20	Standard Curve
O	20	Outer Curve
OO	4	Outer-Outer Curve
D*	8	1/2-Straight
E	6	1/4-Straight
F	11	"Short" Straight
B	13	Full-Straight
A	2	Connector Track

*NOTE: If you are using the Carrera Pro-X in lane-changing system some pairs of standard-length.

need to substitute some "E" 1/4 straights for "D" 1/3 straights (and vice versa) to get the track to fit together tightly. With Carrera, you can use the four-lane locking pins to tightly pull everything together. I have included two terminal tracks so drivers can be positioned on opposite sides of the track so each can serve as a corner marshal.

This plan has a lot to offer in such a small space. There is just about as much track as you could possibly squeeze in, but it should make a great race course. There are tight ess bends at the ends and a sweeping right/left/right ess bend assembled for Carrera's number 4 curves that some cars might take flat out. The plan includes a set of Carrera's massive number 4-size curves to make a giant ess bend. The main straight is more than 12 feet long, and each of the three parallel short straights is more than 7 feet long.

With Carrera track, you can have a four-lane banked turn at the far end. Insert one full straight and two 1/3 straights at "X." Remove the two straights near "Y" and replace them with a single 1/3 straight. This will provide enough straight to get the track in and out of the banked turn. Be aware, however, that some of the longer cars, like Fly's Saleen, may need to be trimmed so the ends do not get hung up on the trough created by the banked turn.

Catalunya, Spain, in 4x16 feet

This 4x16-foot plan combines the best of the Parabola Duo and Parabola Uno 4x8-foot plans from earlier in this chapter. It just happens to be very close to the shape of the Catalunya track near Barcelona, Spain. The Catalunya track has a pair of keyhole curves at each end of the main straight. This compact 4x16-foot plan has a similar design. The track was completed in 1991 and replaced Montjuich Park and Jarama as the site for the Spanish round of the F1 series. The track is set in low, rolling hills with sand gravel traps and grass verges beside the track.

The increasing-radius curves are a delight to drive on a 1/32 scale track because the cars can accelerate quicker as they exit the larger radii of the curve. If you run the track in the opposite direction, the curve becomes a decreasing radius curve that allows you to enter quickly, but demands less speed if you expect to make it through the tight end without deslotting.

These 4x16-foot plans have a decreasing radius turn on one end of the straight and an increasing radius turn on the opposite end of the straight. The combination allows the straight to be the longest possible within the given space. It also provides the driving excitement of an increasing radius turn at the end of the straight. Here, that increasing radius is followed immediately by a tighter curve that is half of an ess bend. The ess bend is followed by a very large radius curve that can be taken flat out with most cars, followed by another ess bend and a decreasing radius turn onto the straight.

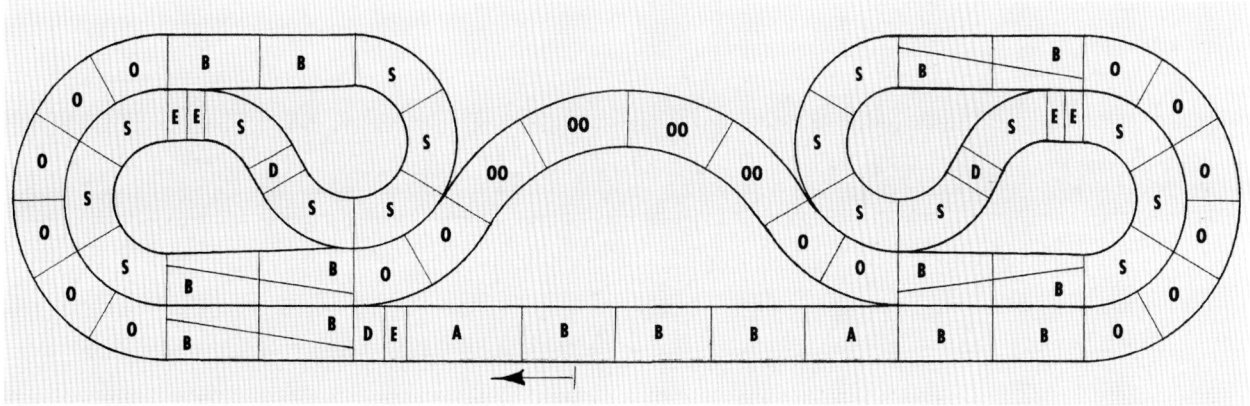

Carrera track required for a 4x16-foot Indy F1 circuit.

Key	Quantity	Description
H	0	1/2 Inner Curve
S	16	Inner Curve
O	16	Middle Curve
OO	4	Outer Curve
OOO	0	Outer-Outer Curve
E	5	1/4-Straight
D	3	1/3-Straight
B	15	Full-Straight
A	2	Connector Track
R	0	Half of Overpass Bridge set

Catalunya in 4x16 feet for Scalextric Sport, Classic, SCX, or NINCO

This version of Catalunya is a very twisting snake-like track that will require far more throttle changes than the Carrera version. There are so many curves in so tight of a space that there was no room for the Scalextric Sport Digital lane-changing tracks. You could replace the three OOO curves and three of the S curves with a pair of half-curves (H) and some straights to fit a lane-changer on the right side of the plan. There's room for a second lane-changer on either end of the straight.

Catalunya in 4x16 feet for Carrera

There are two Carrera Pro-X digital lane-changers on this plan. They can be replaced by two pairs of standard straights.

Double Indy F1 Circuit in 4x16 feet

These plans are essentially two of the 4x8-foot versions with one plan mirrored and the two connected with largest possible radius sweeper curve. The 4x16-foot track can be assembled on two pieces of 4x8 plywood placed end to end.

Both plans include lane-changers, which allow you to run up to four cars at once with the Carrera version and up to six cars with the Scalextric version. The lane-changers are positioned to allow the shortest possible route around the track. Of course, they can also be used for passing.

Double Indy F1 Circuit in 4x16 feet for Scalextric Sport, Classic, SCX, or NINCO

If you opt to assemble the track from Scalextric Classic, Scalextric Sport, or SCX track, I would strongly suggest that you attach the track to the tabletop with Scalextric, SCX, or NINCO clips and/or Shoe Goo or silicone caulking once the track is perfectly aligned.

On the Scalextric Sport plan, you have the option of using either two standard 45-degree curves or one 90-degree lane-changer at the locations marked with part numbers.

Double Indy F1 Circuit in 4x16 feet for Carrera

The Carrera version will be a higher speed track because the curves are larger. The sweeper curve across the center should be particularly fun to drive because it is the center part of a massive ess bend.

If you opt for Carrera's Pro-X digital system, the lane-changers are two lengths of straight with a diagonal line indicating that it is a lane-changing track. You can use either two standard straights or lane-changers at these locations.

CHAPTER 9
REAL RACETRACKS FOR YOUR HOME

The Scalextric Sport (shown) and Carrera versions of Monaco, with its uphills and downhills, is one of the most interesting and exciting tracks I have assembled.

You are racing exact replicas of real racing cars, so why not race on a replica of a real racetrack? The real tracks are usually two or more miles around, which in 1/32 scale, would mean a 330-foot-long racetrack. Even if you had the space, it would be a boring track to drive because the straights would be so long. Most 1/32 scale cars will reach top speed in about 12 to 16 feet, so there's really no point in having a straight longer than that. The tracks in this chapter range from about 35 to 135 feet, but most are 40 to 45 feet per lap.

The plans in this chapter usually include the longest possible straight in the available space. If you have the space, you can increase the length of the straights by inserting pairs of straights on the opposite sides of the plan at the track joints marked "L" on the plans. On some plans, the width can also be increased by adding pairs of straights at the joints marked "W" on the plans.

Finding the Space to Race

All the tracks in this chapter are designed to fit on some combination of Ping-Pong or conference tables or 4x8-foot sheets of plywood so the tables, as well at the track, can be portable. Ping-Pong tables are 5x9 feet, and conference tables with folding legs are available in 2 1/2- and 3-foot widths and in 8-, 10-, and 12-foot lengths. A few of the plans could be made a bit smaller, but most are as tight as possible in the given space. However, feel free to use the plans as a starting point and modify them to sit larger or smaller spaces.

On most of the plans, I have included connector tracks where the controllers plug in on opposite sides of the track. This will allow two drivers to corner marshal cars that leave the slot without running around the track. However, you must be certain that only one controller is plugged into each lane or a short circuit may result. I recommend that

The original Scalextric Sport version of the track from the *Slot Car Bible* was flat with Lowes hairpin tucked next to the back straight. The revised version is much more like driving the real course.

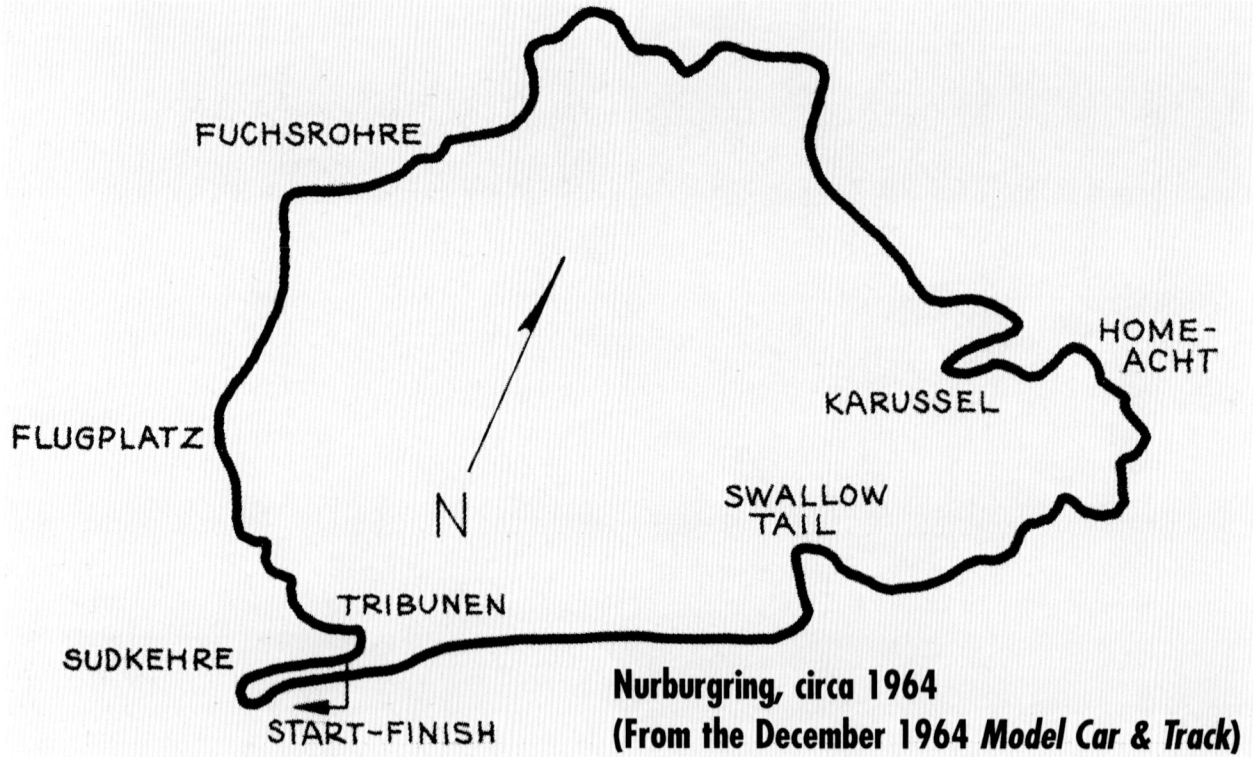

Nürburgring, circa 1964.

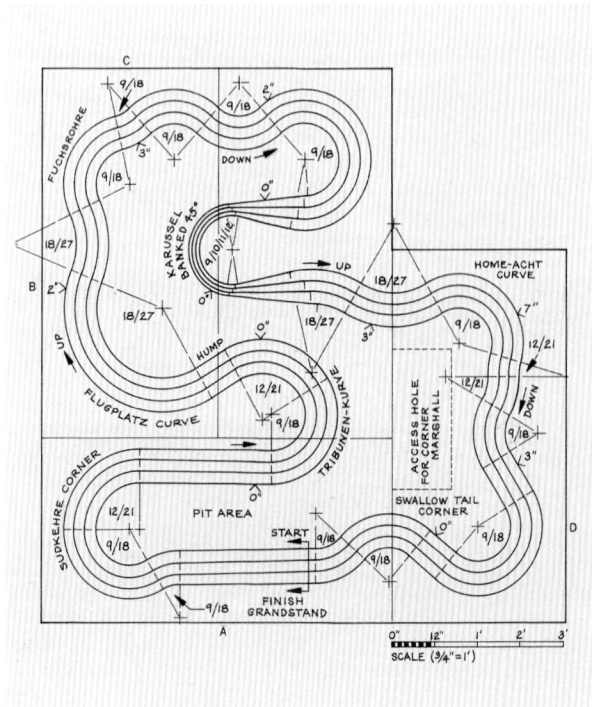

The routed version of the Nürburgring track can be assembled from four 4x8-foot sheets of MDF board or MDO plywood.

you put tape over the socket that is not in use on each connector track.

Which Brand of Track?

Some of the plans in this chapter include variations for the older Revell and Strombecker track sections for routing the track from particle board, MDF, or MDO (as described in *Slot Car Bible*), as well as plans for the currently available Scalextric Sport, Scalextric Classic, SCX, and Carrera.

The plans for the Scalextric track sections can be used for NINCO, but the NINCO track sections are wider and longer, so a bit more space will be needed and you may need some short pieces of straight track to get everything to join together perfectly.

The plans for Carrera track can be used as a guide to assemble the track from Artin track sections because both brands have similar geometry. The Artin sections are much smaller, so the track should require less space. You may need short pieces of straight track to get everything to join together properly.

I recommend that you buy *World Motor Racing Circuits: A Spectator's Guide*, by Peter Higham and

KEY PLAN NO. 2

WIDE LINES INDICATE LANE CENTERS:

THIN LINES INDICATE POINTS WHERE CURVES BEGIN AND END TO GUIDE WHEN ROUTING:

CURVE STARTS AT THIS POINT:

SMALL + INDICATES CENTER OF CURVE:

IN CROWDED AREAS CURVE IS INDICATED:

ALL LANES ARE SPACED ON THREE-INCH CENTERS UNLESS NOTED (I.E., IN CHICANE AREAS).

ALL CURVE RADII ARE INDICATED NEAR CURVE CENTERPOINT (+). IF LANES ARE ON STANDARD THREE-INCH CENTERS, ONLY INNER AND OUTER RADII ARE SHOWN (I.E., A CURVE MARKED: WOULD HAVE RADII OF 9", 12", 15" and 18").

ANY SPECIAL LANE CENTER SPACING ON CURVES IS MARKED.

ANY SUGGESTED CHANGES IN HEIGHT OF TRACK ABOVE LEVEL ARE INDICATED: 2"

(THESE FOUR LANES ARE TWO INCHES ABOVE TABLE TOP LEVEL.)

Key to Markings for Routed, Course

The tracks in this chapter are designed to be routed from particle board, MDO, or MDF board.

Bruce Jones, to learn more about any of these tracks and others. The book does not include plans for Mid-Ohio, Warwick Farm, Oulton Park, Nassau, or South Africa, but the 68 plans include the other tracks in this chapter and dozens more. It has full-color plans for each of the tracks, including most of the famous American ovals and tri-ovals. The plans indicate the gear and speed for each corner. There is also an elevation profile for each course so you can see which parts of the circuit are on hills and which are flat. The history of each track is outlined and describes how the circuit has changed over the years. The results of all the major races are also included.

Two Lanes or Four? Two Cars or Six?

Most of the plans are designed so you can assemble them as four-lane tracks. If you are using digital lane-changing, you'll only need two lanes (to race up to six cars at a time), as described later in this chapter and in Chapter 3. Or you may opt for two lanes, rather than four. If you opt to assemble just a two-lane version of either of these plans, I would recommend you pick the outer two lanes, rather than the inner, because there is a greater variety of curves on the outer two lanes.

Racing Four to Six Cars at Once

Some of the plans in this chapter include the locations of optional lane-changing sections for the

TRACK SECTIONS NEEDED FOR "COLLECTOR" BRANDS

BRAND	SCALE	LAYOUT SIZE	STRAIGHT TRACK REQUIRED*	CURVED TRACK REQUIRED†	AVERAGE LENGTH LAP
Strombecker	1/32 or 1/24	12' X 12'	28 full straight 4 half straight	27 reg. curve 12 half curve 66 outer curve	55'
Kal-Kar	1/32 or 1/24	12' X 12'	12' 4 lane straight section	5½ full circles 4 lane	53'
Varney (2 lane only)	1/32 or 1/24	12' X 12'	22 sections	36 standard	50'
VIP (2 lane only)	1/32	12' X 12'	26 sections	36 standard	51'

These are track sections needed for the collector brands.

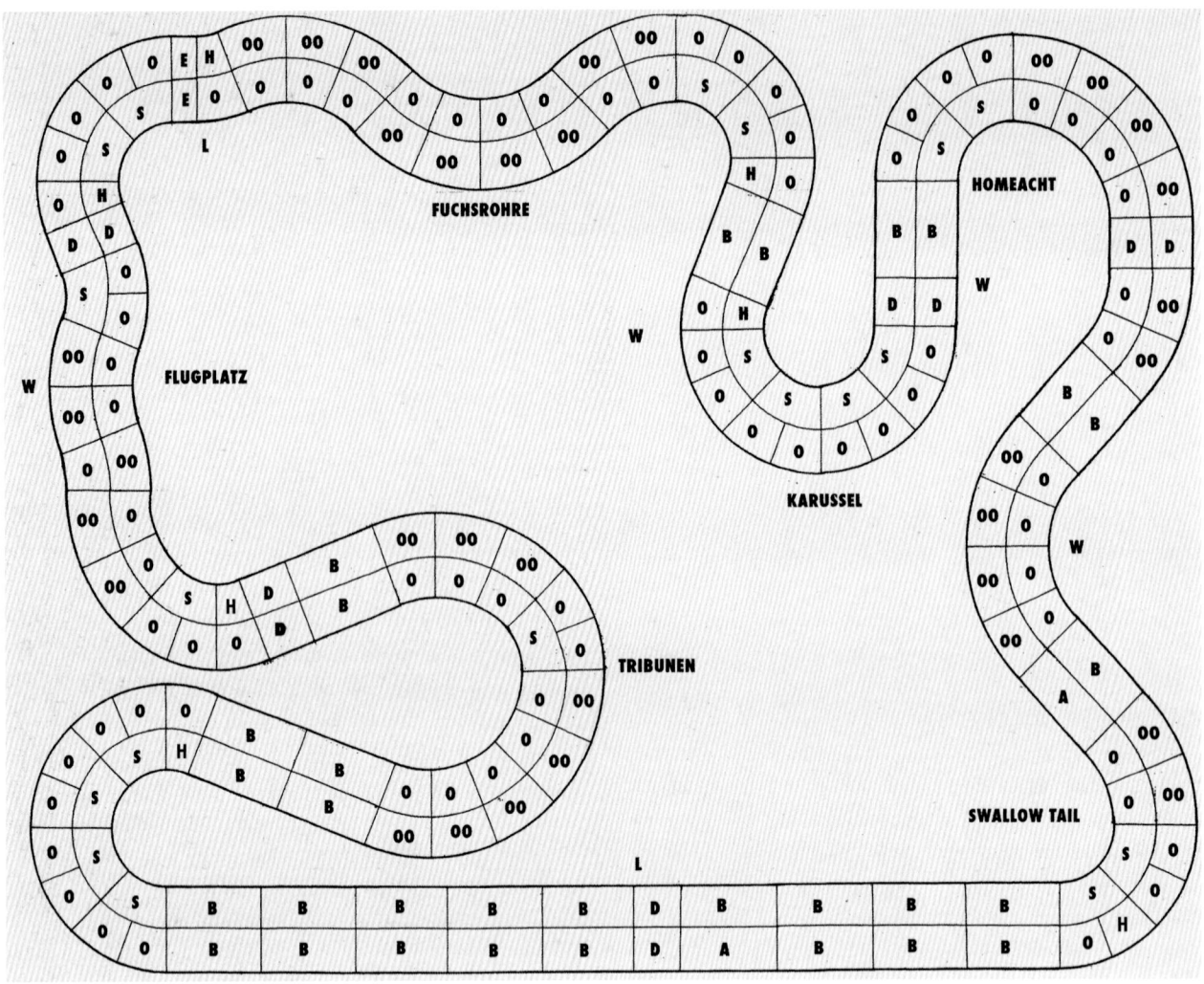

Above and next page: Scalextric Sport, Classic, SCX, NINCO track required for a 12x15-foot Nürburgring circuit.

Key	Quantity	Description
R	2	Sport-brand C8201 Hairpin Curve (see text)
H	1	1/2 Standard Curve
S	7	Standard Curve
V	2	Optional Crossover curves (replaces four pieces of "S")
O	22	Outer Curve
OO	15	Outer-Outer Curve
E	0	1/4-Straight
D	0	1/2-Straight
B	30	Full-Straight
C	4	Sport-brand C8246 Side Swipe Straights (must be used with "R", see text)
A	2	Connector Track

Scalextric Sport Digital system that allows you to run six cars at once, or for the Carrera Pro-X system that allows you to run up to four cars in each lane. These plans include positions for the lane-changing sections to provide what I believe will provide the best replication of real racing. You can add lane changers to most of the plans in this chapter by locating them using the same principles.

You will see that the Scalextric Sport Digital system has lane-changers located only on a pair (90 degrees) of standard curves. The Scalextric system has a half-straight before each curve to provide the location for the track sensors that the car triggers to change lanes. The Scalextric system is then only operational in one direction. There are four different Scalextric lane-changing tracks and the part numbers (7007, 7008, 7009, or 7010) are shown where they might be most effective. I have identified the track sections as standard curves (with an "S"), as well as with the curved diagonal line so you can

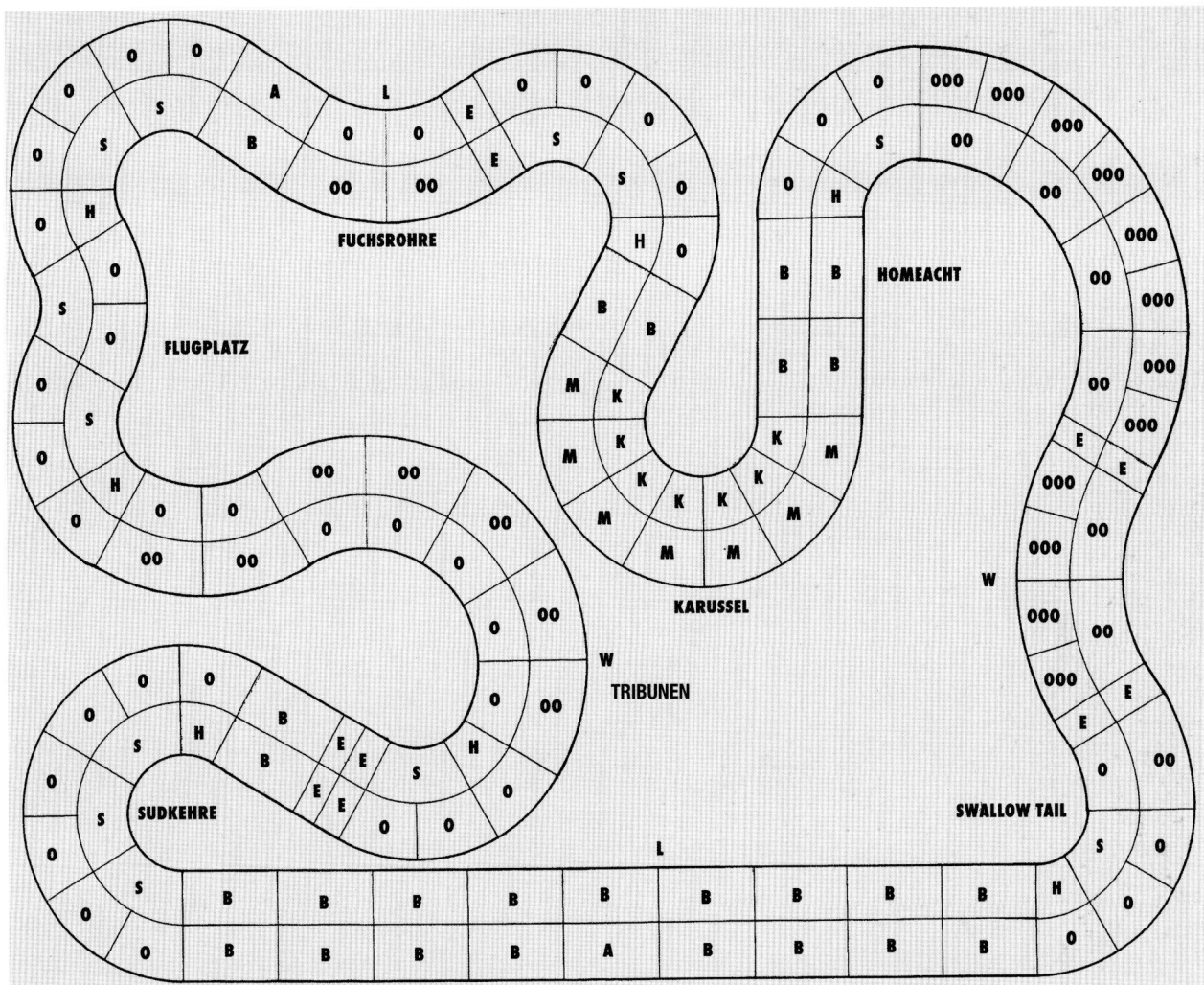

Carrera track required for a 12x15-foot Nürburgring circuit

Key	Quantity	Description
H	7	1/2 Inner Curve
S	12	Inner Curve
K	7	Banked Inner Curve
O	41	Middle Curve
M	7	Banked Middle Curve
OO	16	Outer Curve
OOO	6 pair	(12) Outer-Outer Curve
N	0	Banked Outer Curve
E	6	1/4-Straight
D	4	1/3-Straight
B	26	Full-Straight
A	2	Connector Track

choose either standard or lane-change sections at those locations. I have also provided what should be the proper part number for the lane-changer.

The Carrera system places the lane-changers only on straights and it requires full straights. There are only two Carrera lane-changers, a left and a right. The lane-changers are identified as standard-length straights ("B") on the plan so you can substitute standard track sections if you do not want to use Pro-X. The Carrera Pro-X part numbers for the lane changer section are 30308 for the right and 30306 for the left. These sections are shown on the plans in the direction that works the best. The lane-changers are something you may want to experiment with. You may, for example, prefer to race with the lane changers at the beginning, rather than at the end of the straights.

The Nürburgring

The Nürburgring plans are based on the original road circuit that was opened in 1927 and was

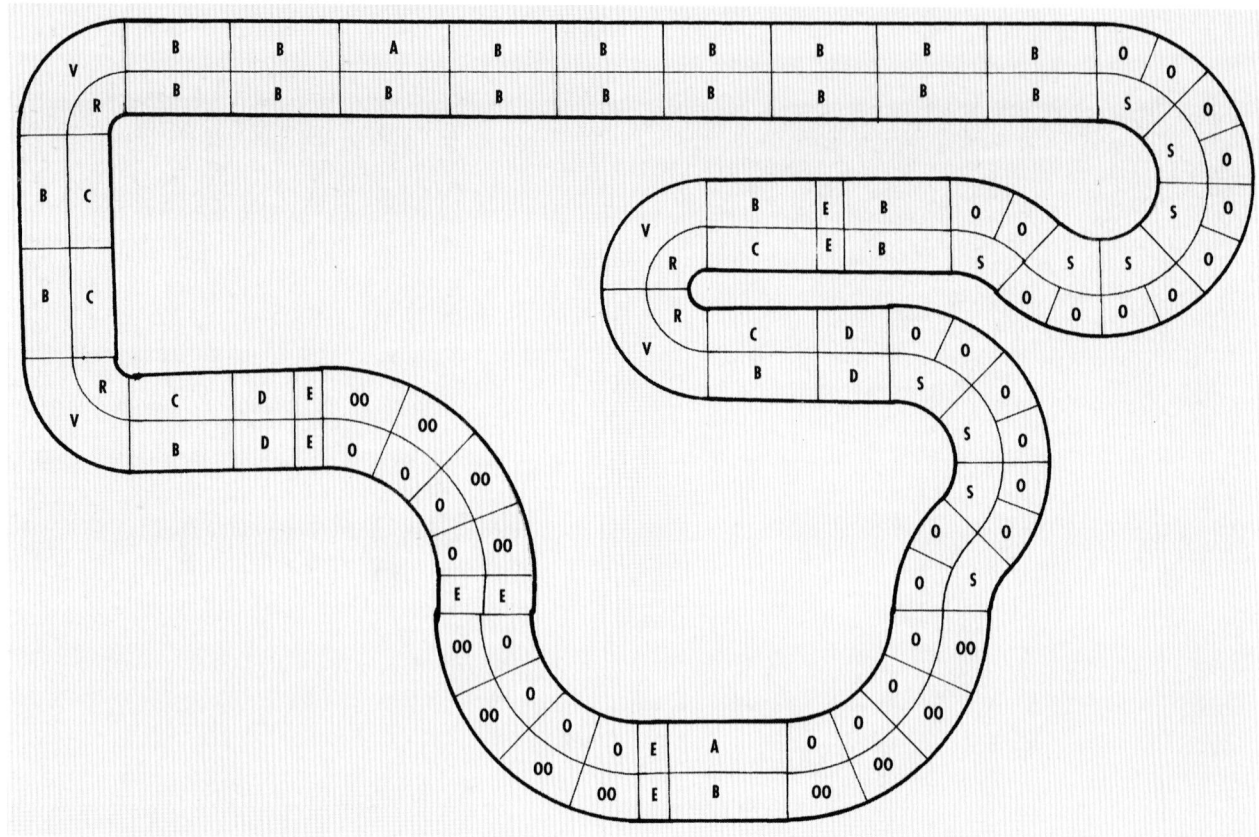

Scalextric Classic, Sport, SCX, or NINCO track required for a 9 1/2x14-foot, four-lane Monaco circuit

Key	Quantity	Description
R	4	Sport-brand C8201 Hairpin Curve (see text)
S	9	Standard Curve
V	4	Optional Crossover curves (replaces four pieces of "S")
O	32	Outer Curve
OO	12	Outer-Outer Curve
E	8	1/4-Straight
D	2	1/2-Straight
B	24	Full-Straight
C	6	Sport-brand C8246 Side Swipe Straights (must be used with "R", see text)
A	4	Connector Track

replaced with the newer purpose-built road racing course in 1984.

The Nürburgring for Scalextric Sport, Classic, SCX, and NINCO

I have tried to include as many broad radius curves as possible to better simulate the actual paths the cars take around the track, rather than imitate the shape of the real track. If you travel around the course clockwise, the Sudkehre is a steady, medium radius curve, but Tribunen is a fast-in, fast-out curve with a tight apex. The esses at Flugplatz are made with the largest radius curves available, as is the sweeping curve through Fuchsrohre. The Karussel could be elevated slightly to simulate the banking on the real curve. Homeacht is an increasing radius turn, leading to another sweeping curve and into the decreasing radius curve at Swallow Tail.

The Nürburgring for Carrera

The Nürburgring for Carrera track utilizes their broad radius curves wherever possible to recreate the speeds of this fast circuit. Traveling clockwise, Sudkehre is a relatively tight corner that leads into an increasing radius curve at Tribunen and a series of fast ess bends at Flugplatz. Fuchsrohre is a medium-radius bend followed by the tighter right curve that leads into the Karussel. The Karussel itself utilizes Carrera's unique banked curves. One of the few banked turns tight enough to warrant the use of that Carrera inner (number 1-size, marked "K" on the plan) track section. The curves leading into and out

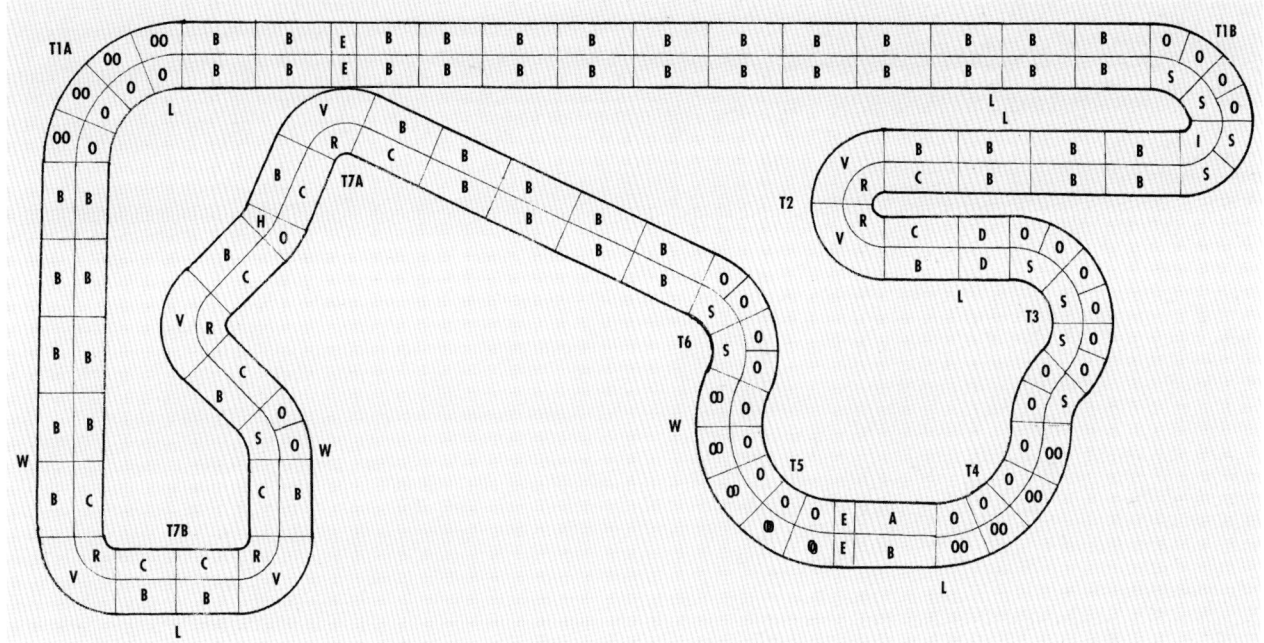

Scalextric Sport, Classic, or SCX track required for a 9x20-foot, four-lane Monaco circuit.

Key	Quantity	Description
I	1	Inner Curve
R	6	Sport-brand C8201 Hairpin Curve (see text)
H	1	1/2 Standard Curve
S	11	Standard Curve
V	6	Optional Crossover curves (replaces four pieces of "S")
O	32	Outer Curve
OO	9	Outer-Outer Curve
E	4	1/4-Straight
D	2	1/2-Straight
B	56	Full-Straight
C	6 pair (12)	Sport-brand C8246 Side Swipe Straights (must be used with "R", see text)
A	4	Connector Track

of the Karussel will both be slightly off camber because there is not quite enough room for the banking to completely flatten out. Homeacht is another increasing-radius curve with the ultra-broad right-hand Carrera number 4-size (marked "OOO" on the plan) curves leading to another number 4-size curve to the right, and down to the decreasing radius turn at Swallow Tail.

Monaco

There are several plans for 9x12- and 9x14-foot versions of Monaco for both Scalextric/Sport/SCX/NINCO and for Carrera track in *Slot Car Bible*. Each of those plans is for a two-lane track. The plans here for Scalextric/Sport/SCX/NINCO illustrate how to expand the two-lane track into a four-lane, and how to expand the track from 9x14 to 9 1/2x20 feet. There is no two-lane 9 1/2x20-foot Scalextric/Sport/SCX/NINCO track here. You'll have to build the outside lane to have the best of Monaco, including the racing line hairpin at Station/Lowes. Also, there is no four-lane version of the Carrera track because that track is too wide to try to squeeze four lanes of Monaco into this relatively small space.

The turns are marked by numbers on the plan to correspond to the similar turns in *Slot Car Bible*. Turns T1A (St. Devote) and Turn T7A (Tabac) are new to the 9 1/2x20-foot versions of Monaco. T1B is Mirabeau, T2 is Station/Lowes, T3 is Portier, T4 and T5 are the sweeper through the tunnel, T6 the chicane, T7A is Tabac, and T7B is Gasworks/LaRascasse.

Monaco for Scalextric Sport, Classic, SCX, or NINCO

The first two plans are four-lane versions of the two-lane track in *Slot Car Bible*. The first fits the same 9 1/2x14-foot space, and the second is expanded to fit a 9 1/2x20-foot space. The larger plan allows Turns T1A and T7A to be included. The track between turns T1B and T2 was revised to allow room for four

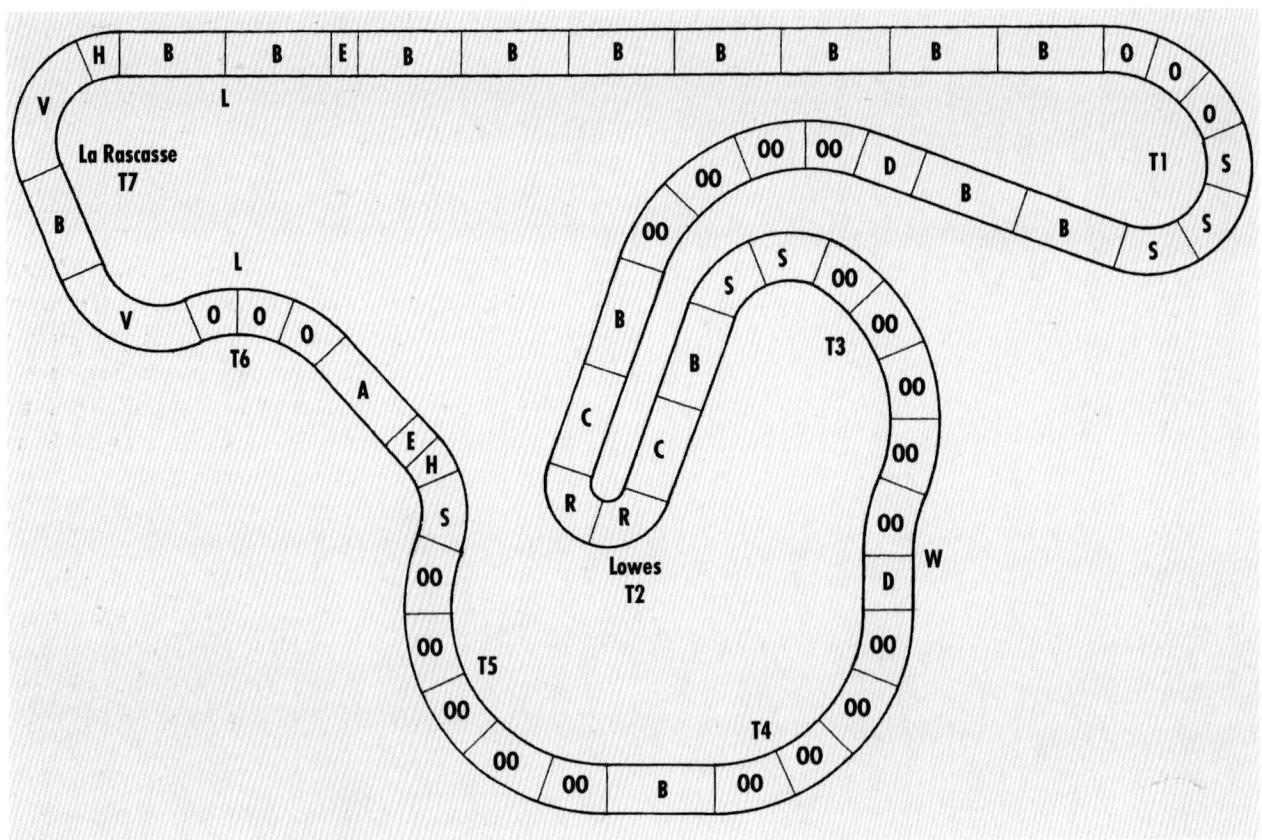

Scalextric Sport, Classic, SCX, or NINCO track required for a 9 1/2x14-foot, two-lane Monaco circuit.

Key	Quantity	Description
I	0	Inner Curve
R	2	Sport-brand C8201 Hairpin Curve
H	2	1/2 Standard Curve
S	6	Standard Curves
V	2	Optional Crossover curves (replaces four pieces of "S")
O	6	Outer Curve
OO	18	Outer-Outer Curve
E	2	1/4-Straight
D	2	1/2-Straight
B	15	Full-Straight
C	2	Sport-brand C8246 Side Swipe Straights (must be used with "R")|
A	1	Connector Track

lanes. I have included the Scalextric Sport number C8201 hairpin (chicaned) curves at "R" in the ess bends with straight chicane track sections (C8246 side swipe straights) at "C," with a set in each lane. If you assemble the track with SCX or NINCO sections, you will need to use standard and outer curves in these areas and replace the straights with half-length straights. I have also indicated that you can use the Scalextric Sport C8201 racing curve crossover at "V" on the inner lane only to provide a racing line through that section of the course.

The third Scalextric/Sport/SCX/NINCO plan for Monaco is the version I assembled with uphills and downhills. You could certainly do that with any of the other versions, as well. I raised the curve at Mirabeau (T1) 9 inches and needed only a relatively mild 8 percent uphill grade down the main straight. The track can then descend 4 1/2 inches to Lowes (T2) and then another 4 1/2 inches to T3. The system, with Woodland Scenics foam products, is shown in Chapter 7 and in *Slot Car Bible*.

The track is an absolute delight to drive. There's an extra curve between Mirabeau (T1) and Lowes (T2) that was needed to get the extra length of track for the descent. The uphill grade increases the effective length of the straight because you can keep it on full throttle for longer than you think because T1 is

This Monaco track has Woodland Scenics supports for the uphills leading to the Mirabeau Hotel in the far upper left, and then downhill to the Lowes hairpin in the far right.

a decreasing radius, so you can dive deeper than it appears at the end of the straight. The descent is surprisingly rapid because of the broad radius between T1 and T2, but you have to brake to pivot the tail of the car around the hairpin at Lowes (T2) before easing the throttle back on full to drift around T3. Back off on the throttle for the jog between T3 and T4, then go back on it for a sustained drift all the way through T4 and T5 (the Tunnel curve at Monaco) where another tight kink can catch you before you accelerate again to T6. Gently negotiate the racing line curve through LaRascasse (T7) before hammering it on up the hill again.

Monaco for Scalextric Sport Digital

The fourth Scalextric Monaco plan includes suggested locations for the Scalextric Sport digital lane changers, but otherwise it is identical to the previous plan. I included a pair of crossover curves at LaRascasse (T1) to include a racing line corner. Those curves were replaced with Scalextric Sport Digital lane-changing tracks.

Monaco for Carrera

This expansion of the 9x14-foot Carrera track in *Slot Car Bible* to 9x20 feet allows room for turns T1A and T7A to be included. I opted for the Carrera number 4 sweeper curves for both of these turns and for the first half on the T4 tunnel curve. This version shows a one-level track, but you can put an uphill down the straight, and a downhill between T1A and T2, as shown in *Slot Car Bible*.

Monaco for Carrera Pro-X Digital

The second plan for Carrera track includes suggested locations for the Carrera Pro-X digital system's two-straight-long lane-changers. You may discover that you prefer the lane-changers in different locations after you have raced on the track for a few hours.

Oulton Park

Oulton Park is an interesting circuit for model car racing because it is possible to duplicate the general challenge of the majority of the circuit's corners. The increasing radius curve at Esso Bend, the sweeping right hander at Druids Corner, and the decreasing radius turn at Lodge Corner are all recreated on the two-lane plans for modern brands of sectional plastic track.

Oulton Park for Scalextric Sport, Classic, SCX, or NINCO

The plan for Scalextric Sport, Classic, SCX, and NINCO track is designed to use the largest possible curves. If you race clockwise, Esso Bend is an increasing radius curve that is fun to drive. The kink at Clay Hill can probably be considered part of the straight because the cars will brake there for the sweeping Druids Corner. Lodge Corner is a tricky decreasing radius curve.

Oulton Park for Carrera

The plan for Carrera track also takes advantage of Carrera's broad curves. The Carrera number 4 curve is used to make an incredible sweeping curve at Druids Corner, at Lodge Corner as the beginning of a tricky decreasing radius curve, and at Esso Bend as

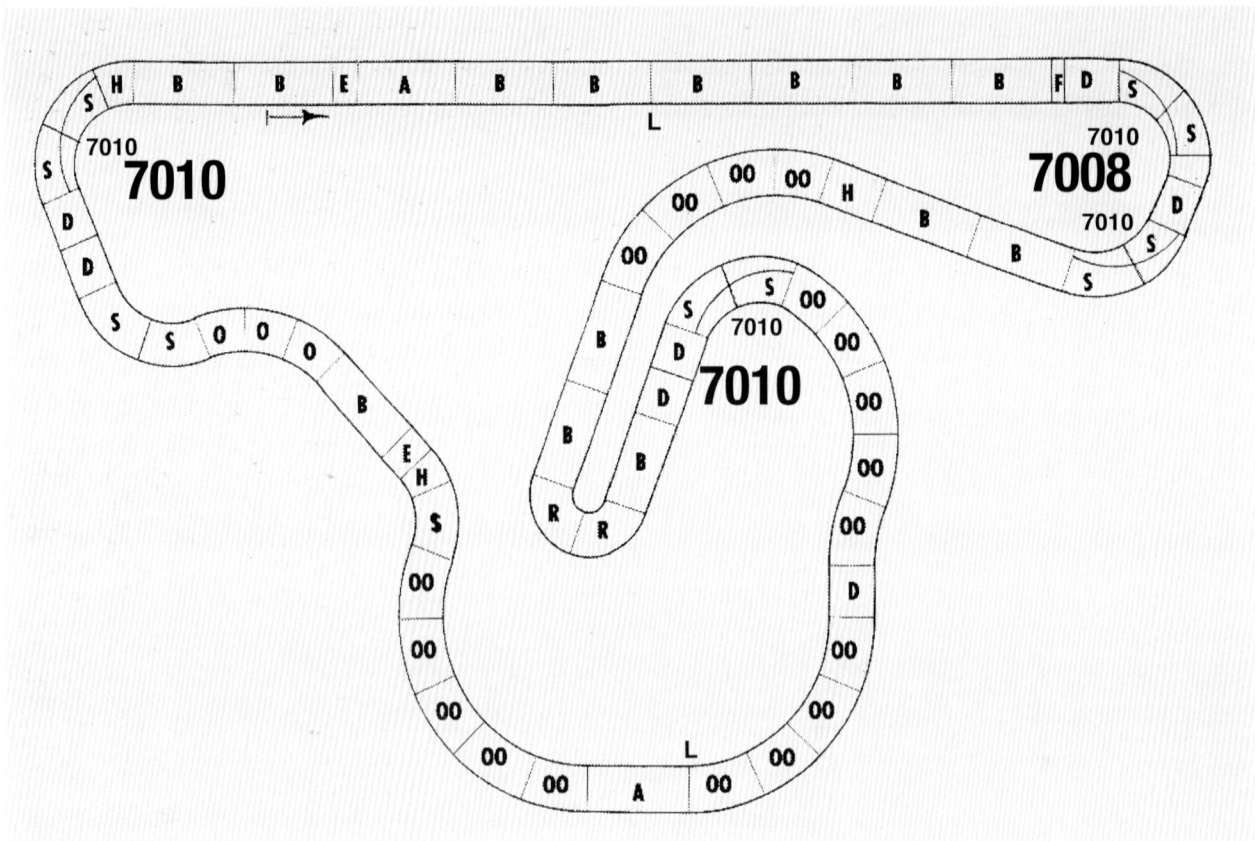

List of Scalextric Sport Track with digital lane-changers required for 9x14-foot two-land Monaco circuit.

Key	Quantity	Description
R	2	Sport-brand C8201 hairpin curve
H	2	1/2 standard curve
S*	8	Standard curves
O	3	Outer curve
OO	18	Outer-outer curve
E	2	1/4 straight
F	1	Short straight
D*	7	1/2 straight
B	12	Full straight
C	2	Side-Swipe straights C8246 must be used with R (above)
A	2	Connector track

*If you are using the Carrera Pro-X lane-changing system, some pairs of standard-length straights ("B") may be placed with Carrera Pro-X lane-changing tracks.

** I originally included a pair of crossover curves at LaRascasse (T1) to include a racing line corner—those curves would be replaced with Scalextrick Sport digital lane-changing tracks.

the exit from an increasing radius turn (if you are racing clockwise around the circuit). The track can be expanded to four lanes by adding two lanes on the inside of the plan.

Road America at Elkhart Lake, Wisconsin

Historically, the Can-Am cars (and their predecessor USRRC cars) and Trans-Am cars thundered around the Wisconsin hills when these cars were new. Road America has a website that will tell you everything you need to know about today's track (http://www.roadamerica.com/).

Road America for Scalextric Sport, Classic, SCX, or NINCO

The Carousel (turns T9 and T10) is assembled from the largest radius curves Scalextric Sport, Classic, SCX, and NINCO have available. I have avoided using any of the inner/inner curves to try and replicate the sweeping curves of the real Road America.

Road America for Carrera

This plan takes maximum advantage of Carrera's range of broad radius curves. The Carousel (Turns T9 and T10) is a decreasing radius curve that should

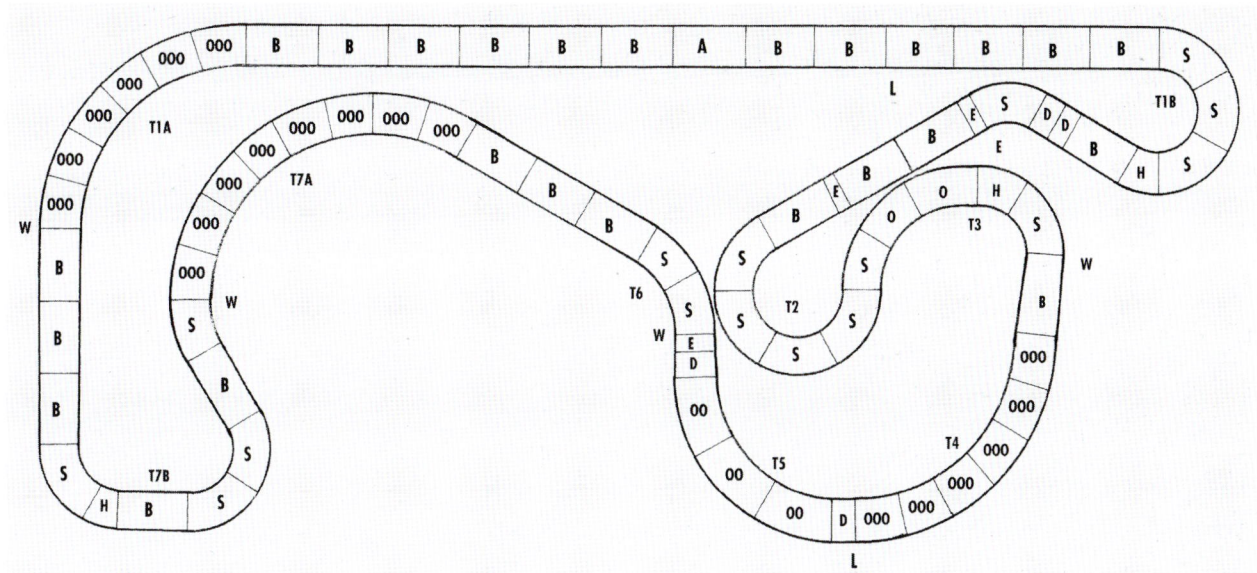

Carrera track with Pro-X digital lane-changers required for a 19 1/2x20-foot, two-lane Monaco circuit.

Key	Quantity	Description			
H	3	1/2 Inner Curve	OOO	10 pair (20)	Outer-Outer Curve
S	16	Inner Curve	E	3	1/4-Straight
O	2	Middle Curve	D	4	1/3-Straight
OO	3	Outer Curve	B	25	Full-Straight
			A	1	Connector Track

The Carrera R4 outer-outer-outer curve (with the borders painted green) on the Monaco track.

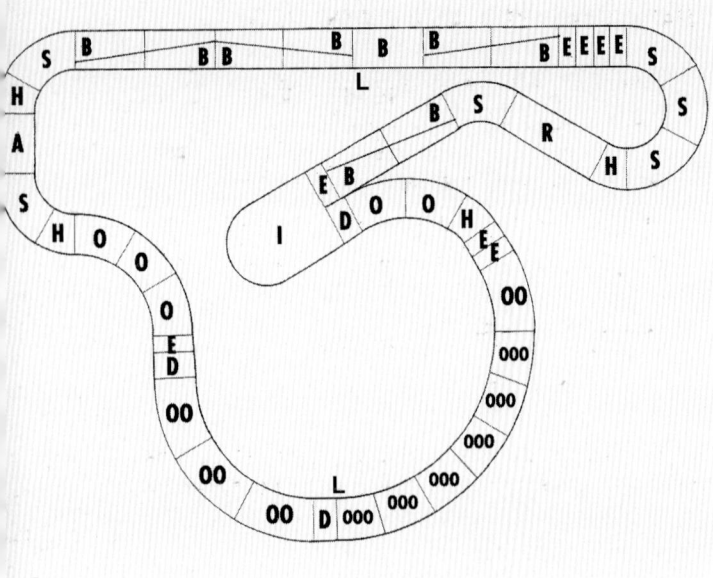

List of Carrera track with Pro-X digital lane-changers required for 8x16-foot Monaco:

Key	Quantity	Description
I	1	Custom-made inner/inner curve from Brad's Tracks
H	4	1/2 inner curve
S	6	Inner curve
O	5	Middle curve
OO	4	Outer curve
OOO	3 pair (6)	Outer-outer curve
E	8	1/4 straight
D	3	1/3 straight
B	8	Full straight
R	1/2	1/2 of overpass set
A	2	Connector track

*If you are using the Carrera Pro-X lane-changing system, some pairs of standard-length straights ("B") may be placed with Carrera Pro-X lane-changing tracks.

provide some exciting powerslides. The kink through Turns T11 and T11A can probably be taken flat-out with most cars. The course is tight through turns T3, T5, T6, and T8, with fast entry and exit from the straight that effectively lengthens the straight.

South African Grand Prix Circuit

The South Africa (East London) circuit was one of the most picturesque of the mid-1960s racing venues, and had an unusual triangular shape. The South African Grand Prix was held at East London Circuit in 1934, 1936–1939, and 1960–1965. In 1966, the South Africa Grand Prix race was moved to Kyalami.

All four plans can be fitted nicely on four sheets of 4x8-foot plywood or braced Styrofoam to fill a 12x16-foot area. The track could fit in a corner, but at least one of the rear edges should be 3 feet from the wall to

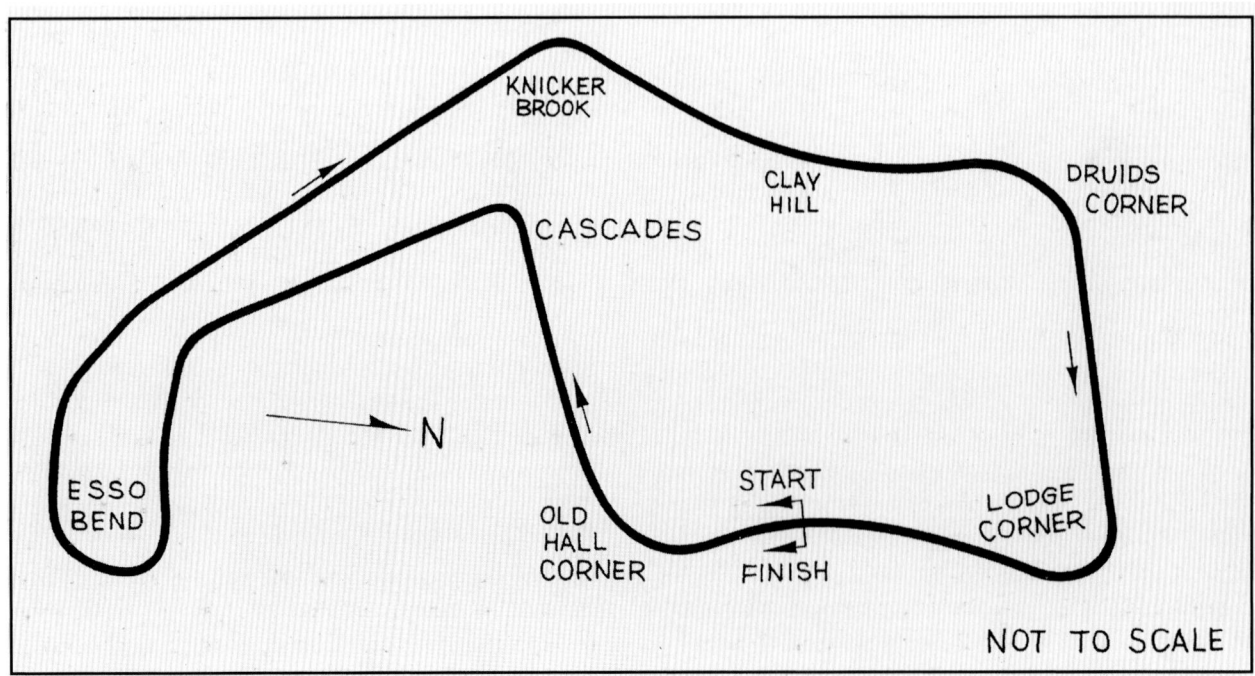

Oulton Park Circuit.

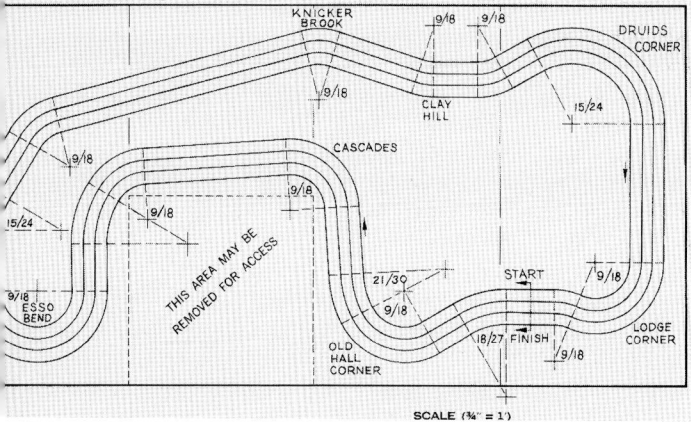

The routed version of the Oulton Park Circuit can be assembled from four 4x8-foot sheets of MDF board or MDO plywood. *From the February 1965 issue of* Model Car & Track

TRACK SECTIONS NEEDED FOR "COLLECTOR" BRANDS

BRAND	SCALE	LAYOUT SIZE	STRAIGHT TRACK REQUIRED	CURVED TRACK REQUIRED	AVERAGE LENGTH/LAP
Strombecker	1/32 or 1/24	8' x 16'	46 full straight 6 half straight	11 regular 8 half 30 outer	34½'
Kal-Kar	1/32 or 1/24	8' x 16'	24½' 4 lane straight	2½ full circles 4 lane	33'
Varney (2 lane only)	1/32 or 1/24	8' x 16'	28 sections	15 standard	40'
V.I.P. (2 lane only)	1/32 or 1/24	8' x 16'	30 sections	15 standard	39'

SCALE (¾" = 1')

The Oulton Park Circuit for Strombecker, Revell, Monogram, or Kal-Kar track for 12x12 feet. *From the February 1965 issue of* Model Car & Track

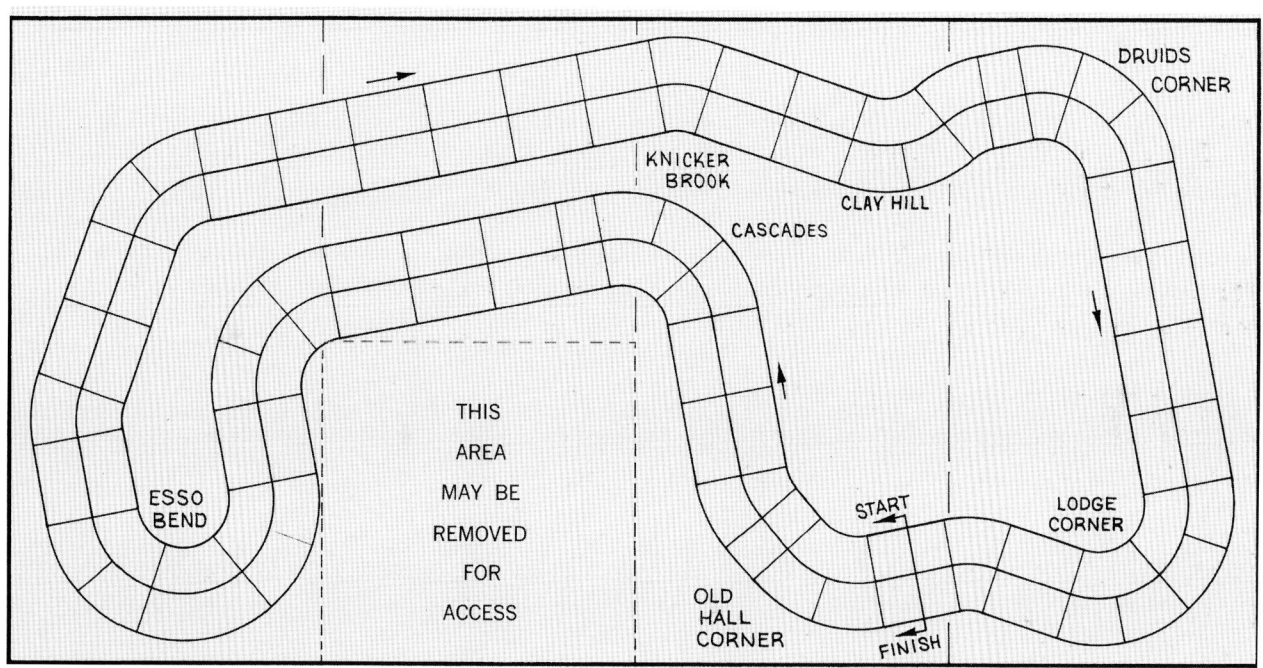

The track sections needed for collector brands.

provide access for the corner marshals, so you may need as much as 15x16 feet or 12x19 feet. The plan would fit easily in one stall of a two-car garage.

South African Grand Prix Circuit for Scalextric Sport, Classic, SCX, or NINCO

The Scalextric Sport, Classic, SCX, and NINCO version of the South Africa circuit has two tight curves at Cocobana Corner and Beacon Bend, with another tight kink at the Esses. The Potters Pass Curve and Rifle Bend are the R4 curves, but you'll certainly have to let off the throttle for Potters Pass Curve, but Rifle Bend might be negotiated at full throttle because the car will still be accelerating. The broad series of right/left/right ess curves through the Esses and Cox's Corner, and the Sweep is interrupted only by the kink at the beginning of the Esses.

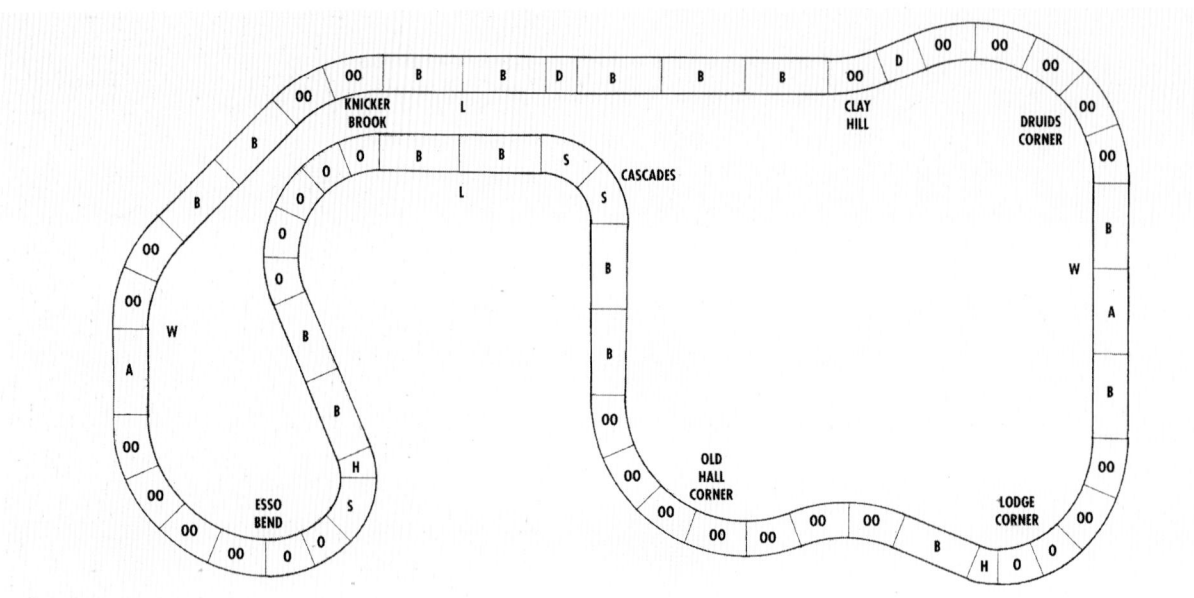

Scalextric Sport, Classic, SCX, or NINCO track required for an 8x15-foot Oulton Park circuit.

Key	Quantity	Description
H	2	1/2 Standard Curve
S	3	Standard Curve
O	9	Outer Curve
OO	23	Outer-Outer Curve
E	0	1/4-Straight
D	0	1/2-Straight
B	16	Full-Straight
A	2	Connector Track

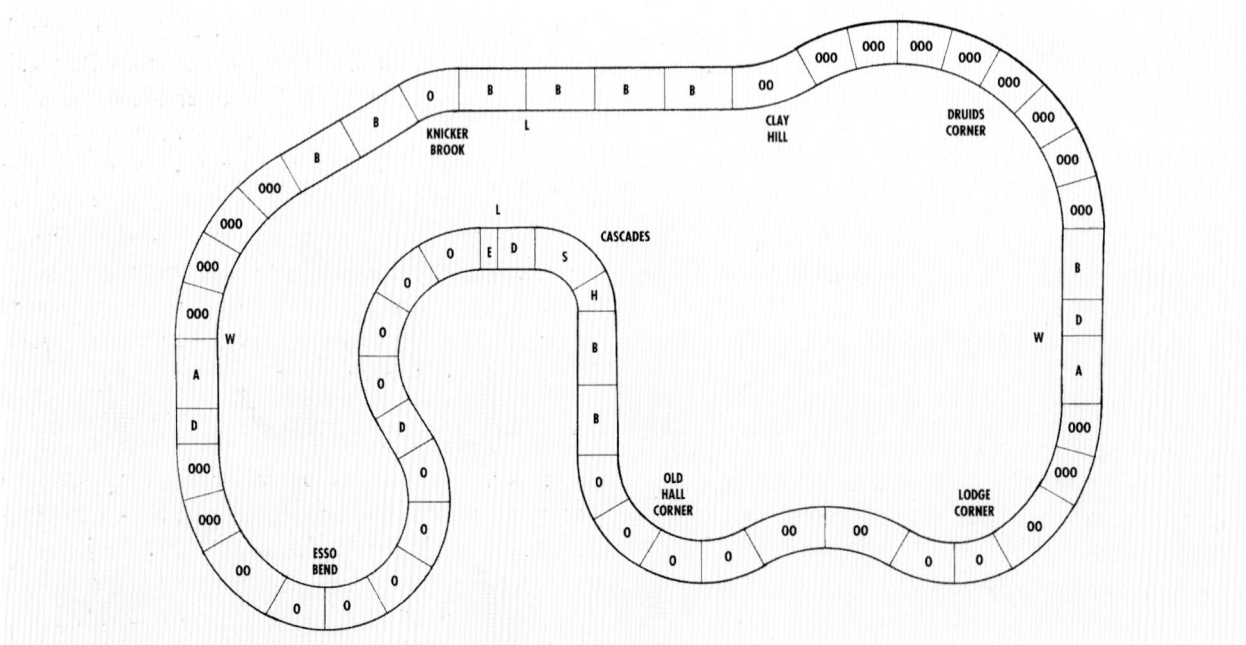

Carrera track required for an 8x15-foot Oulton Park circuit.

Key	Quantity	Description
H	1	1/2 Inner Curve
S	1	Inner Curve
O	41	Middle Curve
OO	15	Outer Curve
OOO	8 pair (16)	Outer-Outer Curve
E	1	1/4-Straight
D	4	1/3-Straight
B	9	Full-Straight
A	2	Connector Track

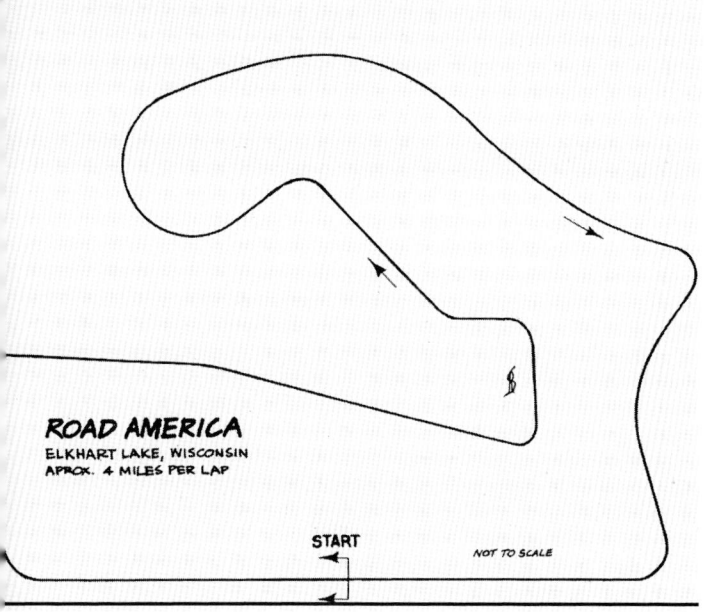

Road America.

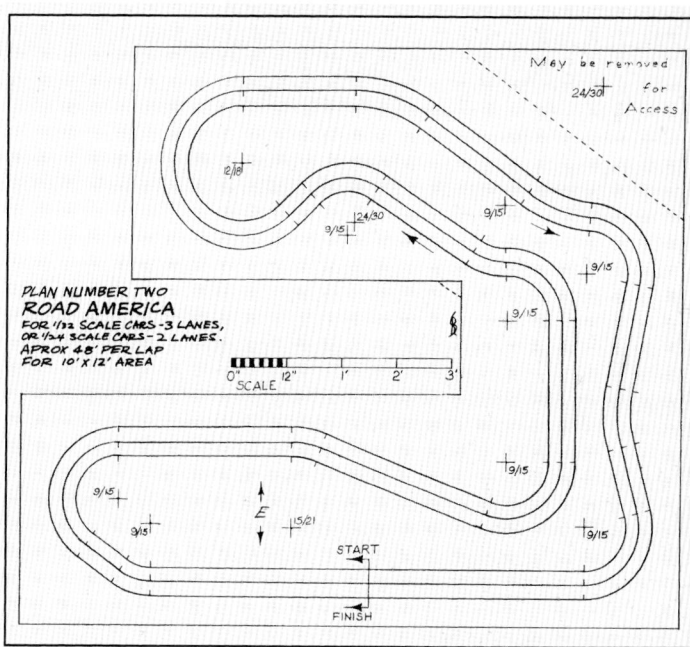

The three-lane routed version of the Road America Raceway can be assembled from four 4x8-foot sheets of MDF board or MDO plywood.

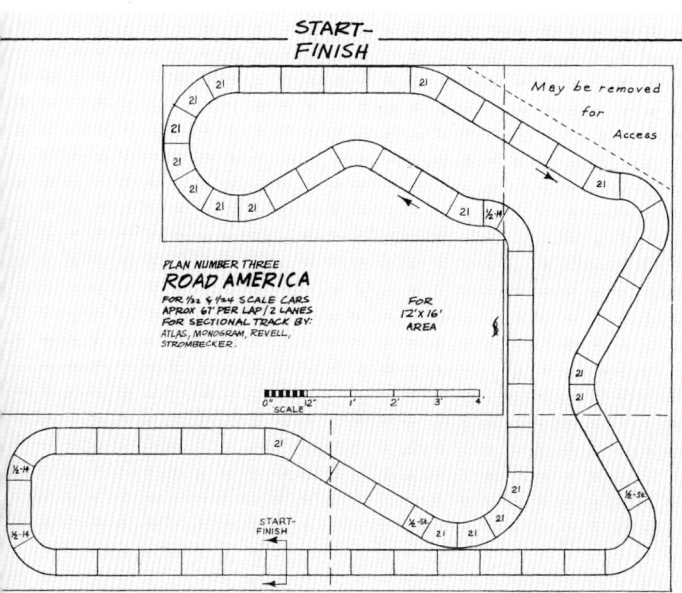

Road America for Strombecker, Revell, Monogram or Kal-Kar track for 12 x 16-feet.
(From the June 1967 Model Car & Track)
This plan for Road America is drawn for use with Strombecker or Kal-Kar track sections; however the same layout idea can be used with any set track using 60-degree segments of a circle for curves (six pieces per circle) if the area using half-curve sections is altered.

Brand	Straight Track Required	Curved Track Required
Strombecker	44 full straight, 2 half straight	7 regular, 3 half, 16 outer
Revell	44 full straight, 2 half straight	7 regular, 3 half, 16 outer

South African Grand Prix Circuit for Carrera

The Carrera version of the South Africa Circuit takes advantage of the flowing nature of Carrera's large radius curves. The Cocobana Corner and Beacon Bend are tight, but you can carry most of the speed from the Main Straight through Rifle Bend and Potters Pass Curve because those two utilize Carrera's broad number 4 curves. Beach Straight is short and it leads into the tight kink at the esses, which then opens into a three-radius curve (from increasing to broad to decreasing) and back into a broad number 4-size curve at the Sweep.

Silverstone

Silverstone is the site of just about every type of road racing from BTCC sedans to current F1 Grand Prix cars. It is also the site of the historic races.

Silverstone for Scalextric Sport, Classic, SCX, and NINCO

The 12x20-foot plans have a long straight across the top with a slight jog in the middle to represent the Maggots, Becketts, and Chapel Curve. This set of curves can be removed and simple straights can be inserted in their place (use two full-length and

This plan for Road America is drawn for use with Strombecker or Kal-Kar track sections, however the same layout idea can b e used with any set track using 60-degree segments of a circle for curves (six pieces per circle) if the area using half-curve sections is altered.

BRAND	STRAIGHT TRACK REQUIRED	CURVED TRACK REQUIRED
Strombecker	44 full straight 2 half straight	7 regular 3 half 16 outer
Revell	44 full straight 2 half straight	7 regular 3 half 16 outer

Track sections needed for collector brands.

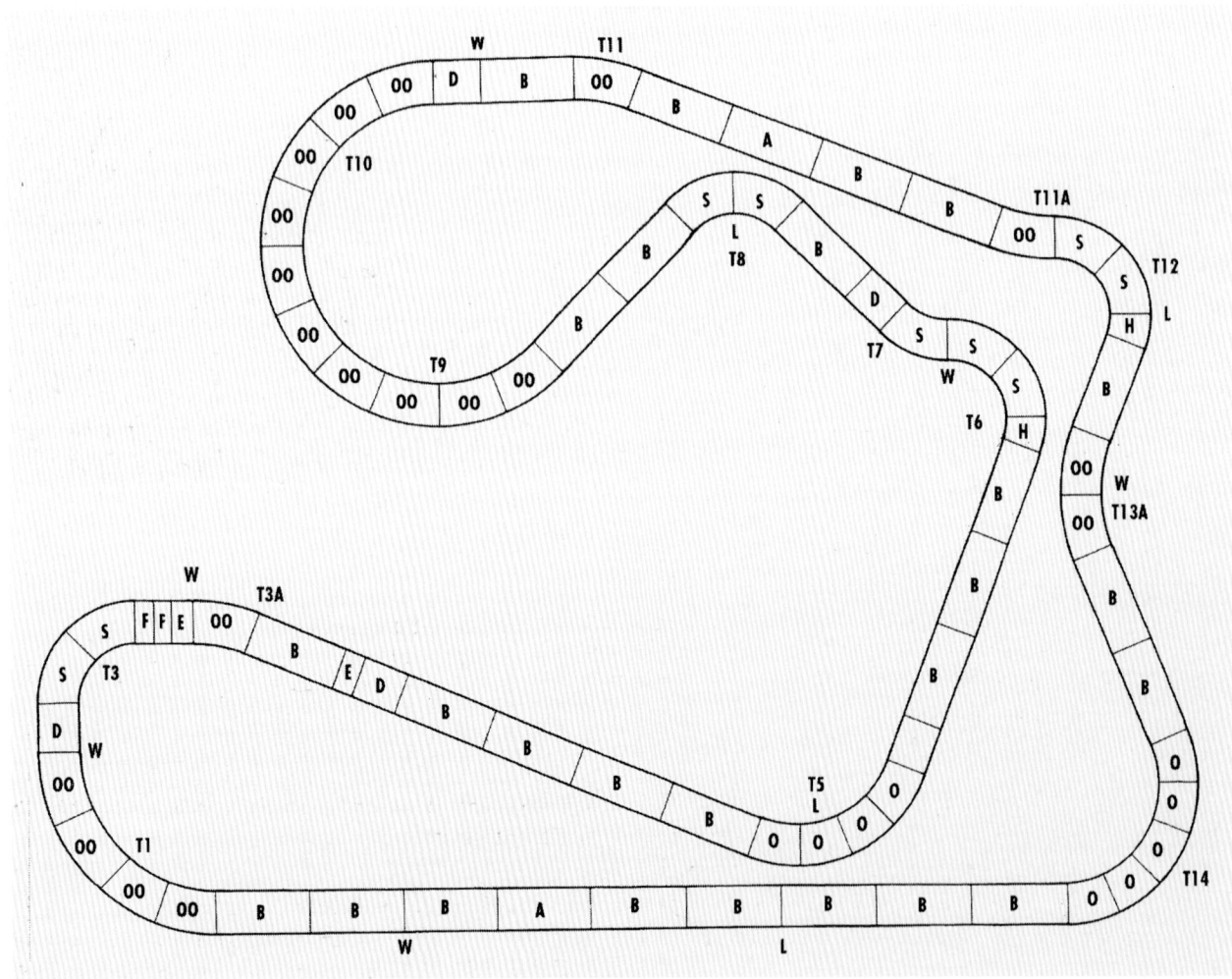

Scalextric Sport, Classic, SCX, or NINCO track required for a 12x16-foot Road America

Key	Quantity	Description
H	2	1/2 Standard Curve
S	9	Standard Curve
O	9	Outer Curve
OO	17	Outer-Outer Curve
F	2	Short Straight
E	2	1/4-Straight
D	5	1/2-Straight
B	25	Full-Straight
A	2	Connector Track

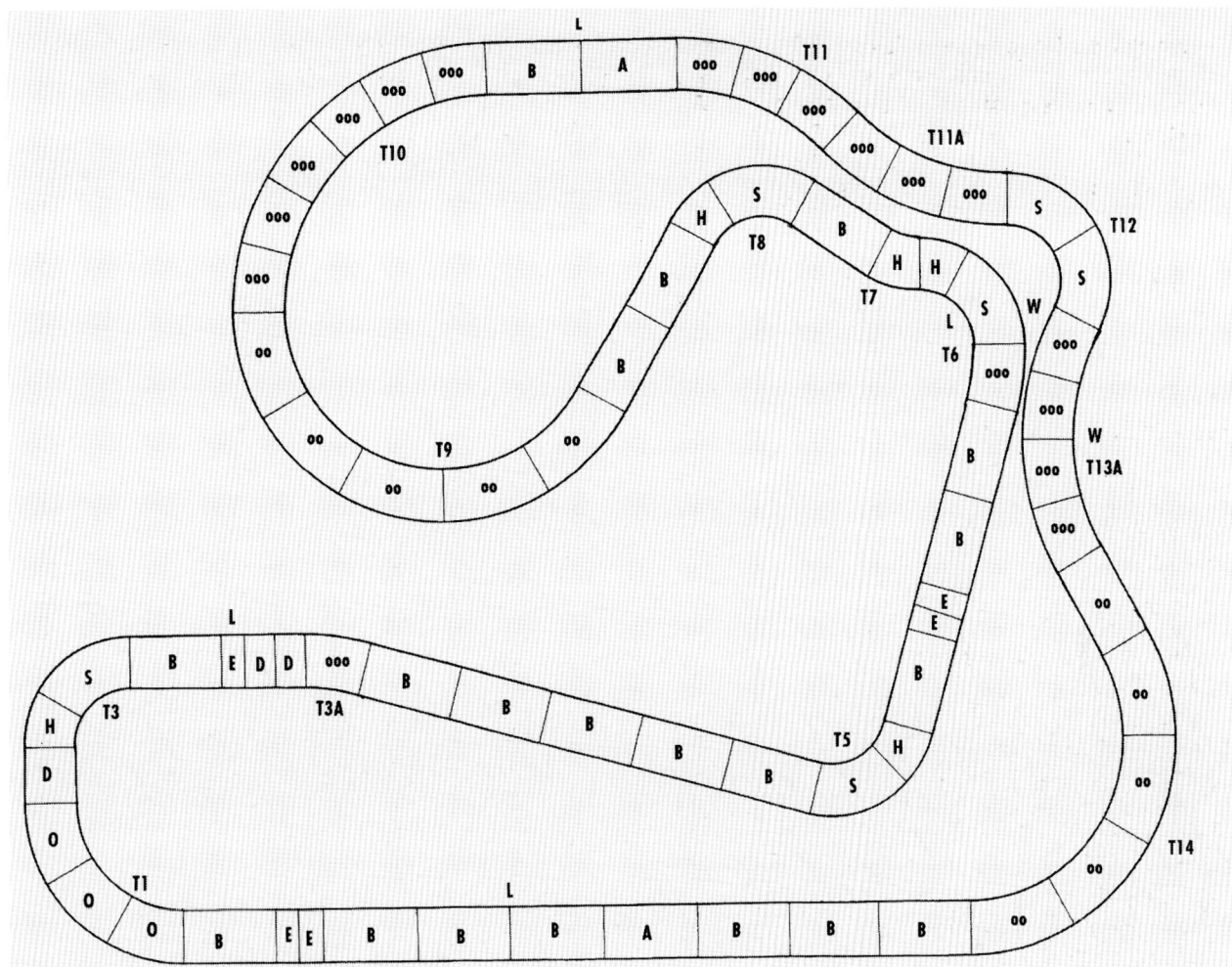

Carrera track required for a 12x16-foot Road America.

Key	Quantity	Description
H	5	1/2 Inner Curve
S	6	Inner Curve
O	3	Middle Curve
OO	9	Outer Curve
OOO	9 pair (18)	Outer-Outer Curve
E	5	1/4-Straight
D	3	1/3-Straight
B	21	Full-Straight
A	2	Connector Track

one quarter-length straight for the Sport/Classic/SCX plans. Before you do, try it as shown and see if the faster cars can negotiate the curves at full throttle. If not, you can move the curves a bit to the right so the cars enter them while still accelerating out of Copse.

Both the Sport/Classic/SCX/NINCO plan and the Carrera plan for 12x20 feet have a variety of increasing and decreasing radius curves (parabolas). On the Scalextric version, the Prior through Brooklands curve is a decreasing radius, and the curve from Luffield through Woodcote is an increasing radius. All the other curves are constant radius.

Silverstone for Carrera

The straight on the Carrera version has 12 pairs of full-length straights and one pair of 1/3-length straights. The plan utilizes all four sizes of Carrera turns to produce an increasing radius curve through Luffield and Woodcote, a decreasing radius curve at Copse, and an increasing radius curve through Club. There's a massive 120-degree sweeper curve through Stowe, and a 90-degree

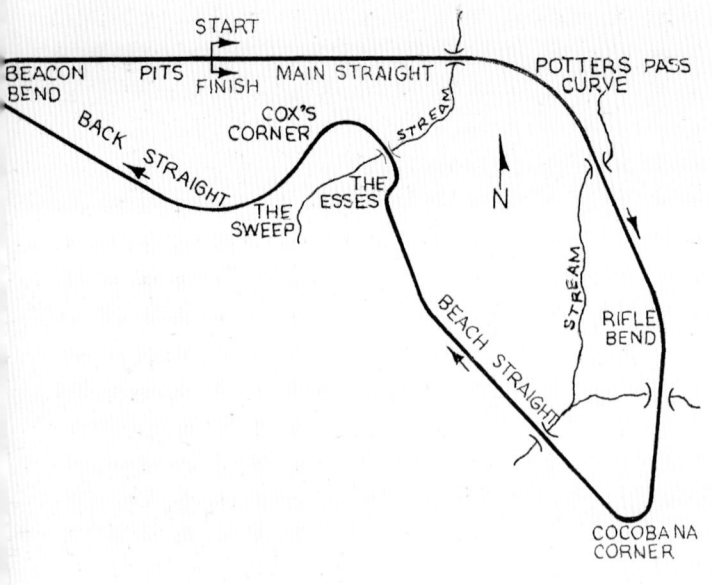

South Africa (East London) Circuit.

Mid-Ohio

The Mid-Ohio Sports Car Course features all types of two- and four-wheeled motor sports, including the Sprint Vintage Grand Prix, the American Le Mans at Mid-Ohio, Grand American Classic, and the SCCA National Championship Runoffs. The plan to route three slots in particle board, MDF, or MDO board has the most accurate shape in an 8x16-foot area. The three plans for plastic sectional track are designed for 12x18-foot area that you can assemble with four 4x8-foot tabletops. The plans for sectional track do not try to duplicate the exact shape of the track. The Keyhole, for example, appears oversized, but it is much closer to the driving experience you would get at the real Mid-Ohio than if I had used hairpin-sized tight curves to mimic the shape of the real Mid-Ohio track. The plan for the real Mid-Ohio course lists

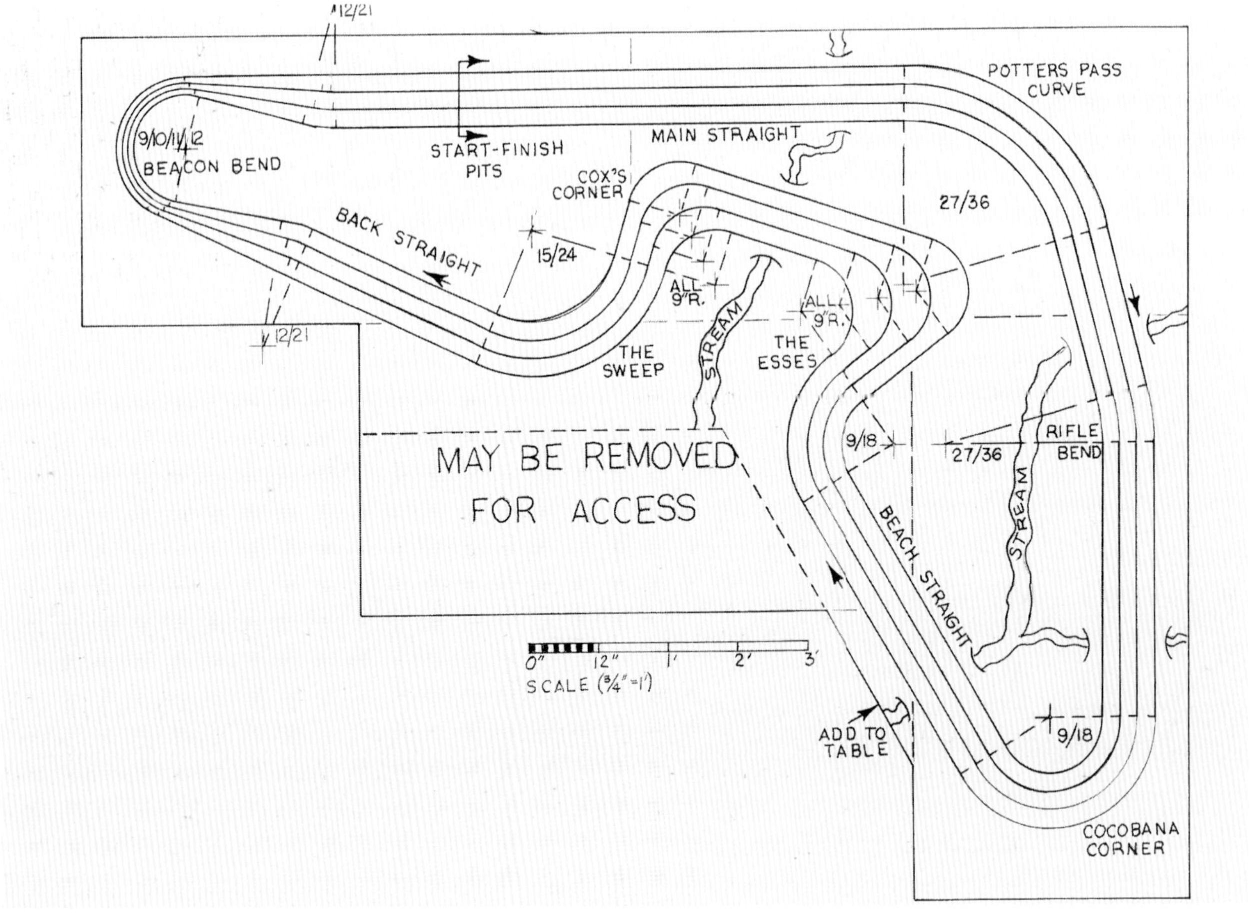

version at Bridge with tight ess bends through Vale and Priory/Vale/Luffield.

The three-lane routed version of the Road America Raceway can be assembled from four 4x8-foot sheets of MDF board or MDO plywood.

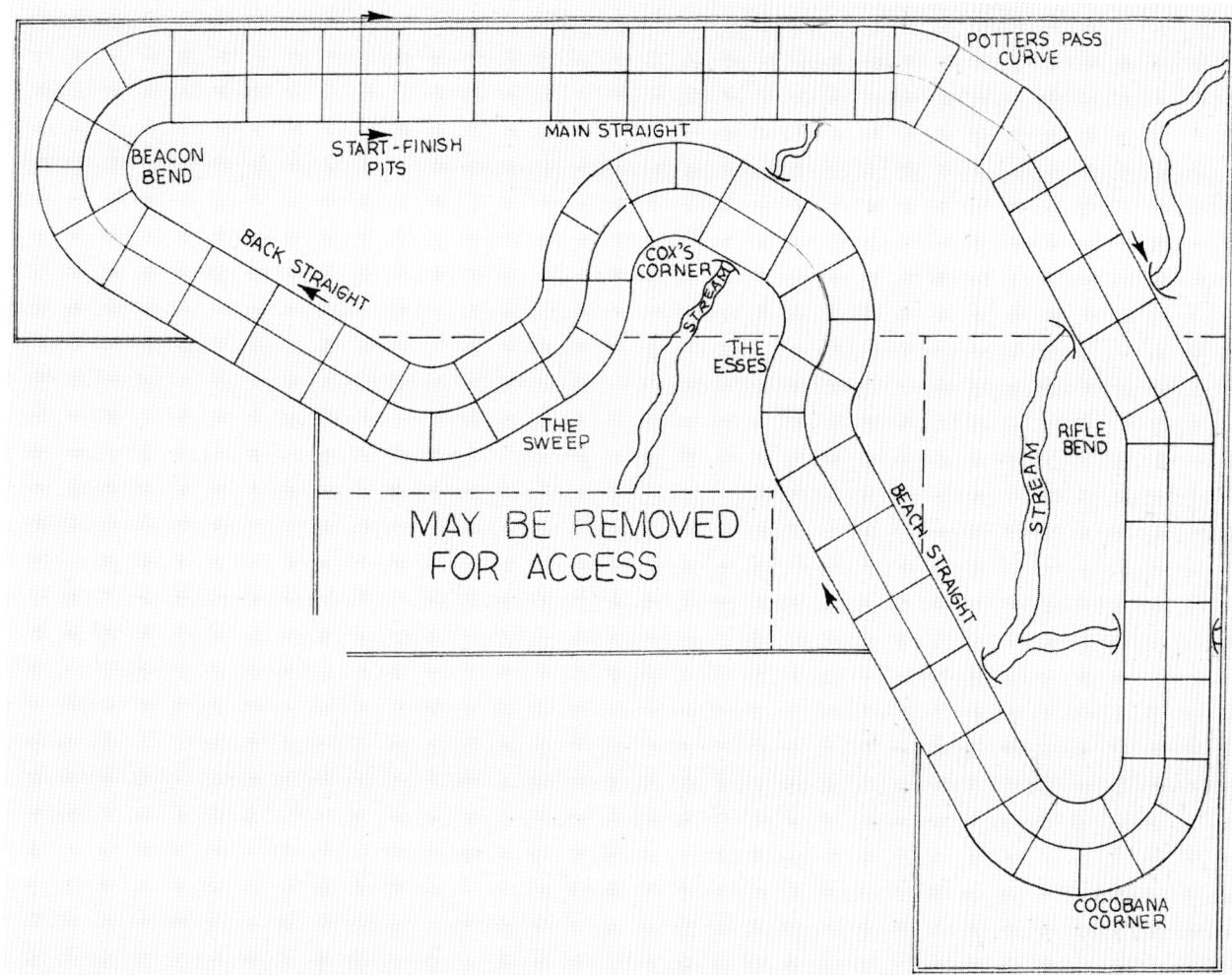

The Road America for Strombecker, Revell, Monogram, or Kal-Kar track for 12x16 feet.

corner flag stations. Stations 4, 5, 6, 12, and 13 are along the straights and are not on the model plans.

Mid-Ohio for Scalextric Sport, Classic, SCX, or NINCO

The second 90-degrees of the Keyhole (T3) is assembled from the largest radius curves Scalextric Sport, SCX, and NINCO have available. The turn at the MG Bridge (T1) is a deceasing radius turn. I have avoided using any of the inner/inner curves to replicate the sweeping curves of the real Mid-Ohio course. The OO-size curves at the Chicane will need to be replaced with two O-size curves and two pieces of short straights to fit two more lanes inside the plan.

Mid-Ohio for Carrera

This plan takes maximum advantage of Carrera's

(Plan No. three is drawn for use with Strombecker or Kal-Kar track sections however, the same layout idea can be used with any set track using 60° segments of a circle for curves (six pieces per circle) if the areas using half curve sections are altered.)

BRAND	SCALE	LAYOUT SIZE	STRAIGHT TRACK REQUIRED *	CURVED TRACK REQUIRED†	AVERAGE LENGTH/LAP
Strombecker	1/32 or 1/24	12' x 16'	56 full straight 4 half straight	10 regular 6 half 26 outer	44 ft.
Kal Kar	1/32 or 1/24	12' x 16'	30' four lane straight	2-1/6 full circles four lane	43 ft.
Revell (2 lane only)	1/32 or 1/24	12' x 16'	35 sections	13 regular	47 ft.
Varney (2 lane only)	1/32 or 1/24	12' x 16'	35 sections	13 regular	47 ft.
V.I.P. (2 lane only)	1/32 or 1/24	12' x 16'	35 sections	13 regular	42 ft.

The track sections needed for collector brands.

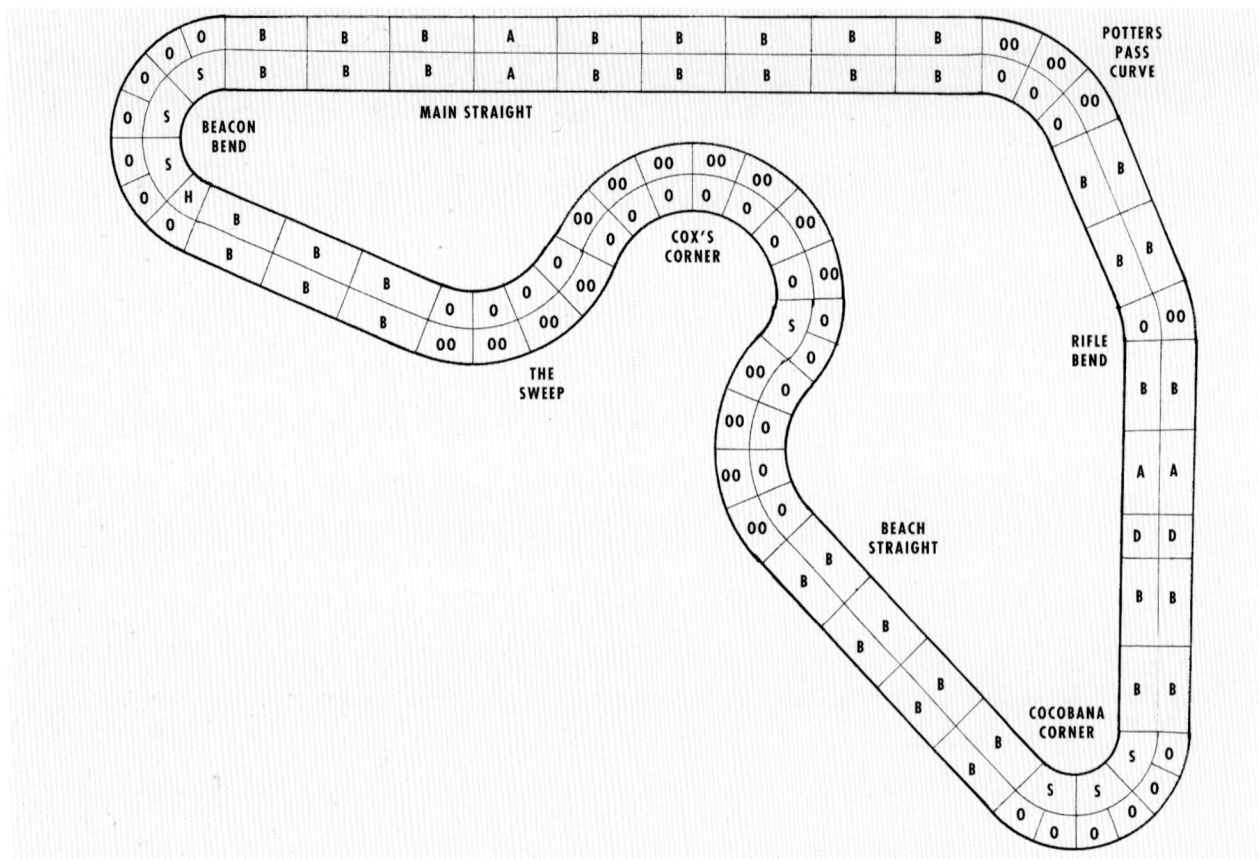

Scalextric Sport, Classic, SCX, NINCO track for a 12x16-foot South Africa circuit.

Key	Quantity	Description
H	1	1/2 Standard Curve
S	7	Standard Curve
O	34	Outer Curve
OO	19	Outer-Outer Curve
F	0	"Short" Straight
E	0	1/4-Straight
D	2	1/2-Straight
B	40	Full-Straight
A	4	Connector Track

range of broad radius curves. The Keyhole (T3) is an increasing radius curve that should provide some exciting powerslides. The plan for Carrera track is designed so two more lanes can be fitted inside the plan.

Daytona International Raceway for Carrera

Carrera's massive number 4-size banked turn (20579) with border (20580) allows you to assemble a massive oval with outer two lanes 7 feet across. I couldn't resist applying the new track to the Daytona International Raceway. No other brand offers such a broad radius curve. There are four other versions of Daytona in *Slot Car Bible*.

You cannot simply replace the number 2 and 3 banks with numbers 3 and 4 because the larger curves change the geometry. Since I had to create an entire new version of Daytona for Carrera, I opted to use the extra space to include more interesting infield curves. If you run the track counterclockwise, turn T2 is a decreasing radius, turn T3 is an increasing radius, and turn T4 is another decreasing radius, but of a different set of radii than T2 and with a quicker exit onto the high bank. Actually, the banking from turn T5 will extend into part of T4. Turns T1 and T4 are high banks.

Sepang, Malaysia, F1 Track

I compressed the Sepang track to fit it in a 9x20-foot area so it would fit into one stall of a two-car garage. Both plans are designed to allow a center access

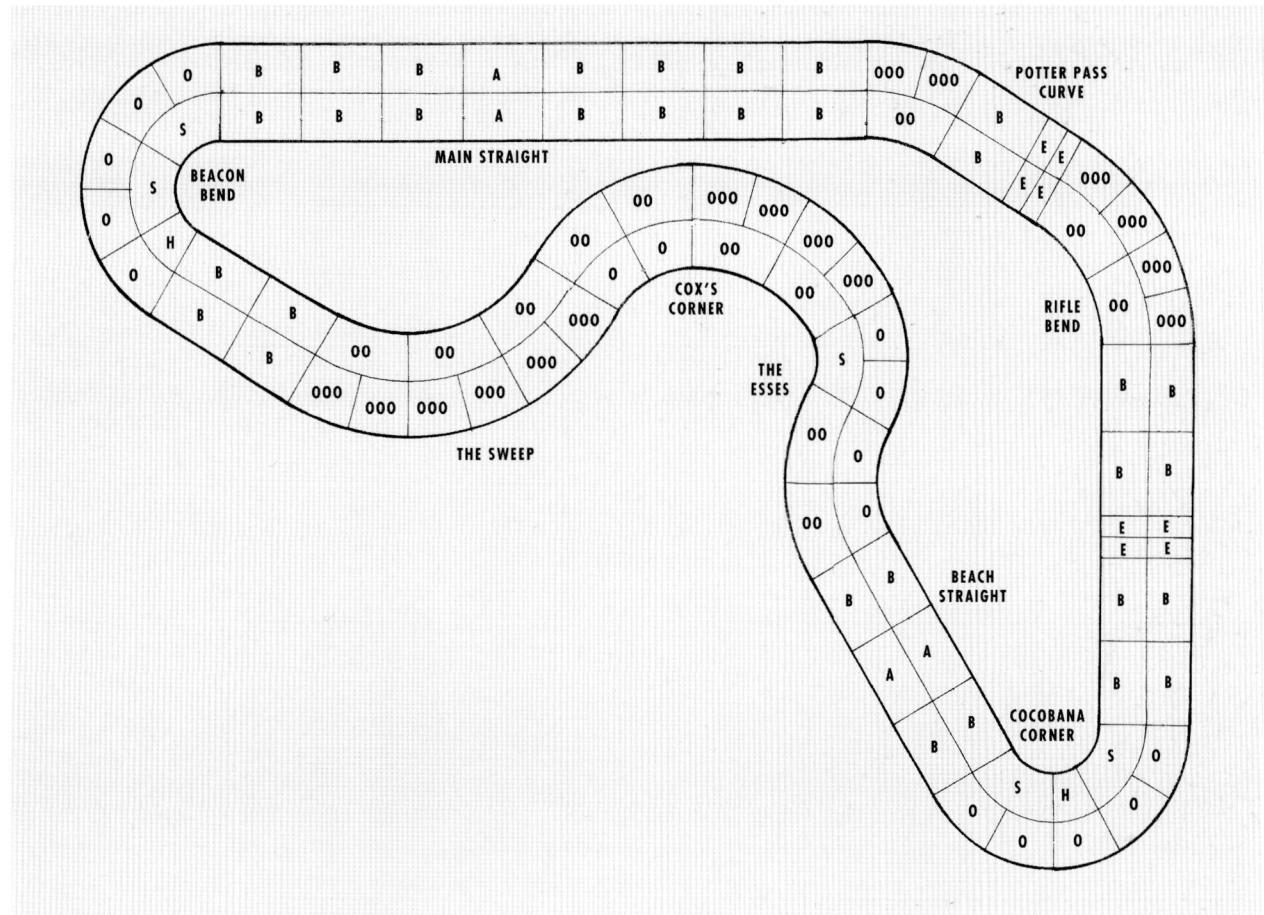

Carrera track required for a 12x16-foot South Africa circuit.

Key	Quantity	Description
H	2	1/2 Inner Curve
S	4	Inner Curve
O	14	Middle Curve
OO	12	Outer Curve
OOO	8 pair (16)	Outer-Outer Curve
E	8	1/4-Straight
D	0	1/3-Straight
B	32	Full-Straight
A	4	Connector Track

aisle, but the Carrera version is a skinny 16 inches wide. With a 9-foot width, you will definitely need access along both long sides, even if you cut holes into the tabletop.

There are examples of 13 of the 15 curves at Sepang on both versions of this track for 1/32 scale racing. Turn 1 is a tight hairpin that opens up before the tight left at Turn 2, followed by a broad sweeping Turn 3. The broad curves are broader on the Carrera version because Carrera has the option of a much larger outer/outer/outer curve. Turn 4 is a quick, tight right-hander followed by a sweeping left-hand Turn 5, and a broad, decreasing radius Turn 6. There was no room for Turn 7, and Turn 10 was also eliminated, resulting in an ess bend through Turns 9 and 11, which is actually much tighter on the Carrera version. There's another tight left at Turn 12, followed by a broad curve at Turn 13, leading into a decreasing radius Turn 14, and down the paint straight to Turn 15 (which is a radius-radius on the Scalextric version). Both plans have two positions for controllers so both drivers can serve as corner marshals.

Sepang, Malaysia, F1 Track for Scalextric Sport, Classic, SCX, or NINCO

The main straight is 16 feet, 9 inches on the Scalextric version, with about an 89-foot lap length.

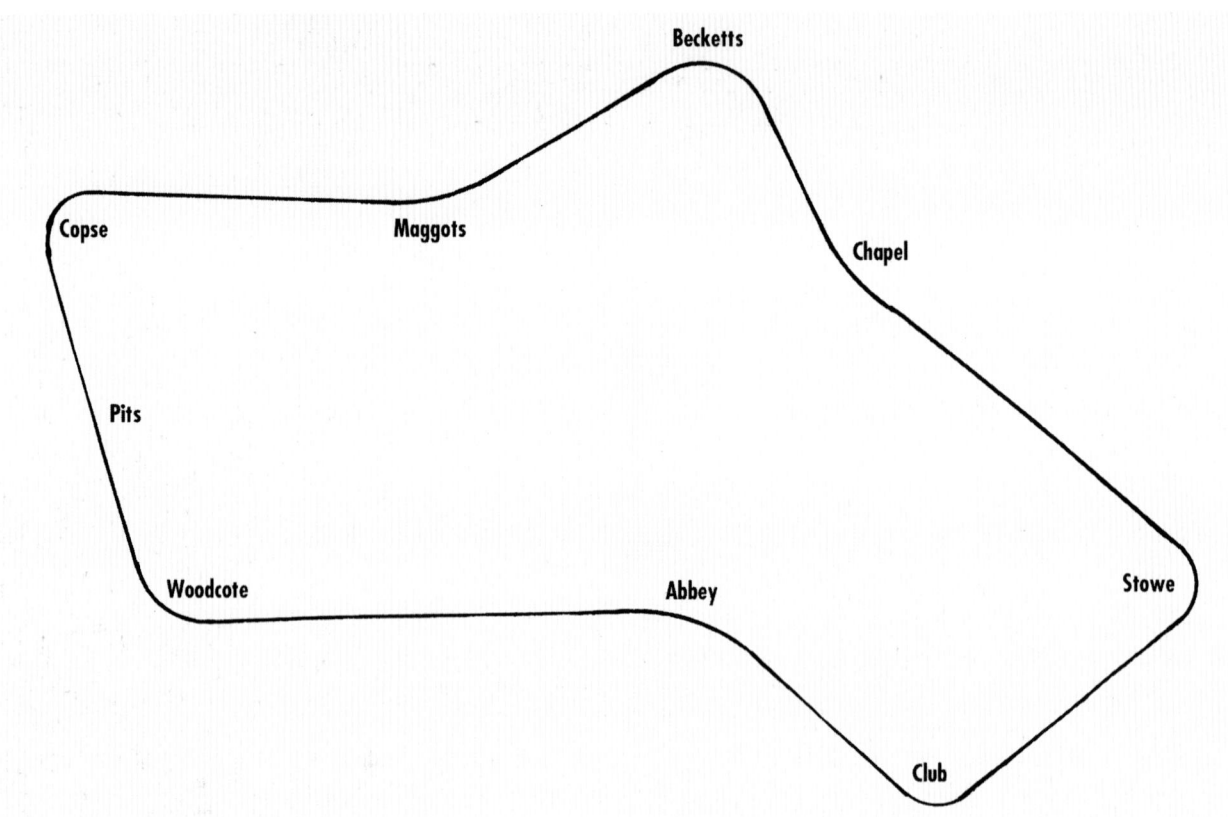

Silverstone, as it was rebuilt in 1991.

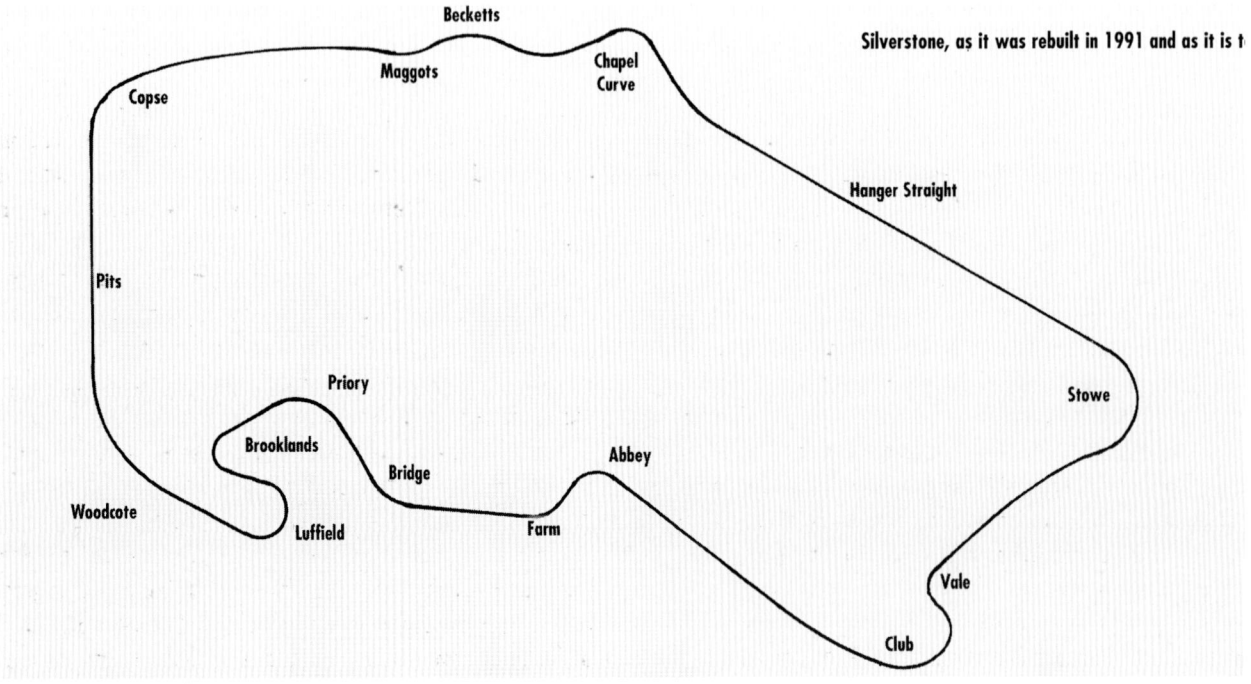

Silverstone, as it is today.

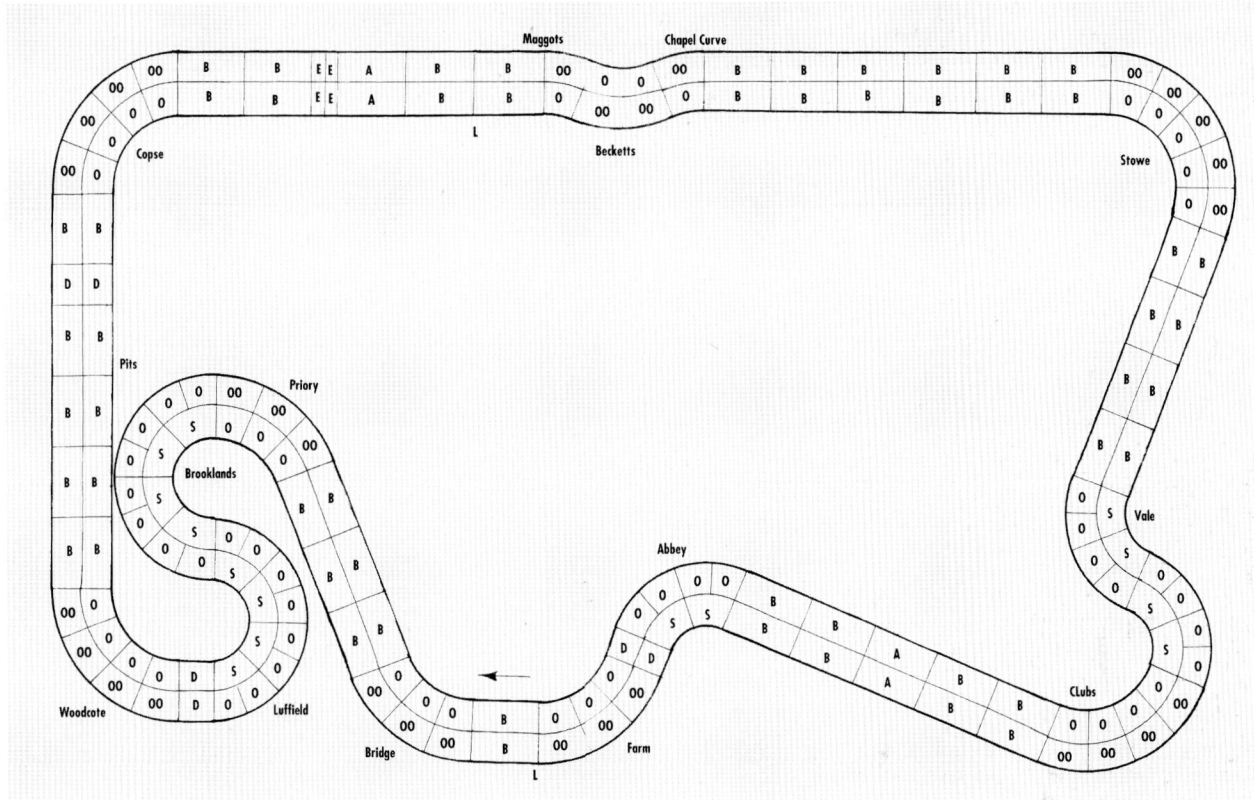

Scalextric Sport, Classic, SCX, or NINCO track required for a 12x20-foot Silverstone circuit.

Key	Quantity	Description		Key	Quantity	Description
H	0	1/2 Standard Curve		F	0	Short Straight
S	14	Standard Curve		E	4	1/4-Straight
O	57	Outer Curve		D	4	1/2-Straight
OO	30	Outer-Outer Curve		B	54	Full-Straight
				A	4	Connector Track

The lane-changing tracks at Turns 4 and 12 allow the cars to take the shortest inside line through the majority of the track. The lane changing tracks at Turns 1 and 4 provide an additional opportunity to pass on this relatively long track.

Sepang, Malaysia, F1 Track for Carrera

The main straight on the Carrera version is 16 feet, 2 inches long, with an 88-foot lap length. The lane changing tracks at Turns 4 and 12 allow the cars to take the shortest inside line through the majority of the track. The lane-changing tracks at Turns 1 and 8 provide an additional opportunity to pass on this relatively long track.

Warwick Farm, Australia, GP Circuit

Warwick Farm was one of the tracks that were used for the winter Tasman series of Grand Prix races in the 1960s. When the European Grand Prix season ended and winter set in, the teams would head for Australia and New Zealand for the winter Tasman series of races.

The track could fit in a corner, but at least one of the rear edges should be 3 feet from the wall to provide access for the corner marshals so you may need as much as 15x16 feet or 12x19 feet. The plan would fit easily in one stall of a two-car garage.

I have drawn this plan as four lanes. With conventional track and cars you can race four cars at once. You can race up to eight cars at once with Carrera Pro-X digital system, and up to 12 cars at once with Scalextric Digital system. If you opt for lane-changers, you might consider using them only on the outer pair of lanes so you can race against conventional cars on the inner two lanes, but you can still race six to eight cars at once. Because of the tight number of turns,

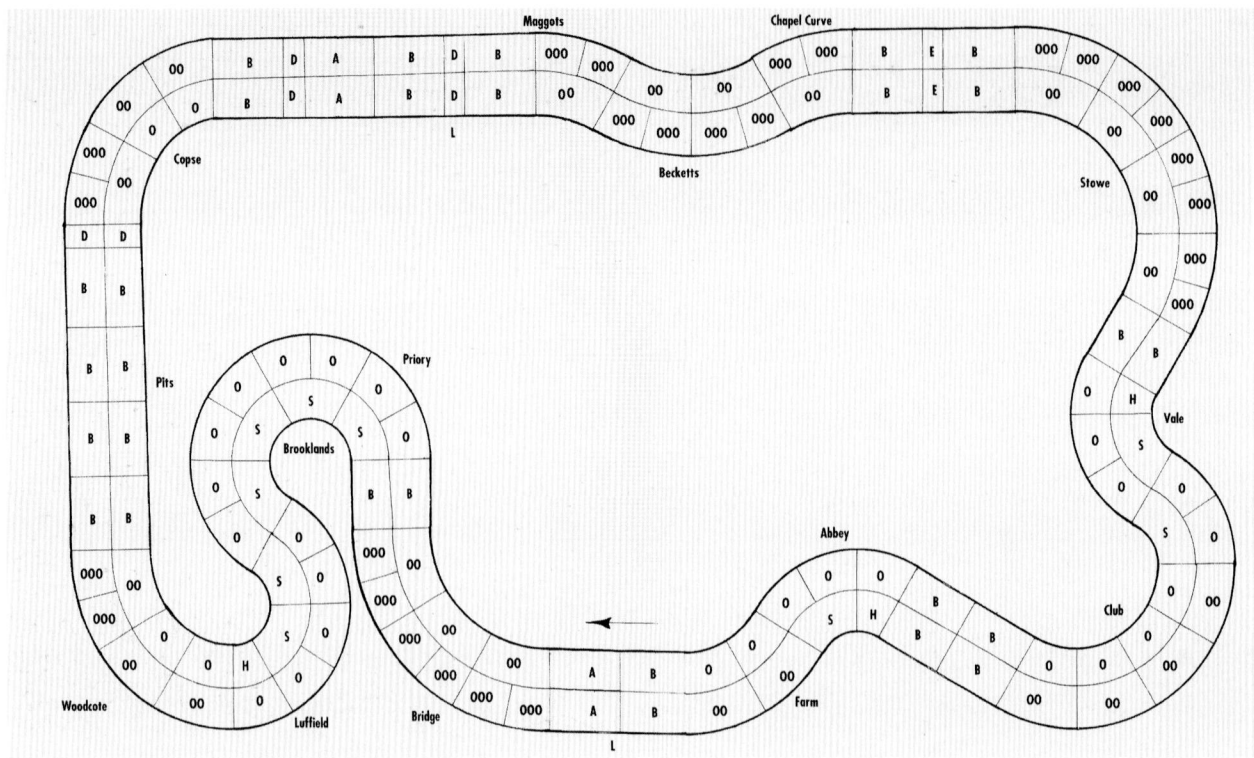

Carrera track required for a 12x20-foot Silverstone circuit.

Key	Quantity	Description
H	3	1/2 Inner Curve
S	9	Inner Curve
O	14	Middle Curve
OO	35	Outer Curve
OOO	13 pair (26)	Outer-Outer Curve
E	2	1/4-Straight
D	6	1/3-Straight
B	28	Full-Straight
A	4	Connector Track

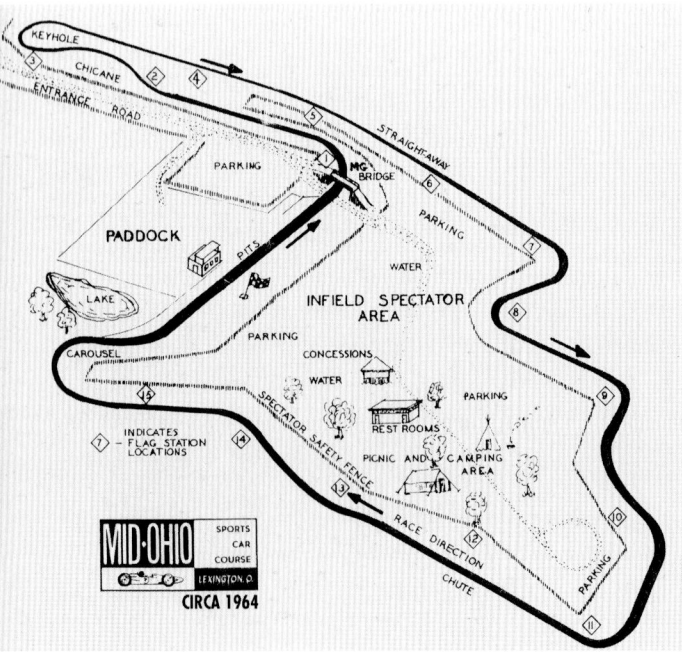

Mid-Ohio.

there was only room for two lane changers on both the Scalextric and the Carrera versions.

Warwick Farm, Australia, GP Circuit for Scalextric Sport, Classic, SCX, or NINCO

There was room for two lane-changers on the Scalextric plan. The Scalextric Sport lane-changers are located on curves, so they are positioned in somewhat different locations than on the Carrera version. On the inner two lanes, the lane changer at Turn 8 allows the shortest route around, and the lane changer at Turn 4 allows the cars back into the other lane. On the outer two lanes, the lane changer at Turn 11 allows the cars to follow the shortest path around the course, and the lane changer at Turn 7 allows the cars back into the other lane for passing. The plan is designed so that when running clockwise, Turns 11 and 14 are increasing radius turns.

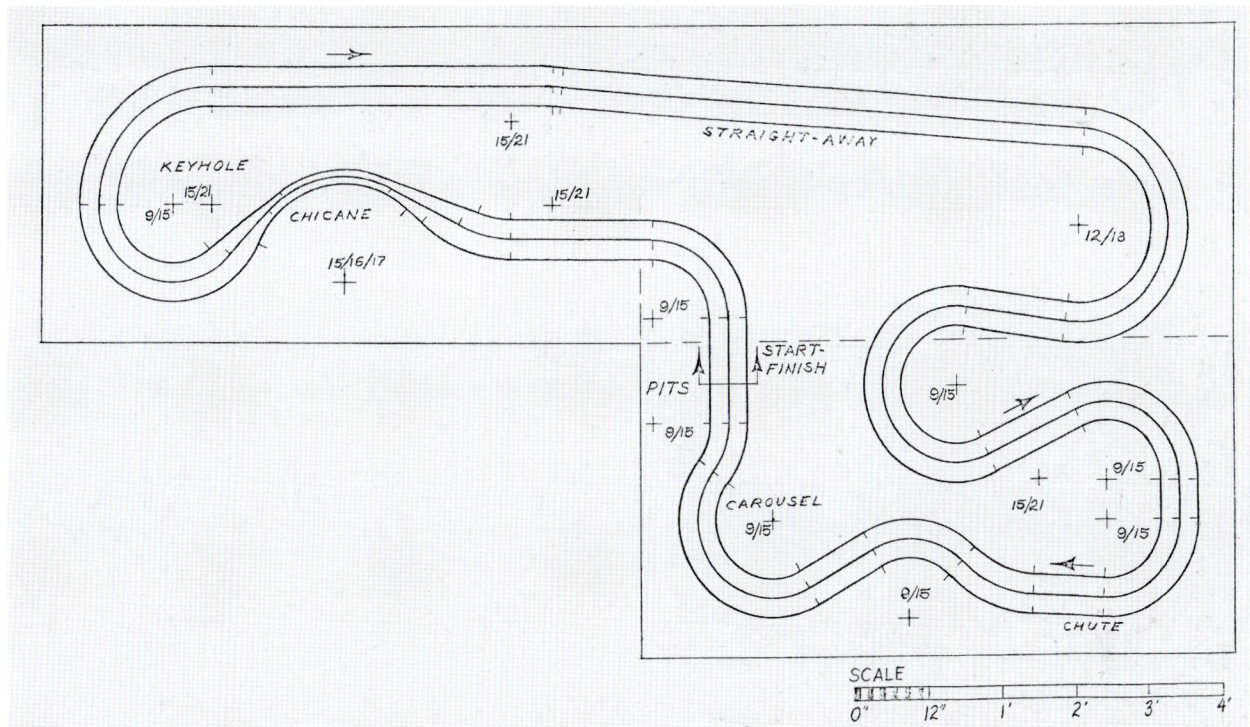

The three-lane routed version of the Road America Raceway can be assembled from four 4x8 foot sheets of MDF board or MDO plywood.

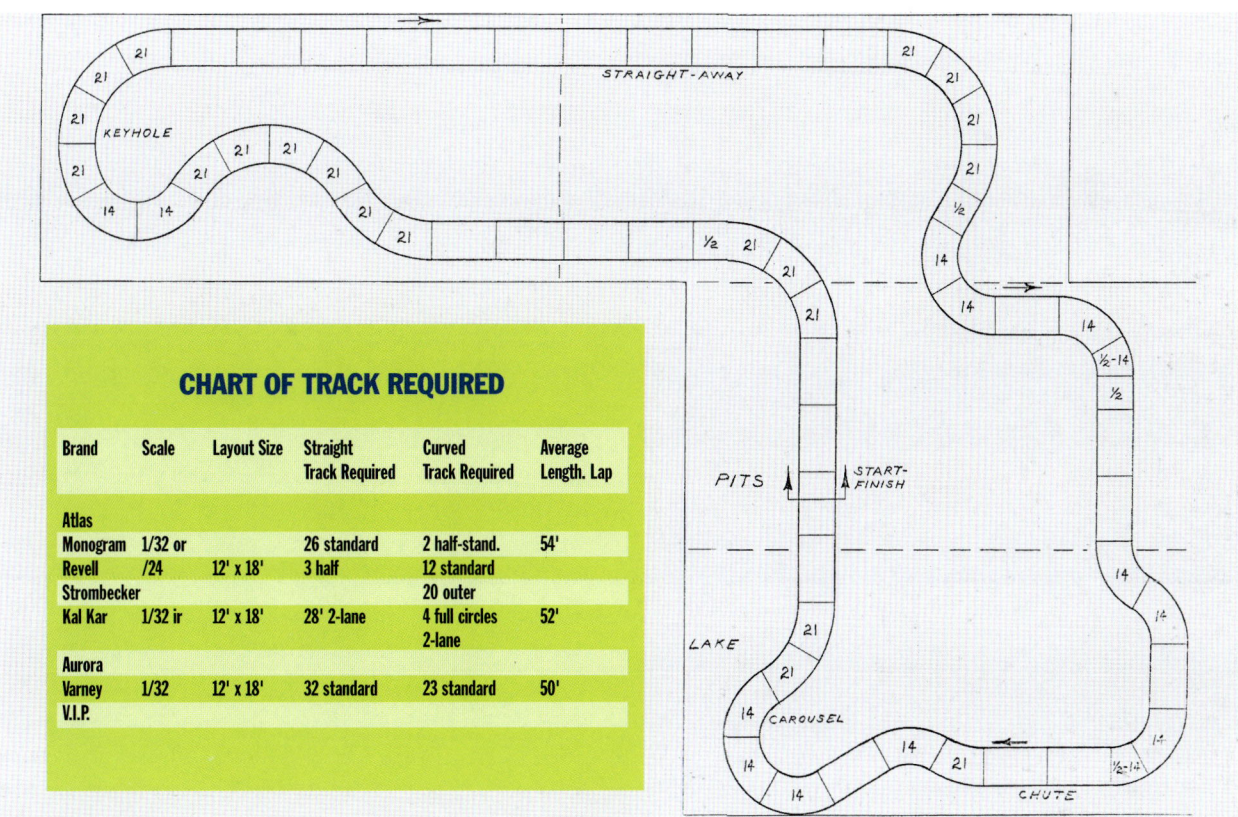

CHART OF TRACK REQUIRED

Brand	Scale	Layout Size	Straight Track Required	Curved Track Required	Average Length. Lap
Atlas Monogram Revell Strombecker	1/32 or /24	12' x 18'	26 standard 3 half	2 half-stand. 12 standard 20 outer	54'
Kal Kar	1/32 ir	12' x 18'	28' 2-lane	4 full circles 2-lane	52'
Aurora Varney V.I.P.	1/32	12' x 18'	32 standard	23 standard	50'

Mid-Ohio for Strombecker, Revell, Monogram, or Kal-Kar track for 12x16 feet.

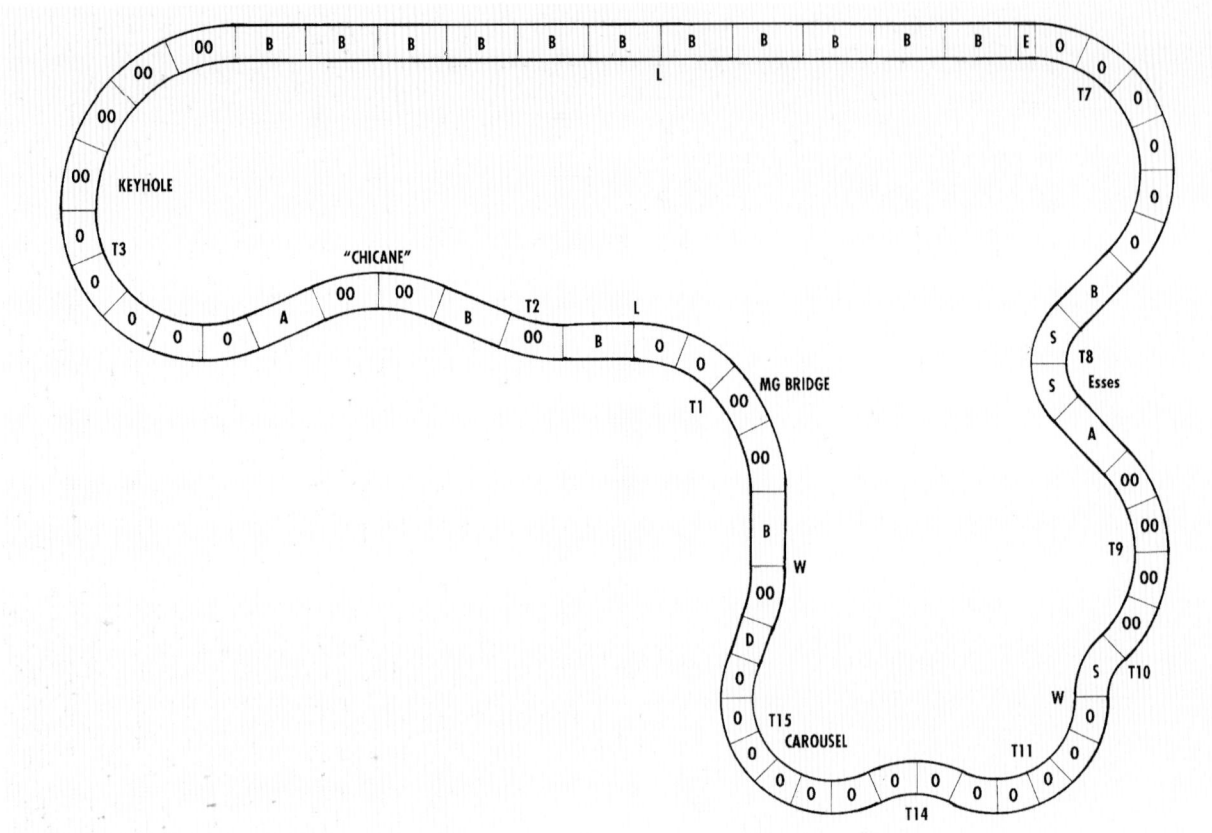

Scalextric Sport, Classic, SCX, or NINCO track required for a 12x18-foot Mid-Ohio.

Key	Quantity	Description
H	0	1/2 Standard Curve
S	3	Standard Curve
O	26	Outer Curve
OO	14	Outer-Outer Curve
F	0	Short Straight
E	1	1/4-Straight
D	1	1/2-Straight
B	15	Full-Straight
A	2	Connector Track

Warwick Farm, Australia, GP Circuit for Carrera

On the Carrera version, the lane-changing tracks at Turn 14 allow the cars to take the shortest inside line through the majority of the track. The lane-changing tracks at Turn 4 allow the cars to get back into the other lane for passing. The plan is designed so that, when running clockwise, Turns 1 and 11 are decreasing radius turns.

Interlagos, Brazil, F1 Track

The Interlagos Track, near Sao Paulo, Brazil, was built in 1954 as a labyrinthine 4.95-mile circuit. It was shortened by removing some of the near-overlapping sections in 1990, and it is now a 2.67-mile course. For model car racers who are always short on square footage, the original track is the one to copy. There are plans of both the original and the modern versions of the real Interlagos in this book. You could remove some sections and duplicate the current Interlagos circuit if you want an accurate simulation of a modern F1 track.

The track will fit nicely in a 12x18-foot area. There are many places where the tracks are far beyond reach. I have indicated areas where 2x4-foot holes should be cut into the tabletop to allow corner marshals to reach some of the otherwise inaccessible areas of the racetrack to replace deslotted cars. An alternative solution would be to use pistol-gripped tongs called "grabbers" that can pick up objects that are out of reach.

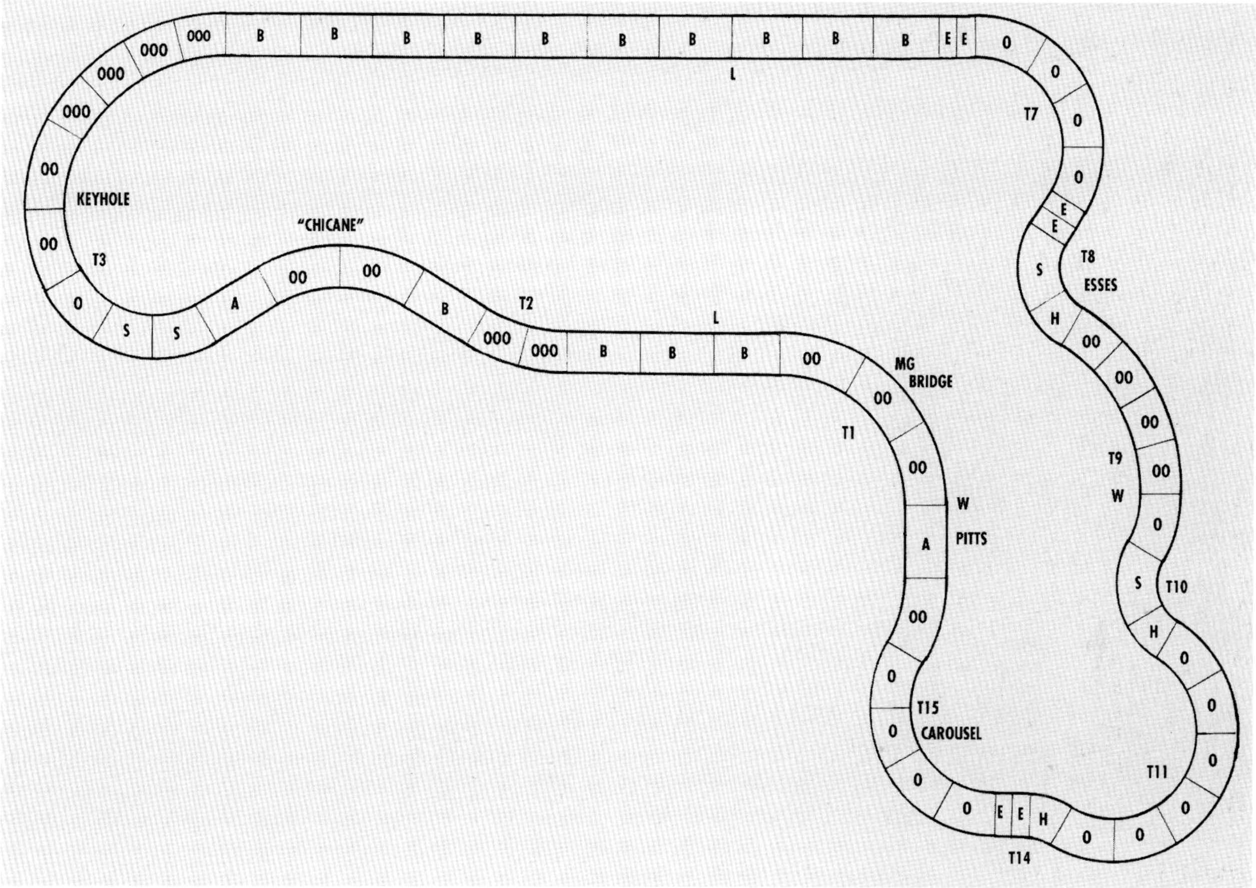

Carrera track required for a 12x18-foot Mid-Ohio.

Key	Quantity	Description
H	3	1/2 Inner Curve
S	4	Inner Curve
O	16	Middle Curve
OO	12	Outer Curve
OOO	3 pair (6)	Outer-Outer Curve
E	6	1/4-Straight
D	0	1/3-Straight
B	13	Full-Straight
A	2	Connector Track

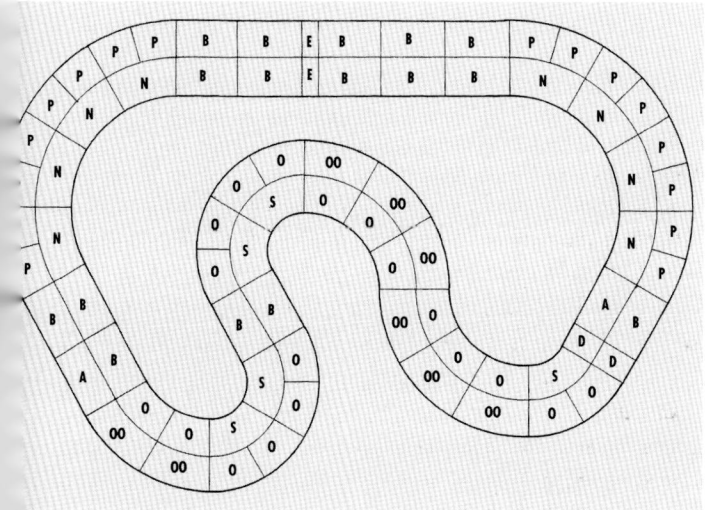

Carrera track required for a 9x15-foot Daytona International Raceway.

Key	Quantity	Description
H	0	1/2 Inner Curve
S	5	Inner Curve
O	18	Middle Curve
OO	8	Outer Curve
N	8	Banked Outer Curve
OOO	0	Outer-Outer Curve
P	16	Banked Outer-Outer Curve
E	2	1/4-Straight
D	2	1/3-Straight
B	16	Full-Straight
A	2	Connector Track

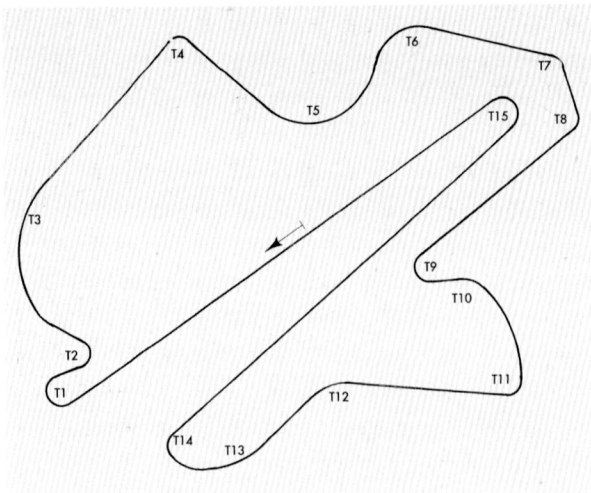

The Sepang, Malaysia, F1 Track.

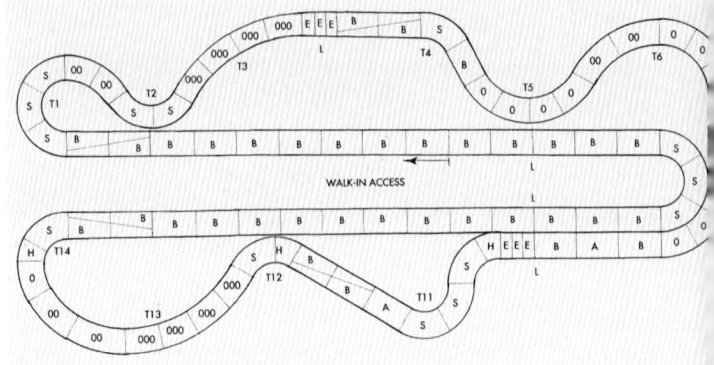

Carrera track required for a 9x20-foot Sepang layout.

Key	Quantity	Description
H	3	1/2 Inner Curve
S	11	Inner Curve
O	11	Middle Curve
OO	6	Outer Curve
OOO	4 pair (8)	Outer-Outer Curve
E	6	1/4-Straight
D	0	1/3-Straight
B*	36	Full-Straight*
A	2	Connector Track

*NOTE: If you are using the Carrera Pro-X lane-changing system, some pairs of standard-length straights ("S") may be placed with Carrera Pro-X lane-changing tracks.

Interlagos, Brazil, F1 Track for Scalextric Sport, Classic, SCX, or NINCO

The Scalextric Sport, Classic, SCX, and NINCO version has the broadest possible curves through all but two of the corners. The track includes four straightaways, two series of 120-degree ess bends, and a series of 90-degree ess bends. With exception

continued on page 183

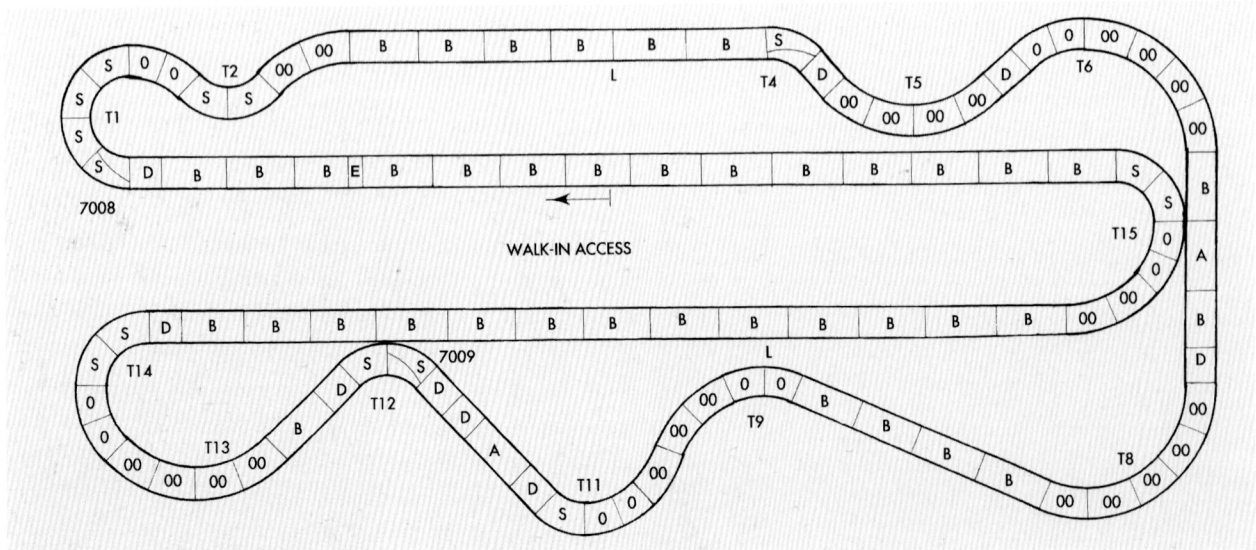

Scalextric Sport, Classic, SCX, or NINCO track required for a 9x20-foot Sepang layout.

Key	Quantity	Description
H	0	1/2 Standard Curve
S*	14	Standard Curve*
O	10	Outer Curve
OO	22	Outer-Outer Curve
F	0	Short Straight
E	1	1/4-Straight
D*	10	1/2-Straight*
B	39	Full-Straight
A	2	Connector Track

*NOTE: If you are using the Scalextric Sport digital lane-changing system, some of these "S" standard curves may be replaced by lane-changing tracks, along with the adjacent half-straight "D" as a sensor track.

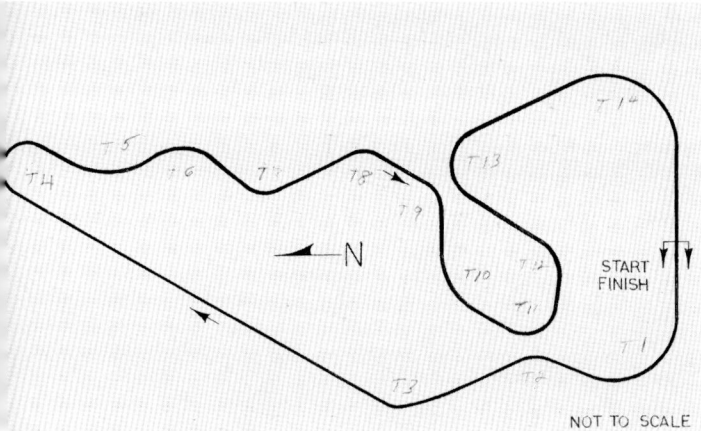

The Warwick Farm, Australia, racetrack.

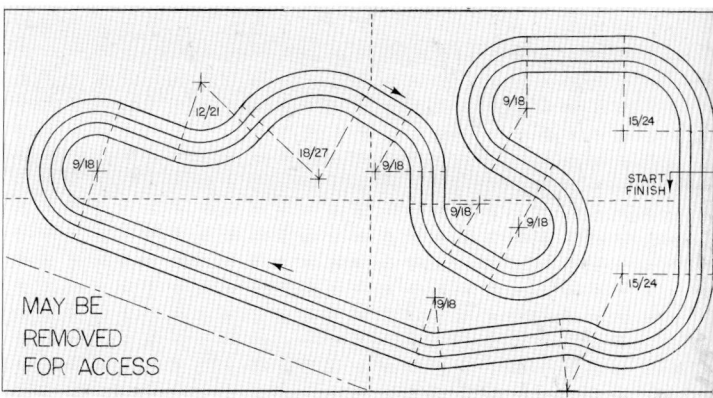

This four-lane routed version of the Warwick Farm, Australia, racetrack can be assembled from four 4x8-foot sheets of MDF board or MDO plywood.

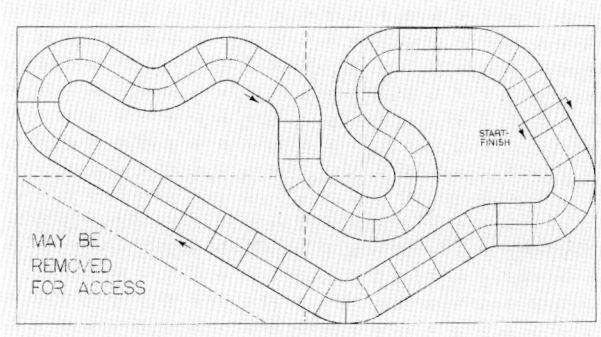

A layout for the Warwick Farm, Australia, racetrack for Strombecker, Revell, Monogram, or Kal-Kar track for 12x16 feet.

WARWICK FARM PLAN NO. 3
Plan number three is drawn for use with Strombecker or Kal-Kar track sections, however, the same layout idea can be used with any set track using 60° segments of a circle for curves (six pieces per circle) if the areas using half curve sections are altered.

BRAND	SCALE	LAYOUT SIZE	STRAIGHT TRACK REQUIRED *	CURVED TRACK REQUIRED †	AVERAGE LENGTH/LAP
Strombecker	1/32 or 1/24	8' x 16'	42 standard 10 half	15 regular 4 half 34 outer	44-1/2 ft.
Kal Kar	1/32 or 1/24	8' x 16'	23½ feet four lane	2-5/6 full circles four lane	44 ft.
Revell (2 lane)	1/32 or 1/24	8' x 16'	28 sections	16 regular	43-1/2 ft.
Varney (2 lane)	1/32 or 1/24	8' x 16'	28 sections	16 regular	43-1/2 ft.
V.I.P. (2 lane)	1/32 or 1/24	8' x 16'	28 sections	16 regular	42 ft.

The track sections needed for the collector brands.

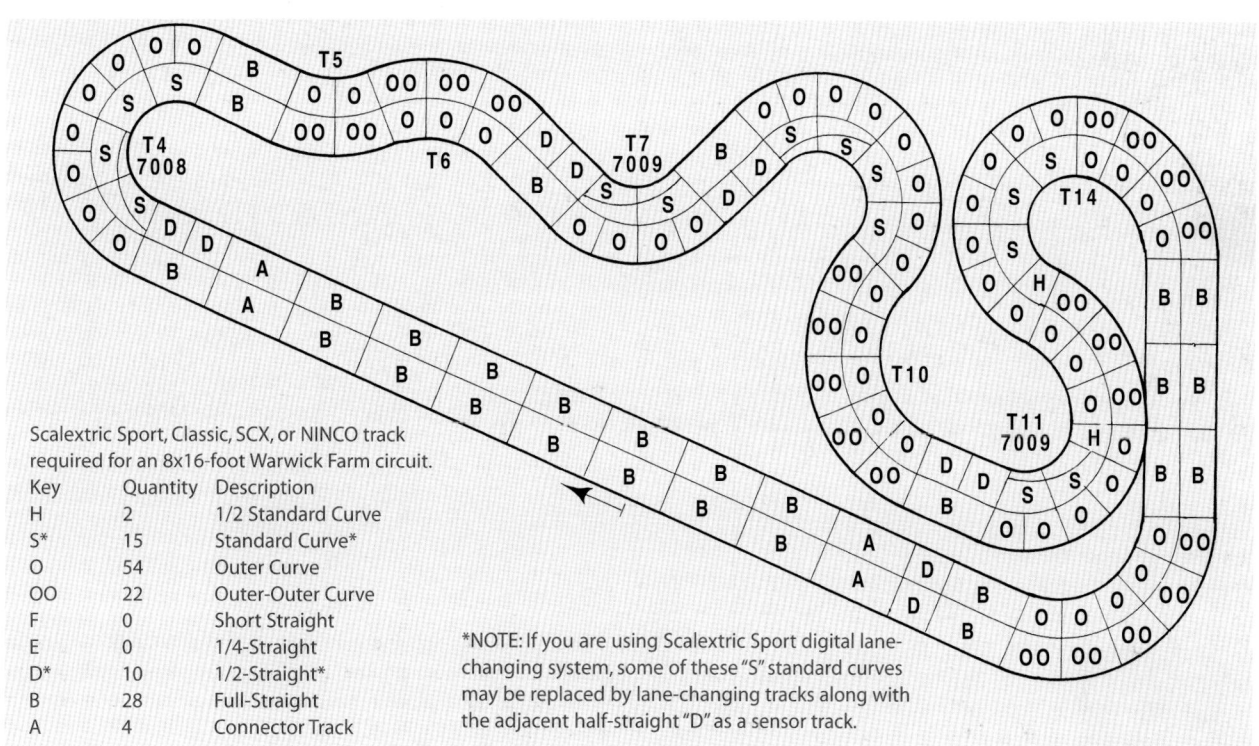

Scalextric Sport, Classic, SCX, or NINCO track required for an 8x16-foot Warwick Farm circuit.

Key	Quantity	Description
H	2	1/2 Standard Curve
S*	15	Standard Curve*
O	54	Outer Curve
OO	22	Outer-Outer Curve
F	0	Short Straight
E	0	1/4-Straight
D*	10	1/2-Straight*
B	28	Full-Straight
A	4	Connector Track

*NOTE: If you are using Scalextric Sport digital lane-changing system, some of these "S" standard curves may be replaced by lane-changing tracks along with the adjacent half-straight "D" as a sensor track.

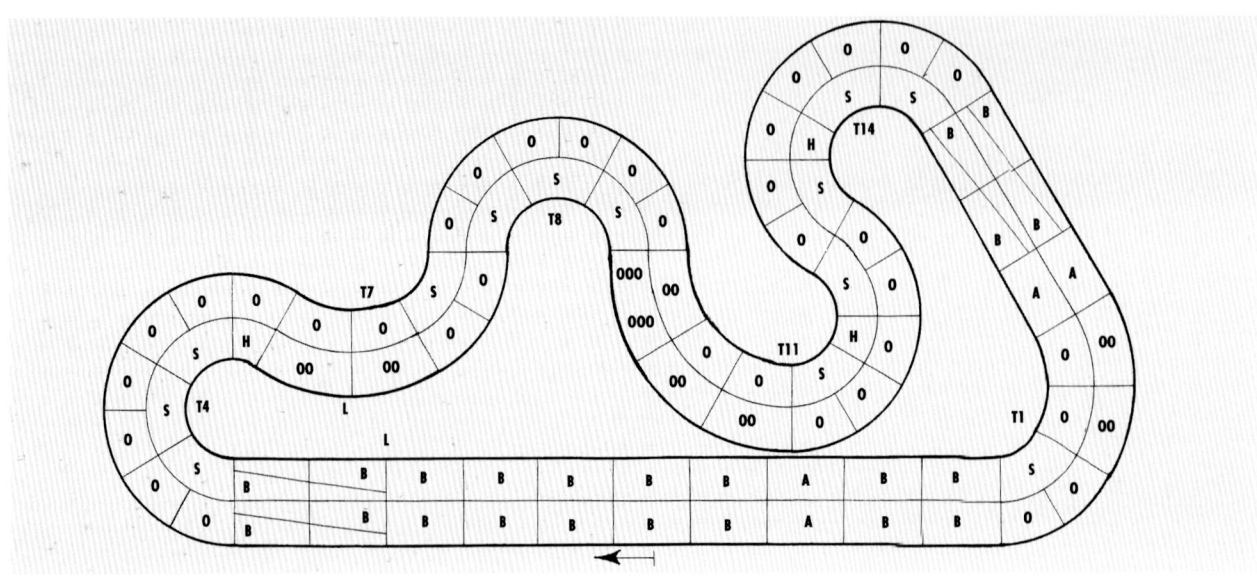

Carrera track required for an 8x16-foot Warwick Farm circuit.

Key	Quantity	Description
H	3	1/2 Inner Curve
S	13	Inner Curve
O	35	Middle Curve
OO	7	Outer Curve
OOO	1 pair (2)	Outer-Outer Curve
E	0	1/4-Straight
D	0	1/3-Straight
B*	22	Full-Straight*
A	4	Connector Track

*NOTE: If you are using the Carrera Pro-X lane-changing system, some pairs of standard-length straights ("S") may be placed with Carrera Pro-X lane-changing tracks.

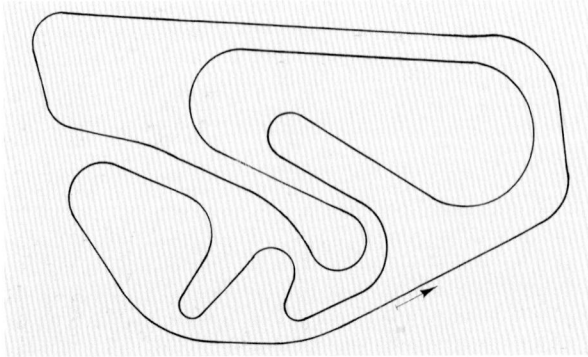

The original Interlagos track as it was from 1954 to 1990.

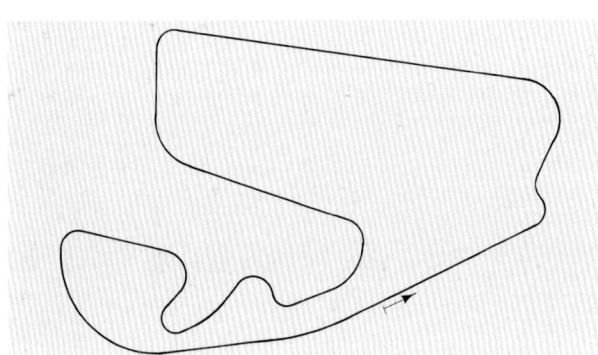

In 1990, the Interlagos circuit was widened and many of the overlapping sections were removed to create this configuration. This is the track that is now used for the Brazilian F1 races.

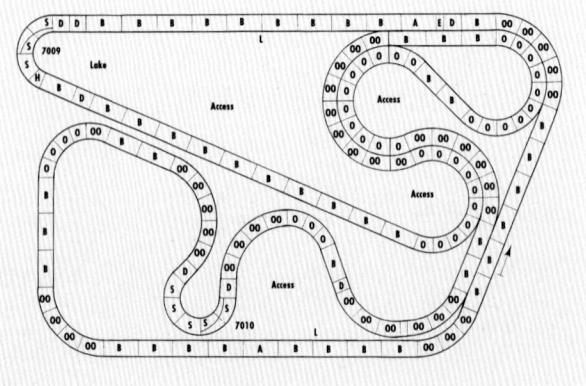

Scalextric Sport, Classic, SCX, or NINCO track required for a 12x18-foot Interlagos track.

Key	Quantity	Description
H	1	1/2 Standard Curve
S*	8	Standard Curve*
O	54	Outer Curve
OO	22	Outer-Outer Curve
F	0	"Short" Straight
E	0	1/4-Straight
D*	6	1/2-Straight*
B	48	Full-Straight
A	2	Connector Track

*NOTE: If you are using Scalextric Sport digital lane-changing system, some 45 degree pairs of the "S" standard curves may be replaced by 90 degree curved lane-changing tracks, along with the adjacent half-straight "D" as a sensor track just before the curve.

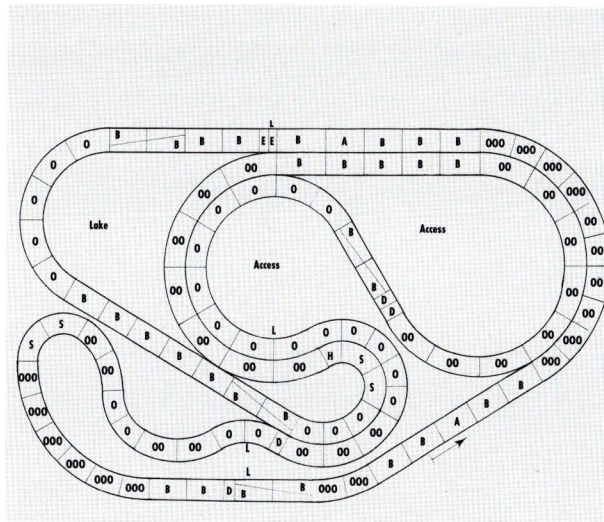

Carrera track required for a 12x18-foot Interlagos track.

Key	Quantity	Description
H	1	1/2 Inner Curve
S	4	Inner Curve
O	26	Middle Curve
OO	722	Outer Curve
OOO	9 pair (18)	Outer-Outer Curve
E	2	1/4-Straight
D	4	1/3-Straight
B*	30	Full-Straight*
A	2	Connector Track

*NOTE: If you are using the Carrera Pro-X lane-changing system, some pairs of standard-length straights ("S") may be placed with Carrera Pro-X lane-changing tracks.

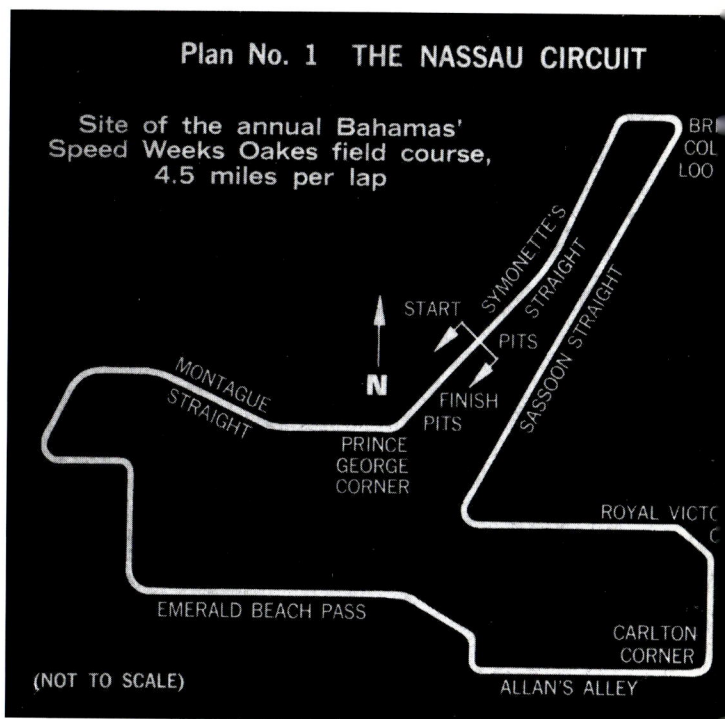

Nassau, Bahamas, circuit.

Brand	Scale	Layout Size	Straight Track Required	Curved Track Required	Average Length/Lap
Strombecker	1/32 or 1/24	12' x 16'	46 full straight, 10 half straight	14 regular, 8 half, 36 outer	47-1/2'
Kal Kar	1/32 or 1/24	12' x 16'	24-1/2 4 lane straight	3 full circles, 4 lane	46'
Varney (2 lane only)	1/32 or 1/24	12' x 16'	32 sections	16 standard	48'
V.I.P. (2 lane only)	1/32 or 1/24	12' x 16'	32 sections	16 standard	48'

Plan No. three is drawn for use with Strombecker or Kal-Kar track sections, however, the same layout idea can be used with any set track using 60° segments of a circle for curves (six pieces per circle) if the areas using the half curves sections are eliminated.

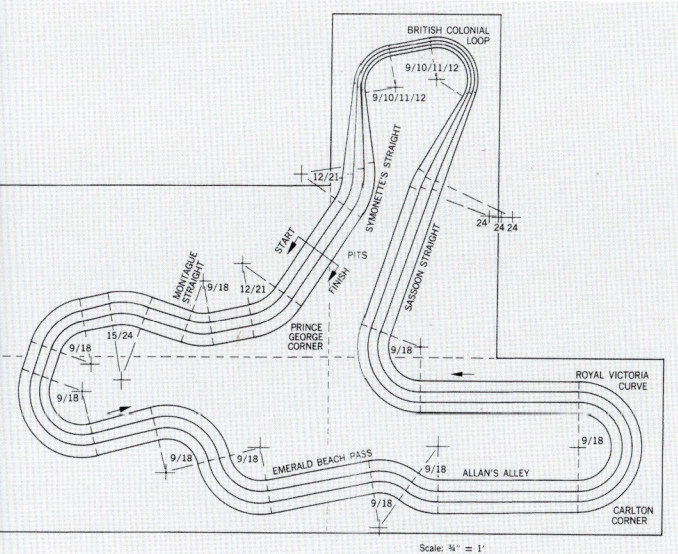

The four-lane routed version of the Nassau Circuit can be assembled from four 4x8-foot sheets of MDF board or MDO plywood.

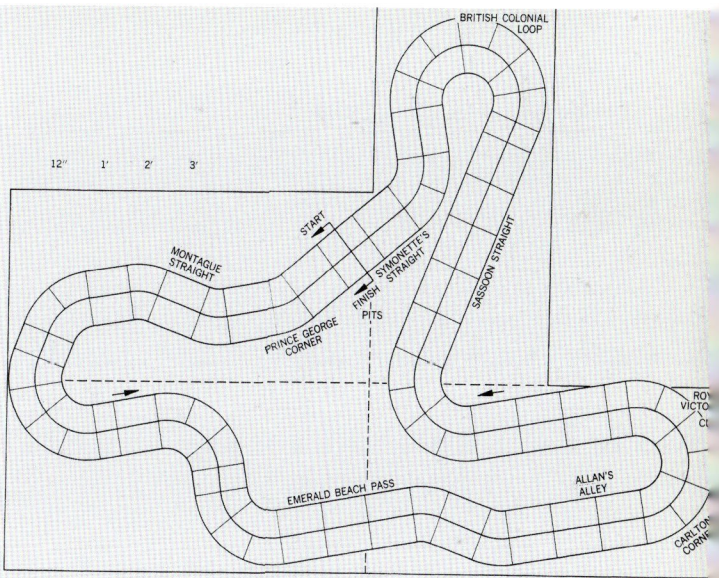

The Nassau Circuit for Strombecker, Revell, Monogram, or Kal-Kar track for 12x16 feet.

(Plan No. three is drawn for use with Strombecker or Kal-Kar track sections, however, the same layout idea can be used with any set track using 60° segments of a circle for curves (six pieces per circle) if the areas using the half curve sections are eliminated.)	BRAND	SCALE	LAYOUT SIZE	STRAIGHT TRACK REQUIRED*	CURVED TRACK REQUIRED	AVERAGE LENGTH/LAP
	Strombecker	1/32 or 1/24	12' x 16'	46 full straight 10 half straight	14 regular 8 half 36 outer	46½'
	Kal-Kar	1/32 or 1/24	12' x 16'	24½ 4 lane straight	3 full circles 4 lane	46'
	Varney (2 lane only)	1/32 or 1/24	12' x 16'	32 sections	16 standard	48'
	V.I.P. (2 lane only)	1/32 or 1/24	12' x 16'	32 sections	16 standard	48'

Track sections needed for collector brands.

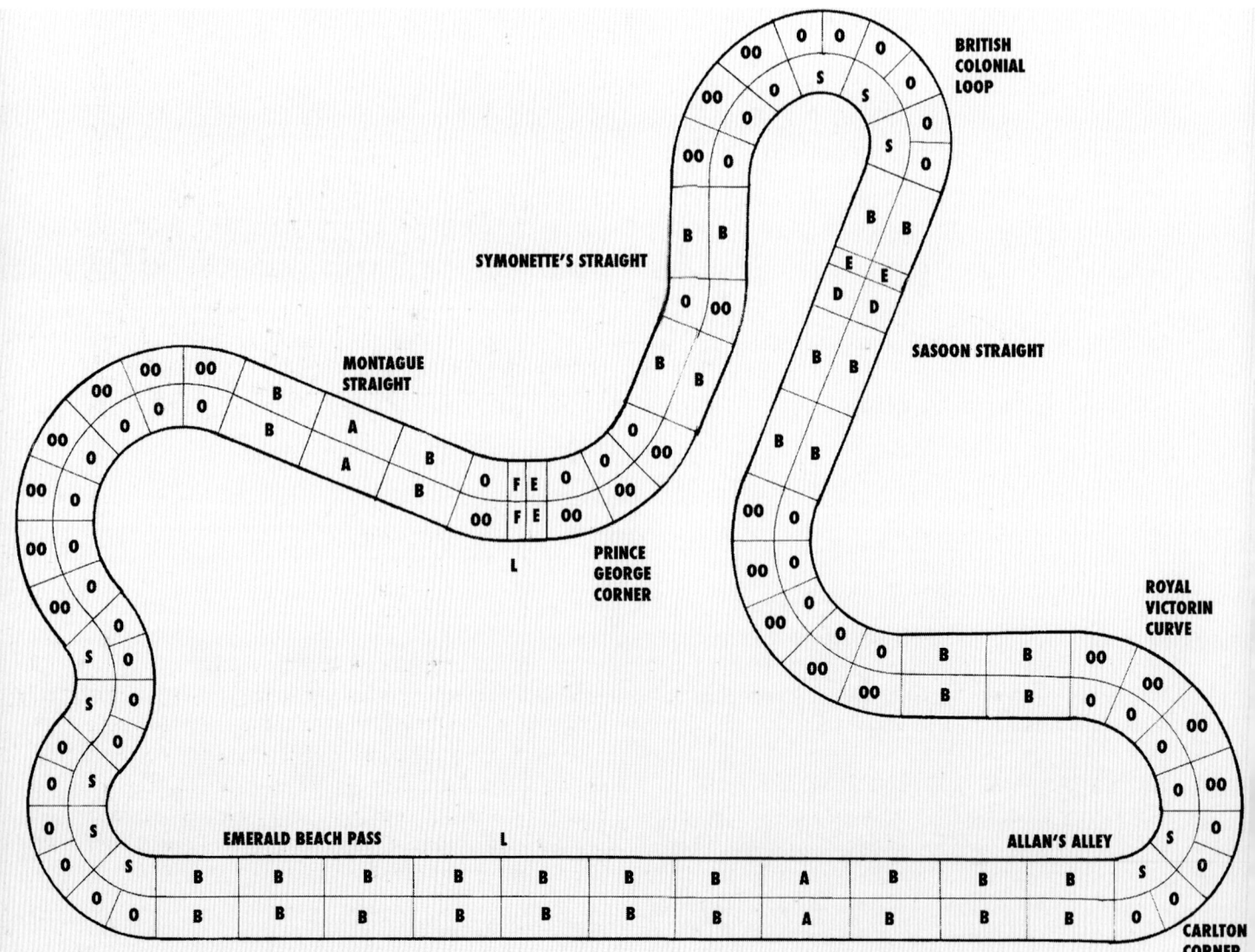

Scalextric Sport, Classic, or SCX track required for a 12x16-foot Nassau circuit.

Key	Quantity	Description
H	0	1/2 Standard Curve
S	10	Standard Curve
O	44	Outer Curve
OO	24	Outer-Outer Curve
F	2	Short Straight
E	4	1/4-Straight
D	2	1/2-Straight
B	38	Full-Straight
A	4	Connector Track

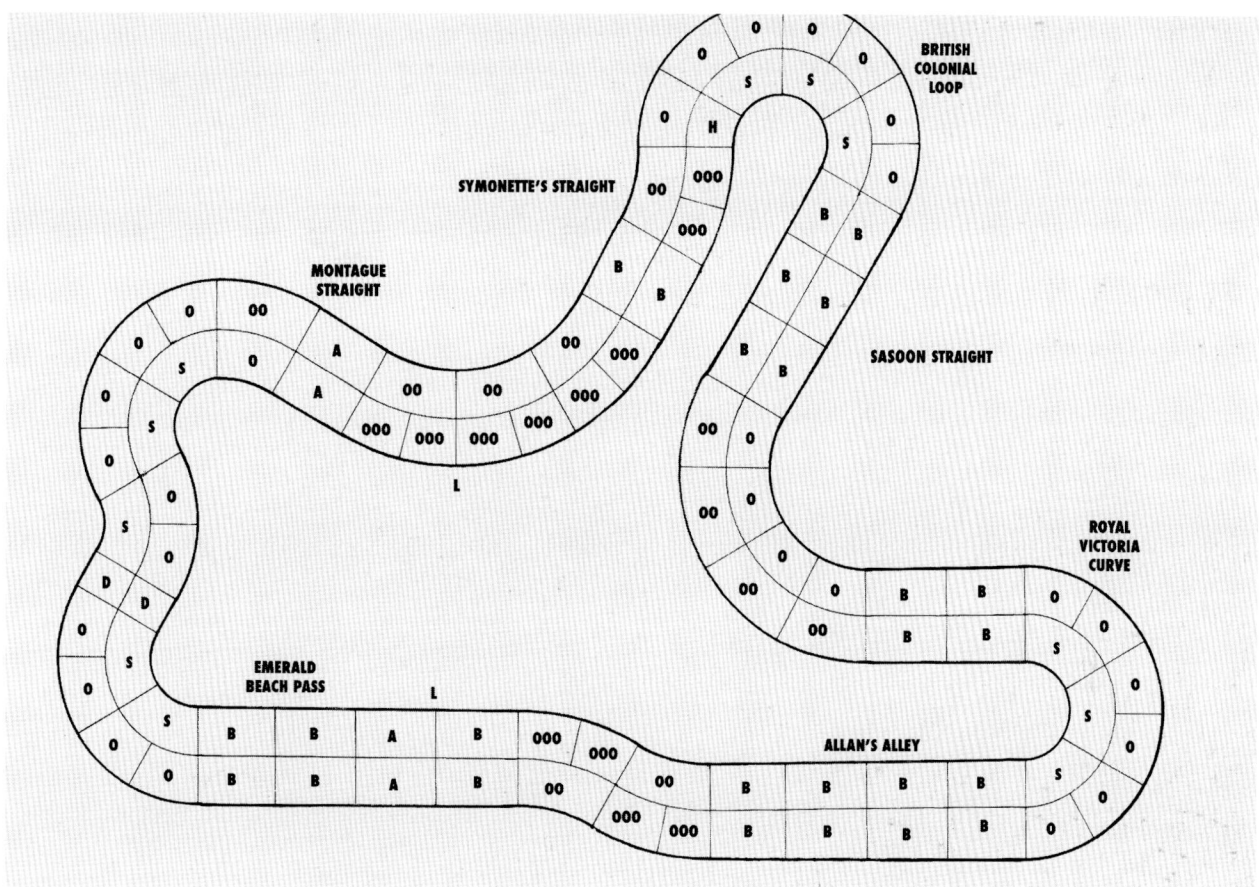

This is a list of Carrera track required for a 12x16-foot Nassau circuit.

Key	Quantity	Description
H	1	1/2 Inner Curve
S	11	Inner Curve
O	28	Middle Curve
OO	11	Outer Curve
OOO	6 pair (12)	Outer-Outer Curve
E	0	1/4-Straight
D	2	1/3-Straight
B	26	Full-Straight
A	4	Connector Track

of a decreasing radius curve (the one leading into the curve marked "7010"), all the curves have a constant radius.

Interlagos, Brazil, F1 Track for Carrera

The Carrera version of Interlagos has even broader radius curves with an incredible 150-degree sweeper at the far right and another 90-degree sweeper at the lower left. The sweeper at the lower left is entered from a pair of large curves, then two standard-size curves, to provide a replica of a curve with tight apex. The 150-degree curve near the lower center is a decreasing radius on the inside pair of lanes, but the outer two lanes are traversed in the opposite direction as an increasing radius turn. All of the other curves on the track are constant radius. There are only two short tight curves on the track.

On the Carrera version, the lane-changing tracks at Turn 14 allow the cars to take the shortest inside line through the majority of the track. The lane-changing tracks at Turn 4 allow the cars to get back into the other lane for passing. The plan is designed so that when running clockwise, Turns 1 and 11 are decreasing radius turns.

Nassau, Bahamas

In the 1950s and 1960s, sports car racers were invited to compete on the island of Nassau in the Bahamas to increase tourist traffic to the islands. The events were held early enough in the season so that by 1963, the list of entries often rivaled Sebring or Daytona as a "first look" at the coming year's racing machines.

CHAPTER 10
SEDAN RACING: NASCAR, TRANS-AM, DTM, AND WRC

Scalextric has offered 2003 NASCAR cars in a variety of paint schemes. These four are on a Carrera banked curve.

To Americans, NASCAR is the best-known form of sedan racing. In Europe, DTM (German Touring Car Championship) and World Rally Cup (WRC) draw the crowds. NASCAR cars are actually pure racing machines that happen to be shaped like sedans.

Australia has its own series, including the V-8 Supercars (Scalextric makes replicas), and Japan has several series of sedan races. The concept of a race car with a sedan body is the basis for the new British SCV8 class with tubular chassis cars and Cosworth 550 horsepower V-8s. The bodies that run in the series include Jaguar's X-Type, Accord, Vauxhaul Vectra, and Peugeot 406.

The German Touring Cars (DTM) are closer to production cars, but they share only a few body panels, grilles, and emblems with the street versions. The shapes of the NASCAR and DTM cars are similar enough to the street versions that you can tell a Taurus from a Monte Carlo (from the grille, if not the shape). The DTM cars' bodies are closer in appearance to stock, but they have fenders that are nearly a foot wider.

Racing Your Daily Driver

There are dozens of real racing classes, many limited to a single country, for just about any type of sedan. In America, there's the SCCA Speed World Challenge series for wheel-to-wheel racing. The small sedan racing sport is more popular in Europe, and the ETCC (European Touring Car Championship—the Super Racing series) offers DTM-style cars but is limited to four cylinders. The BTCC (British Touring Car Championship) is very similar to the ETCC. There are also dozens of similar series in Spain, Germany, France, Finland,

Some examples of the array of racing sedans are (left to right): Scalextric NASCAR Ford Taurus, Scalextric Mercedes DTM CLK, Scalextric Trans-Am Camaro, Carrera Camaro SS396 Muscle Car, NINCO BMW M3GTR, SCX Subaru Impreza WRC, and NINCO New Mini.

Carrera also has Bobby Allison's 1970 Daytona (number 71) that he drove at Riverside and to win the 1970 NASCAR Championship. Carrera also has Dan Gurney's car that competed at Riverside in 1970.

Sweden, Argentina, Australia, and Eastern Asia. Nearly every country has its own series for small sedan racing. There are even more series for one-make sedans series, including the John Cooper Challenge (Scalextric and NINCO have New Minis), the Renault Clio Cup Series (NINCO has the Rally version), VW Polo series (NINCO), Beetle Cup for New Beetles (Scalextric), and others. In the 1960s and 1970s, the 1,000-cc displacement GT Touring car classes were populated by the original Mini-Minor and the Fiat Abarth 1000, which were both made by SCX.

Race Cars that Began Life as Sedans

The American Trans-Am and NASCAR cars of the late 1960s and 1970s were also production bodies fitted with roll cages that served as a second chassis. Trans-Am racing was populated with sedans that ranged from Mini Minors (like the SCX model) to Alfa Romeo GTAs (Fly has them) to Mustangs, Camaros (like the Scalextric models), and 'Cudas (like Carrera's models in Chapter 6).

The larger and more highly modified cars like the BMW M3GTR (a very limited production racer with a V-8 in place of the standard M3's inline 6—NINCO and Fly have it in 1/32 scale) run in the American Le Mans Series (ALMS) GT Class; similar BMWs won the 2003 Grand Am Series GT class and the Speed GT Class of the SCCA Speed World Challenge series. The AMG Mercedes CLK, Opel Astra V-8, and Audi TT compete in the European DTM series. SCX and NINCO offer all three vehicles, and Scalextric has the Mercedes and Opel.

The World Rally Cup (WRC) cars compete on closed sections of both paved and dirt public roads all over Europe and Australia. These are four-wheel-drive versions of some of the more popular compact cars such as the Subaru Impreza, Ford Focus,

Dan Gurney at the Riverside NASCAR road race in 1970.

Mitsubishi Lancer Evo, Hyundai Accent, as well as cars that Americans may not be as familiar with, such as the Citroen Xsara, Peugeot 307, and Skoda Fabia. The cars carry the basic body shell and engine block of the production cars, but are fitted with roll cages that effectively provide a second chassis, and the running gear and engine are highly modified.

The junior versions of the WRC that feed drivers to the series include the Super 1600 Rally series for Toyota Corollas, Fiat Puntos, Seat Cordobas, Citroen Saxos, and the like (NINCO), or the Seat Leons and Hyundai Accents (SCX).

Sedan Racing in 1/32 Scale

There's nothing that says you have to match your model car racing classes or series to those of the real world. An alternative would be to run a small sedan series and throw it open to anything. You can discover, in 1/32 scale, if a Ford Taurus really can outrun a Mercedes CLK.

A Scalextric Trans-Am Mustang and a repainted Carrera 'Cuda are on a 1/32 scale version of Riverside Raceway.

Parnelli Jones' Trans-Am Mustang at the 1970 Laguna Seca race.

SCX has offered the Fiat Abarth in a variety of different paint schemes, including this vintage racing car's Gulf-style orange and blue.

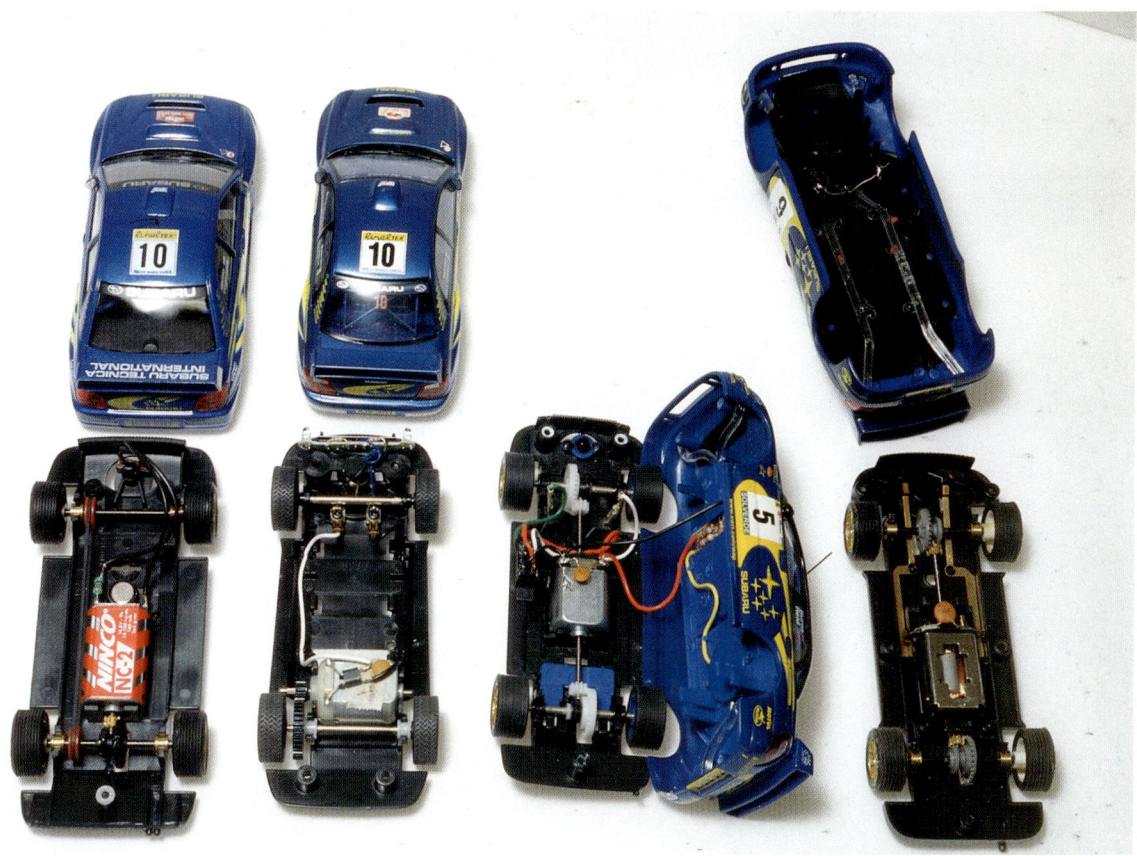

The chassis of the four WRX Subarus (left to right): NINCO, Scalextric, Auto Art, and SCX.

Four Rally Cars

These four model car manufacturers make replicas of the same Subaru WRX Rally car in 1/32 scale. The Auto Art and SCX cars have a geared drive to both front and rear axles. The NINCO car has a conventional rear wheel drive with a pair of pulleys and a belt to drive the front wheels. The Scalextric car is a sidewinder.

The Subaru WRX in the far rear (number 10) is Scalextric, the number 6 car is an SCX, the number 5 car is an Auto Art, and the number 10 in the foreground is NINCO's.

PERFORMANCE

Four WRC Rally Cars

Auto Art	NINCO	SCX	Scalextric
Subaru	Subaru	Focus	Subaru

Lap Times on Sport Monaco track:

| 6.41 sec. | 7.21 sec. | 6.95 sec. | 7.26 sec. |

Lap Times on Carrera Monaco (on page 67, Slot Car Bible):

| 6.73 sec. | 7.24 sec. | 6.85 sec. | 6.44 sec. |

We have performed track test reports, reported by Dan Wilson, on all four brands of Rally cars, but not specifically on the SCX or Scalextric Subarus. Just to be sure, we ran all four cars around the Carrera and Sport Monaco tracks.

CHAPTER 11
YOUR RACETRACKS

Rowland Anselmo's NINCO track has borders on every curve and scale guardrails, spectators, and vehicles.

It's great to collect replicas of real racing cars, but it's much more fun to see them in action. Thousands of people have assembled model car raceways in their homes. Most are assembled from plastic track sections, but a few are cut from particle board, MDF, or MDO sheets with a router, as shown in *Slot Car Bible*. Here are some examples of the kind of track you can have in your home.

Rowland Anselmo's NINCO Raceway

Rowland Anselmo's raceway is one of the tracks in the West Suburban Slot Car Association (WSSCA, http://groups.yahoo.com/group/WSSCA/; http://www.wssca.us) near Chicago. Rowland's raceway is assembled from NINCO track and borders to fill a 12x13-foot tabletop with four lanes of action. The track was designed so carefully that the lap length on any of the four lanes is exactly 67 1/2 feet. Races are run for simulated 24-hour periods (24 minutes per lane is common) with the track illuminated only with cars' headlights and the array of Lionel Train streetlight stanchions.

The track is powered by a Pyramid-brand industrial power pack with 12 amps and a variable 9 to 12 volts—the voltage is usually set to 13.8 to match the wall transformers in most sets. The track lap counting and timing are done on a laptop using the shareware SRM program (http://www.cenobyte.nl/slotracemanager/news.html). A dead strip in each pickup rail provides electrical signals for the counting system. Lap times with out-of-the box cars average about 7.5 seconds, although the group prefers to run cars without magnets.

Russell Cox's Scalextric Raceway

Like many Scalextric enthusiasts, Russell Cox likes both the old and the new. He received his first

Russell Cox's track is assembled from Scalextric Classic track sections, including the out-of-production working pit lane.

The pit buildings on Russell Cox's track are positioned so they serve two parallel straight sections of the track.

Scalextric set as a kid in England before he moved to America. His track combines both today's super realistic cars and the more toy-like offerings that Scalextric offered from the 1950s through the 1990s. Scalextric still offers the plastic pit buildings, tower, and grandstand, but you'll have to search eBay and flea markets for the operating pit stop lane, refreshment stand, fencing, the Dunlop bridge, and many of the cars. The track is fully illuminated with a variety of Lionel train accessory light stands and a light tower.

The track is placed on a tabletop made of 1/2-inch plywood with 1x2-foot braces that rest on sawhorses. The surface is painted green, but the track is not secured to the tabletop, so it's easy to make changes in the track configuration. The wiring for the lights is, however, routed through holes drilled through the tabletop so the wires can run beneath the table.

The pit area is assembled from two Scalextric pits and two Riggen (ex-Strombecker) pit buildings that are still available to dealers through REH. The pits are faced by a row of four Scalextric grandstands.

The track is one of a series that is part of the Houston Scale Auto Racing Club (HSARC, http://www.hsarc.net/). The other clubs in the U.S. are listed on the *Model Car Racing* magazine website at www.modelcarracingmag.com.

Bob Dunkle's Scalextric Sport Raceway

Bob Dunkle's Highland Raceway is about as far as you can get from the commercial raceways. Bob Dunkle considers the hobby to be one of racing miniature replicas of real automobiles, and he has

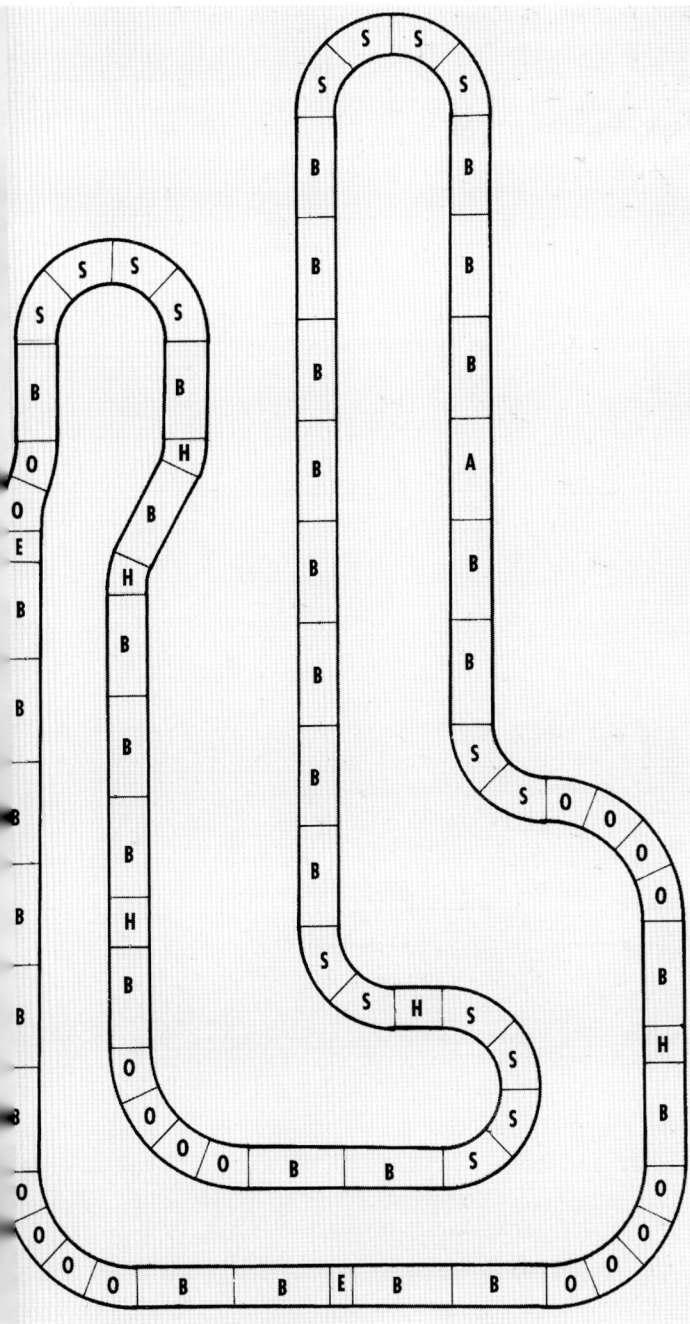

Russell Cox's 9x15-foot Scalextric track. You can assemble a replica from Scalextric Sport, Classic, or SCX track sections. See Chapters 8 and 9 for the key to the letters on the track sections.

road-style with Mountains-in-Minutes rock castings and plaster over the door screen.

Bob's Highland Raceway is one of about a dozen home tracks that are part of a Chicago area club. You can contact them at bdunkle@comcast.net if you live in the area and want to race on a track other than your own.

John MacKenzie's Seattle Hill Raceway

John MacKenzie is one of the most active members of the Puget Sound Slot Racing Association (PSSRA; jicemanmac@msn.com), a group of Seattle/Tacoma racers who have a round-robin series on a half-dozen home raceways. Steven Cobb built the benchwork. MacKenzie's track has been detailed to include the scenes you'd expect on a real racetrack, and the crowd is usually protected by chainlink fences. The four-lane track is about 8x16 feet.

The track is illuminated with a few dozen lights from Art-Kit in Spain. Most of the buildings are in Scalextric's current line or are out-of-production models from the 1960s. The track is powered by an adjustable Samlex 10 amp, 0-30-volt power supply. Lap counting, timing, and scoring are done on a computer with a SlotMaster (www.slotmaster.com) program.

Jim Cusumano's Tabasco Lakes Speedway

Jim Cusumano has applied the scenery building techniques model railroaders use to create a very realistic raceway. The track is Scalextric with SCX inner and outer borders. The average lap length is about 43 feet. The track is also part of a dozen or so groups that host weekly races in the west Chicago suburbs: WSSCA (West Suburban Slot Car Association).

Cusumano built the track on a table with 1x4-foot legs and braces, and a 1/2-inch plywood top. The plywood was cut about 6 inches wider than the track and the plywood is elevated with 1x4-foot supports to create the overpass. The Sport track rests on the plywood and is held in place with a few dabs of silicone caulking compound. The scenery is Hydrocal plaster, which is much harder than regular plaster and less likely to chip. The lake is decoupage casting resin. The pit tower and pit buildings are from Scalextric. Most of the vehicles were found in toy stores.

Bruce Yeoman's Carrera Raceway

Bruce Yeoman created this 7x18-foot, four-lane Carrera track to fill an alcove beside his basement

developed a track to provide both realistic racing action and realistic scenes. The track is assembled from Scalextric Classic track, and it climbs almost a foot from the level main straight. Most of the buildings and accessories are Scalextric, and some are collector's items. The scenery is done model rail-

continued on page 198

The Highland Raceway is a compact 5x12 feet. All of the corners have borders because the club has a non-magnet racing class, and the cars need room to powerslide or drift through the turns.

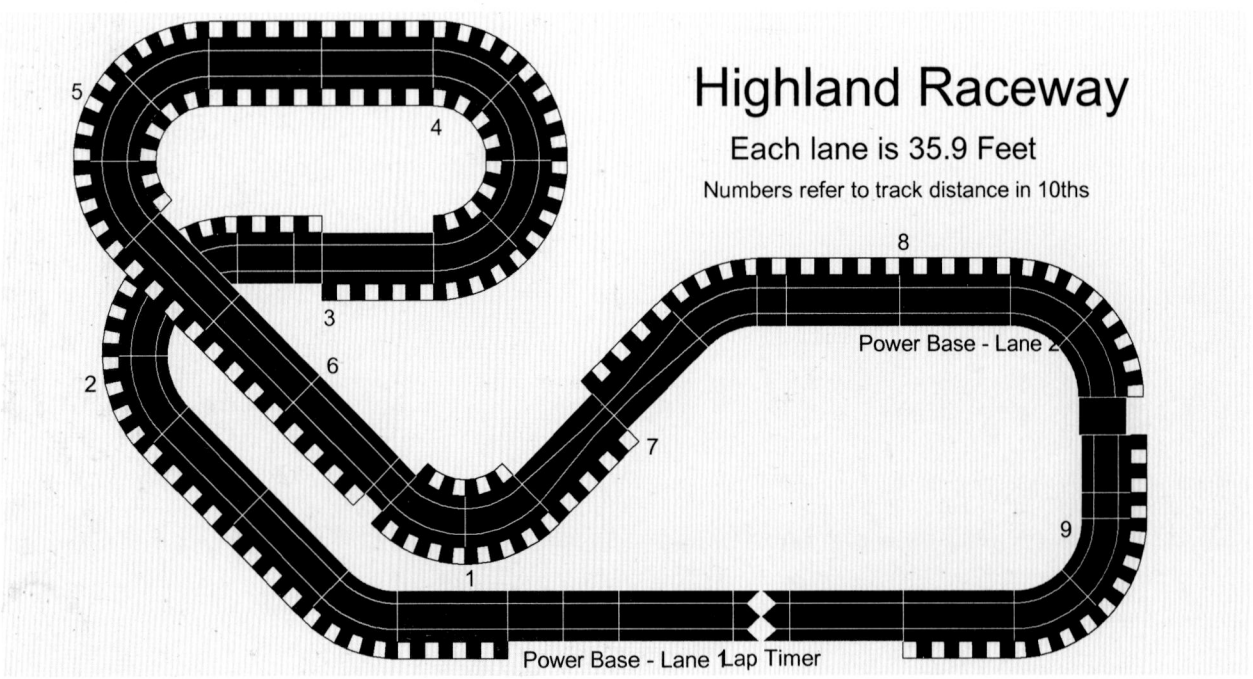

Bob Dunkle's Highland Raceway is assembled from Scalextric Sport track sections.

Bob Dunkle's Scalextric raceway climbs about 9 inches to a tight turn before heading back onto the flats. The trees are Life-Like model railroad accessories. The figures are porcelain and were found on eBay.

The pit buildings and most of the figures on the Highland Raceway are Scalextric and hand-painted MRRC.

Most of the track on the Seattle Hill Raceway is Scalextric Classic with three curves, including the one in the foreground, which was assembled from SCX 3-size curves for the outer two lanes.

The vertical poles on the Seattle Hill Raceway are steel rods with aluminum screen door mesh to simulate a chain-link fence. The cars are a Monogram Cooper-Ford on a modified MRRC Chaparral chassis and a Top-Slot Daytona Cobra coupe on an MRRC chassis with an MRRC Cobra interior.

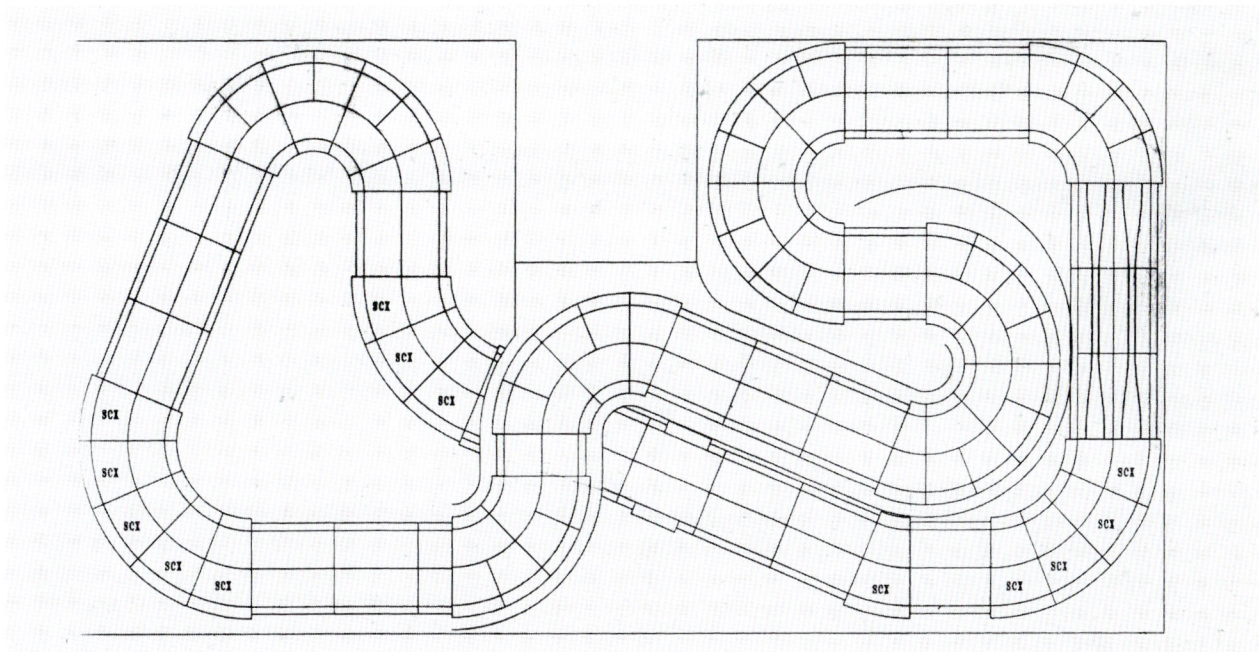

John MacKenzie's Seattle Hill Raceway.

The pit buildings on the Tabasco Lakes Speedway are from Scalextric.

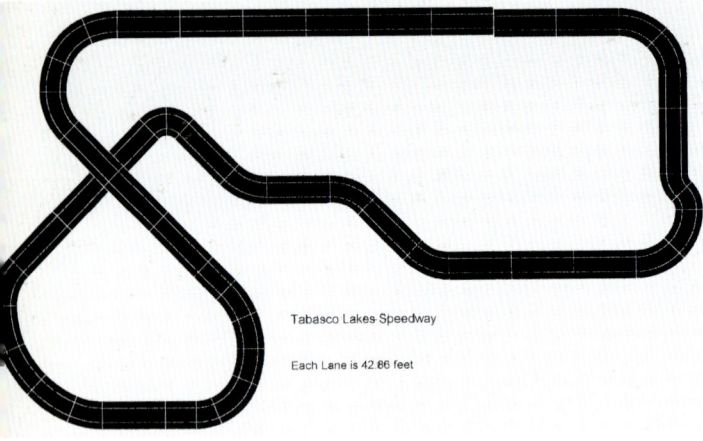

This Tabasco Lakes Speedway is assembled from Scalextric Sport track sections.

den. He painted the borders (skid aprons) to avoid the construction zone look of Carrera's yellow-striped borders. The newer Carrera borders have a red and white herringbone pattern. The layout is placed in a corner, so cars that deslot more than 3 feet from the front edge are replaced using a pistol-grip set of tongs.

The track has several realistic scenes, but none of the scenic texture materials such as sand or sawdust are loose. The track rests on a piece of indoor/outdoor carpet. The trees are model railroad products, and any loose foliage is secured with several coasts of cheap hairspray. The track is illuminated for night racing with building interior lights and lights on poles from a model railroad shop. He

The shelves surrounding the track display a portion of Bruce Yeoman's collection of 1/32 scale model racing cars.

The track loops back on itself without a figure-8-style overpass on Bruce Yeoman's Carrera track. The lap times on the four lanes are nearly identical.

built the pits from sheet styrene. The grandstands are from Scalextric and Artin.

Jimmy Attard's Lane-Changing Northland Raceway

Lane changing was introduced to 1/32 scale racing from Scalextric, Carrera, and SCX in late 2004, but Jimmy Attard has had a lane-changing system for several years. His track was cut from wood with an electric router. The electrical contact comes from self-adhesive copper braid. The system operates on 12 to 18 volts of DC current, just like the 1/32 scale plastic track systems. Jimmy preferred the flexibility of track design that a handmade track offers. He also wanted to try his ideas about forcing the cars to pick the place to pass.

The track design is clever. There are the typical four lanes. Lanes 1, 2, and 3 each have a switch at the hairpin turn to allow them to take a parallel route around the track, which totals seven lanes around the track. Lane 4 has no switch or passing lane and is the center of the seven lanes. The lane spacing around most of the track is so close that you cannot pass unless your car is in the passing lane and the car(s) you want to pass are in the regular lane(s). You have to make a decision once a lap whether to take the passing lane or stay put. The cars only take one lap in the passing lane, and when they get around to

The pit buildings on Bruce Yeoman's track were built from styrene sheet and strip, and the lighting was intended for use on model railroads. The figures are mostly Scalextric and SCX. The three women are from Slot.it.

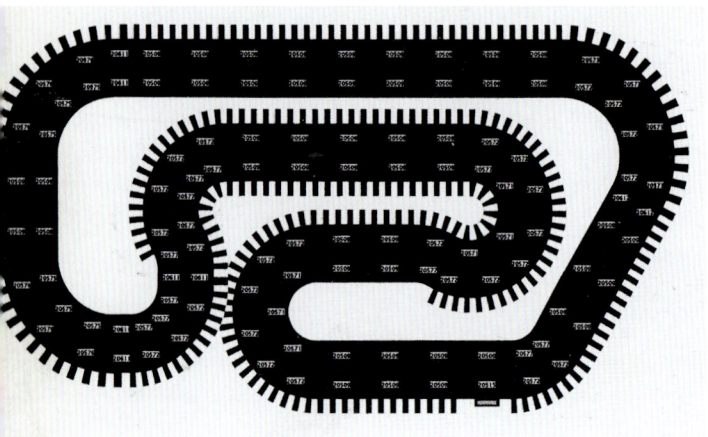

Bruce Yeoman's Carrera raceway.

the hairpin again, they are automatically routed back into their regular lane.

The passing lane switches are small metal flaps that pivot to force the cars from the regular lane to the passing lane. It's about the same system as the lane-changers on the Scalextric Sport Digital and Carrera Pro-X digital lane-changers. On Jimmy Attard's track, however, the lane-changers are operated by stout hand levers, one for each of the three passing lanes, which are pulled much like a shift lever, to change from conventional to passing lane.

Attard's system works. I raced with it. Attard is experimenting with a diode system to allow two cars per lane, with a total of seven per race (the fourth lane car has no passing lane).

A panorama of Northland Raceway. The hairpin turn with the lane-changing switches is visible in both photos. The scenery is only complete in the corkscrew area to the far upper right.

The Northland Raceway has a second set of switches and levers to allow each of the four lanes to be routed into the pits. Like the MESAC track from decades earlier (which was Jimmy's inspiration for his track), the racing rules require at least one pit stop per race.

The Mystique of MESAC

The Miniature Electric Scale Auto Racing Club (MESAC) is one of the legends of model car racing. The track was built in the late 1960s and lasted for less than 10 years. Designed to be the ultimate slot car track, a variety of switches and sliding shunts allowed the MESAC course to be altered into eight different tracks. The photographs here are some of the same shots that caused such a stir in the 1970s. Imagine one track with eight options.

The MESAC track was routed from particle board and used a metal braid for electrical pickup on each of the six lanes. MESAC had switches, but not lane-changing. The switches were metal flaps like Scalextric Sport Digital and Carrera Pro-X digital, but they were used only to route the cars into the pits.

When you looked at the MESAC track, it appeared to offer a number of different course options, as do many full-size raceways. MESAC did offer options. The change from one route to another was achieved with a 4-inch-wide sliding board that had 12 lanes; one set of six for the straight route,

The downhill section on Jimmy Attard's raceway is complete with scenery.

The entrance to the pit lanes on the Northland Raceway, and three cars are heading for the pits.

The one place on the Northland Raceway where the drivers must choose to stay in their lanes or go for the passing lane is the hairpin where small levers in the track direct the cars into their chosen lane.

The slots on the Northland Raceway recreate the path a real car would take into the pits, but it sometimes requires that one slot crosses another.

and another set of six (adjacent to each of the first six) for the curved route. Six of these shunts were fitted to allow the option of the eight different tracks. These sliding shunts proved troublesome because a deslotted car could easily slip into one of the unused dead-end slots to come to an instant stop with a broken guide. Later, the sliding shunts were replaced with flip-over panels that had the six curved routes on one side and the straight routes on the back side.

The tracks were usually changed for each week's races so it was difficult to learn the track. MESAC usually ran two or three championships, and each was based on a real racing class. Some of them could

The legendary MESAC track in Southern California was routed from wood, and the switches lead to the pits.

The MESAC track climbed nearly 3 feet. One of the alternate track-routing areas is visible in dark gray in the upper right.

The levers for changing from straight-ahead to the pit lanes are similar to those used on Scalextric Sport Digital and Carrera Pro-X digital systems.

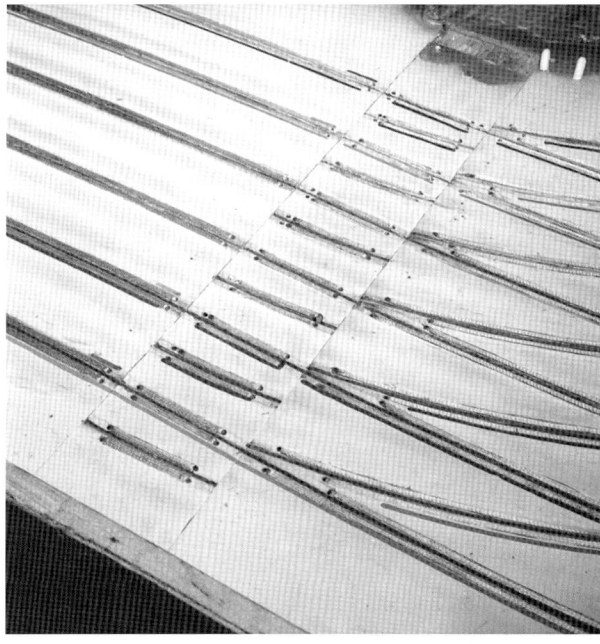
This is one of the sliding shunts used to change the MESAC track configuration.

be obscure, like the "U2" class—the low-cost sports car series of the period. Races for 1930s-era vintage cars were common series, as were current-era sports and Grand Prix series.

What made MESAC so controversial was its very strict adherence to exact scale. It was up to the entrant to prove that his or her car was the correct size by supplying the scrutineers with

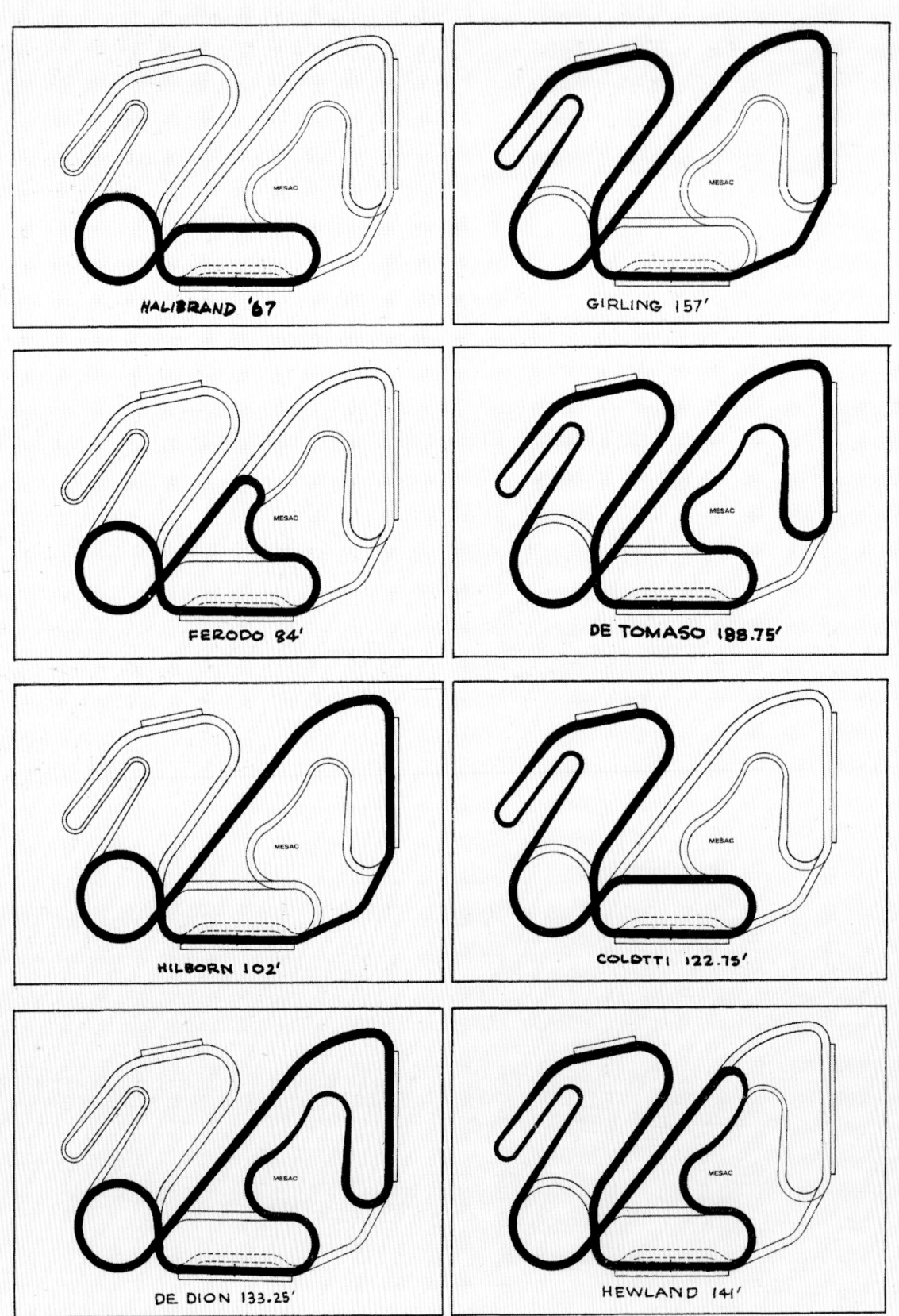

There was no lane-changing on MESAC, but sliding track sections (shunts) allowed the course to be altered to eight different tracks.

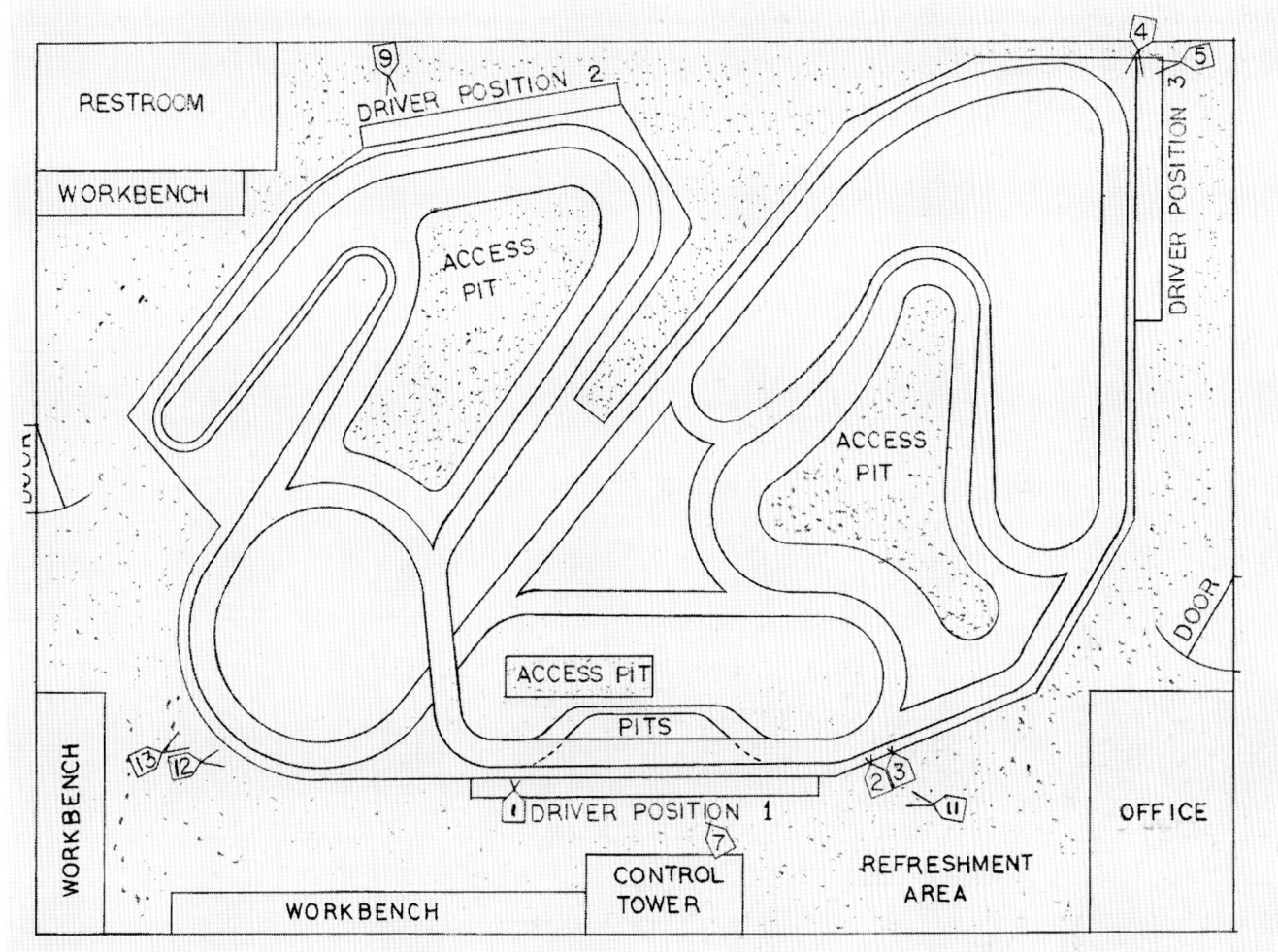

The MESAC track with all the alternate course options, including the pit lanes.

published documentation. Each car was also subject to pre-race *concours d'elegance*, and each car had to score a minimum number of *concours* points to be able to race. All this was a stark contrast to 1/24 scale commercial raceways of the time that pushed further into the "door stop" school of projectile racing. The club was about evenly divided between 1/32 and 1/24 scale events. The same rules of exact-scale applied to both scales.

A visit to MESAC, whether as a spectator or a driver, was an event you would remember. Winning was even sweeter because these were some of the best drivers in Southern California.

CHAPTER 12

HO RACE CAR TRACK TESTS

The Katz-Spa-Ring from Chapter 13 was one of three tracks that were used to provide lap times.

Brad Bowman tested 11 of the popular HO cars on the racetrack. You can compare the numbers he recorded for the cars you currently own to see how much quicker (or slower) another brand might be. Do note that the Tomy T-Jet and Playing Mantis Thunderjet cars have no magnets and, hence, produce much slower times. Also, the Playing Mantis X-Traction has a weak magnetic downforce. Conversely, the Wizzard and BSRT cars have stronger downforce and stickier tires. These Wizard and BSRT cars may not be suitable for a small HO track.

The skid pad test is pretty simple. Drive the car as fast as you can until it spins out or falls off the track. This is an interesting test because it only tests the road-holding ability of the car. Horsepower doesn't matter as long as the car makes enough horsepower for the car to reach a speed that will cause it to break loose. What is very important to note here is that if a car is good at the skid pad test, it doesn't necessarily mean it's going to be drivable on the racetrack, especially if the slot car utilizes magnetic grip.

This skid pad test was performed on the inner lane of a circular circuit made up of Tomy 12-inch-radius corner track sections. The actual radius of the inner lane is 9.8215 inches (9 13/16 inches) or 19.625 inches (19 5/8 inches) in diameter. The distance around one lap of this skid pad is 61.654 inches.

You'll also note that the body doesn't make much of a difference here, but out on the racetrack where the car has to change directions, accelerate, and decelerate, a lighter and lower body will help reduce lap times. If you make changes to your race car that makes it go quicker on the skid pad, the car may lose top speed and yield slower lap times. Also, some drivers don't like a car that feels "too stuck" to the track. They prefer a car that feels "light" or "freed up." Cars that these drivers lap quickly wouldn't do as well

The Tomy T-Jet chassis.

The Mattel chassis is a recreation of the Tyco chassis from the 1970s.

on the skid pad, but are found to be easier (and more fun) to drive by some.

The reason we are doing this is because I know that some major manufacturers of HO slot cars use this test to determine if one brand of chassis is better than their competition. Examine and compare the results from these tests and make your own assessments.

The Racetrack Tests

The cars were tested on the DL Challenge track (see http://www.origin8.com/bradstrack/slotcar.htm), on the Shaunadega tri-oval shown in *Racing and Collecting Slot Cars,* and on the Katz-Spa-Ring, shown in Chapter 13. Not all the tracks were available to test all the cars, but you can extrapolate some comparative times from the cars that were tested on all three tracks.

LAP TIMES ON THE HO DL CHALLENGE TRACK

Car	w/body	w/o body
Tomy T-Jet	6.63 (Camaro)	N/A
Mattel	3.92 (Lumina)	3.62
Tomy Super G plus	3.42 (Jag), 3.17 (F1)	3.05
Old Life-Like	3.49 (Lumina)	3.35
New Life-Like	3.27 (Lumina)	2.95
Tomy SRT	3.38 (Jag)	3.07
BSRT G2	N/A	N/A
BSRT G3	3.22 (Jag) 3.01 (F1)	2.95
Wizzard Patriot P3 (no body)	NA	3.10
Playing Mantis Thunderjet (with Fairlane body)	5.84	N/A
Playing Mantis X-Traction (with Mustang body)	5.02	NA

SKID PAD TESTS

Car	Time	mph
Tomy T-jet	1.65	2.12
Tomy T-jet w/narrow silicones	1.25	2.80
Mattel 440 X-2 Lumina body	0.65	5.39
Mattel no body	0.59	5.94
Tomy SG Plus Jag body	0.50	7.01
Tomy SG Plus F1 body	0.49	7.15
Tomy SG Plus no body	0.46	7.61
Old Life-Like Lumina body	0.55	6.37
Old Life-Like no body	0.51	6.87
New Life-Like Lumina body	0.54	6.49
New Life-Like no body	0.50	7.01
BSRT G2 (.420 diameter tires—Jag)	2.70	N/A
BSRT G2 (F1)	2.52	N/A
BSRT G2 no body	2.37	N/A
BSRT G3 Jag body	0.44	7.96
BSRT G3 F1	0.41	8.54
BSRT G3 no body	0.39	8.98
Wizzard Patriot P3 (no body)	0.41	8.54
Playing Mantis Thunderjet (with Fairlane body):	1.07	3.274
Playing Mantis X-Traction (with Mustang body)	0.96	3.95

NOTES: All times are in seconds.
Jag indicates Jaguar GT-style body. F1 indicates Formula 1-style open-wheel body.

Dynamometer Tests

My dynamometer is a black box with a slave motor that is driven by the race car's rear tires. I connect power to the pickup shoes with two wires and alligator clips. The power is then gradually turned up to a full 18.9 volts.

At load setting 0, there is no load induced by the slave motor. The race car is powered up to 18.9 volts, the lowest setting on my adjustable power supply. The race car will spin the slave motor to whatever it can (high rpm torque), and I note the amount of voltage the slave motor is putting out. Basically, the stronger the race car, the faster it can turn the slave motor; and the faster the slave motor turns, the more voltage it puts out.

At load setting 1, there is a slight amount of load induced through the slave motor. This tests the car's mid-range torque. A strong race car will be able to overcome this resistance and spin the slave motor faster (more voltage output) than a weaker car.

At load setting 2, there is even more load induced. This tests the race car's low rpm torque. A stronger

TEST TIMES FROM THE KATZ-SPA-RING

The track plan can be seen at: www.origin8.com/bradstrack/slotcar.htm.

Car	w/body	w/o body
Tomy T-Jet	29.22 (Camaro)	N/A
Mattel	15.11 (Lumina)	13.67
Tomy Super G plus (timing at 0)	13.04 (Jag), 12.07 (F1)	11.50
Tomy Super G plus (timing adv.)	12.97 (Jag), 11.67 (F1)	11.47
Old Life-Like	12.99 (Lumina)	12.17
New Life-Like	11.55 (Lumina)	11.25
Tomy SRT	12.78 (Jag)	11.40
BSRT G2 (.420 tires, timing at 0)	9.41 (Jag), 8.64 (F1)	8.20
BSRT G2 (.420 tires, timing adv)	8.90 (Jag), 8.41 (F1)	8.15
BSRT G3	10.01 (Jag) 9.61 (F1)	9.51
Wizzard Patriot P3 (no body)	N/A	11.51
Playing Mantis Thunderjet (with Fairlane body):	25.11	N/A
Playing Mantis X-Traction (with Mustang body)	20.10	N/A

TEST TIMES FROM SHAUNADEGA:

Photos of track can be seen at: www.origin8.com/bradstrack/slotcar.htm and shaunadega.com/.

Car	w/body	w/o body
Tomy T-Jet	4.201 (Camaro)	N/A
Mattel	2.861 (Lumina)	2.686
Tomy Super G plus (timing at 0)	2.470 (Jag), 2.395 (F1)	2.388
Tomy Super G plus (timing adv)	2.454 (Jag), 2.383 (F1)	2.376
Old Life-Like	2.306 (Lumina)	2.281
New Life-Like	2.258 (Lumina)	2.240
Tomy SRT	2.212 (Jag)	2.198
BSRT G2 (timing at 0)	1.875 (Jag), 1.697 (F1)	1.659
BSRT G2 (timing adv)	1.749 (Jag), 1.656 (F1)	1.626
BSRT G3 2.004 (Jag)	1.958 (F1)	1.908
Wizzard Patriot P3 (no body)	N/A	2.011
Playing Mantis Thunderjet (with Fairlane body)	N/A	N/A
Playing Mantis X-Traction (with Mustang body)	N/A	N/A

race car will be able to spin the slave motor faster than a weaker one and give a higher reading on the voltmeter.

After any changes that should improve performance are made, the race car is re-tested and the results of those tests can be compared to the previous ones. It can easily be determined if the car

continued on page 213

The Tomy Super SRT chassis.

The Tomy A/FX G-Plus chassis.

The new Life-Like chassis with dot magnets and a plastic shield.

The Wizzard Patriot P3 chassis.

The Playing Mantis X-Traction chassis is similar to the old Aurora Magna-Traction chassis.

The Playing Mantis X-Traction cars are available with a variety of body styles, including replicas of the tuner cars from the film *2Fast 2Furious*.

There is little visual difference between this BSRT G3 chassis and the slightly slower BSRT G2 chassis.

puts out more horsepower if the voltage readings are higher than the numbers in the earlier tests.

Be aware that changing the gear ratio between dyno tests will change the scale of voltage that the slave motor is putting out. If you put a taller (3.0:1 as opposed to 3.5:1) gear ratio in the race car, the rear tires will spin faster at the same given rpm of the engine. This will throw the previous dyno figures out the door. True, the race car will be able to go faster, but it will lose the bottom end and may not come off the corners with as much torque.

Each motor has an optimum torque band, and each circuit requires the proper gear ratio to maximize the effectiveness of this power band. It's also true that a stronger race car will drive the slave motor with more force than a weaker car with a taller gear ratio installed in each. I wanted to point out that the dyno should be used to measure the strength of the motor and any efforts made to reduce friction in the race car, and not necessarily determine the best gear ratio.

DYNAMOMETER TEST RESULTS

Chassis	Load setting	Voltage reading	Chassis	Load setting	Voltage reading
Tomy T-Jet	0	1.157	(timing at 0)	1	1.77
	1	0.700		2	1.38
	2	0.496	BSRT G2	0	3.28
Mattel	0	2.40	(timing adv)	1	1.85
440 X-2	1	1.33		2	1.44
	2	1.06	BSRT G3	0	2.60
Tomy	0	2.39		1	1.497
Super G plus	1	1.42		2	1.200
(timing at 0)	2	1.10	Wizzard Patriot P3 (no body)		
Tomy	0	2.93		0	2.330
Super G plus	1	1.60		1	1.398
(timing adv)	2	1.28		2	1.061
Old Life-Like	0	2.72	Playing Mantis Thunderjet		
	1	1.33	(with Fairlane body)		
	2	1.08		0	1.231
New Life-Like	0	2.40		1	0.452
	1	1.39		2	0.319
	2	1.09	Playing Mantis X-Traction (with		
Tomy SRT	0	3.08	Mustang body)		
	1	1.68		0	1.488
	2	1.34		1	0.516
BSRT G2	0	3.17		2	0.361

CHAPTER 13
HO TRACKS AND 11 TRACK PLANS

A recreation, in every detail, of how Lowe's hairpin appeared at Monaco in the mid-1960s on Jason Boye's LeMonzaco. All the cars in the photos are Boye's Models (lemonzaco@aol.com) cast-resin bodies on a Mattel chassis. Car 21 is a 1967 Ferrari 330P4, car 8 is a Ford GT40 Mk II, car 7 is a 1967 Lola T70 Mk III, and car 8 is a 1968 Ford GT40.

There's more action and excitement per square foot with HO cars and track. A 4x8-foot board is plenty of space for an HO track, but 4x8 feet is a real squeeze for 1/32 scale cars and track. Just to prove the point, there's a selection of HO track plans in this chapter and all fit on a 4x8-foot board.

HO Super Tracks

If you have more space, you can create a truly spectacular HO raceway. You have three choices of track. You can use the Tomy A/FX track, perhaps supplemented with some of the 18-inch diameter curves available to dealers through REH Distributors. Or you can buy one of the commercial routed tracks from Brad's Tracks, Wizzard, or Brystal. Or route your own track from PVC sheet as described in the *Slot Car Bible*.

Carl Schorle's A/FX Raceway

Carl Schorle considers HO cars to be realistic miniatures, and not just race cars. He wanted a track that was as realistic as the cars. For his group of racers, the magnet-free T-Jets are the cars of choice. The track is assembled from Tomy A/FX pieces with fiberboard cut to match the outline to provide borders around all the edges for the cars to slide out on. The edges of the table are surrounded with fiberboard that extends about 2 inches above the track to keep the cars from tumbling off the tabletop and onto the floor.

The track is scenic with signs cut from advertisements and attached to 0.040-inch styrene strip walls. Many of the buildings are Aurora or Atlas plastic kits from the 1970s that Schorle bought new, but unfortunately none are currently available. The trees are Life-Like HO model train products. The spectators are also model railroad figures from Preiser, Atlas, and others.

Slugger Canady's Hillclimb

Racetracks can provide a variety of challenges, but Slugger Canady's hillclimb is an incredible challenge. You could consider it a Monte Carlo Rally driver's worst nightmare, but it is a delight to drive, as long as the car doesn't have much front or rear overhang. The vertical curves are formed from matched pieces of Tyco's out-of-production uphill and downhill overpass track sections end-to-end.

Canady's cars of choice are some of the long-out-of-production rally cars from Tomy. Some of the dune buggies and Jeeps seem to like the course, too.

The scenery is concrete. Canady is in the concrete business and he just happened to have some handy.

continued on page 218

Carl Schorle's A/FX Raceway is completely sceniced.

These A/FX cars have been repainted and detailed by Carl Shorle.

The scenery on Slugger Canady's hillclimb layout is blown concrete.

The vertical curves on Slugger Canady's track are formed from matched pieces of Tyco's out-of-production uphill and downhill overpass track sections end-to-end.

Gary Merrifield's Rattlesnake Raceway

Gary Merrifield opted for HO model car racing as the video game of its day. Back in the 1970s, the Autoworld mail order catalog was his "Holy Grail." About eight years ago, Merrifield rediscovered HO racing and combined a few leftover pieces with some relatively inexpensive (at the time) collector pieces to build the racetrack of his dreams.

During his sabbatical from racing, Merrifield built a few HO model railroads and became familiar with what realism can look like in a smaller scale. He elected to recreate an HO raceway as it might have looked in 1970. That meant he could use buildings (and cars) from firms such as Faller, Atlas, and Minic that have long ceased production of model car accessories. The track is assembled from A/FX sectional track and powered by a variable voltage filler power supply with a Trackmate photocell-triggered

Rattlesnake Raceway is an 8x16-foot adaptation of a classic Aurora Clubman track from the long out-of-print *A/FX Handbook*.

This portion of the track is completely different from the Aurora Clubman track plan. The barn is a current production (ex-Revell) kit with a Plasticville hot dog stand and gas station, an Atlas hot dog stand, and an Aurora curved bleachers—all out-of-production kits.

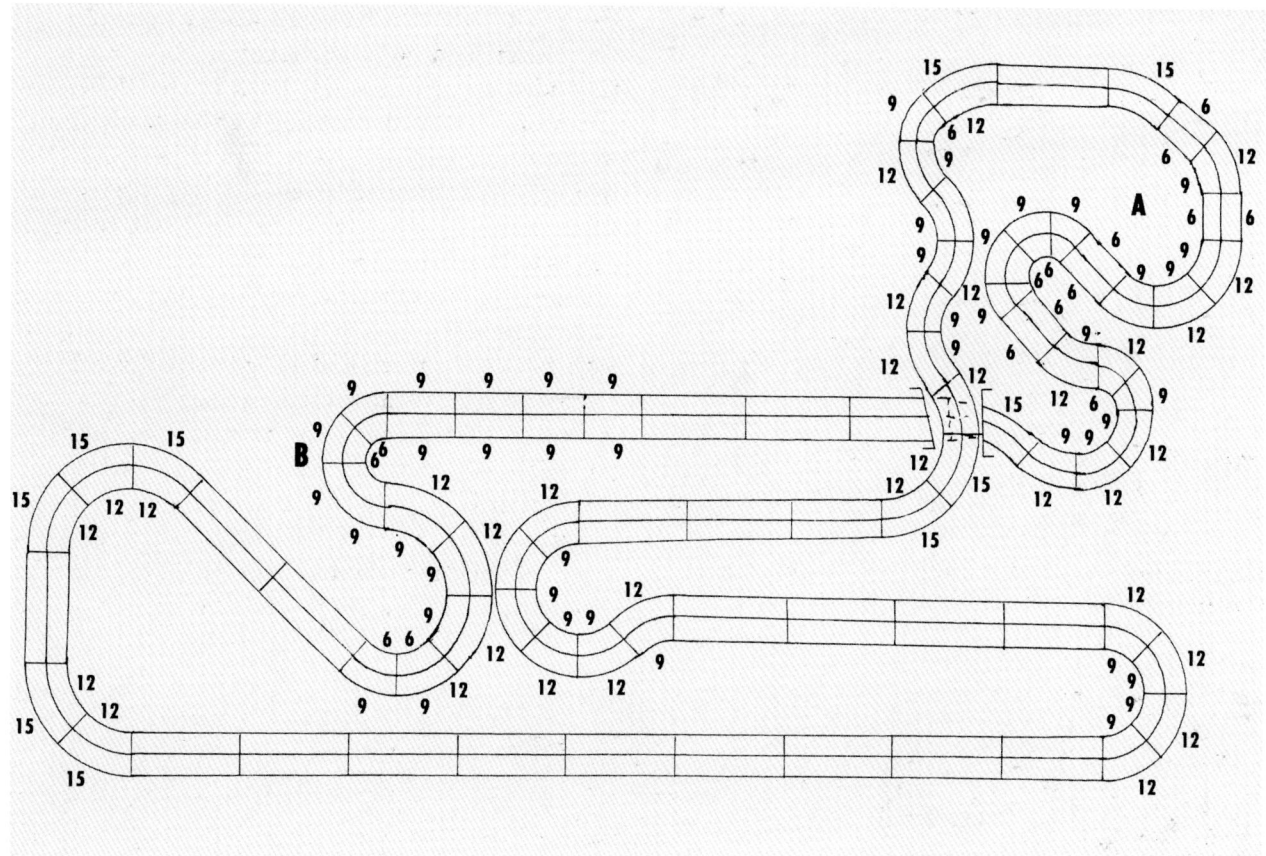

You can assemble the Rattlesnake Raceway as is. If you would prefer a 9/12 curve at "A," remove the pair of side-by-side 6-inch straights at "A." The straights are all 15 inches unless marked.

lap timing and counting system on an old 486 computer. It works flawlessly.

Jason Boye's LeMonzaco

The LeMonzaco track was constructed as a state-of-the-art raceway using Tomy/A/FX track sections with the rails removed. Many of the sections were sliced to allow for larger than standard radii.

The scenery and structures are all built from scratch with materials from various model railroad supply firms. The people are all 1/76 scale, which is known as 4mm scale in England. Most British model railroads are built to 4mm scale so there are plenty of people and details available from British hobby shops. All the figures were repainted to match trackside workers, mechanics, and spectators.

The local club raced on the track for nearly a decade, but unfortunately Jason had to move. The track was never designed for transport, so it was destroyed.

The Katz-Spa-Ring, A Real Racetrack

If you took a real Daytona Cobra and shrunk it to 1/32 or 1/64 size, you'd have the appearance of the Monogram or A/FX models. If you took a real race track and shrunk it to 1/64 size, you'd have the Katz-Spa-Ring. This is the first model racetrack I have seen that is more realistic than most of the cars that race on it. Usually it's just the opposite; the track is a bit go-kartish compared to the dead-accurate model racing cars.

Brad Bowman, of Brad's Tracks (http://www.bradstracks.com/ or http://www.origin8.com/bradstrack/slotcar.htm), built the track and Jason Boye created the scenery. The track was owned by the late Greg Katz. The three worked together to first create a track that could be raced on with the turns within reach of corner marshals. Fortunately, they had room for a 10x31-foot track in Greg's rec room.

Their goal was to build a real racetrack, not a model. A real racetrack would be about two miles around, would follow the contours of the land,

Turn 1, with the end of the pit complex, infield car park (with Ferrari and Porsche clubs dominating), a giant Goodyear tire, tunnel into the paddock, 3-D billboard, amusement park, and the chicane in the background.

provide suitable run-off areas for the safety of the spun-out cars, and have Armco and concrete barriers to protect the spectators. The circuit was designed to include corners with apex turns, increasing radius turns, decreasing radius turns, and both banked and flat turns. In general, it was the same design practices a typical county road department would use to design a two-lane road, including provisions for drainage. Remember, this was to be a real racetrack, only smaller.

Boye and Bowman collaborated on the circuit design. Inspired by their local real raceways, Laguna Seca and Sears Point (which both have raced), the pair wanted to recreate the dramatic elevations and roller coaster–like challenge these tracks present to racing drivers, but on a miniature scale. Katz's 15x35-foot addition to his house provided ample room for the layout to emulate the spectacular topographical nature of these tracks in scale. Boye took a design cue from the old Nurburgring and laid out two adjoining straights along the front edge of the layout. These straights, a 20 1/2-foot pit straight and a 23-foot front straight, account for 44 feet of the total 171-foot lap length. The design moves the cars up from zero elevation along the main straight to 22 1/2-inches (120 scale feet) at the highest point. The track takes nearly half a lap to get up and down several slopes before reaching the top at the appropriately named Summit Corner. Of the circuit's

A 1966 Ford GT40 Mk II, a 1964 Shelby Daytona Coupe and a 1968 Ford GT40 race along the harbor front. LeMonzaco's pit complex and crowded paddock fill the background.

An overall view of the twisty bits at LeMonzaco. From the left, progressing around the circuit, there's a double right turn, then a left at the Saint Devote (Monaco) complex with a Ferrari 330P4, Ford G40 Mk II, and Lola T70 Mk III negotiating the left Beau Rivage corner, with a long sweeping uphill to the left at Mirabeau (Monaco). The circuit winds downhill through Lowe's hairpin (Monaco) to the right-left at the Mirabeau Inferior turn to disappear through the long tunnel (Monaco). The course then flicks left along the harbor front with cars precariously close to a real water hazard.

171-foot lap length, only 16 feet are on the layout's tabletop.

The table to support the track is constructed using conventional model railroad layout-building practice with eight separate tables that fasten together so the track can be moved if necessary. To allow the joints of these sections to bisect the circuit at 90 degrees, these table shapes are anything but rectangular and took a full month to construct. Four removable access hatches were also constructed to facilitate work and any future maintenance requirements on the layout's central area. When the track starts to climb, it is supported by vertical risers cut from 1/2-inch plywood.

Bowman laid most of it with a single rail, leaving gaps only where he has determined they are needed for expansion and contraction. The track is also fed with four sets of feeder wires to prevent any voltage drop, regardless of how far the cars are from the power source. The circuit's 171-foot lap length is divided into three timing sectors. Each of the four lanes of the track is wired with four dedicated lap timers (one for laps completed and overall lap time) so that the three sectors can be timed individually, just like a current Formula 1 race circuit. At the moment they are using some long-out-of-production Aurora A/FX electronic control stations Bowman wired to perform the three-sectors and total lap timing and counting.

For the scenery, Boye decided to use fiberglass over wire cloth attached between the track edges because of its qualities of strength, lightness, and relatively fast construction. After the wire cloth was attached to the track edges, three layers of fiberglass were laid up. This process

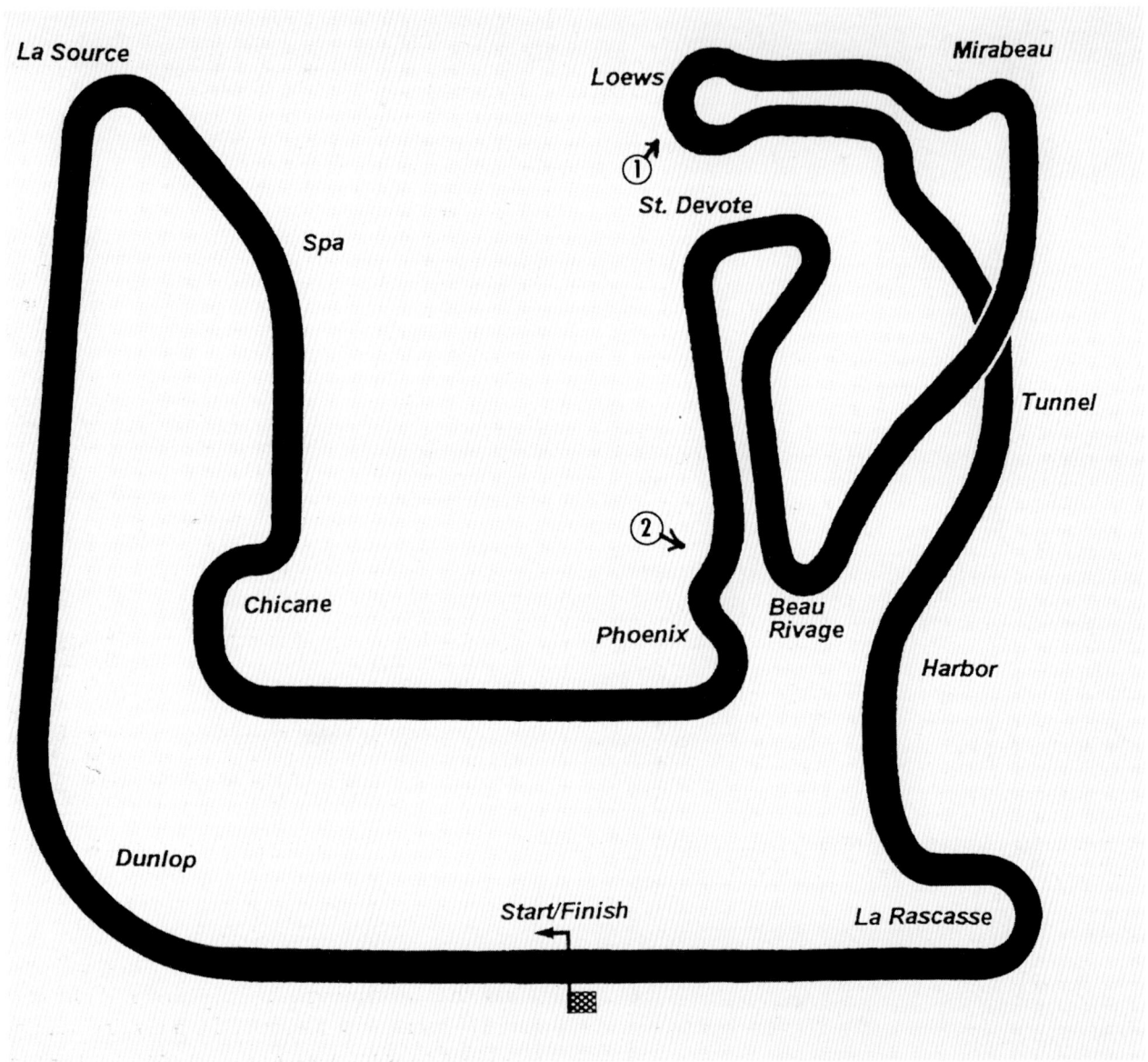

The LeMonzaco track plan.

bound the entire elevated portions together and added great strength and rock-solid stability. When the final layer of fiberglass resin was applied, Perma-scene (from a model railroad store) was liberally sprinkled onto the wet resin. When cured, the excess Perma-scene was vacuumed away. Celuclay instant papier-mâché was mixed with earth-tone latex paint and applied over the Perma-scene.

This track really does drive like a real race course. It is eerie to watch a car going at exactly the same speed you'd expect if you were watching from a helicopter, except that you are doing the driving from that elevated perch. The speeds vary, as they would with real cars. A stock Super-G (with sponge/silicone tires) racer can fly around in about 10 seconds, while a tuned T-Jet can make it in about 17 seconds. Very much like the difference between an Audi R8 and a Cobra around Road America, Laguna Seca, or Watkins Glen. It's always risky to apply real time to models, but if you multiply 10 and 17 seconds by 64 to bring the lap times up to the real world, it works out be about 1:04 for the Audi R8, and 1:48 for the

On the Katz-Spa-Ring, the four large openings are access pits and the scenery that will cover them are not yet in place. This is looking from Turn 1 (the chicane) with Summit Corner in the far upper center.

Looking from Summit Corner with the dramatic drop under the bridge leading to the Eau Rouge and Radillon turn complex (right-center). The esses snake their way down and up to the crossover bridge along the right.

Cobra. It is still too fast, but it looks right. I have to say that, assuming equal lap times, if the cars were 1/32 scale, the speeds and lap times would be very close to what would be a bit over a mile-long road course. The driver positions are near the center of the main straight, so the cars are never more than 15 feet from any driver. It is a bit of a squint with HO cars, but it works.

HO Track Plans for 4x8 feet

All these plans are designed to fit on a 4x8-foot piece of plywood. All can be extended in either direction by adding pairs of straights on opposite sides of the track. If you have room for a 4x16-foot track, you can usually find a place where four sets of 8-foot-long straight tracks can be inserted to add 32 feet to the lap length.

The plans are drawn to match Tomy A/FX dimensions, but Mattel or Tyco track sections can

continued on page 227

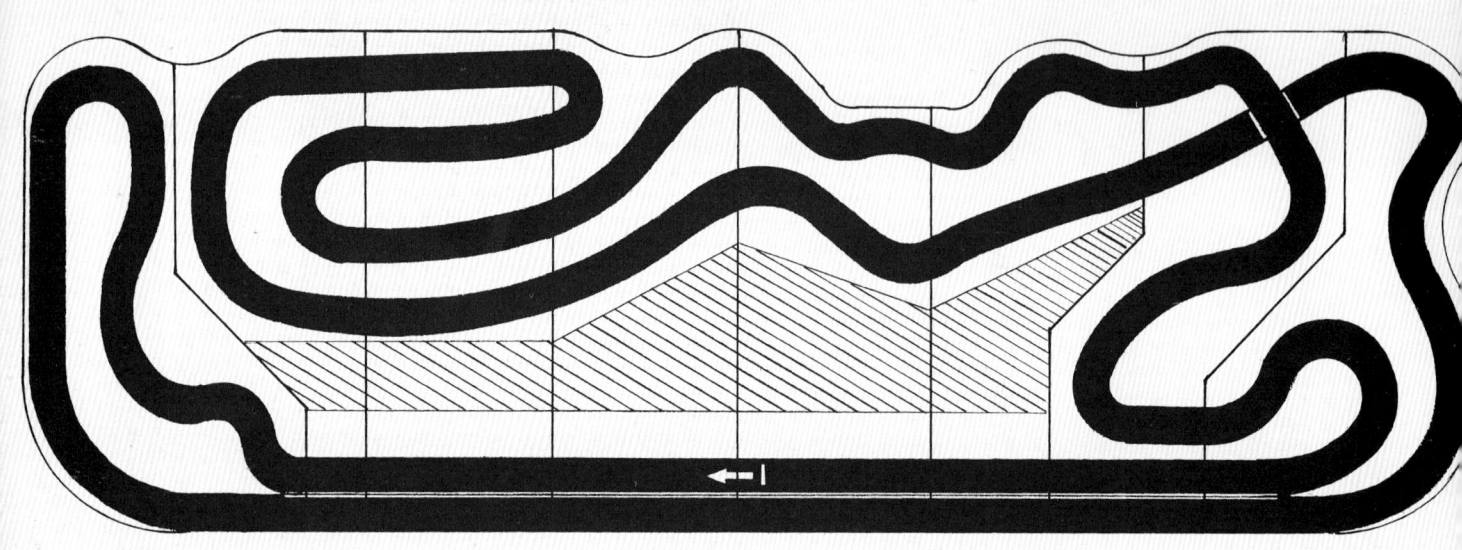

The Katz-Spa-Ring is shown in 10x31 feet. This is the closest thing to a plan because the corners were all designed in place. The track is actually built on eight separate tables, each about 3x10 feet, so it can be moved if necessary.

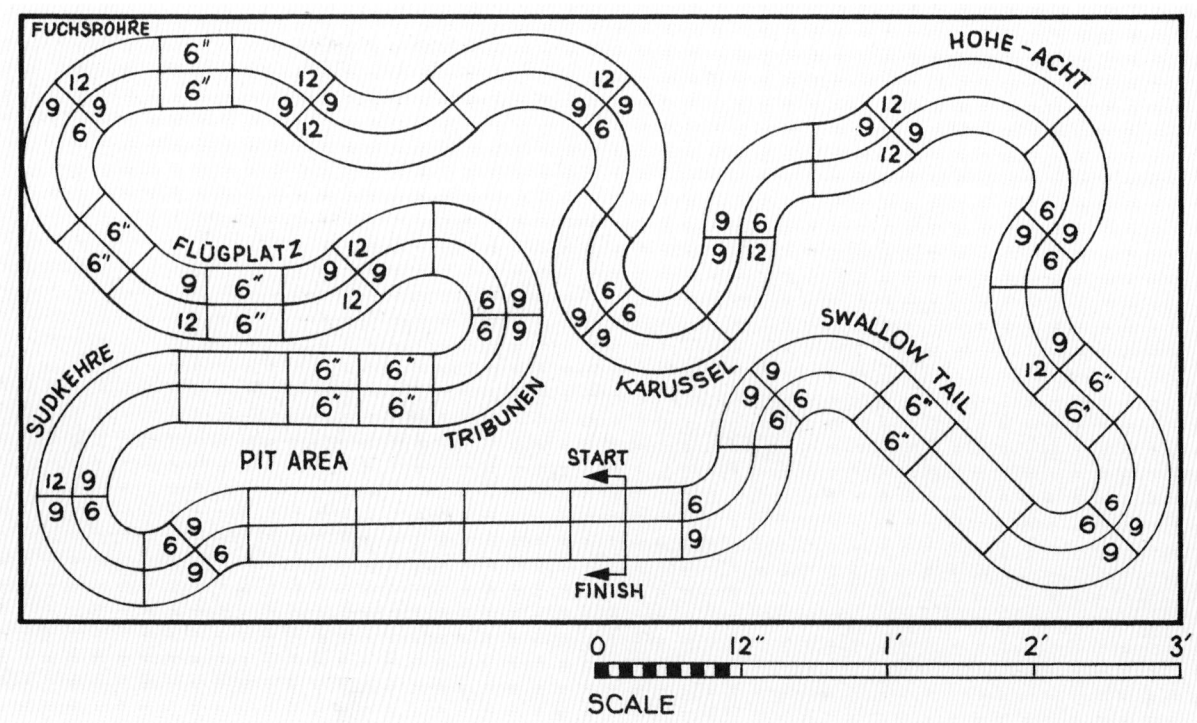

Track sections required for HO Nurburgring in 4x8 feet.

Quantity	Description
0	3-inch Straight
14	6-inch Straight
12	9-inch Straight
5	6-inch 45-degree Curve
12	6-inch 90-degree Curve
16	9-inch 90-degree Curve
13 1/2	9-inch 45-degree Curve
9 1/2	12-inch 45-degree Curve

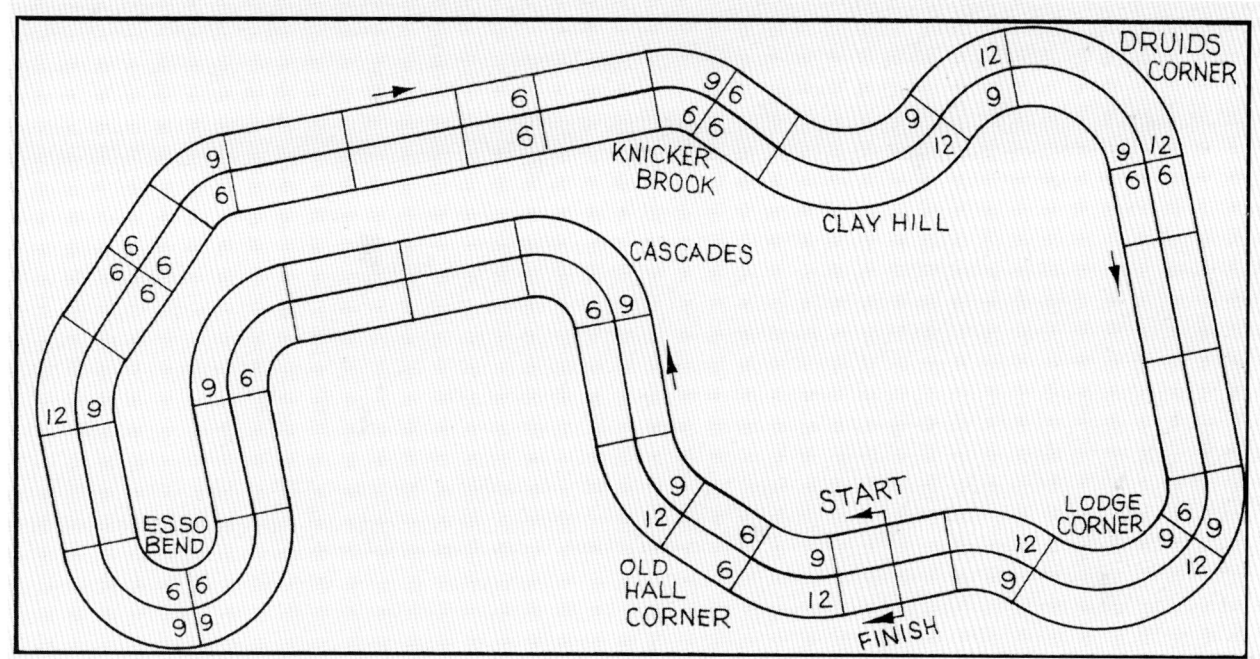

Track sections required for HO Oulton Park in 4x8 feet.

Quantity	Description
0	3-inch Straight
10	6-inch Straight
22	9-inch Straight
3	6-inch 45-degree Curve
4	6-inch 90-degree Curve
7	9-inch 90-degree Curve
6 1/2	9-inch 45-degree Curve
9 1/2	12-inch 45-degree Curve

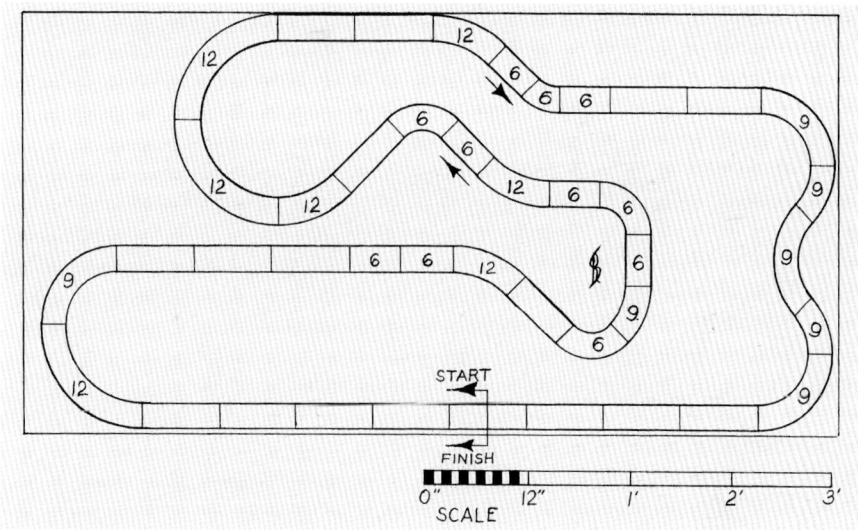

Track sections required for HO Road America in 4x8 feet.

Quantity	Description
0	3 inch Straight
6	6-inch Straight
17	9-inch Straight
1	6-inch 45-degree Curve
3	6-inch 90-degree Curve
4	9-inch 90-degree Curve
3 1/2	9-inch 45 degree Curve
3	12-inch 90-degree Curve (use 45-degree curve)
4 1/2	12-inch 45-degree Curve

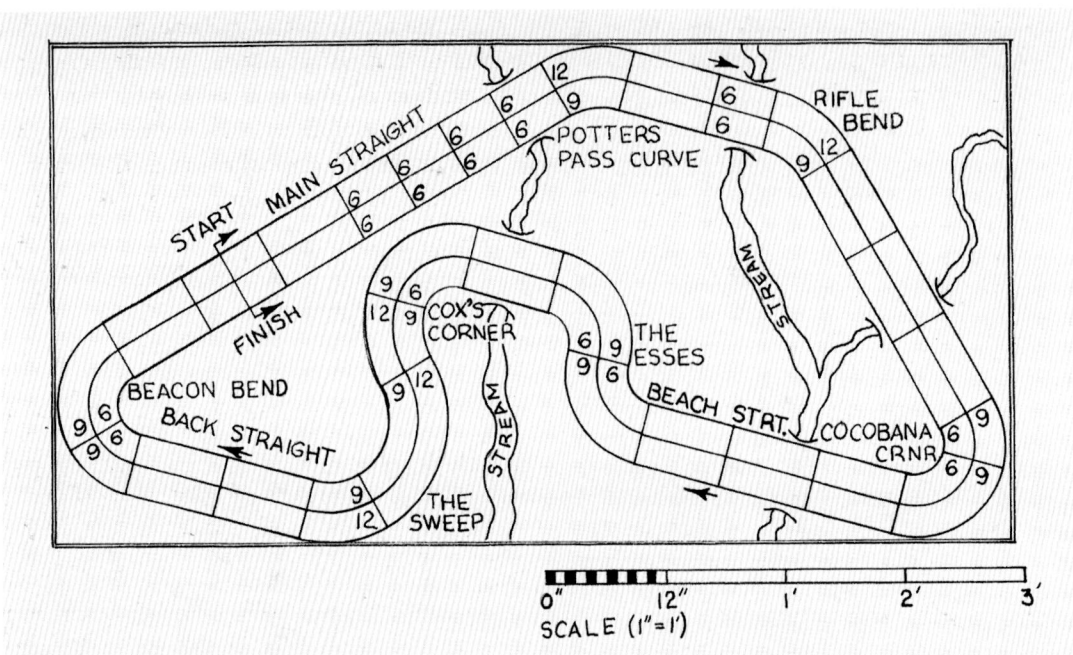

Track sections required for HO South Africa in 4x8 feet.

Quantity	Description
0	3-inch Straight
10	6-inch Straight
26	9-inch Straight
2	6-inch 45-degree Curve
5	6-inch 90-degree Curve
6	9-inch 90-degree Curve
6 1/2	9-inch 45-degree Curve

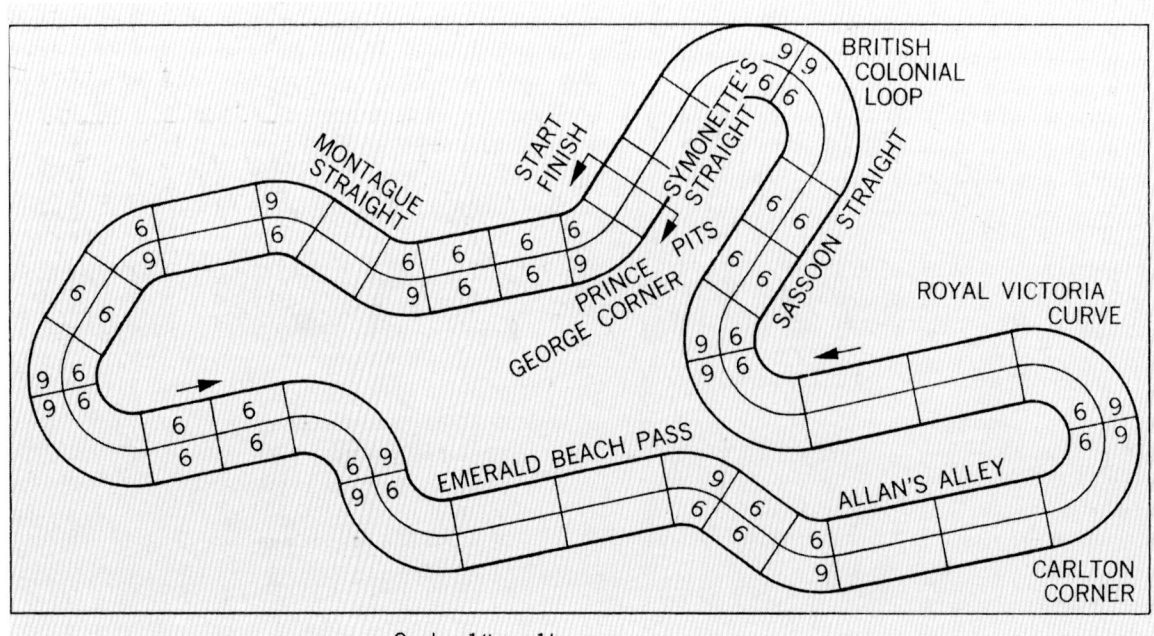

Track sections required for HO Nassau in 4x8 feet.

Quantity:	Description:
0	3-inch Straight
22	6-inch Straight
14	9-inch Straight
7	6-inch 45-degree Curve
8	6-inch 90-degree Curve
8	9-inch 90-degree Curve
7 1/2	9-inch 45-degree Curve

be substituted on most. I used the 6- and 9-inch lengths for the straights so you could assemble the circuit from any brand of HO track, but you can substitute 12-inch straights if they are available in the brand you prefer.

Most of these plans are designed for four lanes. The Silverstone plan, however, is designed for six lanes and is about as much track as you can squeeze into just 4x8 feet.

None of the plans include the 18-inch diameter curve that is available to dealers from REH Distributors. You can usually fit the 18-inch curve outside any 15-inch curve by removing 6 inches of straight on the opposite end of the track.

There is information on the real tracks that these plans have recreated in Chapter 9. You can compare how well the real track is recreated in 1/32 scale to these HO versions.

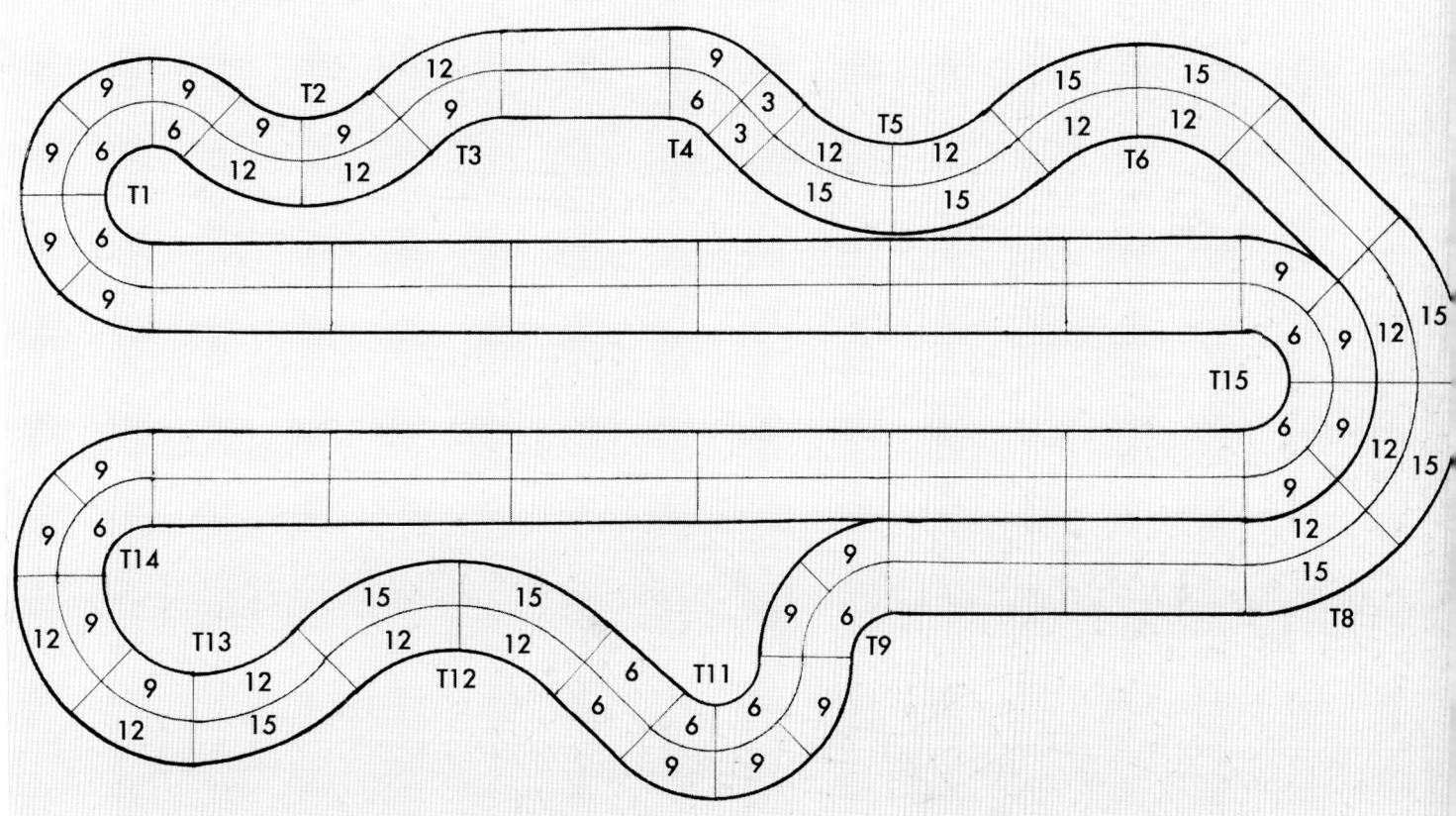

Track sections are required for the HO Sepang, Malaysia, circuit in 4x8 feet.

Quantity	Description
2	3-inch Straight
0	6-inch Straight
0	9-inch Straight
32	12-inch Straight
3	6-inch 45-degree Curve
6	6-inch 90-degree Curve
22	9-inch 45-degree Curve
15	12-inch 45-degree Curve
10	15-inch 45-degree Curve

INDEX

1964 289FIA Cobra, 9
1970 AAR Trans-Am 'Cuda, 92, 93, 94
A2M, 100
Allard, Sydney, 104
Allison, Bobby, 186
ALMS, 11
Anselmo, Rowland, 190, 191
Artin, 49, 122, 199
Art-Kit, 193
Attard, Jimmy, 199, 200, 201
Austin-Healey 100S Le Mans Racer, 98, 99
Auto Art, 17, 34, 59, 189
Axles, front, 108–110
Bauer, 100, 123, 124, 127
Beetle Cup Series for New Beetles, 186
Bodies, plastic, 110, 111
Body damage, 89
Bodywork, 61
Bowman, Brad, 113, 219–221
Boye, Jason, 10, 113, 214, 219–221
Brabham, Jack, 89
Braids, 52, 56, 59, 60, 110
British Touring Car Championship (BTCC), 185
Buildings, Carrera modern-era, 124, 129
Bunkey, Steve, 105
BWA, 63–66
Cadillac-Allard, 103, 104
Canady, Slugger, 215–217
Cardboard structures, 123, 124
Carrera, 6, 13, 15, 17–19, 30, 31, 34, 45, 47, 49, 62, 63, 66, 68, 70–72, 74, 76, 77, 79, 81–83, 85, 86, 92, 107, 117, 123, 126, 130, 132–134, 136–147, 149, 150, 152, 155, 156, 159, 160, 164, 165, 167, 169–171, 173, 174, 176–178, 180, 183–186, 188, 189, 193, 198–200
Carrera F1, 70, 84, 87, 89
Carrera Monaco, 121, 122
Carrera Pro-X, 28, 31–35, 37, 38, 40, 46, 148, 149, 154, 155, 161, 162, 173, 180, 181, 200, 203
CART, 16, 60, 69, 86, 87
Castroneves, Helio, 96
Chassis, 49
    Brass, 108

    Building, 105
    Iso-Pivot, 108, 110
    Mattel, 208
    Pin-guide, 109, 110
    Plastic, 106
    Pro-Track, 106
    Super-tuned TSRF, 107–110
Tomy T-Jet, 207
Chrome, 97, 98
Classic Indy Roadster Kit, 105
Cobb, Steven, 193
Color, 90, 91
Cox, Russell, 110, 191, 192, 193
Custom-built models, 100
Cusumano, Jim, 193
de Lespinay, Philippe, 107
Decal, custom, 90
Digital racing, 31, 32
Dirt, "real," 122–124
Display models, 105
Dolan, Tom, 15
DTM (German Touring Car Championship), 185
Dunkle, Bob, 121, 192, 194, 195
Dynamomter tests, 209, 213
Electric Dream, 55, 60
European Touring Car Championship (ETCC), 185
Extensions, 135
Ferrari F2001 F1, 91, 92
Fly, 19, 26, 34, 48, 72, 74–76, 79–85, 89, 107, 108, 123, 148
G&G Osterero, 12
Gears, 62, 63
Grand National, 28
Guide shoe, 59
Gurney, Dan, 89, 92, 94, 186, 187
Higham, Peter, 152
Hillclimbs, 118, 121, 122, 215–217
Historic Racing Replicas, 19, 84
HO, 68, 85, 100, 106, 116, 124, 127, 207, 208, 215, 218
Houston Scale Auto Racing Club, 192
Indianapolis 500, 96
Indy Grips, 65, 66, 77, 81, 82, 86
IRL, 16, 69, 75, 86, 87
Isaac, Bobby, 8
Jeffords, Jim, 103

John Cooper Challenge, 186
Jones, Bruce, 153
Jones, Parnelli, 188
Kal-Kar, 163, 165, 169, 175, 179, 181
Kaplan, Ronnie, 103
Katz, Greg, 219
Lane-changing, 9, 34, 35, 37, 40, 42, 45, 46, 154
Lawrence, Chuck, 106
Le Mans, 11, 8, 18, 75, 81, 82, 86, 115
Le Mans Miniatures, 12, 66, 100
LeMonzaco, 10, 113, 214, 219
Louvers, 100
MacKenzie, John, 102, 193, 197
Macklin, Lance, 100
Magnetic downforce, 68, 69, 71–73, 77
Marlboro-sponsored racers, 94, 96
MAXI-Models, 18, 59, 88, 100
Merrifield, Gary, 218
Miniature Electric Scale Auto Racing Club (MESAC), 201–205
MMK, 17, 18, 76, 79, 81, 100
Model Car Racing magazine, 11, 24, 32, 37, 72, 108, 135
Modelmaker 289FIZ Cobra, 101–103
Modelmaker, 9, 100
Monogram, 14, 19, 34, 48, 64, 67, 74, 76–78, 81, 105, 110, 116, 163, 165, 169, 175, 179, 181, 196, 219
MRRC, 34, 59, 65, 67, 74, 75, 77, 78, 100–103, 105, 1125, 126, 195, 196
NASCAR, 8, 68, 72, 75, 86, 107, 115, 123, 184–187
NINCO, 15–17, 20–23, 32, 34, 49, 58, 63, 66, 71, 72, 74, 76, 79, 81–83, 85, 86, 97–99, 100–108, 110, 115, 122, 124, 133, 135, 139, 139–141, 144–147, 149, 152, 154, 156–160, 163–167, 169–171, 173, 174, 178–180, 182, 185–187, 189, 191
NINCO CART, 70, 85
NINCO Classic, 106
NINCO Digital, 47
NINCO F1, 70, 87
Noisy Muse, 100, 102, 103
Ortmann, 58
Paddock, scenes, 123
Painting, 91

be substituted on most. I used the 6- and 9-inch lengths for the straights so you could assemble the circuit from any brand of HO track, but you can substitute 12-inch straights if they are available in the brand you prefer.

Most of these plans are designed for four lanes. The Silverstone plan, however, is designed for six lanes and is about as much track as you can squeeze into just 4x8 feet.

None of the plans include the 18-inch diameter curve that is available to dealers from REH Distributors. You can usually fit the 18-inch curve outside any 15-inch curve by removing 6 inches of straight on the opposite end of the track.

There is information on the real tracks that these plans have recreated in Chapter 9. You can compare how well the real track is recreated in 1/32 scale to these HO versions.

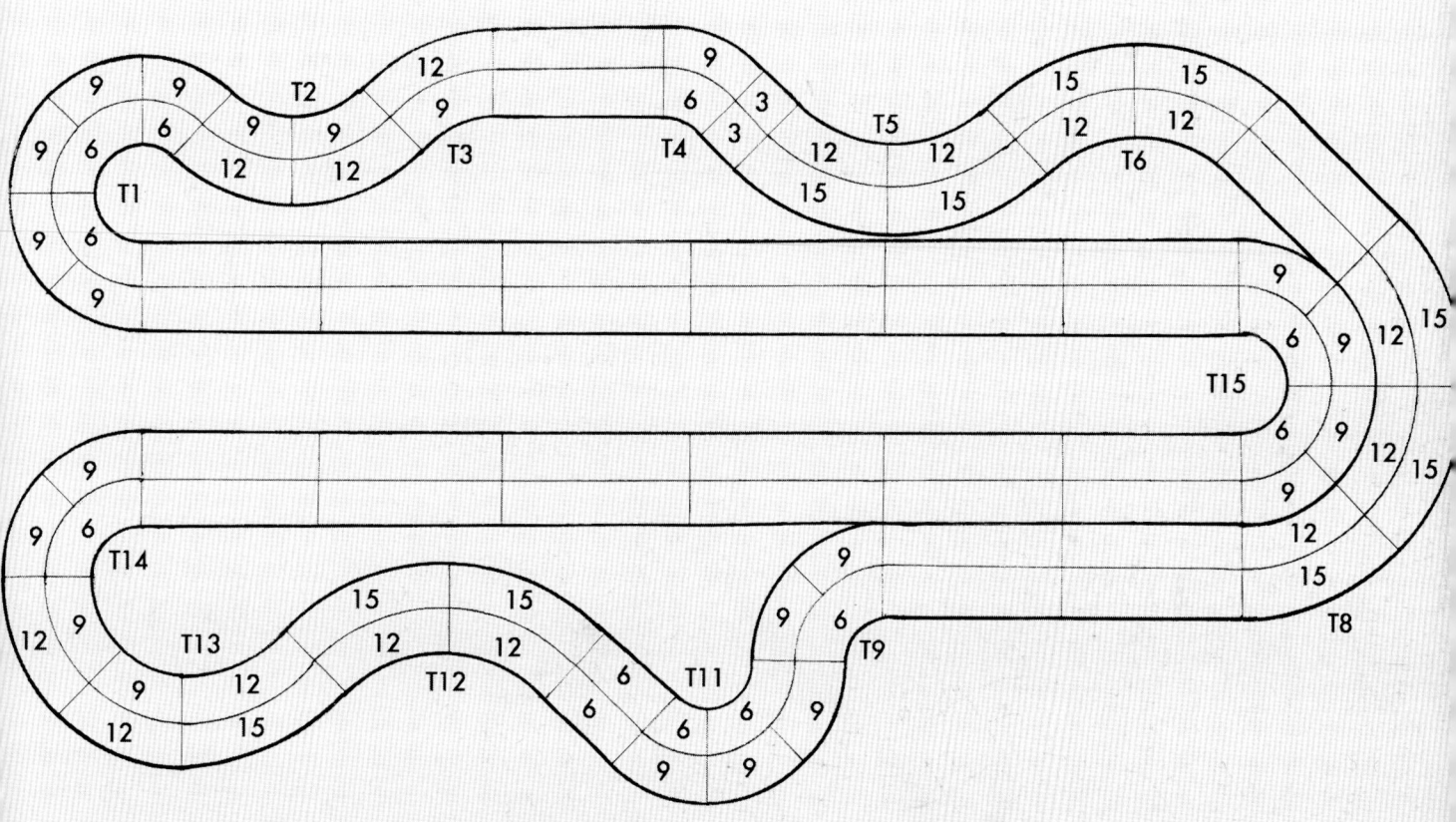

Track sections are required for the HO Sepang, Malaysia, circuit in 4x8 feet.

Quantity	Description
2	3-inch Straight
0	6-inch Straight
0	9-inch Straight
32	12-inch Straight
3	6-inch 45-degree Curve
6	6-inch 90-degree Curve
22	9-inch 45-degree Curve
15	12-inch 45-degree Curve
10	15-inch 45-degree Curve

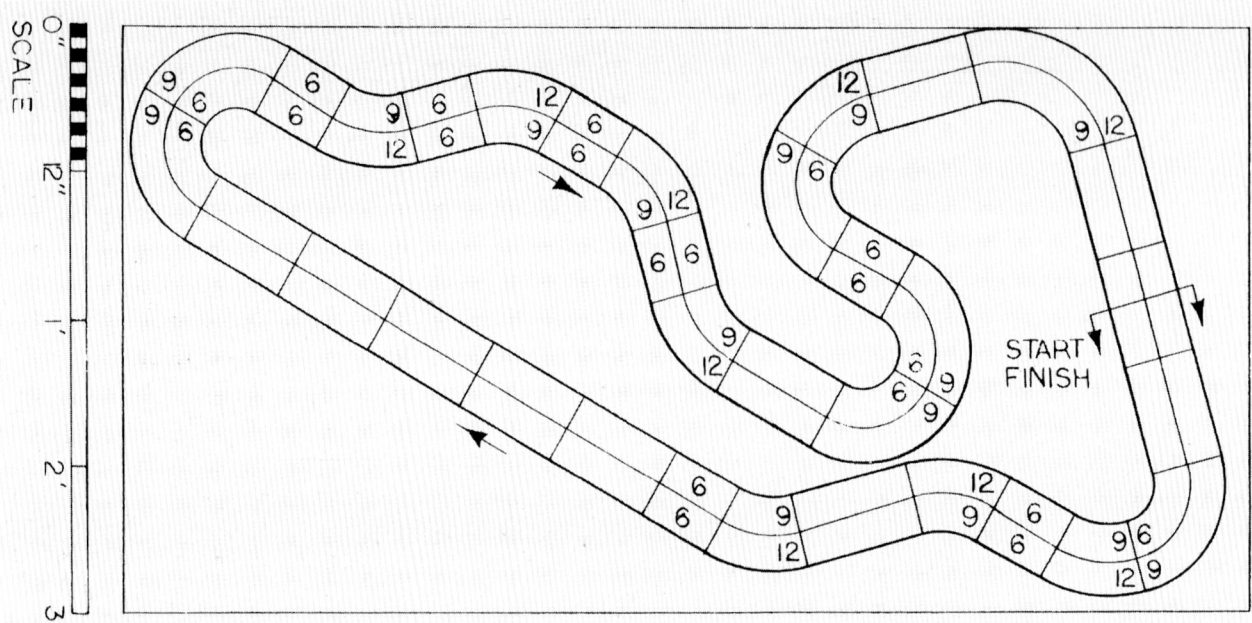

Track sections required for the HO Warwick Farm, Australia, circuit for 4x8 feet.

Quantity	Description
0	3-inch Straight
14	6-inch Straight
22	9-inch Straight
0	12-inch Straight
0	6-inch 45-degree Curve
6	6-inch 90-degree Curve
7	9-inch 45-degree Curve
7	12-inch 45-degree Curve
1	12-inch 90-degree Curve

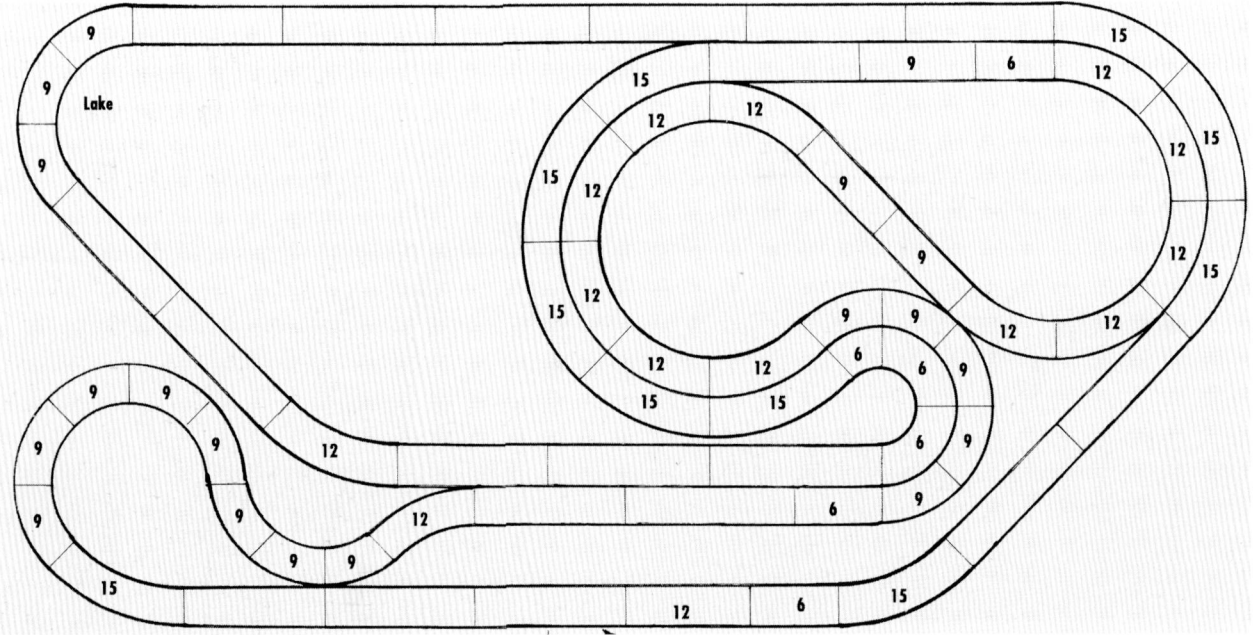

Track sections required for HO Interlagos, Brazil, circuit for 4x8 feet.

Quantity	Description
0	3-inch Straight
2	6-inch Straight
3	9-inch Straight
20	12-inch Straight
1	6-inch 45-degree Curve
2	6-inch 90-degree Curve
16	9-inch 45-degree Curve
13	12-inch 45-degree Curve
10	15-inch 45-degree Curve

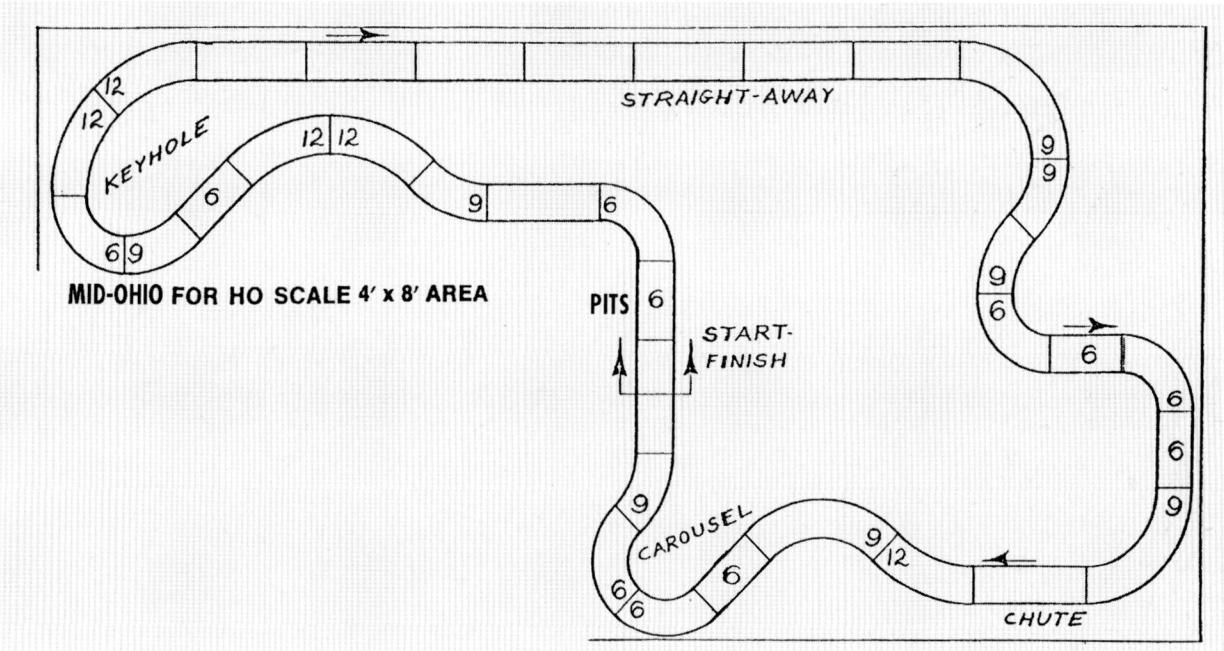

Track sections required for HO Mid-Ohio for 4x8 feet.

Quantity	Description
0	3-inch Straight
5	6-inch Straight
10	9-inch Straight
0	12-inch Straight
0	6-inch 45-degree Curve
6	6-inch 90-degree Curve
5	9-inch 45-degree Curve
3	9-inch 90-degree Curve
5	12-inch 45-degree Curve

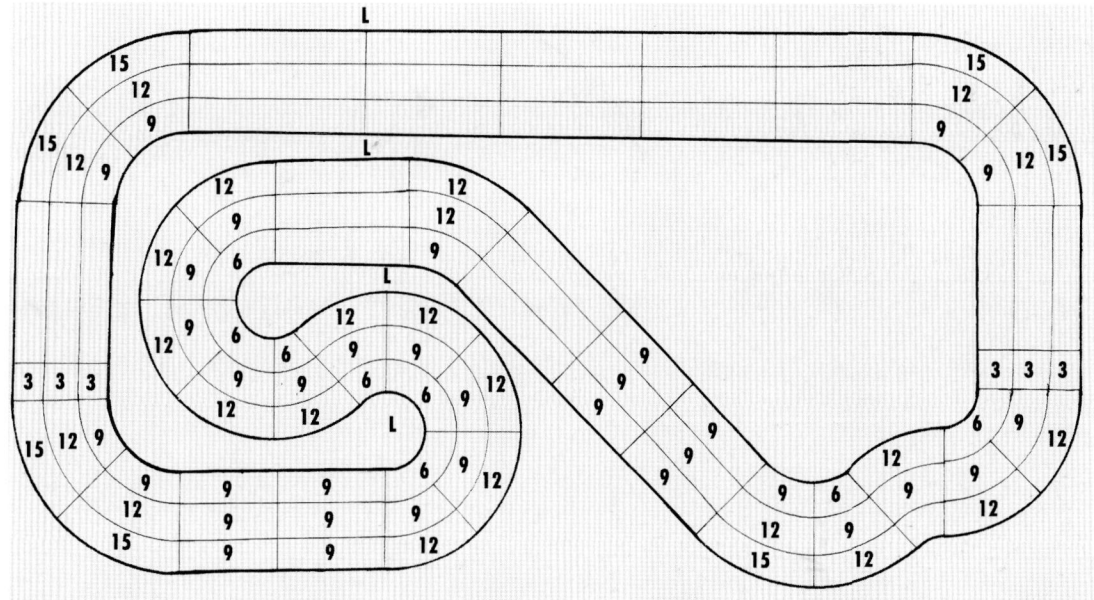

Track selections required for HO Silverstone for 4x8 feet.

Quantity	Description
6	3-inch Straight
0	6-inch Straight
12	9-inch Straight
27	12-inch Straight
4	6-inch 45-degree Curve
5	6-inch 90-degree Curve
22	9-inch 45-degree Curve
22	9-inch 90-degree Curve
8	12-inch 45-degree Curve

INDEX

1964 289FIA Cobra, 9
1970 AAR Trans-Am 'Cuda, 92, 93, 94
A2M, 100
Allard, Sydney, 104
Allison, Bobby, 186
ALMS, 11
Anselmo, Rowland, 190, 191
Artin, 49, 122, 199
Art-Kit, 193
Attard, Jimmy, 199, 200, 201
Austin-Healey 100S Le Mans Racer, 98, 99
Auto Art, 17, 34, 59, 189
Axles, front, 108–110
Bauer, 100, 123, 124, 127
Beetle Cup Series for New Beetles, 186
Bodies, plastic, 110, 111
Body damage, 89
Bodywork, 61
Bowman, Brad, 113, 219–221
Boye, Jason, 10, 113, 214, 219–221
Brabham, Jack, 89
Braids, 52, 56, 59, 60, 110
British Touring Car Championship (BTCC), 185
Buildings, Carrera modern-era, 124, 129
Bunkey, Steve, 105
BWA, 63–66
Cadillac-Allard, 103, 104
Canady, Slugger, 215–217
Cardboard structures, 123, 124
Carrera, 6, 13, 15, 17–19, 30, 31, 34, 45, 47, 49, 62, 63, 66, 68, 70–72, 74, 76, 77, 79, 81–83, 85, 86, 92, 107, 117, 123, 126, 130, 132–134, 136–147, 149, 150, 152, 155, 156, 159, 160, 164, 165, 167, 169–171, 173, 174, 176–178, 180, 183–186, 188, 189, 193, 198–200
Carrera F1, 70, 84, 87, 89
Carrera Monaco, 121, 122
Carrera Pro-X, 28, 31–35, 37, 38, 40, 46, 148, 149, 154, 155, 161, 162, 173, 180, 181, 200, 203
CART, 16, 60, 69, 86, 87
Castroneves, Helio, 96
Chassis, 49
    Brass, 108
    Building, 105
    Iso-Pivot, 108, 110
    Mattel, 208
    Pin-guide, 109, 110
    Plastic, 106
    Pro-Track, 106
    Super-tuned TSRF, 107–110
Tomy T-Jet, 207
Chrome, 97, 98
Classic Indy Roadster Kit, 105
Cobb, Steven, 193
Color, 90, 91
Cox, Russell, 110, 191, 192, 193
Custom-built models, 100
Cusumano, Jim, 193
de Lespinay, Philippe, 107
Decal, custom, 90
Digital racing, 31, 32
Dirt, "real," 122–124
Display models, 105
Dolan, Tom, 15
DTM (German Touring Car Championship), 185
Dunkle, Bob, 121, 192, 194, 195
Dynamomter tests, 209, 213
Electric Dream, 55, 60
European Touring Car Championship (ETCC), 185
Extensions, 135
Ferrari F2001 F1, 91, 92
Fly, 19, 26, 34, 48, 72, 74–76, 79–85, 89, 107, 108, 123, 148
G&G Osterero, 12
Gears, 62, 63
Grand National, 28
Guide shoe, 59
Gurney, Dan, 89, 92, 94, 186, 187
Higham, Peter, 152
Hillclimbs, 118, 121, 122, 215–217
Historic Racing Replicas, 19, 84
HO, 68, 85, 100, 106, 116, 124, 127, 207, 208, 215, 218
Houston Scale Auto Racing Club, 192
Indianapolis 500, 96
Indy Grips, 65, 66, 77, 81, 82, 86
IRL, 16, 69, 75, 86, 87
Isaac, Bobby, 8
Jeffords, Jim, 103
John Cooper Challenge, 186
Jones, Bruce, 153
Jones, Parnelli, 188
Kal-Kar, 163, 165, 169, 175, 179, 181
Kaplan, Ronnie, 103
Katz, Greg, 219
Lane-changing, 9, 34, 35, 37, 40, 42, 45, 46, 154
Lawrence, Chuck, 106
Le Mans, 11, 8, 18, 75, 81, 82, 86, 115
Le Mans Miniatures, 12, 66, 100
LeMonzaco, 10, 113, 214, 219
Louvers, 100
MacKenzie, John, 102, 193, 197
Macklin, Lance, 100
Magnetic downforce, 68, 69, 71–73, 77
Marlboro-sponsored racers, 94, 96
MAXI-Models, 18, 59, 88, 100
Merrifield, Gary, 218
Miniature Electric Scale Auto Racing Club (MESAC), 201–205
MMK, 17, 18, 76, 79, 81, 100
Model Car Racing magazine, 11, 24, 32, 37, 72, 108, 135
Modelmaker 289FIZ Cobra, 101–103
Modelmaker, 9, 100
Monogram, 14, 19, 34, 48, 64, 67, 74, 76–78, 81, 105, 110, 116, 163, 165, 169, 175, 179, 181, 196, 219
MRRC, 34, 59, 65, 67, 74, 75, 77, 78, 100–103, 105, 1125, 126, 195, 196
NASCAR, 8, 68, 72, 75, 86, 107, 115, 123, 184–187
NINCO, 15–17, 20–23, 32, 34, 49, 58, 63, 66, 71, 72, 74, 76, 79, 81–83, 85, 86, 97–99, 100–108, 110, 115, 122, 124, 133, 135, 139, 139–141, 144–147, 149, 152, 154, 156–160, 163–167, 169–171, 173, 174, 178–180, 182, 185–187, 189, 191
NINCO CART, 70, 85
NINCO Classic, 106
NINCO Digital, 47
NINCO F1, 70, 87
Noisy Muse, 100, 102, 103
Ortmann, 58
Paddock, scenes, 123
Painting, 91

Two-color, 94–97
Paris-Dakar, 122
Pattos, 105
P-B-L Hot Shoes, 58
Pendle, 105
Penske, Roger, 94
Petrolati, Greg, 100, 103, 104
Pickup shoe, 59, 60
Pink-Kar, 14, 77, 110, 111
Pits, 123, 125, 126, 127
Plasticville, 218
Playing Mantis, 207, 212
Pollack, Bill, 103, 104
Power slides, 115
Pre-Add, 100
Preiser, 125, 126, 128, 129
Preparation, 49–51
ProRace, 23
Pro-Slot, 71, 85
Pro-Slot F1, 70, 87
Proto Slot-Kit, 100
Pro-Track, 22, 59, 63–66, 105–107
Puget Sound Slot Racing Association, 193
Puma Paws, 65, 66, 77, 81, 82, 86
Racers, 105, 106
Racetrack tests, 208, 209
Racing, multiple cars, 153, 154
Rear axle slop, 61, 62
Renault Clio Cup Series, 186
Reprotec, 74, 77
Resilient Resins, 100
Revell, 67, 110, 116, 163, 165, 169, 175, 179, 181, 218
Richter, Roy, 104
Riggen, 116, 192
Road racing, 1950s-era Sports/GT/Le Mans, 79
Russo, Rocky, 104, 108
Scalextric Challenger, 7, 29, 30
Scalextric Classic, 15, 30, 31, 70, 76, 84, 113–116, 122, 131, 133, 135–149, 152, 154, 156–160, 163–167, 169–171, 173, 174, 178–180, 182, 191, 193
Scalextric, 6, 11, 15, 30, 23, 38, 45, 51, 52, 59, 61, 65, 66, 69, 71–76, 78, 79, 81–83, 85, 86, 89, 90, 96, 103, 105, 107, 123, 124, 130, 184–186, 188, 189, 191–193, 195, 197, 199, 200
Scalextric F1, 70, 71, 87
Scalextric IRL, 16, 70, 71, 84, 86, 87, 96
Scalextric Sport Digital, 30–38, 40, 43, 44, 45, 46, 47, 76, 154, 159, 200, 203
Scalextric Sport Track, 113–116, 120–124, 131, 133, 135–152, 154, 156–160, 163–167, 169–171, 173, 174, 178–180, 182, 192, 193
Schorle, Carl, 215, 216
SCX, 6, 15, 24, 45, 49, 57–59, 62, 63, 66, 70, 76, 82, 83, 85, 86, 107, 114, 115, 118, 122, 123, 125, 127, 131, 133, 135–149, 152, 154, 156–160, 163–167, 169–171, 173, 174, 178–180, 182, 185–189, 193, 196, 199, 200
SCX Digital, 31–34, 37–42, 44–46
SCX F1, 71, 60, 86, 87
Seattle Hill Raceway, 102
Sebring, 11
Shoot-outs, 75
    1960s-era Sports/GT/Le Mans, 76, 77, 78, 80
    1970s-era Sports/GT/Le Mans, 80–82
    Modern-era Sports/GT/Le Mans, 82
    Open-wheel F1/CART/IRL, 83, 84
    Ten-car grand prix F1/CART/IRL, 86, 87
Skid aprons, 116, 135
Skid pad tests, 207, 209
Slot Classics, 13, 74, 100, 105
Slot Sports, 60, 61
Slot.it, 24, 26, 34, 58, 62–66, 82, 83, 107, 200
SlotMaster, 193
Spa, 11
Spirit, 26, 34, 72, 76, 80, 81, 83, 84
Strombecker, 116, 163, 165, 169, 175, 179, 181, 192
Super Slot, 55
Suspension, three-point, 58
Ten-count penalty, 46
Tire numbers, 86
Tires, 85
    Silicone rubber, 53, 77, 78, 83, 84
Titus, Jerry, 105
Top-Slot, 17, 100, 196
Track
    4x8-foot four-lane, 135, 136
    Borders, 116, 135
    Brand, 133, 134, 152
    GB, 76, 81, 84, 123, 126, 129
    HO plans, 223–229
    HO Super, 215
    Joints, loose, 117
    Portable or permanent, 131, 132
    Space, 131
    Test results, 25, 27
Tracks
    A/FX Raceway, 215, 216, 219
    Aurora Clubman, 218
    Brands Hatch, 11
    Catalunya (Barcelona) F1, 147–149
    Darlington Raceway, 143, 144, 146
    Daytona International Raceway, 170, 177
    DL Challenge, 208
    Double Indy F1, 148, 149
    Highland Raceway, 194, 195
    Indy F1 Circuit, 136, 138, 141, 142
    Interlagos, Brazil, 142–144
    F1, 176, 180, 181, 183
    Katz-Pa-Ring, 113, 206, 208, 209, 219–224
    King Snake Raceway, 145, 146
    Laguna Seca, 94, 123, 188, 222
    LeMonzaco, 221, 222
    Mid-Ohio, 153, 168–170, 174–177
    Monaco, 6, 123, 128, 150, 157–159, 161, 189, 214
    Nassau, Bahamas, 153, 181–183
    Northland Raceway, 199–202
    Nürburgring, 152, 154–156
    Oulton Park, 153, 159, 162–164
    Parabola Duo, 138, 139, 148
    Parabola Uno, 140, 148
    Rattlesnake Raceway, 218, 219
    Riverside Raceway, 8, 11, 186, 187
    Road America, 160, 162, 165–168, 175, 222
    Seattle Hill Raceway, 193, 196, 197
    Sepang, Malaysia F1, 170, 171, 173, 178
    Shaunadega, 208, 209
    Silverstone, 139, 140, 165, 167, 172–174
    South Africa, 153, 162, 163, 165, 168, 170, 171
    Super 8 Raceway, 140, 141
    Tabasco Lakes Speedway, 197, 198
    Warwick Farm, 153, 173, 174, 176, 179, 180
    Watkins Glen, 11, 135, 222
Traction, 67, 68
Trans-Am, 103, 186
TSRF, 26, 105
Vanquish, 27
VW Polo Series, 186
Walker, Chris, 60
Weights, 75, 78, 79
West Suburban Slot Car Association (WSSCA), 191, 193
Wheels, 53, 54, 58, 64–67
Wicker, Fred, 103
Williams, 16, 17
Wilson, Dan, 15, 108–110, 189
Wizzard, 207, 211World Rally Cup (WRC), 122, 123, 125, 185–187
Yeoman, Bruce, 193, 198–200

Other MBI Publishing Company titles of interest:

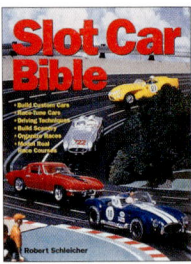

Slot Car Bible
ISBN 0-7603-1153-6

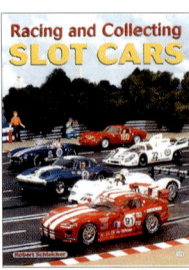

Racing and Collecting Slot Cars
ISBN 0-7603-1024-6

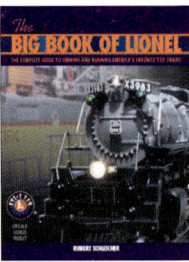

The Big Book of Lionel
ISBN 0-7603-1826-3

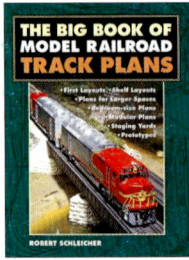

The Big Book of Model Railroad Track Plans
ISBN 0-7603-1423-3

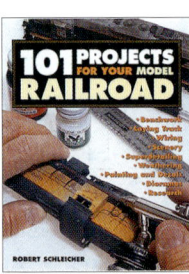

101 Projects for your Model Railroad
ISBN 0-7603-1181-1

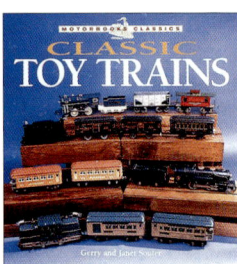

Classic Toy Trains
ISBN 0-7603-1367-9

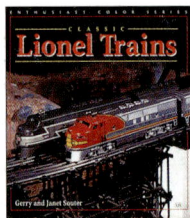

Classic Lionel Trains 1900–1969
ISBN 0-7603-1138-2

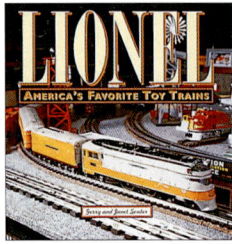

Lionel: America's Favorite Toy Trains
ISBN 0-7603-0505-6

Modern Lionel Trains
ISBN 0-7603-1596-5

Find us on the internet at www.motorbooks.com   1-800-826-6600